The Right Word in the Right Place at the Right Time

Wit and Wisdom from the

Popular "On Language" Column in

The New York Times Magazine

William Safire

Simon & Schuster   *New York   London   Toronto   Sydney*

SIMON & SCHUSTER
Rockefeller Center
1230 Avenue of the Americas
New York, NY 10020

SIMON & SCHUSTER and colophon are registered trademarks
of Simon & Schuster, Inc.
For information about special discounts for bulk purchases,
please contact Simon & Schuster Special Sales:
1-800-456-6798 or business@simonandschuster.com

Designed by Jeanette Olender

Manufactured in the United States of America

1   3   5   7   9   10   8   6   4   2

Library of Congress Cataloging-in-Publication Data
Safire, William, date.
The right word in the right place at the right time : wit and wisdom from the popular
"On language" column in The New York times magazine / William Safire.
p.   cm.
1. English language—Usage. 2. English language—Style. I. New York times magazine. II. Title.
PE1421.S2334 2004
428—dc22   2004045355
ISBN 0-7432-4244-0

For Jacques Barzun,

with thanks for all his comments herein.

We must make up our minds what we mean by usage. If it be defined merely as the practice of the majority, we shall have a very dangerous rule affecting not merely style but life as well, a far more serious matter.

QUINTILIAN, first century AD

INTRODUCTION

We will come to *sodomy* in a moment. To stagger together through today's column about grammatical possessiveness, you and I must agree on the difference between a gerund and a participle.

Take the word *dancing*. It starts out as a form of a verb: "Look, Ma, I'm *dancing*!" When that word is used as an adjective to modify a noun—"look at that *dancing* bear!"—it's called a participle.

But when the same word is used as a noun—"I see the bear, and its *dancing* isn't so hot"—then the word is classified as a gerund. (From the Latin *gerundum,* rooted in *gerere,* "to bear, to carry," because the gerund, though a noun, seems to bear the action of a verb.)

We give the same word these different names to tell us what it's doing and what its grammatical needs are. Two great grammarians had a titanic spat in the 1920s over the use of the possessive in this sentence: "Women having the vote reduces men's political power." H. W. Fowler derided what he called "the fused participle" as "grammatically indefensible" and said it should be "Women's having"; Otto Jespersen cited famous usages, urged dropping the possessive and called Fowler a "grammatical moralizer."

Comes now Supreme Court Justice Antonin Scalia with the latest manifestation of this struggle. An Associated Press account of his stinging dissent in *Lawrence v. Texas,* in which the Court struck down that state's anti-sodomy law, quoted Scalia out of context as writing, "I have nothing against homosexuals," which seemed condescending. His entire sentence, though, was not: "I have nothing against homosexuals, or any other group, promoting their agenda through normal democratic means."

Note the lack of apostrophes after *homosexuals* and *group* to indicate

1

possession; Fowler would have condemned that as a "fused participle." Such loosey-goosey usage from the conservative Scalia, of all people?

"When I composed the passage in question," the justice informs me, "I pondered for some time whether I should be perfectly grammatical and write 'I have nothing against homosexuals', or any other group's, promoting their agenda,' etc. The object of the preposition 'against,' after all, is not 'homosexuals *who are* promoting,' but rather 'the promoting *of* (in the sense of *by*) homosexuals.'

"I have tried to be rigorously consistent in using the possessive before the participle," Scalia notes, "when it is the action, rather than the actor, that is the object of the verb or preposition (or, for that matter, the subject of the sentence)."

But what about his passage in *Lawrence,* in which he failed to follow Fowler and fused the participle?

"I concluded that because of the intervening phrase 'or any other group,' writing 'homosexuals' "—with the apostrophe indicating possession— "(and hence 'any other group's') would violate what is perhaps the first rule of English usage: that no construction should call attention to its own grammatical correctness. Finding no other formulation that could make the point in quite the way I wanted, I decided to be ungrammatical instead of pedantic."

But his attempt to be a regular guy backfired. In a jocular tone, Scalia observes: "God—whom I believe to be a strict grammarian as well as an Englishman—has punished me. The misquotation would have been more difficult to engineer had there been an apostrophe after 'homosexuals.' I am convinced that in this instance the AP has been (unwittingly, I am sure) the *flagellum Dei* to recall me from my populist, illiterate wandering. (You will note that I did not say 'from me wandering.')"

My does beat *me* before that gerund *wandering*. Robert Burchfield, editor of the third edition of *Fowler's Modern English Usage,* writes, "The possessive with gerund is on the retreat, but its use with proper names and personal nouns and pronouns persists in good writing."

Now let's parse Scalia's self-parsing. In his refusal to say "from me wandering," *wandering* is a gerund. When a personal pronoun comes in front of a gerund, the possessive form is called for: say *my,* not *me.* This avoidance of a fused participle makes sense: you say about the above-mentioned bear "I like *his* dancing," not "I like *him* dancing," because you want to stress not the bear but his action in prancing about.

In Scalia's dissent in the Texas sodomy case, *promoting* is a gerund, the object of the preposition *against.* His strict-construction alternative, using apostrophes to indicate possession—"against homosexuals', or any other group's, promoting"—is correct but clunky. He was right to avoid it, and is wrong to castigate himself for eschewing clunkiness.

There would have been another choice, however: put the gerund ahead of the possessors. Try this: "I have nothing against the promoting of their agenda by homosexuals, or by any other group, through normal democratic means." That would not only avoid the confusing apostrophes, but follows "I have nothing against" with its true object, the gerund *promoting*—and would make it impossible for any reporter to pull out a condescending "I have nothing against homosexuals."

There's always a way out.

Regarding your proposed solution to my gerundial problem (to wit, "I have nothing against the promoting of their agenda by homosexuals, or by any other group, through normal democratic means"): It is so obvious that of course I considered it. Two problems. (1) I do not like to have a relative pronoun preceding its antecedent, as in "the promoting of their agenda by homosexuals." (2) More importantly, English remains a language in which emphasis is largely conveyed by word order, and the emphasis in my sentence was upon homosexuals' promoting, not upon (where your alternative places it) the promoting by homosexuals. Surely you can sense the difference.

Justice Antonin Scalia
Supreme Court of the United States
Washington, D.C.

Acronymania.   Who affixes glorious names to acts of Congress—with words whose initial capital letters spell out a hard-selling acronym?

When you ask a spokesman for the House Judiciary Committee who in the vast federal establishment came up with the USA PATRIOT Act, you get a bravely bureaucratic, "It was a collaborative bipartisan effort of the full committee." That'll be the day. When you press further, you discover that a partial coiner was a determinedly anonymous staff member of the Senate Judiciary Committee who called the initial antiterrorism statute the Uniting and Strengthening America Act. (USA—get it?)

But USA is a set of initial letters pronounced individually, not forming an acronym that can be pronounced as a word or is already a word. The key to infusing the quickly drawn legislation with a rousing title in which the flag fairly flapped came from House Judiciary. A junior staff member there named Chris Cylke achieved acronymic immortality by coming up with this inspiring moniker: Providing Appropriate Tools Required to Intercept and Obstruct Terrorism Act of 2001. Put it all together, and it spells PATRIOT.

Now join the House contribution with the Senate's name, and you get Uniting and Strengthening America by Providing Appropriate Tools Required to Intercept and Obstruct Terrorism—the USA PATRIOT bill, promptly signed by President Bush into law and, with a label like that, hard to criticize in any way.

This posed a challenge to the professional acronym-creators at the Pentagon, home of FATE (Fuse Arming Test Equipment, though often embarrassingly confused with a different program, Female Acceleration Tolerance Enhancement). Within that Puzzle Palace, an accidental acronym was formed when the phrase Global War on Terrorism became popular among military briefers and point-sheet writers. This group of words was initialized, as is the custom with all Department of Defense phrases; unfortunately, it produced GWOT, universally pronounced with a rising inflection as "Gee-what?" The image it projects is of a brass hat scratching his head, however, which is why the phrase may be dropped from internal DOD communications.

More recently, the Students for Global Justice and other opponents of globalization who demonstrated peacefully at the World Economic Forum in New York were organized under the banner of the Anti-Capitalist Convergence. However, the initials ACC hold no meaning for anyone outside the NCAA's Atlantic Coast Conference, and *capitalism* is not the dirty word it used to be. To deal with questions raised by the bigwigs huddling in the Waldorf-Astoria, some anarchists, Marxists and other image-makers converged to create International ANSWER. The title is an acronym of Act Now to Stop War and End Racism. Executives inside the Waldorf suspected that the demonstrators created the title to fit the word.

Some acronyms are standing the test of time. In 1960, as optical scientists were studying *maser*—from Microwave Amplification by Stimulated Emission of Radiation—along came the bright idea of amplifying a highly coherent beam of light, promptly dubbed a *laser*. (Tangent: Will somebody explain to me why every focus is now *laser-focused*? Lasers can guide, ignite, heat, drive and print, but focus? This is the hottest compound adjective around today, leaving all other focuses fuzzy. In Enron's 2000 annual report, the company claimed to be "*laser-focused* on earnings per share," at which point I should have become suspicious. End of tangent; this column is determinedly *laser-unfocused*.)

In Jennet Conant's book *Tuxedo Park,* about a social setting in which key scientists worked during World War II, the origin of *radar* is recounted: United States Army scientists used RPF, for "radio position find-ing," while the British preferred R.D.F., for "radio direction finding." The Navy liked "radio detection and ranging," or RADAR, which the British ac-cepted by 1943. That's a partial stump word, using a first syllable and then initials; a purer stump word is *hazmats,* familiar to drivers of trucks con-taining nitroglycerine and similarly hazardous materials.

A pure acronym—NIMBY, "not in my backyard"—long ago took hold among zoning lawyers and environmentalists. MADD—Mothers Against Drunk Driving—has become well known, spoofed by DAM, Mothers Against Dyslexia. The recent spate of acronymania (and do not write that as acronymphomania) can be combated only by resolute ridicule. A car-toon in *Punch* showed marchers under a banner titled COCOA, the Coun-cil to Outlaw Contrived and Outrageous Acronyms. This was topped by Jack Rosenthal's satire in the *New York Times* calling for the Action Com-mittee to Reform Our Nation's Youth Morals.

Several years ago I described a condition in professional voice users analo-gous to exercise asthma. That condition is not related to exercise itself, but rather to the airway drying that is associated with hyperventilation from ex-ercise. We noted that some singers, who have an exquisite sensitivity to sub-tle changes in airflow, had an analogous condition. Even though they might have had no other signs of asthma, when they were treated, their voice issues improved. I labeled this Airway Reactivity Induces Asthma in Singers (ARIAS).

John R. Cohn, MD
Thomas Jefferson University
Philadelphia, Pennsylvania

Adjust That Season.   Alistair Cooke rang me up to say, "Do something about *seasonable* when you mean *seasonal.*" (I use the Britishism *rang me up* instead of *phoned* because my nonagenarian friend is a BBC stalwart.) When I wrote recently that a week in January had been "*unseasonably*

warm," another reader, John Connor, e-mailed: "Shouldn't the word be *un-seasonally*? To me, *unseasonable* implies that you can't add salt or pepper."

No; as even the most roundheeled permissivists admit, "There ain't no *unseasonal.*" *Seasonable* means "normal for that time of the year"—icy in February and muggy in August. I am now shopping for cruise clothes because that is what will soon be *seasonable*, although cruises make me seasick. By extension, it has come to mean "apt, timely, opportune."

Contrariwise, *seasonal* has nothing to do with such suitability; rather, its meaning is "occurring in a particular season of the year," like "*seasonal* unemployment." That honking you hear overhead is the "*seasonal* migration of geese." If you're talkin' winter, spring, summer or fall, you're talkin' *seasonal;* only if you're talkin' about what's right and proper for those times are you correct to use *seasonable.*

Just as *seasonable* is a big word with weather forecasters, *seasonal* is a favorite of economists. The great economist Herbert Stein, familiar with the works of T. S. Eliot, used the right word many years ago when he seasoned his prediction to taste: "The poet tells us that April is the cruelest month, but *seasonally* adjusted, January is the cruelest month."

The Agnostic Bit.   "Bits are *agnostic*," Bill Gates, self-dethroned boss of Microsoft, told Forbes's *ASAP* magazine. "They don't care how they get where they are going—only that they arrive in the right order and at the right moment."

William Marmon of Chevy Chase, Maryland, demands a ruling as soon as possible: "Has *agnostic*—'holding the belief that the ultimate reality on matters such as the existence of God is unknowable'—been successfully morphed by high tech to mean 'indifferent'? Everywhere one hears the word used in this perverted manner. Where do you stand?"

Hier stehe ich, in the phrase of one unwaveringly opinionated Worms dieter. In theology and usage, I react religiously.

The etymology of *agnostic* is plain. It's Greek for "not known." Here's how it was coined to describe the position held by people who are neither atheists nor believers: "It was suggested by Professor [Thomas] Huxley at a party . . . one evening in 1869, in my hearing," wrote R. H. Hutton in 1881. "He took it from St. Paul's mention of the altar to 'the Unknown God.' "

Henry Kissinger, in his 1979 memoirs, *The White House Years,* was among the first to give the word a metaphoric stretch: "I favored European unity, but I was *agnostic* about the form it should take." The intended meaning (I have always been able to read Henry's mind) was more "non-committal" than either "undecided" or "indifferent." In 1983 Warren Buffett, the investor, treated the word as a verbal shrug: "I look at stocks, not markets. I am a market *agnostic.*"

Broadbandniks in the computer world have adopted that stretch toward neutrality. "We will deliver 'infrastructure *agnostic*' solutions," announced Steven Francesco, CEO of N(x) Networks, "that can handle both voice and data and be deployed over virtually any network." (The odd-looking company name is pronounced "nex" or "nix"; the new agnostics, professing a hands-off attitude, sometimes take a negative approach.)

Another computer executive, holding that the alliance of Dell and Red Hat came as no surprise, commented, "They've always been operating-system *agnostic.*" At Microsoft, Gates's usage gives the reheated term about bits a sense of "indifferent" to the point of "uncaring."

Can we ever know if this new meaning—as in "Frankly, Scarlett, I'm *agnostic*"—will overtake the theological sense?

Sure we can. Give the voguish jargon a little time; this anomie-tooism will pass because it is a highbrow term that lacks specificity. *Neutral* passively takes no side; *noncommittal* suggests a more active refusal to take a side; *indifferent* describes a mild state of apathy; *unconcerned* imputes aloofness; and *uncaring* has a hint of cruelty. But the new *agnostic* wanders all over the lot.

And Done With.   Peter Mandelson, a minister in Tony Blair's Labor government in Britain, admitted misleading the press about helping a contributor get a passport. After this led to a great media furor, Blair's controversial *éminence grise* was forced to resign. Then, to refashion his tattered reputation after what he called "a trivial error," the longtime spinmeister launched what the British press calls a *fightback,* a colorful term that may or may not lead to a *comeback.*

A cabinet colleague, Clare Short, promptly kicked the downed man with "He wasn't accurate, didn't speak the truth, let himself down and the government. Peter Mandelson is *over.*"

To *be over* is current British and American slang for "to be finished, washed-up, done with, kaput." The predecessor phrase from the '80s is *history,* as in "Forget him—he's *history.*"

Now *history* is over. However, *over*—as in "like, so *over*"—is a Valley Girl expression from the '80s that has shown remarkable legs for what seemed to be a nonce term, outlasting both *history* and *been there, done that.* Toward the end of the second millennium, *so 1999* had a brief run, and *so second millennium* surfaced briefly, but both were too tightly tied to a specific date to have staying power.

The Yogi lesson drawn by dialectologists on both sides of the pond: *over* ain't over till it's over.

In the, uh, rarified vernacular of the world of professional wrestling, "over" means "popular," as in "The Rock is still amazingly over, while daring aerialist Essa Rios could pop the crowd in his hometown."

Rhonda Reddy
Santa Monica, California

Anticounter.   Are we engaged in *antiterrorism* or *counterterrorism*?

Antiterrorism, according to the Department of Defense *Dictionary of Military and Associated Terms,* is "defensive measures used to reduce the *vulnerability* of individuals and property to terrorist acts, to include limited response and containment by local military forces."

Counterterrorism is "offensive measures taken to prevent, deter and respond to terrorism."

How to respond to September 11? Doves prefer *antiterrorism;* hawks plump for *counterterrorism.*

Arab street.   Peppered by questions from senators about why the Bush administration supported a Saudi monarchy that oppressed political or religious dissenters, Secretary of State Colin Powell gave a reply that struck many as puzzling: "Unto dust thou shalt return the day you stop representing *the street.*" He explained, "When you don't have a free, democratic system, where the street is represented in the halls of the legislature and in the executive branches of those governments, then they"—the Saudi rulers— "have to be more concerned by the passions of *the street.*"

Members of PAW—the Poetic Allusion Watch—instantly caught the secretary's "unto dust" drift. The allusion was to Henry Wadsworth Longfellow's "Dust thou art to dust returnest, / Was not spoken of the soul." The poet, in turn, was referring to the passage in Genesis 3:19, "Dust thou art, and into dust shalt thou return," often cited on Ash Wednesday and at funerals.

Powell's message limited itself to the prayer's "dust to dust" portion. His import was that if a Saudi monarch were to go against *the Arab street,* he would soon find himself dead.

"Does this *Arab street* phrase refer to the person (or suicide bomber) in the street," asks Bianca Carter of Slingerlands, New York, "or is there a broader meaning?"

The *street,* from the Latin for "paved path," has many metaphoric senses. Financiers use it to mean Wall Street, the home of the New York Stock Exchange; those thrown out of work use *on the street* to mean "unemployed" (and in a recession, many in the financial Street are on the street). To those in prison, *the street* means "outside," the place to live in freedom. To those hunting for bargains, *street* becomes an attributive noun modifying *price,* meaning "what it actually is selling for, no matter what the price tag says."

In political usage, to get to the point, *the street* began in 1831 as "the man in the street," or average person. In the 20th century, that meaning changed to "those demonstrating in the street." That sense spread to a more general "popular opinion" but often still carries a connotation of "the incendiary emotions of the mob."

The first use of *the Arab street* I can find is in a December 1977 issue of *American Political Science Review*. "The existence of nuclear weapons in the region," wrote Steven J. Rosen, "will induce moderation and a revolution of declining expectations in *the Arab 'street.'*" Though it does not seem to be working out as Rosen hoped, the phrase he spotted caught on. A decade later, G. H. Jansen in the *Los Angeles Times* recalled that during the Suez crisis of 1956, "*'the Arab street'* in every Arab capital pulsated with popular demonstrations." The quotation marks then disappeared as the phrase took hold in the language and gained complexity:

"There was not one but many different *Arab streets*," wrote David Pollock in 1992. Professor Samer Shehata of Georgetown agrees: "The term *Arab street*, which is not used in the Arab world, divides countries into just two factions, but it's much more complicated than *the Arab street* versus the authoritarian regime."

"The phrase used to be *'the Arab masses*,'" recalls a Middle East expert who prefers to remain anonymous because he is passing along only an impression. "With the eclipse of the Soviet Union, that phrase disappeared because *Arab masses* has too much of a Marxist-Soviet-Communist tilt to it, and it was replaced by *the Arab street*."

Does *the Arab street* reflect popular opinion in the Arab world or just the opinion of extremists carrying banners and burning flags? Is there a silent majority that is not in agreement with demonstrators, as there often is in the West? Nobody can say for sure, but the phrase, as used by Secretary Powell, means "the opinions of people governed by an autocratic regime and unable to express their views through elected representatives."

It should not be confused with *street Arab*, a derogatory term for "urban vagabond, homeless urchin," as used in 1887 in Arthur Conan Doyle's first Sherlock Holmes tale: "I therefore organized my *street Arab* detective corps," which later evolved into fans styling themselves "the Baker Street Irregulars."

Asymmetry. "*Asymmetric warfare,*" said Maj. Gen. Perry Smith, retired, "is the term of the day." President Bush evidently agrees: "We need to re-think how we configure our military," he told his first prime-time news conference, ". . . so that we more effectively respond to *asymmetrical* responses from terrorist organizations."

The prime user is Secretary of Defense Donald Rumsfeld. After noting recently, "We really are going to have to fashion a new vocabulary" to de-scribe the new kind of warfare, he told reporters that he had long been talking of "*asymmetrical* threats" like "terrorism and ballistic missiles, cruise missiles, cyberattacks." When Tim Russert of *Meet the Press* tried to pin him down further with "What are *asymmetrical* methods?" Rumsfeld came up with the same examples but not a definition.

Let's begin with *symmetry,* meaning "in balance; in proportionate arrangement," often implying a beauty that flows from such regularity. The middle syllable is *met,* its root in the Greek *metron,* "measure," which acts as a fulcrum in a nicely balanced word. William Blake used it most memo-rably in his 1794 poem "The Tyger," concluding, "What immortal hand or eye / Dare frame thy fearful *symmetry?*" (Making the last syllable, which sounds like *ee,* rhyme with *eye* was poetic license.)

Asymmetric (or *asymmetrical,* equally correct, so I use the shorter one) has the obvious dictionary definition of "not symmetric" and the slang meaning of "out of whack," but a less pejorative sense is developing: "off-beat, intriguingly unbalanced."

Asymmetrical warfare is defined by the Defense Department as "coun-tering an adversary's strengths by focusing on its weaknesses." Michael Krepon wrote in the May-June 2001 issue of *Foreign Affairs* that "*asymmet-rical warfare* allows a weaker opponent to level the playing field by un-orthodox means."

The earliest citation of the phrase I can find, and one that suggests ear-lier military use, is by Robert Fox, a reporter for the *Daily Telegraph,* in 1991. He quoted a British commander, Lt. Col. Mike Vickery, who compared the coming allied attack on Iraq to an unconventional maneuver by the 14th Hussars in the Peninsular War, as the English under the future duke of Wellington drove the French out of Spain: "The regiment was detailed to move round the flanks, sneak round the back, you might say, to harry the rear and baggage train. It was what today we call *asymmetric warfare*." (A trophy of that unconventional engagement in 1813 was a solid silver chamber pot given by Napoleon Bonaparte to his brother Joseph.)

In the past decade, the phrase was applied to war that might be waged against a superpower. Clinton's defense secretary William S. Cohen, in a farewell speech in January, defined it as "indirect, but highly lethal, attacks on our forces and our citizens, not always from nations but from individuals and even independent groups."

Until recently, the meaning was limited to the application of surprise force by a terrorist against a stronger force's vulnerability, but ever since the Sept. 11 attack, Pentagonians have been applying *asymmetric warfare* to the kind of commando and anti-guerrilla techniques, drawing heavily on intelligence data, to be used against Taliban forces in Afghanistan—using non-superpower strength to go after a weaker foe's vulnerabilities. The idea is to fight *asymmetry* with *asymmetry*.

Lopsidedness (from *lop,* "to sever") is in fashion, too: "Only squares will be wearing straight hems next spring," writes Holly Finn in the *Financial Times,* "but fear not. Done well, an *asymmetrical* hem looks sexier."

Attention All Alliterators. "Apt alliteration's artful aid"—Charles Churchill's famous foray was not wholly alliterative, since not all the first letters are pronounced the same way—is alive and well on the political scene.

You need at least a triple to qualify as an apt alliterator. At a conference of the Center for the Study of the Presidency, Senator John Breaux of Louisiana described his centrist alliance with a fellow centrist Democrat, Senator Joe Lieberman, as "the Kosher-Cajun Caucus."

According to the man who taught me English in sophomore year at prep school, the Charles Churchill phrase you quote, with or without its flaws, would not represent alliteration. For alliteration, the initial letters have to be consonants. When the initial letters are vowels, the gimmick is called assonance. *

John Strother
Princeton, New Jersey

*Correct in origin, but usage usurped.—W.S.

B

Baldfaced. As the 2000 campaigners practice their endgamesmanship, each side accuses the other of *baldfaced* lies. In some instances, the accusers prefer *barefaced* lies, and in a Virginia race, the mouth-filling modifier has come out sounding like *boldfaced* lies.

Where does the truth lie? (Yes, in this instance, the truth does *lie;* unless your subject is a hen, *lay* must have an object.)

It seems that the unadorned *lie* no longer has its old puissance. Time was, that word was so inflammatory as to need a euphemism: *fib* was the slang gentler, *prevarication* the bookish term. But to score as an emphatic charge, it now needs an adjective. "That's a *dirty* lie" used to have a ring to it, but that adjective is now almost exclusively applied to jokes and lyrics. "*Damned* lie," once popular, is too closely associated with statistics.

The denunciator has a menu from which to choose: *outright* is forthright, *blatant* has a ring to it, *flat* is sharp (though it is often mistakenly replaced by *flat-out,* which lacks the disapproving connotation) and *flagrant* lends itself to mispronunciation by stumbling speakers as *fragrant.*

What is a designated finger-pointer to do when this anti-dissembly line turns out no insightful inciting to outrage? Into vituperation's void steps *baldfaced,* giving the lie to the new listlessness of the overused *lie.* At the request of Robert and Claudia Wasserman of Remsenburg, New York, let us deconstruct the campaigners' favorite counterpunch intensifier.

Shakespeare coined first *barefaced* and then *boldfaced*. The first referred to beardless youth: "Some of your French Crownes have no hair at all," Quince tells Bottom in *A Midsummer Night's Dream* as he casts a play, "and then you will play *bare-faced*." The meaning of *barefaced* was clearly "without whiskers," which led to senses of "unconcealed, open." In time, this innocent lack of disguise took on the color of shamelessness. In Laurence Sterne's *Tristram Shandy* (1760), we have, "See the *barefaced* villain, how he cheats, lies, perjures, robs, murders!" (This is the sense today's political campaigners have in mind.)

A year after his 1590 coinage of *barefaced*, Shakespeare, in *Henry VI, Part 1,* had Lord Talbot speak of "proud desire of *bold-faced* Victory" after he rescues his son, John, on the French battlefield; that meant "confident," a sense that soon turned into "impudent," as confidence so often does. Not until 1884 did the Italian printer Giambattista Bodoni use *boldface* to describe a darkly thick, or bold, typeface, which looks **like this** and is easily distinguished from lightface type.

From *bare* and *bold* to *bald:* the etymology of *baldfaced* should interest angry animal rights advocates. All the early uses referred to animals: in 1648, "a *bawld-facd* heighfer"; in 1677, "a sorrel Mare . . . *bald-faced*"; and in 1861, "our *bald-faced* hornet." And of course, the symbol of America was "the *bald* eagle." In its original sense, *bald* did not mean "hairless, shiny-pated, cueball-like, suedeheaded." It meant "white." The top of our symbolic eagle's head is not featherless; the last time I patted one, its head and neck were covered with smooth white feathers. In the 13th century, the *balled coot* was a water bird with a white mark on its forehead, lingering in the lingo today in the simile *bald as a coot. Baldfaced* whiskey was a 19th-century Americanism for pale, raw liquor, and a *boiled, biled* or *bald-faced* shirt was a cowboy's go-to-meetin' white shirt. The Celtic *bal* meant "a white mark," and the Sanskrit *bhala,* "forehead," from the Indo-European *bhel,* "white, shining." Had enough? At bottom, it's white. That's why horses with white markings on their noses are often called Old *Baldy,* same as the snow-covered mountain.

In current use, then, *baldfaced* lie is the most popular because it sounds most resounding; *barefaced* lie continues to run strong with no connotation of any pursuit of the hirsute; and *boldfaced* lie sounds like a printer's error. In every case, kill the hyphen.

Barnburner.   "I know where the *rats in the barn* are," shouted Al Gore on the stump in Muskegon, Michigan. "And you know what? The *rats in the barn* know that I know, and that's why they're coming out trying to stop us."

He repeated this lively rural phrase in Fond du Lac, Wisconsin, and it was broadcast far and wide in coverage of the Democratic campaign. (Perhaps it subliminally evoked the split-second use of the word *rats* in a GOP television spot.) It has the sound of an old Americanism, but is nowhere to be found in the dialect dictionaries.

"Don't ask Congress to *rid your barn of rats,*" wrote William Raspberry in the *Washington Post* in 1993. This was the sinister meaning that Gore evoked, but when coupled with *old,* the phrase has another, almost affectionate, sense. "Once you . . . get to be an *old rat in a barn,*" Representative Willis Brown of North Carolina told an Associated Press reporter asking about term limits, "you do not want to be dislodged."

The figure of speech was cornered again when Zell Miller of Georgia—this month elected a U.S. senator but in 1998 departing the Statehouse—said in an aw-shucks way that he and those governors who accompanied him into retirement were nothing but "*old rats in a barn.*"

The invasive rodent has still another sense in its tail: to *have a rat in the garret,* according to the *Century Dictionary,* is "to be slightly crack-brained: same as 'to have a bee in one's bonnet.' "

How do you rid your barn of rats? One drastic approach is to burn the barn down. In a sermon in 1629, Thomas Adams said, "The empiric to cure the fever, destroys the patient; so the wise man, to burn the mice, sets fire to his barn." This related metaphor was heard on MSNBC just before the election, as the anchor Brian Williams said: "By all accounts, we have a *barnburner* of a presidential election on our hands. That would make this *barnburner* eve." That was a use of *barnburner* in one current sense: ripping along as excitingly as "a house afire" or some such spectacular event.

A more traditional sense is "one who is uncompromising, rigidly principled"—who sees politics as the art of the impossible.

The *Barnburners* in the early 1840s were the reformist, radical faction of New York State Democrats led by former President Martin Van Buren, who adamantly opposed slavery. They were given that derisive nickname by the Hunkers (so called because they "hunkered" or "hankered" after national office), who favored the annexation of Texas, which extended slavery westward.

The Hunkers ridiculed Van Buren's antislavery stand "in the manner of the Dutch farmer who burned his barn to destroy the rats." In 1848, Van Buren's *Barnburners* bolted the Democratic Party to join the Free-Soilers, and Van Buren's candidacy delivered election victory to the Whig Zachary Taylor. That uncompromising, abolitionist coalition later named itself Republican.

In the recent contest, Ralph Nader, in rejecting Democratic compromises on issues central to many liberals, could be said to have been the *barnburner.* Some Democrats recalled Adlai Stevenson's admonition in 1952 in a different context, warning of excess in combating subversion: "We must take care not to burn down the barn to kill the rats."

In 2000, Al Gore did not propose to burn down the barn, nor did he say precisely who the unwanted inhabitants were, but he did make it clear he knew where the metaphoric rats could be found.

Bated Breath.   "The people of Congo," said Levy Mwanawasa, the president of Zambia, last month in his capital of Lusaka, "are waiting with *baited breath* for a positive outcome of the Sun City talks." That's how Agence France-Presse spelled the adjective modifying the noun *breath.*

The same week, the *Independent* newspaper of London, recapping memorable quotations of Margaret Thatcher in a review of her new memoir, *Statecraft,* chose this famous 1980 example: "To those waiting with *bated breath* for that favorite media catch phrase, the U-turn, I have only one thing to say: You turn if you want to—the lady's not for turning." (That was a rhyming reference to the title of Christopher Fry's 1948 play about a woman's resistance to a witchcraft trial, *The Lady's Not for Burning*.)

Meanwhile, Reuters reported from Tokyo that "shares edged up by midday as investors waited with *baited breath* for a government package."

Which is correct in modifying *breath*—*bated* or *baited*? A search of the Dow Jones database covering the past twenty-five years shows 5,520 uses of *bated* and 1,289 uses of *baited*. In a world of toleration and permissiveness, both are thus correct, right? Wrong. A mistake is a mistake, and there is no *i* in *bated*. (Contrariwise, you cannot leave out the *i* in "*baiting* a hook," from the Old Norse *beita*, "to cause to bite," which will work on fish if you *bait* the hook properly.)

What's the basis of *bated*, which we never hear in the present tense? It is a clip of *abate*, from the Old French *abattre*, "to beat down," and now it means "to moderate, subside, reduce, ebb." In connection with breathing, it means "shorten" or "hold." When you *abate* your breath, you hold it in anticipation of some breathtaking event.

The coiner was Shakespeare in his 1596 *Merchant of Venice*, in which Shylock says to Antonio, "Shall I bend low and in a bondman's key, / With *bated breath* and whispering humbleness, / Say this: / 'Fair sir, you spit on me on Wednesday last?' "

Synonyms—more precisely, similar metaphors—for *bated breath* include *butterflies in the stomach*; the British *get the wind up*; the 17th-century *on tenterhooks* (the frame on which a tent's cloth is stretched); *have one's heart in one's mouth*, from Homer's *Iliad*; and *on pins and needles*, an 1810 coinage about the tingling sensation from sitting on them. In Yiddish, this feeling is expressed as *shpilkes*. The extreme is *screaming meemies*, which *Picturesque Expressions* by Laurence Urdang notes originated as a World War II nickname for German rocket shells and is now often confused with the phrase *streaming media*.

In *bated breath*, we have a clear-cut case of widespread misspelling. It's no controversy; forget *baiting* unless you're fishing or taunting. And yet I anticipate mail on this item. A dozen or so readers, afflicted with raging e-mailitis, will ask: "How come President Mwanawasa's first name is Levy? That doesn't sound Zambian." To get ahead of the querying curve, I called the Zambian Embassy. They haven't called back. You can imagine in what state I'm waiting.

Bravo for saying about bait/bate *that the frequent, ignorant confusion is a mistake and not to be condoned.*

But I think that your list of equivalents to "bated breath" is too inclusive. It takes no account of motive. "Bated breath" results from deliberate purpose—wanting to remain hidden, hoping for a much-desired answer. Something makes us hold our breath; whereas "butterflies in the stomach" or "heart in one's mouth" comes unbidden, and so does "getting the wind up" (as the passive sense of getting *implies). As for "tenterhooks" and "pins and needles" they also are consequences of external events or others' actions. Finally, "screaming meemies" require a great deal of breath and are the contrary of the bated supply.*

Jacques Barzun
San Antonio, Texas

Between Prexies.   Here's a word that pops up every four or eight years: *interregnum.* The Latin means "between reigns." The *interregnum,* or *interregencie,* originally meant the interval when a throne or position of leadership was vacant, as between the death or removal of one sovereign and the accession of the next. This invited trouble, as in the Cromwell era. William Blackstone, in his 1765 *Commentaries,* held that in England "the king is made a corporation to prevent in general the possibility of an *interregnum* or vacancy of the throne."

The word now means "an intermission in the order of succession" and, more generally, "a breach of continuity." Specifically, in the United States, it means "the period between the election of a new president and his inauguration." But it is not limited to political power: the breakfast-table autocrat Oliver Wendell Holmes wrote, "Between the last dandelion and violet . . . and the first spring blossom . . . there is a frozen *interregnum* in the vegetable world."

The word, lest we forget, is spelled with two *r*'s. It produced a spin-off during the transition from Jimmy Carter to Ronald Reagan, which wags called the *interreaganum*.

Bialy.   Thanks to Mel Brooks, creator of *The Producers*—one of the few smash-hit musicals without one popular song—the word *bialy* is rising on America's horizon.

His central character is Max Bialystock. That name gives a vaguely Eastern European flavor to the role of the unscrupulous impresario out to bilk investors by producing a surefire flop.

That's because there is a place named Białystock. It is a city of about a quarter million residents located in northeast Poland; its most famous sons were the Soviet diplomat Maxim Litvinov and the microbiologist Albert Sabin. Its most famous product is known locally as the *Bialystoker kuchen* and to the hungry world as the *bialy*.

A *bialy* is to a bagel what Białystock is to Vladivostok—that is, a world apart. A *bialy* is a round, saucer-size *pletzl*, "flat bread" (rhymes with *pretzel*), that has its center mushed in to form a depression made delectable with bits of onion.

The food critic Mimi Sheraton explored this mouthwatering subject last year in a book titled *The Bialy Eaters: The Story of a Bread and a Lost World*. Although *bialy* means "white" in Slavic languages, the cakelike bread does not get its name from its dusting of white flour; rather, the Polish mountainside, or *stok,* is on what we would call the White River, which gives its name to the city. That city, in turn, gives its name to the fragrant roll and to the fictional Broadway producer.

Sheraton describes the tenderly crusty roll as "characterized by an indented center well that is ringed by a softer, higher rim, all generously flecked with toasted onions and, at its most authentic, with a showering of poppy seeds." It has, she adds with a certain reverence, "an affinity for sweet butter and fluffy cream cheese."

This department does not shrink from controversy: one should neither slice nor toast a *bialy*. Smear whatever you like over the onions in the well;

bakeries these days use up their poppy seeds on bagels, which can be toasted, but the seeds mess up the toaster. If you like your breakfast bread hot, bake the center-depressed *pletzl* for five minutes or so until its edges look threatening. (I don't know at what heat; this is a language column.) The newly popularized word is pronounced "bee-AH-lee."

Big Applesource.   Controversy rages over who coined *the Big Apple* as a moniker for New York.

The earliest citation is in Edward Martin's 1909 book, *The Wayfarer in New York*. Martin, a founder of the Harvard *Lampoon* and first editor of the humor magazine *Life*, was writing about the attitude of the Midwest toward the metropolis: "Kansas is apt to see in New York a greedy city. . . . It inclines to think that *the big apple* gets a disproportionate share of the national sap."

The *Random House Historical Dictionary of American Slang* notes an absence of capitalization or quotation marks in this citation and thinks it "probable that the 1909 quotation represents a metaphorical or perhaps proverbial usage, rather than a concrete example of the later slang term." I dunno about that; capitalization is not necessary in coinage, and quotation marks only would suggest an earlier use.

The etymologist Barry Popik, with fresh support from the phrase detectives Fred Shapiro and Gerald Cohen, has long been campaigning to give coinage honors to John J. Fitzgerald, a turf writer. He wrote in the *New York Morning Telegraph* on Feb. 18, 1924: "There's only one *Big Apple*. That's New York." After Fitzgerald popularized the term, crediting it to African-American stable hands in New Orleans in 1920, the columnist Walter Winchell picked it up in 1927. A decade later it became the name of a Harlem nightclub and a dance.

Popik makes a strong case, but I'd credit Martin with coinage and Fitzgerald with independent recoinage and early popularization. But you pays yer money and you takes yer cherce (from an 1846 cartoon in the British magazine *Punch*).

⁊

Blip.   "We don't react to day-to-day *blips*," said James Gorman, a Merrill Lynch sales chief. On *Wall Street Week,* Louis Rukeyser dismissed "some renewed jitters in the wake of a *blip* in retail sales."

As a linguistic plunger, I invested heavily in *blip*s two decades ago. "*Blip* has good upside potential," it was noted in this space in 1982, when a White House spokesman shrugged off bad financial news with "We had one bad *blip* today." Since then, the usage of this onomatopoeic word has soared as jargonauts in a variety of fields embrace it, and I remain bullish on *blip*s because the word satisfies a need for "sudden, minor shock; meaningless interruption."

The earliest senses were "a quick blow, accompanied by a popping sound" and "a twitch." The *Dictionary of American Regional English* exhumed its origins: "Brer Rabbit draw back wid his fis', he did," wrote Joel Chandler Harris in his 1880 Uncle Remus stories, "en *blip* he tuck 'er side er de head." In 1894, Mark Twain in *Tom Sawyer Abroad* wrote, "We took him a *blip* in the back and knocked him off."

Dashiell Hammett kept that sinister sense in his 1929 *Maltese Falcon,* introducing a verb form: "You could have *blipped* them both." In our electronic age, *blip* overtook *pip* to mean "a point of light on a radar screen to locate a searched-for object." On television and later computer screens, the noun denoted any sudden surge of sound or light, often caused by an electrical interruption. When this was done deliberately to expunge an expletive, it was called a *bleep.*

Because the spot of light or pop of sound was tiny, the word soon connoted smallness or insignificance as the metaphor was extended.

In the 2000 campaign, when George W. Bush used a vulgarity near an open mike, the *Dallas Morning News* noted the difference between a minor slip and a major blunder: "Analysts differ over whether it is a soon-to-be-forgotten *blip* or a *blooper* with staying power." Electronic media that wanted to shield their listeners *bleeped* the *blip.*

Do not sell this short word short, as it can be used to describe sudden, transitory moves in any direction. Diplomats have long found it a useful word to minimize troubling changes: commenting on reversals in peace negotiations in 1972, Henry Kissinger said there "may be *blips* up and down." But dismissal as a *blip* can invite response from editorialists who deride attempts to play down major events. As Watergate scandals came to a head in 1974, the *New York Times* wrote about President Nixon, "Can he really be so uncomprehending that he considers it, to use his word, a mere '*blip*'?"

Though some language mavens cautiously rate *blip* as a market outperformer, I'll still call it a buy.

As for "bleep," you failed to mention it lasts longer than a "blip," which is only momentary (or, in the language of today, possibly "momentous"). Also, the Slang Dictionary's "origin" is probably mere coincidence: "blip" is virtually onomatopoeic, and that is its most likely origin.

Laurence Urdang

Old Lyme, Connecticut

I was a bit disappointed to see you perpetuate the misuse of the word "expletive."

While the word came into widespread use upon the publication of the Nixon tapes, which made "expletive deleted" a common term, it has been widely misused.

There is nothing about an expletive, per se, that would require it to be deleted or "bleeped." An expletive is merely an exclamation, which may be obscene, but "ain't necessarily so!"

For example, if I were to say, "Oh, fudge!" or "Gosh!"—those would be expletives, but would not be obscene and would not require deletion. If, however, I were to say, "Al Gore is a lying sack of [deleted]," the word in brackets would be an obscenity, but would not be an expletive!

Misuse of a word, no matter how widespread, should not change its meaning. If you allow this to happen you are promoting the "if you can't beat 'em, join 'em" school of semantics. Look at what that attitude has already done to words like "infer," "hopefully" and "fulsome." It's up to purists like you and me to resist it.

Stuart Tarlowe
Rosedale, Kansas

Body Man.   The political lexicon is suddenly being enriched. For years, *the man* has been the president, perhaps associated with *main man,* from Black English. Now *the man* has a man of his own with an official job title.

"Here's a new entry," says Eric Schmitt, the *New York Times* reporter who covers Vice President Dick Cheney (sometimes referred to as "the P.M.," or prime minister, or less reverently by President Bush as Big Time, recalling Cheney's famous response to a joshing derogation of another of our journalistic colleagues). "It's *body man.*"

Cheney's *body man,* reports Schmitt, is Brian McCormack, an earnest young guy from New Jersey who considers himself a jack-of-all-trades. He carries Big Time's coat, passes him messages, "keeps him up to date and on time" and generally sticks close by to do whatever errand or task Cheney needs done.

A *Times* reporter who covers the president, Frank Bruni, says that George W. Bush's *body man* is Logan Walters, retained in that key post from the campaign. Walters jots down addresses for thank-you notes, declines gifts worth more than fifty dollars and holds the cell phone that keeps his boss reachable by his inner circle. (Sign of intimacy: a cow on the Bush ranch, born on the aide's birthday, is named Logan.)

The informal job title is not to be confused with *the man with the briefcase,* the ever-present carrier of the codes needed by the president to respond to a hostile missile launch. It is more specific and intimate than *gofer,* a term applied to any aide ready to "go fer" coffee or do other menial tasks.

The earliest citation I can find after a quick rattling of the cages is from a 1988 article by Susan Trausch of the *Boston Globe:* "Every candidate has a *body man,* someone who fulfills a kind of mothering role on the trail. The *body man* makes sure the candidate's tie is straight for the TV debate, keeps his mood up and makes sure he gets his favorite cereal for breakfast." The columnist Chris Matthews, who used the phrase in print in 1989, recalls that JFK's *body man* was David Powers.

The phrase suggests that the aide does not deal with the president's mind. However, the title was given more dignity recently by Mary McGrory in the *Washington Post*. "Thanks to *The West Wing*, the classy television series," she wrote, "everyone knows what a *'body man'* is. He's the one who hovers over the Big Man, making sure his suit is pressed, his shoes are shined and his speech is stapled in order." Then the columnist, aware of the power of access, gave the job a prestigious boost: "He's also a press secretary without portfolio, a policy adviser and a diplomat who keeps the locals from pestering the boss."

The *body* in *body man* is an attributive noun, which means it does the job of an adjective—as in *body suit, body blow* and *body snatcher.*

I thought that main man *was merely an embellishment of* man, *which I have been led to believe became a black term of address in order to counteract the racist put-down,* boy.

Laurence Urdang
Old Lyme, Connecticut

Broadband.   His necktie was defiantly ripped away. His old-fashioned mustache was shaved off. All but rocking on the soles of his feet and snapping his fingers to illustrate his with-it-ness, the new boss of AOL Time Warner Inc. announced to the world, "I am a *broadband* person."

As if that transmogrification were not enough, Gerald M. Levin—until now a fairly dignified executive—added plaintively, "I'm an *interactive* guy." But *interactive* is yesterday's word, for years meaning "acting upon each other" and then meaning "reciprocating by electronic means"; now used mainly by aging Wunderkinder straining to keep pace, it awaits the coinage of its opposite, *interinactive,* "a one-way flow of data." Hip, connected e-lexies in this winter of our content provision focused on his *broadband* personhood.

That word has a glorious history in the northern dialects of Britain.

"The verie euill thoughts of the wicked," wrote Zachary Boyd in *Last Battell,* his 1629 masterpiece, "in that day shalbe spread out and laide in *broadband* before the face of God." James O. Halliwell, in his 1847 *Dictionary of Archaic and Provincial Words,* reminded us that a band was a space twenty yards square, and *broad-band* was "corn laid out in the sheaf on the band, and spread out to dry after rain."

Over three centuries, the *band* evolved from a marked-out strip of land into "a range of radio frequencies or wavelengths." In 1956, W. A. Heflin's *U.S. Air Force Dictionary* defined *broadband* as "a band having a wide range of frequencies." In our time, it morphed into a medium that not only transmits a wide range of radio, video and data signals, but also can carry other independent channels in their own bandwidths, or space on the band. (On these multiple spaces the communicators still seem to lay out wet corn.)

Then metaphor began to beat the *broadband.* The adjective (sometimes hyphenated) is still used to describe multiplex communications networks, but in more sweeping terms. "In a *broad-band* world," wrote Andrew Sullivan in the *New York Times,* "even the distinctions among telephone wires, cables and satellites will be erased. There will be one cultural-economic tube." The *Milwaukee Journal Sentinel* wrote of "the *broad-band* war, the struggle over who will control the ability to deliver seamless streams of data to consumers."

And now, in an interinactive linguistic breakthrough, Mr. Levin has extended the metaphor from networks to human beings. "I am a *broadband* person" means more, in my view, than "I work in an industry characterized by simultaneous transmission of multiple channels." It means that he sees himself as a person with *broadband* personal characteristics—able to think, speak, gesture, persuade, broadcast and data-disseminate in an unlimited way, while chewing gum at the same time.

Look at yourself, dear reader. Are you a *narrowband* person, cribbed, cabin'd and confined in a strait gate—or are you the sort whose mind ranges far out over the amber waves of corn? By rejecting the "verie euill thoughts of the wicked," you, too, can mega-merge yourself into a *broadband* person.

If that's your choice, move quickly to so identify yourself, because telecommuning lingo changes fast, and *broadband* is sure to be crowded out soon.

Bundling.   The great American counterspook, Paul Redmond, left a word-news tip in the dead drop that is my answering machine: "Check out *bundling*."

Old-timers remember that word fondly from their spooning days. "*Bundling* was originally courting in bed," noted an 1874 British slang dictionary, "the lovers being tied or bundled up to prevent undue familiarities. The practice still obtains in Wales."

This 1781 term for an early form of what is now called "safe sex," apparently pioneered by the prudent Welsh, was derived from the Old English *bindan*, "to bind together," and was later applied to "men and women sleeping together, where the divisions of the house will not permit of better or more decent accommodation, with all their clothes on."

Fast-forward to the Arizona legislature in 1956, which prohibited "*bundling* or combining various limited benefit insurance policies." The pejorative connotation grew when the Justice Department in 1975 accused IBM of charging anticompetitive prices for *bundling* hardware and software services. The European Community repeated the complaint in 1981, and John Tagliabue defined the word in the *New York Times*: "the practice of what is called *bundling*—selling the elements of a computer system as a package to prevent competitors from supplying them at perhaps better conditions."

Today the term obtains, to use the archaic verb, in the Microsoft case, as a federal judge ruled that the company illegally *bundled* its Web browser with its Windows operating system. In my legal-etymological interpretation, the company is appealing on the grounds that separate divisions wrapped up in bed together, fully clothed, are not making love.

Thus do old terms find new uses in the brave new wide Web world. For example, the trade name SPAM—created in 1937 by Hormel Foods out of the first and last letters of "spiced ham"—has, when uncapitalized, come to

mean "junk e-mail," with a second sense of "the random posting of adver-
tisements on computer bulletin boards."

A fanciful speculation about the metaphoric reason for the adoption of
spamming by the computer world can be found in the excellent *Newton's
Telecom Dictionary,* sixteenth edition: "the term is derived from a brand of
pink, canned meat that splatters messily when hurled." (A spokesman for
Hormel vociferously denies this, and tests run at the Safire Semantic
Kitchens confirm that uncanned SPAM, when hurled against a wall at a
normal speed, bounces rather than splatters.)

Cache, pronounced "cash," from the French verb *cacher,* "to hide," came
to mean "a hiding place for valuables"; it was especially applied to holes
dug to conceal provisions and ammunition. (One reason given by the Pentagon for the U.S. incursion into Cambodia in 1969 was to capture buried
arms, causing the Nixon aide Len Garment to ask, "Can you check a
cache?")

In usage by the new lingo, information is *cached* by placing it closer to
the user to make it more accessible, which also places less strain on limited
computer and network resources. The meaning has changed from the sinister "hiding place" to a more positive "nearby holding place."

A *cookie* originated as a small Dutch cake and became the term for a
baked morsel to be passed around after the *canapés* have been devoured.
The metaphoric origin of *cookie* in computerese is obscure, but its meaning is "a text file placed on a computer's hard disk by an Internet server to
track the client's habits and tastes." Marketers say it provides convenience
and unexpected choices to clients; privacy guardians warn that a *cookie* can
follow a customer's movements around the Web to create an invasive profile.

A *cookie pusher* was a term coined in World War II to be a derogation of
diplomats who attended too many receptions; now it is an exponent of
"targeted marketing."

Attendant began as "one who waits upon or accompanies," as in Milton's
"Lest sin Surprise thee, and her black *attendant,* Death." After adoption by
airlines of *flight attendant* when *stewardess* was taken as sexist, the word
was snapped up by technologists and now has two meanings. The first is

"an inexpensive computer that leans heavily on its connection to more sophisticated computers." The second meaning bothers me. "An attendant is an operator of a phone system console," lexicographer Harry Newton reports. "Typically, it's the first person in a company to answer an incoming call. That person *attends* the phone system; when the company's phone is answered by a machine, that's an *automated attendant*."

What's the matter with *operator*? My mother was a telephone *operator* and proud of it. An *operator* suggests an active, purposeful, hands-on person engaging with a device or system; an *attendant* is more passive, sometimes just hanging around "in waiting." The machine, or system, that is operated is secondary to the human in charge, but the phone system that is merely *attended* is the master.

Hello, Central?

Anent (ahem) your column on technological borrowings: I believe that in its cybersense, "cache" is pronounced with a long "a," as in "case."

Allan M. Siegal
The New York Times
New York, New York

Another current context for bundling is the device for getting around campaign contribution limits of $5,000 from a PAC or $1,000 from an individual. Emily's List is the best-known liberal practitioner of collecting a bunch of checks for one candidate and handing them over all at once to show that you're worth more than $1,000 or $5,000, but various corporate operatives do it, too.

Adam Clymer
The New York Times
Washington, D.C.

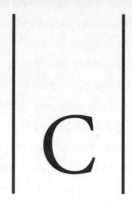

Can a Pig Fly?   The modifier universally adopted by journalists and political figures to describe our aircraft was *lumbering*.

After one jingoistic *New York Times* columnist described the Aries as
having been "*lumbering* along at about 350 mph," another *Times* pundit
sensitive to loaded words noted coolly that "U.S. sources have insisted that
the Chinese fighter planes must have been at fault, because they are so
much nimbler than our *'lumbering'* surveillance plane."

Lumbering soon achieved code status for "it couldn't have been our
fault." "We had a slow, *lumbering,* relatively unmaneuverable aircraft," said
House International Relations Committee Chairman Henry Hyde; "they
had a fighter plane." Larry Eagleburger, the heavyset, slow-moving former
secretary of state, asserted, "You know, our aircraft is a slow, *lumbering*
thing."

Origin is the Swedish *lomra,* "to resound," and *loma,* "to walk heavily";
Middle English picked up the imitative word (like *rumbling, crumbling,
cumbrous, ponderous*) in the 14th century as *lomeren.* A clip of the last syllable led to *lumber,* a collection of useless goods, like old wooden tables
and chairs, that impede movement. British slang still uses *lumbered* to
mean "laden, weighed down, encumbered."

No wonder our unapologetic servicemembers call it "the flying pig."

Cardinal Placement.   A *New Yorker* editor wonders about "the westward title migration" of cardinals. "How come it always used to be Francis Cardinal Spellman and Richard Cardinal Cushing and now all of a sudden it's Cardinal Edward M. Egan and Cardinal Bernard F. Law?"

This is the least of the church's problems. The 1999 *New York Times Manual of Style and Usage* reports, "Church authorities no longer place *Cardinal* between given name and surname." In a 1987 column in this space irreverently but respectfully titled "Long Time No See" (the archaic *see* is the "seat of power"), I quoted His Eminence Johannes Willebrands, who is today the chamberlain of the College of Cardinals, as cheerfully waving off the placement of the title between his first and last names with "We don't do that anymore."

But many still do: the archbishop of New York, identified by the *Times*, the Associated Press and most television reporters as "Cardinal Edward M. Egan," last month signed his vigorous denunciation of the abuse of children with a traditional "Edward Cardinal Egan." As with pronunciation and usage, it's a matter heavily influenced by style.

Carpe Diem.   Justifying his plans for transition planning during the vote-counting turmoil, Governor George W. Bush said that it was important "to show the American people that this administration will be ready to *seize the moment*." Two weeks later, in his first speech as president-elect, he told the nation, "We must *seize the moment* and deliver."

This is a case for PAW. The Poetic Allusion Watch is maintained in this space to call attention to the roots of our current metaphors that are expressed in flights of vaguely remembered poetry. Whether the Republican candidate knew it or not, he was alluding to a phrase in an ode by the Roman poet Horace: *Carpe diem, quam minimum credula postero,* "*Seize the day,* put no trust in the future."

At its first citation in English, Lord Byron in 1817 took the phrase to mean, in his words, "never anticipate." That philosophical approach was akin to Robert Herrick's 1648 "Gather ye rosebuds while ye may," expressed much later in the song "Enjoy Yourself (It's Later Than You

Think)." The literary critic Northrop Frye wrote in 1957 that Horace's *carpe diem* was "based on a moment of pleasure in experience."

But two strange things happened to Horace's phrase on its way to political oratory. First, the day was radically shortened to an hour and finally to a moment. This may have been influenced by Ernest Hemingway's promulgation of the Spanish phrase *el momento de la verdad,* "moment of truth." More to the point, the meaning expressed by *carpe diem* shifted from the hedonistic "live it up while you have the chance" to an exhortation to be bold, recalling Shakespeare's "tide in the affairs of men, which, taken at the flood, leads on to fortune." The two U.S. presidents who did most to fix the speeded-up phrase in the current political lexicon were Richard Nixon and Bill Clinton. In his State of the Union message in 1971, Nixon said, "If we act boldly—if we *seize this moment,*" we could close great gaps, and he warned in 1972 that "if we failed to *seize this moment,*" we would be untrue to generations yet unborn.

When asked why he named his 1992 book *Seize the Moment* rather than quote his own frequent use, Nixon said: "I quoted from a poem that Mao Zedong had written in which he said, 'Seize the day, seize the hour, because many things urgently remain to be done.' . . . We should *seize the moment,* not for Communism, but for the victory of freedom."

Clinton became so enamored of the phrase that he used it eleven times on the final day of his 1996 campaign for re-election: "Will you *seize the day* tomorrow and help us expand family leave?" he asked voters in Cleveland. "Will you *seize the day* and help us balance the budget? . . . You've got to *seize the day* and help us reform health care. You've got to *seize the day.*"

In the years following that multiple seizure, Clinton went for the accelerated form adopted by Nixon. In the summer of 2000, he urged Republican senators to "*seize this moment,* to stop the delays." Meanwhile, GOP Senator John McCain was reminding his Republican colleagues of their obligation "to *seize this moment* to help build a safer, freer and more prosperous world." Democrats hastily snatched the phrase back: soon after Bill Bradley said "I feel an urgency to *seize this moment,*" Al Gore asked voters in New York, "Will we *seize this moment* to extend prosperity and share it widely, or will we just lavish more on those who need it least?"

The phrase in the Horace ode, its meaning twisted from "live it up" to "be bold" in Mao's accelerated corollary, is now enshrined in the book of golden political clichés. Because I did not want Bush's repetition of it to go unnoticed, I thought the time ripe, the day upon us and the hour propitious to take this opportunity to . . .

I know you'll get a lot of mail from Horace lovers on this. You mention the translation of carpe diem *in English as "seize the day." In fact, the original Latin verb* carpere *means "to pluck." Rather than the fairly abrupt, "beat out the competition" feel of "seize the day," the original more properly connotes a gentler, more thoughtful "harvest the day," make the best of what time we have, etc. Caverley's 1861 translation, for example, beautifully renders the end of the poem as, "Mistrust To-morrow, catch the blossom of To-day."*

Henry Martin

New York, New York

Carvilification.   In his book *Stickin': The Case for Loyalty,* James Carville seemed pleased that he had been called "Clinton's *gunsel*" by the columnist Richard Cohen. "I'm sure I am one," the Clinton loyalist and henchman observed in a footnote. "I just don't know what it is."

Filling those voids in vocabulary is the scholarly public service demanded by readers of this column.

American moviegoers first became familiar with the word when spoken by Humphrey Bogart, playing Dashiell Hammett's hard-boiled private detective, Sam Spade, in *The Maltese Falcon.* Bogie looked contemptuously at the young bodyguard played by Elisha Cook Jr. and told Sydney Greenstreet, "Keep that *gunsel* away from me."

Most readers of *Black Mask* magazine in 1929, when the story first appeared, and moviegoers in the 1940s thought that *gunsel* was a variant of *gunman.* It is not; in a 1965 article, the mystery writer Erle Stanley Gardner revealed why Hammett used it.

The editor of *Black Mask,* Joseph Shaw, was on guard against the use of vulgarisms by his writers. Hammett, eager to slip one by, had a character describe his activity as "on the gooseberry lay," tramp lingo for "stealing clothes from clotheslines," its connotation larcenous but not vulgar.

"Shaw wrote Hammett telling him that he was deleting the 'gooseberry lay' from the story," Gardner recalled, "and that *Black Mask* would never publish anything like that. But he left the word *gunsel* because Hammett had used it so casually that Shaw took it for granted that the word pertained to a hired gunman. Actually, *gunsel,* or *gonzel,* is a very naughty word with no relation whatever to a bodyguard."

The term in tramp slang is derived from the Yiddish *gendzl,* or "gosling"; the young goose symbolized a homosexual boy. An earlier use was defined in *American Speech* in 1933 as "*Gonzel,* Catamite" (a corruption of the name of Jupiter's cupbearer, Ganymede).

"All the writers of the hard-boiled school of realism," noted Gardner, "started talking about a *gunsel* as the equivalent of a gunman. . . . The aftereffects of that joke are still seen in American murder stories."

And in columns by pundits who mean no such thing. And in books by impervious loyalists.

Celibate.   A debate rages over whether sexual abuse is related to celibacy. On an Easter telecast of *Meet the Press,* the Reverend John McCloskey said the church was "looking for people who are capable of living the celibate life, who are capable of living a chaste life." What's the difference between *celibacy* and *chastity*?

Plenty; you can be one without being the other. The *Catholic Encyclopedia* defines *celibacy* as "the renunciation of marriage . . . for the more perfect observance of chastity."

To be *celibate* is to be single, to be unmarried, the priestly purpose of which is to remain chaste. To be *chaste,* from the Latin *casta,* "morally pure," is to deny all sexual intercourse. The goal of *celibacy,* not the state of *celibacy,* is *chastity*.

Now here comes the semantic problem. In many cases, people in all walks of life choose to be *celibate* because they do not like the notion of living all the time with people of the opposite sex, or with people of their own sex; they just prefer the single life. If, in so living, they abjure all sexual intercourse, they are both *celibate* and *chaste*. But if they fool around occasionally or even regularly, as millions do, they can rightly claim to be *celibate* without being *chaste*.

Thus, if the object of desire is asked, "Will you?" and replies, "I'm *celibate*," that is not a proper declination; it may only be an indication of housing condition. "I'm *chaste*," however, slams the door.

Unfortunately when you turned to "celibacy" and "chastity" you erred. In Roman Catholic moral theology, which is relevant here, these terms are not used in the way you say that they are. You tell us that one can be celibate without being chaste. Better you had turned this around: One can be chaste without being celibate. That is, to be celibate (which can be described independently of marriage) one must refrain from sexual intercourse. To be chaste one need not unless he is unmarried or widowed. In other words, for married couples their chastity—conjugal chastity—is expressed by affectionately achieving coitus. What makes a married person unchaste is committing an act such as adultery.

Ronald Colvin
Philadelphia, Pennsylvania

I think you're a bit too liberal in your view of what chaste means. It is quite possible to be unchaste in marriage—by excessive sexual indulgence, perpetual search for means to heighten pleasure, and anything like animal violence that disregards the partner in the act. I know that the current view of sex is unbridled recreation, but that fact is the very reason why the word chaste is quasi obsolete and often equated with marital infidelity.

Jacques Barzun
San Antonio, Texas

Surely, chastity does not require total abstinence from sexual intercourse. Among many examples, Emilia, bemoaning her mistress' murder (Othello, Act V, Scene II), "Moor, she was chaste; she lov'd thee cruel Moor." Don Juan, in Shaw's Man and Superman, *refers to the "chastity" of the much-married*

Doña Ana to make precisely this point, indeed. There is clearly a mode of morally sanctioned (positively) sexual intercourse which does not erase chastity. The removal, for obvious purpose, of the chastity belt by the husband did not make his lady unchaste.

M. H. Rodman, MD
Winchester, Massachusetts

❦

Census 2000.   Ten years ago this week, I received in the mail a census form that began, "Please use a black lead pencil only." Naturally, I objected to the loose placement of the *only,* preferring "use only a black lead pencil" or the even more direct and simple "use a black lead pencil."

This year, reflecting the leap forward in technology, the United States Census 2000 says, "Please use a black or blue pen." I have a blue pen that writes with black ink; I suppose that's OK. But I also have a black pen that writes with red ink; is that impermissible?

The clear intent is "use black or blue ink." But if the Bureau of the Census, conscious of literal correctness, wrote those words, millions of people unfamiliar with the details of writing instruments would respond: "I don't use ink; I use a ballpoint pen. Does this mean I have to fill this out with a fountain pen? There'll be big inkblots all over the form. What do they want from my life?"

Therefore, I give the census-form writers a little leeway. In return, they try not to make the same mistakes twice. The 1990 form concluded with the admonition "Make sure you have . . . filled this form completely," and I complained that it was possible to *fill in* or *fill out* a form, but not to simply *fill* a form because a form is not a bucket. In the 2000 form, the error is averted by the adoption of the "Thank you for not smoking" trick: "Thank you for completing your official U.S. Census form." It seems friendlier and is not subject to attack by nitpickers in this space.

However, our intrepid people counters cannot be counted on for the correct use of commas. Turning to the first question in the long form, and aided by my fellow nitpicker Jeff McQuain, we read "people staying here on April 1, 2000 who have no other permanent place to stay . . ." If a date in mid sentence uses a comma, then another comma must follow the year: "on April 1, 2000, who . . ."

Later, the form directs, "Start with the person, or one of the people living here who owns . . ." This cries out for a balancing comma: "person, or one of the people living here, who owns . . ." Better still, forget the commas in that sentence entirely: "Start with the person or one of the people living here who owns . . ." Use two commas to separate the phrase or no commas if it does not need separation.

This comedy of commas continues with "What is this person's age and what is this person's date of birth?" The two independent clauses call for separation by a comma after *age*. (An even better fix is to obviate the need for a comma by shortening it to "What are this person's age and date of birth?")

And the form writers are tensed up. Right at the start, the past tense is used in "How many people were living or staying in this house . . . on April 1, 2000?" Then the tense is switched to the present with instruction to include them "even if they have another place to live." Gotta be this or that: *are* and *have* or *were* and *had*.

The Parallel Construction Workers Union should file a grievance about the way a question about occupation is phrased: "patient care, directing hiring policies, supervising order clerks, repairing automobiles, reconciling financial records" are the examples given. The last four of those listed begin with gerunds; why, then, does "patient care" have no *-ing*? To be in proper parallel, it should be "caring for patients."

At least that was a series of examples not masquerading as a sentence; correctly, with no verb, no period was placed at the end. However, in what is called the ancestry question (more precisely the lineage question), we read "Italian, Jamaican, African Am., Cambodian, . . . Taiwanese, Ukrainian, and so on." The "and so on" tries to make it all-inclusive, but there is no verb to make it a sentence—and yet in this instance a period is put at the end. No style is followed. And why, when no other group is followed by "Am.," is "African" so designated—and without a hyphen to boot?

Hats off to the writers for sticking to past practice in identifying aboriginal Americans as "American Indians" and not the confusing "Native

Americans." That last could mean anyone born in America, in contrast to "Naturalized Americans," citizens born elsewhere. Past designations as Eskimo and Aleut are now lumped together as "Alaska Native."

Thus, the sensitive question of "What is this person's race?" has three main categories: (1) the above "American Indian or Alaska Native," which follows (2) "white" and three choices of names for (3) the other—"Black, African Am., or Negro." The Census Bureau explains that the terminology changes with each generation and that "Negro" was put in so that older members of the group would not feel outdated. What about whites from South Africa? I presume the form presumes that they will choose to describe themselves as white. In a triumph of inclusive self-differentiation, eleven other racial groups are listed, from "Asian Indian" to "Samoan," with blank space left for anyone to write in "Some other race."

Language has its limitations. In the question about relationships, the form includes, among others, "Husband/wife, Natural-born son/daughter, Adopted son/daughter." That "Natural-born" seems awkward; obviously it is there to distinguish between what the Bible colorfully called "the fruit of one's loins" and an adopted child. But with artificial insemination and test-tube babies in the mix, what is natural and what is not?

The delicious bureaucratic euphemism POSSLQ is gone. "Persons of the Opposite Sex Sharing Living Quarters," which appeared in the 1990 census, has been replaced by two categories: "Housemate/Roommate," who shares living quarters "primarily to share expenses," and the new "Unmarried Partner." Says the bureau: "Mark the 'Unmarried Partner' box if the person is not related to Person 1, shares living quarters, and who [*who* should be dropped] has a close personal relationship with Person 1."

Prediction: In the 2010 census, this last category will be listed as "Lovers." Also, the form writers will be warier about their use and abuse of commas.

The main objection I found to the Census Form—the grammatico-usage-style matters aside—was that it asked about the people living in the house on April 1, 2000. So I held on to the form for mailing on or after the 1st, since, God knows, anything can happen in a week.

Then publicity started appearing about how everyone had to send in the form BY April 1st. I don't have at hand the birth and death rates in the U.S., but I assume the former outdoes the latter since things seem to be getting more and more crowded, but there surely must be a difference between the figures for, say, the 25th of March, when I completed the form, and the 1st of April.

I am sure that the people at the Census Bureau are well-intentioned and trying very hard; but it is a pity that they really haven't a clue as to what in hell they are doing or in the simple rudiments of communication.

Laurence Urdang
Old Lyme, Connecticut

In counting the mistakes contained in the United States Census, you seem to have made one of your own. You use the phrase "obviate the need for . . ." This appears to me a redundancy, as the common meaning of obviate *is "to make unnecessary." To make a need unneeded is surplussage at its best. You have suggested many ways the Census could eliminate excess verbiage; so too could have you.*

Andrew J. Heimert
Washington, D.C.

If one wants to get the structure across, unforgettably, one would say, "use black pencil, only." That is more demanding and retentive. A pause in the expression, if oral, and a comma before the last word achieves the result in the interim between instruction and performance.

Judge Milton Pollack
U.S. Senior District Judge
U.S. District Court
New York, New York

Chad.   The word of the year is *chad*. Its current sense is defined in the *Dictionary of American Regional English* (*DARE*) as "the small bit of paper released when a ballot is punched or a paper punch is used."

This meaning of this single-syllable noun was a mystery to most when it first poked its head through the tape of language in the counting of ballots in Florida. But some Californians were familiar with it. In 1981, the *Los Angeles Times* reported, "What the city is trying to avoid is a repeat of April's Great *Chad* Chore, when more than 40,000 ballots had to be recounted because their *chads*—the punched-out portions—failed to break loose."

At that time, one of *DARE*'s lexicographers noted that the word "is used only by people in the ballot-counting business, not by other users of computer cards, who seem to call the same bits of cardboard 'confetti.' " But according to Peter Graham, now university librarian at Syracuse, who served early in his career as a keypunch operator, "We had what we called a *chad* box underneath the key punch. We resisted calling it 'confetti' because the small bits of paper, when they caught on your clothes, would not dislodge." Graham notes that the noun was then construed as plural, on the analogy of *chaff*, but today's ballot counters are referring to *chads*, construing the word *chad* as singular.

The first use in this sense is in the files of Merriam-Webster: "The small discs, called *chads*," noted the *RCA Review* in 1947, ". . . are perforated only sufficiently to permit the *chads* to rise like small hinged lids in response to the sensing pins of a transmitter."

A presidential election appeared to hinge on those hinges. Their near-infinite variety was listed by Katharine Q. Seelye in the *New York Times:* "Variants include *dimpled chad* (bulging but not pierced), *pregnant chad* (attached by all four corners to a ballot that is either bulging or pierced), *hanging chad* (attached by a single corner), *swinging-door chad* (attached by two corners) and *tri chad* (attached by three corners)." Bruce Rogow, an attorney for Florida election supervisors, explained with a straight face, "Pregnancy does not count in Palm Beach County, only penetration."

Other meanings exist. The oldest is from the Middle English *ich hadde,* pronounced *shad* or *chad,* meaning "I had" (and legitimizing the *Wall Street Journal* headline, "*Chad* Enough?"). According to the Venerable Bede, an especially humble priest became St. *Chad* (and his feast day is March 2, for those ballot counters who want to celebrate it). And the nation of *Chad,* formerly part of French Equatorial Africa, took its name from Lake *Chad,* from a word in the Nilo-Saharan language of Kanuri meaning "an expanse of water." According to the 14th-century Arab historian Ibn Khaldun, traders stopped in what is now northeastern Nigeria to take on water.

But now let's see where the sense of "small bit of paper" comes from. Merriam-Webster took a shot at it in the *Third Unabridged* as derived from the Scottish for "gravel," but its current etymologists think that may have been guesswork. The *Century Dictionary,* published in 1889, reported this meaning: "A dry twig, same as *chat,*" a variant of *chit,* which is both a seed and a bit of writing, and noted that *chat* potatoes were "small potatoes." A related sense found in provincial English dialect was "dry, bushy fragments found among food," construed as plural.

Thus we see how *chad, chit* and *chaff* are related in the sense of "small residue." The frequency of usage of *chad* will plummet, but the word will be forever associated with the thirst for votes in the campaign of 2000.

Back in the days when teletype machines used yellow punched paper tape (I'm not sure what time period; '30s, '40s, '50s, probably; any Western Electric survivor in Skokie, Illinois, could tell you), the little round circles of paper that were punched out and discarded were called "chat," and the metal part that collected the chat and dropped it into a collection box was called a "chat chute."

Jack E. Garrett
Jamesburg, New Jersey

Class Warfare.   After the Democratic presidential nominee posed the choice in the election as being between "the people" and "the powerful," he was chastised by GOP leaders as advocating *class warfare.*

"Al Gore launched out talking about populism," charged Karl Rove, Governor Bush's chief campaign strategist, "about *class warfare.*" The next day, on the stump, the GOP standard-bearer himself denounced his opponent as "a candidate who wants to wage *class warfare* to get ahead." Unfortunately, much of the sting in the charge was lost because Bush was seen and heard on television pronouncing the phrase as "class war fore," inviting derision.

Who coined the phrase? The *Oxford English Dictionary* spotted a heading of *class warfare* in George Bernard Shaw's *Fabian Tract 41,* written in 1892; it was not picked up until 1927, when Aldous Huxley, in an essay in *Proper Studies,* wrote about "those who would interpret all social phenomena in terms of *class warfare.*"

However, a useful new database—the Making of America, a joint project of Cornell and the University of Michigan—permits detailed examination of 19th-century American texts. Assiduous research by Kathleen Miller, my research assistant, reveals a use of the phrase in London's Aug. 17, 1867, *Spectator.* The editorialist urged "some grand effort to settle the Irish question" and put forward a conservative idea about land reform, noting that there was "no confiscation in this plan, no plea for raising that cry, no summons to *class warfare.*"

From that day to this, the charge of instigating *class warfare* has been used as an antidote to populist ideas.

Clean Your Clock.   At Super Bowl XXXVI, if history is a guide, one team will decisively defeat the other.

Fans (and advertisers) can hope for a *nail-biter,* defined as "a close contest that causes rooter tension," as used in January 2002 by Elvis Grbac, the Baltimore Ravens' quarterback: "Our games are just *nail-biters,* and they come down to whoever has the ball at the last second to win it." This hyphenated word appears to have produced both *nail-nibbling,* "the action of nervously chewing on one's fingernails," and *ankle-biter,* "an annoying critic."

Synonymous with *nail-biter* is the older *cliffhanger,* a 1937 coinage about unresolved plots. This was rooted in films presented in a series of episodes that always left the hero in a precarious situation, like hanging from the edge of a cliff with the villain stomping on his fingertips, thereby forcing moviegoers to return for the next installment.

A close game with high scores is also called a *barnburner,* a 1960s sports usage based on an old political epithet. In 1840, the radical antislavery wing of New York State's Democratic Party, led by Martin Van Buren, was dubbed the *barnburners* by conservatives after "the Dutch farmer who burned down his barn to destroy the rats."

The above-mentioned quarterback Grbac (a Croatian name pronounced "GER-bots," which he pronounces "GER-back") and his team lost in the playoffs to the Pittsburgh Steelers, 27–10. That loss was described by the *Washington Times* somewhat unkindly as a *rout,* a noun better applied that week to the 45–17 loss by the Green Bay Packers to the St. Louis Rams. Worse, the Ravens, last year's Super Bowl champions, were derided by the headline writer as having been *defeathered,* a metaphoric fate to which Ravens fans would mutter "nevermore."

However, if one team dominates (having come to play, in announcers' jargon, against a team that is *flat,* a reference to carbonated water with the fizz gone), it will be said to have *romped,* an intransitive verb that has for three centuries meant "won easily."

Gone are the mid-century days when the ring announcer in heavyweight fights would offer a dignified version of "may the better man win." Harry Balogh, after introducing the champion Joe Louis and the opponent often called "the bum of the month," would say, "And may the superior pugilist emerge victorious." No such ironic niceties anymore: today, the victor on the field of play will have *creamed, buried, mopped the floor with, shellacked, annihilated, humbled* or otherwise *embarrassed* the losing side.

The verb *to cream* in this destructive sense was first cited in a 1929 *Princeton Alumni Weekly*—"Say, if he opens his mouth, I'll *cream* him"— and then described as "an essential part of any toughie's vocabulary." Its metaphoric origin is either in "to pour cream over, thus humiliating" or in "to remove the cream from, thus leaving a thin milk" (today regarded as desirably low-fat, which is why the locution is on the decline).

The *New York Times* chose *whipped* over *creamed* in recounting the recent Green Bay defeat (*whip-cream* is not yet in use, but give it time), while other headline writers liked *drub,* probably from the Arabic *darb,* "to beat."

But the most extreme—and to some, most mysterious—expression of such merry mayhem is *to clean their clocks.* "This phrase is being used by TV newscasters," writes Stuart Zuckerman of New York, "to describe everything from a one-sided victory in sports to the U.S. bombing in Afghanistan. What's the origin?"

Clock-cleaning is indeed rampant. "If we try to play by Marquess of Queensberry rules," said General Brent Scowcroft during the recent anti-Taliban campaign, "we're going to get our *clock cleaned.*" Mark Mednick, coach of California's Irvine High girls' volleyball team, told the *Orange County Register* that in the battle with Torrance High, "in the third game, they *cleaned our clock,* but then Hillary Thomson had some clutch digs."

Break the phrase apart for close study. *To clean* gained a sense of "to clean out" in 1812, applied to victims of thieves or gamblers. In a few years, a slang meaning of *clean* became "to drub, defeat, wipe out."

Now take up *clock* in its verb form, as in "clock him one." When I expressed puzzlement about this years ago, British readers pointed out that as a clock had a face, to *clock* someone was to hit him in the face or elsewhere on the head. That led to the slang term *fix one's clock:* an O. Henry story in 1904 had the line "I reckon we'll *fix your clock* for a while."

In Latin, *clocca* means "bell." (A *cloche* hat is bell-shaped.) The clock registered time by striking a bell, and that act of noisily striking or hitting was also expressed in the verb *to clock.* In baseball, "he really clocked it" refers to the hard-hit ball; in football, "he really clocked him" is said over the sprawled-out form of the well-tackled runner.

Thus was developed *to clean* (defeat, thrash, trounce) *one's clock* (face, head, person). Earliest citation so far: In 1959, the novelist Sam Cochrell wrote this dialogue: "Don't give me that guff. You're not a corporal anymore." "I don't have to be a corporal to *clean your clock.*"

More specific usages abound, from the sexual ("to deliver complete satisfaction") to the automotive ("to pass another vehicle at great speed"). In all, the essential meaning remains: "to whomp, clobber, slaughter, pulverize" and all the other evocations of thoroughness expressed in *clean your clock.*

"Ankle-biters" started out as an annoyed epithet for small neurotic dogs that

attacked visitors and tradesmen and mailmen and paperboys by trying, literally, to get a bite or bites out of their ankles. If you had spent any time delivering papers (or mail, or magazines, or grocery store circulars), you would have met a number of ankle-biters during your career. There was also an occasional thigh-biter and crotch-biter and arm-biter among the larger dogs.

In cookery, isn't there a role for "to cream," meaning to puree until the product is as close as possible to the consistency of cream? Maybe a chef was the first one to threaten to "cream" an adversary, presumably, in such a hypothetical context, a cretin who had criticized his cooking or infringed on his domain.

John Strother
Princeton, New Jersey

I believe that in boxing circles—and other places too—the phrase is: "May the best man win." You have grammarized it, for the sake of the children, I suppose.

Jacques Barzun
San Antonio, Texas

I was a tad surprised not to find "eat [someone's] lunch" in your list. Oh well, one cannot let the complete be the enemy of the excellent.

Saul Rosen
Rockville, Maryland

Clintonisms.   "Bill Clinton is a relic of another age," the essayist Lance Morrow wrote in *Time* magazine, "like the 20s party boy F. Scott Fitzgerald stranded in the landscape of the Great Depression."

I rise today to our immediate past president's linguistic defense. Let me tell you about the very articulate. They are different from you and me. The Lexicographic Irregulars, asked in this space to choose the phrases that Bill Clinton would be remembered by, responded with words that evoke an era of intense controversy and vituperation. Respondents included his critics and his speechwriters, those nostalgic for the time of prosperity and peace as well as for the days of whine and nosiness.

The most memorable Clintonism or Clintonym (a coinage of F. Gwynplaine MacIntyre) chosen by a plurality of entries was a sentence that thrilled every semanticist, grammarian and syntactician in the nation: "It depends on what the meaning of the word 'is' is."

The words that raised parsing to a fine art were spoken under oath to a grand jury. They were about a statement made by the president's lawyer during a deposition about the relationship with a White House intern, in which the lawyer asserted, "There is absolutely no sex of any kind." Clinton pointed out that because his attorney had been speaking only in the present tense, the statement was true: "It depends on what the meaning of the word 'is' is," he explained, adding, "Actually, in the present tense, that is a true statement." That is indisputable: during the deposition, no sex of any kind was taking place between them.

What made the sentence so memorable? Part was the exquisite nature of the literal reading, taken by Clinton critics to be an infuriating example of legalistic slipperiness. Another part was the unique juxtaposition of the quoted *is* with the unquoted *is*. The sentence would not have had the same puissance—indeed, it might not be destined for the next edition of *Bartlett's Familiar Quotations*—had it concluded with "the meaning of 'is' was."

"I feel your pain," an expression of compassion often associated with psychiatric jargon, was the runner-up in this sample (which has an accuracy estimated at plus or minus sixty points). The remark was ad-libbed at a March 26, 1992, campaign rally as part of a riposte to an AIDS activist who angrily accused the candidate of avoiding the issue. The candidate, who later became a champion of gay rights, came back with "I feel your pain, I feel your pain, but if you want to attack me personally . . . go support somebody else for president." He ameliorated that with "I know you're hurting, but you won't stop hurting by trying to hurt other people."

Tied for second place, thanks to its repetition thousands of times on television, is his statement of Jan. 26, 1998: "I did not have sexual relations with that woman, Miss Lewinsky." What made it memorable was not only its unequivocal tone but also its accompaniment by a wagging finger. More than the words, the stern digit fixes it firmly in the national memory.

A charge leveled by Hillary Rodham Clinton at her husband's nattering, battering cottage industry of vilifiers makes it into the political lexicon. On Jan. 27, 1998, during the month that the most memorable Clinton locutions were launched, the first lady told a television interviewer, Matt Lauer of the *Today* show, that she and her husband were targets of "a vast, right-wing conspiracy." (That is most frequently written without a comma between the adjective *vast* and the compound adjective *right-wing;* such an error is not attributable to Mrs. Clinton but to the vast right wing.)

"I didn't inhale," which was widely quoted in derision early in the Clinton era, seems to be on the decline in quoted recollection. Regarding the use of drugs, Governor Clinton of Arkansas said in 1992 that "when I was in England I experimented with marijuana a time or two, and I didn't like it. I didn't inhale it and never tried it again." (The phrasal verb *experimented with* became the operative term in such admissions, giving the action an almost scientific connotation, rather than *smoked* or *used.*) It was the careful plea of guilty with an explanation—of smoking but not inhaling—that struck many as ludicrously clever, but the phrase was overtaken by "'is' is."

Clinton enthusiasts are proud of "The era of big government is over," spoken in his 1996 State of the Union address, a stunning statement from a Democrat, somewhat tempered by "but we cannot go back to the time when our citizens were left to fend for themselves." This was described by his public-opinion aide, Richard Morris, as *triangulation,* the positioning of a politician above two contending ideologies, a geometric updating of "stealing the opposition's clothes."

Another Clintonism that those who remember his administration fondly like to recall is the campaign semislogan, "It's the economy, stupid." This was a sign posted by his campaign manager, James Carville, and not a statement by the candidate. Clinton did say in his stump speeches, "My responsibility is to grow this economy," which was effective though it drew the ire of grammatical purists who objected to the use of the intransitive verb *grow* in a transitive form.

Students of regional dialect recall with fondness Clinton's use of Ozark expressions. The most memorable of these was spoken at a Feb. 15, 1992, rally where the Arkansas governor said that he hoped people would see him "working hard, reaching out to them and fighting until the last dog dies." (As *'til the last dog is hung*, this has been traced to a 1902 novel set in Michigan.) Clinton also contributed this proverb to the political lexicon: "Even a blind hog can find an acorn."

Perhaps the most poignant of the memorable Clintonyms was recalled by Uzi Amit-Kohn of Jerusalem. In a farewell to Yitzhak Rabin on Nov. 5, 1995, after the Israeli leader's assassination, Clinton said, "*Shalom, chaver,*" which translates from the Hebrew as "Good-bye, friend" or "Peace, friend."

These statements are hardly the relics of a forgotten age. But as F. Scott Fitzgerald wrote in his notebook, "There are no second acts in American lives." And "show me a hero, and I will write you a tragedy." And in *The Great Gatsby,* his unforgettable "So we beat on, boats against the current, borne back ceaselessly into the past."

You mention Clinton's "unique juxtaposition" of is *with* is. *This brought to my mind my favorite juxtaposition of a form of being: "Let* be *be the finale of seem," from Wallace Stevens's "The Emperor of Ice Cream." I just wanted to return the favor.*

Dennis Lawson
Seymour, Connecticut

Codgertation.   Thirteen out of 100 Americans are over 65; only 4 of those 100 are "wired seniors," keyed into the Internet. But good news for older readers of words in all forms comes in a new book from a couple of heavy hitters in brain science. No age group is coming online faster than the Social Security set, and a recent survey shows that especially goes for women.

When information in spoken form is presented rapidly, older people don't understand it as easily as their children do. A fast-talking newscaster is not comprehended well by most older listeners and viewers (to whom advertisers' messages are directed). But Guy McKhann, MD, of Johns Hopkins and Marilyn Albert, PhD, of Harvard Medical School, authors of *Keep Your Brain Young: The Complete Guide to Physical and Emotional Health and Longevity,* write, "Since you read at your own speed and can go back over what you read, speed has less influence on your understanding of written material."

That explains an eye-opening development in the world of the Netties. "One advantage of the computer is that it depends on the written word," write Albert and McKhann, who are happily married and read to each other every night. "Given the fact that vocabulary and reading ability do not decline and may even improve with age, it's not surprising that the fastest-growing group of new computer users in the United States is over the age of 65."

We're allowed to read that again. Let it sink in. For information comprehension, the written word beats the rat-a-tat-tat of cable cubs and cuties any day. That's why you see those letters crawling along the bottom of your screen.

Cold Case Squad.   What has become of Chandra Levy? The question about this missing person is triggered by the FBI's grim refusal to accept the phrase *Cold Case squad.*

Last summer, before the nation's attention turned away from the vanished congressional aide, Jim Stewart, a CBS reporter, said that "the FBI officially transferred the Chandra Levy investigation to its *Cold Case unit,* which has historically handled only the toughest of cases that have few clues. . . . *Cold case* means cold leads, few tips and little to go on."

The FBI responded with an angry news release referring proudly to its *Major Case squad* and coldly noting, "It is not correct to call this squad the 'Cold Case' squad."

Following this up, I was informed by an FBI spokesman, "It has always been the *Major Case squad. Cold Case squad* is used by the media, not by us. The squad that we have in our office is called the *Major Case Homicide squad*. We do not call it a *Cold Case squad*."

And as for you journalists who don't accept our official law enforcement terminology—freeze!

Come Heavy.   What's a *goomah*, and how does it differ from a *goombah*? Is the adjective *skeevy* somehow related to the slang noun for underwear, *skivvies*? Does the *come-heavy* Mafia talk on television give you *agita*?

These are words from the HBO television series *The Sopranos*, which I first turned to hoping to hear a rendition of the mad scene in *Lucia di Lammermoor*. The show is centered on a relentlessly foulmouthed fictional Mafia family with the surname of Soprano. My interest is in the writers' adoption of a lexicon that is loosely based on Italian words, a little real Mafia slang and a smattering of lingo remembered or made up for the show by former residents of a blue-collar neighborhood in East Boston.

"*Goombah* is derived from *compare,* 'godfather' or 'dear male friend,'" says Frank Renzulli, co-executive producer and a writer of the show. "Southern Italians tend to make the *c* a *g*, so *compare* becomes *gompare*. Dropping the last letter is very Neapolitan, so it becomes *goompar* and then *goombah*." Robin Green, another executive producer (it's hard to figure from the titles who is the show's *capo di tutti capi*), contrasts the "godfather" meaning of that word with *goomah*, which she defines as "mistress." She adds, "The language we're using is from the neighborhood, a street language that's bastardized Italian—American forms of Italian words."

I ran *goomah* past Jimmy Breslin, the *Newsday* columnist who wrote *The Gang That Couldn't Shoot Straight,* and he confirms the "alternative wife" sense. While I had him on the phone, I tried *come heavy,* which Jimmy defined as either "bring money" or "come armed"; the show's legion of executive producers prefer the latter.

Agita means "acid indigestion." In that regard, *skeevy* comes from *schifare,* "to disgust." The name of the mob leader's boat is *Stugots,* which *Entertainment Weekly* defined as "idiot," but which has a meaning closer to the Spanish *cojones,* "the courage symbolized by primary male sex characteristics."

That should be enough to get you through a couple of episodes, unless the other endless, unoriginal obscenities get you down. HBO's parent company, Time Warner, had a useful glossary of what the executive producers call their mobspeak on its Web site, but the understandably offended National Italian American Foundation all but *mock-whacked* the corporate brass who—suddenly afflicted with *agita*—removed the offensive page.

Compassion.   In the case of *PGA Tour v. Martin,* the Supreme Court held (7–2) that the game of golf would not be fundamentally altered if a handicapped contestant in a tournament was allowed to ride in a golf cart. Because the game was played in a place of public accommodation, the Americans With Disabilities Act applied, and the court upheld judges who directed the Professional Golfers Association to let the golfer Casey Martin ride.

Justice Antonin Scalia began his dissent with this sentence: "In my view today's opinion exercises a benevolent compassion that the law does not place it within our power to impose."

The term *benevolent compassion* puzzled Noam Cohen, executive editor of Inside.com and a former copy editor at the *New York Times*. Like many who assume that I am one to whom the high court's decisions about language can be appealed, he wrote to me: "I was wondering what you made of Justice Scalia's use of the term *benevolent compassion*. Isn't that redundant? Can there be a 'malevolent compassion'?"

My appellant—a member of an elite group of tautology-spotters that calls itself the Squad Squad—noted that *Merriam-Webster's Tenth Collegiate Dictionary* defines compassion as "sympathetic consciousness of others' distress together with a desire to alleviate it." Writes Cohen: "That would seem to have benevolence tied to its very nature. What's weird is that the offending sentence was the first in Scalia's particularly stinging dissent—he must have thought about it."

I agreed; he must have. A judge noted for his pungently precise prose doesn't modify a noun with a closely related adjective without thinking it through. What was his original intent? So I put it to Justice Scalia directly: "Was it, as the members of the Squad Squad suggest, redundant? Or were you differentiating from some other kind of compassion?"

"I am shocked and dismayed (shocked and dismayed!)," Scalia tongue-in-cheekily replies, "by the suggestion in your note of June 10 that my reference to 'benevolent compassion' can be absolved of redundancy only if I was 'differentiating [that] from some other kind of compassion.'"

Note his bracketed *that,* which is a correction of the English in my note. By inserting *that,* he indicates that the verb *differentiate* should be transitive. I used it without an object; common usage has made that intransitive form correct, but it is not preferred in formal writing. I can defend my intransitive usage—gee, it was only in a scribbled note—but here I am on the defensive, which is surely what Scalia had in mind. (At least he bracketed a suggested correction rather than a humiliating [*sic*]. In return, I have not *sic*'d his use of "was differentiating" when the contrary-to-fact subjunctive called for *were.*)

"I shall assume," he continues, "that such differentiation is impossible— that compassion is always benevolent—though that may not be true. (People sometimes identify with others' suffering, 'suffer with' them—to track the Latin root of *compassion*—not because they particularly love the others or 'wish them well'—to track the Latin root of *benevolence*—but because they shudder at the prospect of the same thing's happening to themselves. 'There, but for the grace of God, go I.' This is arguably not benevolence, but self-love.)"

I suspect that my frequent plunge into etymology in this column has just been satirized, but maybe I flatter myself. He goes on in true Supreme Court style to restate the question at hand about *benevolent compassion* and to address it:

"But assuming the premise, is it redundancy to attribute to a noun a quality that it always possesses?" Scalia's opinion: "Surely not. We speak of 'admirable courage' (is courage ever not admirable?); a 'cold New England winter' (is a New England winter ever not cold?); the 'sweet, green spring' (is springtime ever not sweet and green?). It seems to me perfectly acceptable to use an adjective to emphasize one of the qualities that a noun possesses, even if it always possesses it. The writer wants to stress the coldness of the New England winter, rather than its interminable length, its gloominess, its snowiness and many other qualities that it always possesses. And that is what I was doing with 'benevolent compassion'—stressing the social-outreach, maternalistic, goo-goo character of the court's compassion."

Let me interrupt here to footnote the meaning and etymology of *goo-goo*, which some may mistakenly take as akin to *gooey*. This was the derisive appellation given by the *New York Sun* in the 1890s to local action groups calling themselves "Good Government Clubs"; New York City Police Commissioner Theodore Roosevelt castigated fellow reformers who voted independent as "those prize idiots, the *Goo-Goos*."

I have just returned from northern Greece, where I read, in the International Herald Tribune, *your piece on my redundancy. It was a nice job, and I am flattered that you thought my analysis not only correct but also worthy of recounting.*

By the way, I did not include the bracketed "that" as an intentional jab—it was just the way I was accustomed to using the verb "differentiate." Honi soit qui mal y pense. The Latin etymology was likewise not an intentional parody: I happen to think it useful, and knew that you, of all people, would not consider it out of place. You were correct, however, that my reference to "off-the-cuff thoughts" was (shall we say?) something of an exaggeration.

I hope you will not think it ungrateful if I observe that you are wrong about my use of indicative "was" instead of the subjunctive "were." "Were" would have been appropriate if my sentence had read "my reference 'differentiating [that],'" etc. In fact, however, I wrote, "can be absolved"—and that takes a "was."

Justice Antonin Scalia
Supreme Court of the United States
Washington, D.C.

Philosophers have made the distinction you and Justice Scalia seemed to be striving for when you discussed whether "benevolent compassion" was tautologous. They differentiate between defining characteristics and accompanying characteristics. All elephants may be gray, but grayness is not a defining characteristic of an elephant, merely an accompanying one.

David Kahn
Great Neck, New York

As you analyzed Antonin Scalia's sentence, I kept waiting for you to attack his use of the word "it." Justice Scalia was quoted as saying: "In my view today's opinion exercises a benevolent compassion that the law does not place it within our power to impose." That "it" seems incorrect to me—and also to my husband, the ex-English professor. If we're right, why didn't you dispute the usage? And if we're wrong, we'll just shut up.

Gerry Muir
Mamaroneck, New York

Justice Scalia, wrong in so many other ways, was correct in using "was" rather than "were" in the sentence "(My use) of benevolent compassion can be absolved of redundancy only if I was differentiating (that) from some other kind of compassion," because the event actually occurred. "Were" is hypothetical, suggesting that he might be contemplating some differentiating but hadn't actually done it.

Then to my shock and dismay, in regarding the opening line, ". . . the Supreme Court held . . . that the game of golf would not be fundamentally altered if a handicapped contestant . . . was allowed to ride in a golf cart," I fear that you commit the error yourself. Here, "were" is clearly correct, because golfers were (supposedly) not riding in carts before the sentence was handed down.

Eric Conger
Weehawken, New Jersey

Justice Scalia's statement that "the very essence of 'giftness' . . . is being free" brings to mind a case in law school more than fifty years ago. The Mary

Carter Paint Company had advertised buy two, get one free. *The Supreme Court held that this was not false advertising, as in the context is meant only free of extra cost.*

For this matter, not every gift is really free. The gift of liberty, a performer's gift, many others require sacrifice and diligence.

Robert Obrecht

Old Saybrook, Connecticut

Justice Scalia referred to a past question, hence "was." You, contrary to fact, prescribed "were." But that is present subjunctive, cf "If I were you." A pox on both your clauses. If I had been you (hard swallow) I would have suggested a past subjunctive form, "If only I had been differentiating . . ." Justice Scalia began his dissent with this sentence: "In my view today's opinion exercises a benevolent compassion that the law does not place it within our power to impose." Speaking of redundancy, what's with that "it"?

Carl d'Angio

Mount Vernon, New York

I don't accept Justice Scalia's argument as he has made it. There is a distinction between denotative meanings of words (what I think he must mean when he says "distinctive characteristic *that the noun conveys") and their* connotations. *Justice Scalia chooses* admirable courage *as his first example, remarking,* "is courage ever not admirable?" *It stereotypically is, which is why* admirable courage *is a cliché. But it is not redundant in the way that* brave courage *and* intrepid courage *are, even though the etymologies of the noun and both adjectives are quite distinct, because the meaning of* courage *denotes the qualities that* brave *and* intrepid *do.*

On a different tack, he chooses winter *and* spring, *words that have gigantic semantic fields, with several denotational and connotational meanings, and countless metaphorical extensions. We can talk about* winter *in its astronomical sense and comment about both typical and atypical meteorological conditions associated with that period (warm versus cold New England winters); we can speak about* winters *in our souls and* springs *in our hearts without reference to temperature or colors because those words have been as-*

sociated with a vast lexicon of metaphors for psychological states since literature began, if not conversation.

But I am even more interested in Justice Scalia's take on the word compassion itself. He paints a picture of "compassionate" persons who flee, shuddering, from those who are suffering because they fear the same will happen to themselves. He contrasts this with benevolent compassion, described as "social-outreach, maternalistic, (and) goo-goo . . ." Well, I think it's now clear: the differentiation is not between malevolent compassion and benevolent compassion: it is between benevolent compassion and conservative compassion. Many of us have been wondering about this "conservative compassion" for a long time and will now be able to correct the inferences when we next hear it.

One other point: You correctly point out that Justice Scalia failed to use the subjunctive (was rather than were differentiating). But what about your opening sentence? ". . . (I)f a handicapped contestant in a tournament was allowed to ride . . ." Why not were allowed? They are precisely the same with respect to clause construction, and both require the subjunctive, playing by the old rules. (I quite agree that the English subjunctive has receded, at a galloping pace, out of our modern speech and taken its last refuge in the prose of literati well into their dotage. Alas.)

Marcia Haag
Assistant Professor of Linguistics
University of Oklahoma
Norman, Oklahoma

I agree with Justice Scalia that compassion is not always benevolent. I think that Dido had sympathetic consciousness of another's distress but she was, I believe, also saying to Aeneas who was in the harbor ready to leave her, "I'll give you something to remember me by." She then stabbed herself and jumped onto a burning pyre. Justice Scalia was, perhaps, making reference to Aristotle's notions of the audience's engagement at a tragic drama. The audience may be saying and feeling, "There but for the grace of God go I." Or, "Better s/he than me." This is where the catharsis of pity and terror is felt by *the audience.* Catharsis *now carries the taint of scientism made fashionable by the Freud-bashers.*

The Justice was stressing the "social-outreach, maternalistic, goo-goo" character of the court's decision. I could go back and read his original statement of "benevolent compassion" with a different ear. I can hear "be-NEVolent" with the second syllable drawn out in a sticky sweet tone. This is much like the distinction between "LIGHThousekeeping" and "lightHOUSEkeeping."

Frank Kermode tells us that the language of Hamlet *is dominated by doubles (as in* sticky sweet*) of all kinds. The figure of speech is hendiadys. This means, literally, one-through-two.* Law and order, kith and kin, house and home *are well known examples. Hamlet was preoccupied with questions of identity, sameness, and the union of separate selves—joined opposites. I think that the Justice was responding to the cry of redundancy the way Hamlet responded—with strain, stress, as if the parts were related in some not perfectly evident way. Justice Scalia was being very Aristotelian in referring to the essence of compassion. Aristotle differs from Plato in his belief that certain things in the natural world embody essences.*

Donald J. Coleman, MD
Pittsburgh, Pennsylvania

With reference to your exchange concerning possible redundancy in the phrase "benevolent compassion," I thought you might be interested in an earlier exchange between a distinguished journalist (certainly no redundancy there) and a distinguished Supreme Court Justice (no redundancy even there) concerning a possible redundancy—and one particularly close to home (or the office) for Justice Scalia.

In 1935 Herbert Bayard Swope wrote to Chief Justice Hughes, complaining about the legend "Equal Justice Under Law" on the new Supreme Court building. He accused Hughes of "having permitted tautology, verbosity, and redundancy, each of which is an abomination in good usage." (I'm struggling to determine whether this passage violated his own rules.) Hughes wrote back on February 4:

Immediate judgment. Indictment quashed.

The distress that led to your complaint may be somewhat allevi-ated if for a moment you will free yourself from the tyranny of the blue pencil and consider the history of the law. "Equal Justice" is a time-honored phrase placing a strong emphasis upon impartiality—an emphasis which it is well to retain . . .

The letters are in volume 5B of the Hughes papers, in the Library of Congress; the exchange is reported in Merlo Pusey's biography of Hughes.

I wonder whether Hughes was correct under Justice Scalia's test. Equality in some sense is a characteristic that justice always possesses—that, at any rate, was Hughes's point—but at least arguably it is not "the distinctive characteristic that [justice] conveys." That strikes me as a close question, though. Certainly, the standard-of-justice icon, which has generated some scholarly interest, suggests that impartiality is in fact "[t]he essence of [justice]." I confess that I have difficulty applying this essentialist standard, which reminds me somewhat of the question whether walking is essential to golf.

Richard D. Friedman
University of Michigan Law School
Ann Arbor, Michigan

While discussing your thrusts and parries with Justice Scalia, both of you committed a no-no when you misused the word differentiate. *Many style books warn about using* differentiate *instead of* distinguish. *One differentiates when doing calculus, a physician uses a differential diagnosis when comparing similar diseases, and an electronic circuit can be made to differentiate a train of pulses. Please cease and desist!*

Robert Schroeder
Trenton, New Jersey

Connect!   Why did the Pulitzer Prize–winning historian Joseph Ellis, whose accuracy in writing about the framers of the Constitution remains unchallenged, tell his students fanciful fabrications about his supposed military service in Vietnam?

Edmund Morris, a historian whose fictionalization of parts of his biography of Ronald Reagan drew critical fire, tried to explain in an op-ed article Ellis's strange departure from the truth. "I am loath to speculate what private motives Professor Ellis may have had," Morris began, and then speculated, "but as a fellow communicator, I can understand his urgent desire—Only *connect!*—to convey the divisiveness of the '60s to a generation rendered comatose by MTV."

The literati immediately caught Morris's allusion to E. M. Forster's 1910 novel, *Howards End*: "She would only point out the salvation that was latent . . . in the soul of every man. Only *connect!*" Forster's exhortation is repeated later to emphasize the desperate need for communication among human beings: "Live in fragments no longer. Only *connect*, and the beast and the monk, robbed of the isolation that is life to either, will die."

That extended meaning of *connect* goes far beyond the original "to conjoin, link, fasten together." In the lexicon of reaching out, it has become the vogue term for "to establish rapport" and beyond that, "to feel a surge of mutual understanding," sometimes all the way to "have a sensation of instant intimacy."

On Valentine's Day, Jeff Wise of the American Dating Association told ABC's Alison Stewart, "The No. 1 question-complaint that we get from people is 'I went on a date, had a great time, we totally *connected*—but he never called me back again.' "

What does it mean to "totally *connect*"? A youthful source tells me: "The phrase can be used for friends or lovers. It implies not only a certain commonality but also a genuine comfort level. It's when someone is easy to talk to or hang out with; there's a certain flow or vibe. In the past, we called it 'chemistry' or 'a spark of electricity.' If a date didn't work out, it's not my fault or his fault, we just didn't *connect*."

Source of the new sense, my young friend thinks, "is from something high-tech, like an Internet connection. We say, 'How fast is your connection?' To *connect* implies speed, immediacy, getting in touch globally—

something you want to happen right away, that you want to feel without missing a beat. It causes a bit of pressure, this expectation to feel something right away."

The need for speed in the connection between individuals is influenced by the demand for fast action from computers. "For many young people, there are those moments of frustration when they start up their computers and have to wait to get online," notes Christine Lindberg, managing editor of Oxford University Press's American dictionaries. "Finally you're satisfied, you've gone online, you're connected, you've got friends out there in the ether waiting to *connect* with you. And anywhere they go, online or off, teenagers feel that potential of making an instant connection."

When young people take up with a word, can politicians fearing a *disconnect* be far behind? "A relationship was begun," said Senator Richard Durbin of Illinois about the meeting between President George W. Bush and the Russian president, Vladimir Putin, "and that is critically important for those two leaders of Russia and the United States to *connect*." Condoleezza Rice, the national security adviser, reported that "both men *connected* on a kind of sense of humor." And for years, though not in a strictly interpersonal sense, candidates for office have been measured on their ability to "*connect* with the voters."

Before its intergenerational sense took over, the verb had a variety of meanings. Jonathan E. Lighter's *Random House Historical Dictionary of American Slang* lists the sports use, "to hit a baseball hard," citing pitcher Christy Mathewson's 1912 "When [Joe] Tinker . . . *connects* he hits 'em far." Another informal sense is "to succeed," as in the novelist James T. Farrell's 1933 use, "My wife and I want a kid . . . but . . . I just can't *connect*." Best known is the underworld use, "to make a purchase of illicit goods, especially narcotics." This was immortalized in noun form in the 1971 movie title *The French Connection*.

These days, the verb's popularity illustrates the need not to feel alone. That desire never to be out of touch is touching. "In teen-think," reports Sheila Anne Feeney of New York's *Daily News,* "owning a pager means you are so important you cannot be disconnected from the collective pulse of your peer group even for a moment. You Are *Connected*."

❦

Control Freak.   William Hague, leader of the Tory opposition in the House of Commons, rose to denounce the prime minister: "Tony Blair is the *control freak* who has lost control." In an editorial about the devolution of power to Wales, Britain's *Daily Telegraph* noted, "Tony Blair has acknowledged that he has occasionally acted like the *control freak* his opponents accuse him of being."

The charge has equal puissance on this side of the Atlantic. The Senate Democratic leader, Tom Daschle, used the phrase to describe his Republican counterpart, Trent Lott. And during the recent presidential primary elections, the *Austin American-Statesman* quoted an unidentified aide to Governor Jane Dee Hull of Arizona as derogating Senator John McCain in these words: "The senator gets very heated about things. He's a *control freak.*"

The favored political attack phrase means "one obsessed by the need to dominate; a person driven by the urge to be in total command." It is not as serious a blast as *totalitarian* and does not carry the sexual overtone of *dominatrix,* but—by suggesting the control is for control's sake rather than for any rational purpose—imputes more neuroticism than *micromanager.*

That is because *control* as a noun has become a double-edged sword. To be *out of control* is to approach what used to be called "raving mad," but at the other extreme is the grim-faced, white-knuckled *control freak,* with his obsession to extend untrammeled authority into every detail of others' lives.

Meanwhile, the meaning of the slang noun *freak*—first recorded in Finley Peter Dunne's 1895 "Mr. Dooley" in the *Chicago Evening Post* as "the deluded ol' *freak*"—has also been getting quirkier with the passage of time. A century ago, it meant "eccentric" or "abnormal," as in the carnival *freak show* exploiting specimens of obesity or dwarfism, and later as an adjectival synonym for "aberrational," "deviant" or "hard to imagine," as in "*freak* accident."

In the 1960s, it was adopted in drug lingo as a verb, to *freak out,* meaning "to rave under the influence of hallucinatory drugs." It was then applied as a noun in *speed freak* and *acid freak*. In his 1977 book, *Dispatches*, Michael Herr, who had covered the Vietnam War for *Esquire* magazine, applied the term *control freak* to "one of those people who always . . . had to know what was coming next." The term became favored by Hollywood screenwriters and producers dealing with that war; it was repeated in the 1978 film *The Deer Hunter* and in 1979's *Apocalypse Now*. By 1986, the meaning softened to "enthusiast, aficionado, maven," and Steven Spielberg freely confessed to *TV Guide*, "I'm a *control freak*." (In the same way, language mavens call themselves *word freaks*.)

In current use, the meaning of the combination of *control* and *freak* has veered toward "neurotic." In the *Boston Globe* in 1992, Matthew Gilbert noted how crowds prized the singer Madonna's "*control-freakishness*." Writing four years later about Barbra Streisand, the *Sunday Times of London* could not decide whether she was "America's greatest female singer or a power-mad woman whose *control-freakishness* makes working with her all but impossible save from a kneeling position."

That latest interpretation of *freakishness* as "off the deep end" is why Senator Daschle, when asked about his use of *control freak* about Senator Lott, hastily backed off: "I say it in a light-hearted way. I don't mean he is a *freak*. I'm just saying he's a control *nut*." In Senate rhetoric, evidently *nut* is far less pejorative than *freak*. That reflects general usage; to be *nutty* is to be mildly crackbrained and is often used in self-description of too-earnest advocacy: I readily call myself a "privacy *nut*," but would not flagellate myself as a "privacy *freak*."

A *nut* is a *freak* you kind of like. Loosey-goosey descriptive lexicographers, with their anything-goes passivity, deride prescriptive pop grammarians like me as *control freaks*, but I look bemusedly at those round-heeled dictionary writers as *common-usage nuts*.

Coordinates.   I was in a meeting with Joshua Lederberg, the Nobel laureate who has long been preeminent in biodefense. When asked by another scientist where he could be reached the following week, Lederberg passed along a card with a crisp "Here are my *coordinates.*"

There's a useful word for these times. Instead of saying, "Here's my business address, along with e-mail address, private e-mail address, fax number, pager number, cell phone, office phone, home phone, pager-scheduler and the digital answering machine with caller ID next to my bed," I can now lump together the whole modern communications litany with "my *coordinates.*" This locution will prove especially helpful to people whose business cards run three pages.

The origin of the noun is in geometry. George Crabb in 1823 defined *co-ordinates* (now dropping its hyphen) as "a term applied to the absciss and ordinates when taken in connexion," later better known as the magnitudes that determine the position of a point; geographers and navigators still later used *coordinates* to describe the use of longitude and latitude in locating a spot on the globe.

People in the military, accustomed to map terminology, have taken to using the plural noun to mean "precisely where a person is." Secretary of Defense Donald Rumsfeld, asked, "Do you have any better handle on where bin Laden is?" replied, "I have a handle, but I don't have *coordinates.*" (This is not to be confused with the sense used in the fashion world, as "colors and materials that blend harmoniously and are intended to be worn together." Rumsfeld wears suits and rarely appears in *coordinates.*)

Recent citations in the extended sense of "how to reach me" are Canadian: checking on her Quebec "citizenship," Arabella Bowen wrote in the *Gazette* in Montreal in 1999 that a voter-registration official looked at her documents and "confirmed my *coordinates.*" A year later, Rosa Harris-Adler wrote in the *Ottawa Citizen,* "I walked into one of the dry cleaners in my new neighborhood . . . and gave the guy behind the counter my *co-ordinates.*"

That sense of personal location has flashed around the world. In Moscow this year, at a news conference called to expose corruption in the Ministry for Atomic Energy, Ivan Blokov of Greenpeace charged that "pressure was put on all the members of that faction who voted against the amendment. I can give you the *coordinates* of people who can confirm this." The Russian word used was *koordinatu*.

The origin may be in satellite coordinates, the space equivalent of latitude and longitude, which news media need to get a "feed" from a satellite; the phrase is bandied about by White House press secretaries. An alternate theory: "*Coordinates* has been part of the *Wired* parlance since at least 1996," reports William O. Goggins, deputy editor of the magazine *Wired*. "My gut read"—presumably his instinctive response—"is that an, if not the, origin of this locution is 'Star Trek.' Think transporter room."

The Russian word you mentioned is spelled koordinaty, *not* koordinatu. *The former is the plural form, and the latter is the dative case of the singular.*

Russians have been using this word for a long time in the sense of "contact information." When I was a kid in the '70s, it was already an old people's joke, so the usage is probably quite old. It certainly came about before the age of wireless communications. It probably comes from sailor's parlance—one would ask a girl her coordinates to hint at one's adventurous occupation. I would not be surprised to find that Russian borrowed the use of the word from another language, too. While borrowing a word is a relatively rare occurrence, borrowing another use of an existing word is much more common cross-fertilization of languages, and could be traced to some mistakes a nonnative speaker makes that native speakers find interesting.

My coordinates:

Alexander "Sasha" Sidorkin
Bowling Green State University
Bowling Green, Ohio

I think you missed the true origin of coordinates. *It is a French import, which explains your tracing it to bilingual Canada. It has long been standard and common in French, and appears in any full-sized French dictionary, under the entry "coordonner."*

And there is good reason. The notion of coordinates was invented by the seventeenth-century French mathematician and philosopher René Descartes, the same fellow who thought that he was. *When he turned his attention to the question of* where *he was, he came up with what we mathematicians call to this day the Cartesian coordinate system.*

Evans Harrell
Georgia Institute of Technology
Atlanta, Georgia

𝒞

Cover Story. Within a week of the terrorist attack, George W. Bush went to the Islamic Center in Washington and said, "Women who cover their heads in this country must feel comfortable going outside their homes." In remarks to State Department employees on October 4, President Bush spoke warmly of "stories of Christian and Jewish women alike helping *women of cover,* Arab-American women, go shop because they're afraid to leave their home."

At a televised news conference a week later, he reprised this ecumenical theme: "In many cities when Christian and Jewish women learned that Muslim women, *women of cover,* were afraid of going out of their homes alone . . . they went shopping with them . . . an act that shows the world the true nature of America." He repeated that phrase, *women of cover,* calling "such an outpouring of compassion . . . such a wonderful example."

The *cover* is a veil that expresses Muslim piety. The *hijab,* meaning "cover, curtain," can range from a floral kerchief that leaves the face exposed, to the *niqab, abbaya* or in Persian, *chador,* which covers the whole body except the face, to the *burka,* as worn in Afghanistan, which covers everything. "To have good *hijab*" is a general term meaning "to be properly covered." Some Muslim women believe that the cover need not be worn outside the mosque. The linguistic question: in describing the wearers of the veil, is it *women who cover,* as the president first used it, or *women of cover?*

Sue Obeidi, at the Muslim Public Affairs Council, uses *women who cover, women who wear the scarf* and *women who wear hijab*. She is unfamiliar with *women of cover,* and I cannot find it in databases.

It's possible that the president coined the phrase; if so, it was on the analogy of *women of color,* a description adopted by many nonwhites. (Though *colored people* is dated and almost a slur, *people of color* is not in the least offensive.) The substitution of *who* with *of* in the cover category introduces a nice parallel to the *women of color* phrase; we'll see if it takes.

Crying Woof!   "We can sell all the *woof tickets* we want," the Washington Wizards' basketball forward Juwan Howard said, but "it's about performance out there. . . . We've got to get it together."

"Any idea what Juwan Howard is talking about?" Joe Anderson of Arlington, Virginia, asks.

As early as 1985, Clarence Page of the *Chicago Tribune* defined *selling woof tickets* as "an invitation to fight." In 1996, Jane Kennedy of the *San Francisco Examiner* called it "telling lies." In the *Atlanta Journal-Constitution,* Betty Parham and Gerrie Ferris wrote in 1992, "Although its origin is uncertain, '*woof ticket*' is a somewhat dated phrase that refers to an outrageous or exaggerated boast meant to intimidate or impress the listener." *Woof* is a Black English pronunciation of *wolf.* According to Geneva Smitherman's 1994 *Black Talk,* a *woof ticket* is "a verbal threat, which one sells to somebody; may or may not be real. Often used as a strategy to make another person back down and surrender to what that person perceives as a superior power."

Tom McIntyre, professor of special education at Hunter College in New York, noted nearly a decade ago: "*Woofing* is especially effective against those who are unfamiliar with it and don't realize that it is most often 'all show and no go.' . . . The menacing behavior can usually be defused and eliminated by informed, tactful action." He advised teachers to "look secure and self-assured while you withdraw."

In the context of the basketball star Howard's remarks, *woof tickets* are not to be bought; on the contrary, he uses the phrase to show that performance, and not intimidating attitude, is needed to "get it together."

A woof ticket is a provocation: a threat, accusation, insult, or other statement that is sufficiently injurious to justify violent retaliation. It comes from the verb "to woof." Thus a student who can no longer find his pencil might turn to a nearby kid and say, "'ey why you takin' ma pencil, man?" The accused might reply, "You woofin'?" In white talk, "Do you want to make something of it?"

The origin had nothing to do with "wolf." The metaphor was of a barking watchdog ("woof, woof!"). It was assumed that the one doing the woofin' expected his recipient (the woofee, as it were) to feel the same fear a person would have when confronted by an aggressive barking dog, and to back away from confrontation with the same prudent concern for self-preservation.

The phrase "woof ticket" was most often heard in the context of the never-ending game of trading humorous insults, what sociologists call "the dozens" but we have always referred to as "rank-out sessions." Speaker A might start off with, "Maaaan, in yo' house, the roaches are so big the rats carry switchblades!" Speaker B could return the volley with a comparable rank-out, such as "Ya'll live in the only house I know where you can stand on the roof and get hit by a truck!" an amusingly oblique but recognizable reference to the ubiquitous urban structure more generally known as the sewer.

A woof ticket need not lead to fight or flight, however. One who is truly skilled at the repartee of "ranking out," or who correctly sizes up the woofer as having more bark than bite, could manage to keep things verbal rather than physical, for example with mockery: "He swear he bad! He rank you out so low you can play handball off the curb!" That is, "He thinks he's tough; his insults are truly hurtful! He can really make a person feel small!"

By the 1970s, "woof ticket" had disappeared from the speech of young black Americans, though it may still be remembered among those who are old enough. I can't think of any other expression that I would consider its direct successor, though the practice of verbal provocation certainly survived both in life and art. In fact I recall a friend my age using the expression about 1973, and then remarking that he hadn't heard anyone say it in a long time. I've since read that "woofin' " is still sometimes used among jazz musicians to describe the back-and-forth challenges between instrumental soloists. If it is true that "woof ticket" did not emerge into the mainstream print media until the 1980s and 1990s sources you cited, I would consider it a fascinating example of a short-lived slang locution entering written usage decades after it had achieved obsolescence in its original oral context.

Peter Jeffery
Princeton University
Guilford, Connecticut

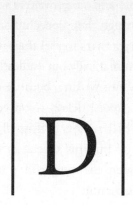

D

Dash It All. The stately colon, the confiding parenthesis and the gently pausing comma demand to know: What's behind today's big dash to the dash? Why has this *lingua interruptus*—expressing uncertainty, jerking the reader around, setting up startling conclusions, imitating patterns of speech—come to dominate our prose?

In the preceding paragraph, I used a pair of dashes to interrupt a sentence and insert supplementary material that gave the question meaning or—to writers, at least—urgency. I could as easily have used a pair of parentheses, specifically designed for the purpose of graceful interjection of useful explication. In the sentence beginning this paragraph, I could again have used parentheses ("parens" to friends) or even commas to separate the mild interjection of "to writers, at least," but I didn't. Why not? Because I have fallen into the habit of trying too often to make writing read like speaking.

The spoken sentence is filled with uttered second thoughts, changes of direction, lurches off on tangents and similar twists. That's because we say what we think as we think it, and thoughts have a way of tumbling over one another, and we stick them in our flow of words as each notion comes to us. In this age of raw transcription, art strains to imitate life, and artful writers feel the pressure to mirror the speech patterns of yammering people by imitating their higgledy-piggledy outpouring of unedited thoughts.

That transcribed-speech technique is fine for writers of fiction and is especially apt for playwrights and screenwriters who reveal the characters' characters realistically through their speech. Some characters blurt their thoughts, showing honesty; others weasel their words, showing duplicity; yet others expostulate grammatically but endlessly, showing off. Writers of drama must write speech, not writing, because real people do not speak writing. Hence we have pauses, delays—you get my drift?—half-stops, restarts, stammering and exclamatory grunts (ugh!) and drifting off into pre–dot-com ellipses . . . To put this speech in written form—that is, to transcribe it—we have seen the powerful punch—pow! right in the kisser—of illustrative punctuation.

Good dramatic writers are in favor of whatever turns the reader on. In an 1863 poem, Emily Dickinson, writing in the halting voice of a woman dying, used the dash to signify gasping for breath: "I am alive—I guess— / The Branches on my Hand / Are full of Morning Glory— / And at my finger's end— / The Carmine—tingles warm— / And if I hold a Glass / Across my Mouth—it blurs it— / Physician's—proof of Breath— / I am alive ..."

In our time, the writing of Tom Wolfe has made stylish use of the dash; he combines it with italics and the mid-sentence exclamation point to indicate herky-jerkiness or panic in thinking. In an article in the current *Harper's* deriding the critics of American "triumphalism," the iconoclastic Wolfe steps into their shoes to write, "After the Soviet archives were opened up—I mean, damn!—it looks like Hiss and the Rosenbergs actually *were* Soviet agents—and even the Witch Hunt, which was one of the bedrocks of our beliefs—damn again!— . . ." That's the use of fictional internal monologue in a nonfiction article, and the dash does its job of chopping up the speech.

But writers of narrative and exposition, as well as those who present fiction in the third person, choose to use the language in the voice of the writer and not of a character. The written sentence, which is not to be confused with the spoken sentence that has been transcribed, gives its creator a chance to rethink the ideas that have come off the top of the head, to reassemble them in an orderly series, to snip off the stupidities and shoot the strays, thereby to marshal a cogent argument or paint a striking image.

On Punctuation Highway, the writer-as-speaker is a dasher, only half-braking at every stop sign; the writer-as-writer measures every pause, uses a comma for the speed bump and a semicolon to proceed with caution at the balancing of closely related complete thoughts, as in this sentence. The colon, a strict setter-up of things to follow, is like an arrow that says "Now watch this" to the reader, but it is too often replaced by the do-anything dash.

Professor Richard Veit of the University of North Carolina at Wilmington disagrees with me about the danger of the *em,* which is the typographer's term for the length of the dash: it's as long as the letter *M* in the same font. "Technically, no function of the *em* couldn't be handled by other punctuation—comma, colon, semicolon, period or parentheses," he notes. "The impact of the *em* is not syntactic but visual. Its shape and length demand a pause and impart drama. It sets up a punch line in a way a colon cannot. Arthur Wallace Calhoun put a code of the Old South into words in 1918: 'A woman's name should appear in print but twice—when she marries and when she dies.' " That was then; now, just as women appear in print a lot, the dash appears too often. I acknowledge that dashes can be useful—say, to add an example—and are surely more emphatic than parentheses (without the sly sharing of confidence with the reader). And the dash is *indispensible* for surrounding a list that already contains commas—weakly beginning a sentence with a conjunction, misspelling *indispensable,* and incorrectly using a comma before the *and* preceding the final item in a series—but undiluted dashiness has become the mark of the slapdash writer who fails to take the trouble to differentiate among the pauses of punctuation.

Writing is different from speaking. Organize your written thoughts so that you don't have to stud your sentences with asides, sudden additions, curses or last-minute entries. Limit your use of the dash to its indisp—to those functions where it beats the other punctuation pauses—or else.

I very much enjoyed—as usual—your witty, learned, and enlightening discourse on the subtle properties of the dash in modern punctuation. Your keen analysis displayed a good deal of dash—not to put too fine a point on it—

and you doubtless did not dash it off in a jiffy, as it were. Nonetheless, your resident Latin censor—dash it all—must have been dozing when he allowed a certain lapsus calami *(aka "slip of the pen") to pass his watchful eye. You will probably receive a sack full of mail from all your faithful admirers who finished a semester of Latin, so my humble contribution will by now be merely old hash—no rhyme intended.*

I am, of course, referring to your allusion concerning "lingua interruptus," which, I am almost tempted to suspect, you might have dangled before your eager readers as a tempting bait. As you see, I am one of the innocents who fell for your ruse.

By now, I have no doubt, you have been lectured ad nauseam *about this petty point, so I shall just briefly confirm what you already know; i.e., that the term in question ought to be either "lingua interrupta"—or, stylistically more preferable—"oratia interrupta," or, if you insist on "interruptus"—and who would not under such circumstance—the noun ought to be "sermo," which is masculine, and thus in agreement with the adjective. For in Latin, which has three grammatical genders, nouns and adjectives must agree, to make a proper, if not dashing impression.*

Hoping you will not look askance at this punctilious observation on behalf of what is, after all, a dead lingua.

Bodo Reichenbach
Arlington, Massachusetts

I am sure that we are agreed that coitus interruptus *should be avoided by all means.*

Lingua interruptus should also be avoided, because it is incorrect. It should be lingua interrupta, *of course.*

Gerardo Joffe
San Francisco, California

Date War.   Language is expressed in writing with a series of symbols. When people cannot agree what the symbols stand for, all is confusion. We find ourselves gesticulating wildly in a Tower of Babel.

Ah, you say, but globalization and Internetting will fix all that. Computers inside a little translating bug in our ear will enable us all to understand one another instantly. Or English will become everybody's second language until a universal language takes over someday.

Oh, yeah? (That's based on the Sanskrit for "Izzat so?") Then how come all the nations of the world, marching into the new millennium, can't agree on what date of the month this is? A furious tug of war is going on between Europe and America that dwarfs the banana wars in importance, threatens the Atlantic Alliance and paralyzes the U.N. But nobody is willing to face up to the Date Debate.

What's today? Unless we're Chinese or Hebrew or some other civilization with its own calendar, we can all agree it's the fifth day of the month of March in the year 2000. And we also agree that it's easier to put that date in a combination of words and numerals: *March 5, 2000.*

Unless, of course, you're in the military. Then it's *5 March 2000,* saving valuable commas needed for investment in missile research and—more to the point—nicely separating the numbers with a word.

But we're all in a hurry; who wants to take all the time to write out the whole word signifying the month? Since March is the third month, we substitute the number 3 for the word's interminable five letters. So *March 5, 2000* is shown as *3/5/2000.* (Unless you like hyphens—then it's *3-5-2000.* Or unless you prefer voguish periods, now called dots, as the *Times Magazine* finger-snappingly does; then it's *3.5.2000,* which has been further shortened to *3.5.00.*)

This simple act of reducing a date to its shortest elements is the cause of the semiotic War Between the Continents now threatening to end globalization as we know it. "In the United States," writes Dr. Alan D. Legatt of White Plains, New York, "a date written as *1/2* would mean Jan. 2, while in Europe it would mean the first of February."

So today's date—the fifth day of the third month in the run-up to our brand-new third millennium—is written in America as *3/5/00.* (I'm a slasher, not a hyphenator or a dotter.) But in Britain and throughout Europe, those same numerals signify an entirely different date: the third day of the fifth month, or *May 3, 2000.*

Big difference. March goes out like a lamb; rough winds do shake the darling buds of May. Even worse, when President Bill Clinton sends a cheery note to Prime Minister Tony Blair and dates it 4/11, the Yank is thinking of April 11 but the Brit thinks it is November 4. This is sure to contribute to Anglo-American misunderstanding; if it leads to one leader standing the other up at a scheduled summit meeting, it could put a strain on the special relationship.

To resolve this problem before it discombobulates transatlantic e-mail and drives the editors of the *International Herald Tribune* to distraction, a nongovernmental organization that calls itself ISO has put forward a recommendation. The name is an acronym formed by the rejiggered initials of the International Organization for Standardization, headquartered in Geneva; ISO is rooted in the Greek word for "equal," and this outfit seeks to get everyone to agree on the same symbols for the same things. To avert date warfare, ISO recommends that we all start with the year, followed by the month and finally the day. Today's date, in ISO format, is *2000-3-5.*

As they like to mutter in the Pentagon, I nonconcur. Who are these cookie-pushing cookie cutters of an unelected international bureaucracy to tell America's native speakers that we must conform to the linguistic *diktats* of Continental Common Marketeers and sovereignty-grabbing European Unionists? Do the Brits think that English is a better language than Merkin? ISO may call me a lationist, but I reject this backdoor attempt to force American check writers to date our support of the IMF in a way alien to our ways.

If those one-worlders in Geneva are so het up about standardization, why don't they adopt the American system? A millennium and a half from now, the standardeers will be writing the second of January in the year three thousand four hundred and fifty-six as *3456/1/2,* while we will write it as *1/2/3456,* which will be a real kick.

The Brits, on the verge of giving up their pound for the euro, are losing their regard for tradition, but when it comes to habits, Americans—even those who prattle about the need for great change at election time—hate change. It was hard enough for some of us to memorize the month-day-year sequence in the first place (if I have that order right); we don't need to reprogram our minds just because some professional smoother-outers want everybody in the world to march in lockstep.

Hawks, finding geopolitical significance in this coming symbolic dust-up, will cry: if being a sole superpower does not give us hegemony in the writing of dates, why go to the expense of being a superpower at all? Doves, taking a less bellicose line, will coo: diversity is more precious than uniformity.

I say: By jingo, let's stick to our slashes and hold fast to the American Way of Dating. To the standardizers, we should refuse to give a centimeter. Write today's date as *3/5/00* and let the rest of the world complain about us being out of date, out of step, out of time and out of sorts. So what if we miss a few appointments? We will be striking a blow for dialectical uniqueness, icono-clastic individuality, national sovereignty and international confusion.

Only make it a convention to use Roman numerals for the month and every-body can go his own sweet way. Your jingoism in the matter of dating is wor-thy of Stephen Decatur.

Jacques Barzun
San Antonio, Texas

Diplolingo. The diplomatic oxymoron of the year was issued by the Egyptian president Hosni Mubarak, attempting to put the best face on a disappointing summit meeting between President Clinton and the Syrian dictator Hafez al-Assad. "It's a step forward," said Mr. Mubarak, "although there was no progress."

Dirigiste. "Financial markets and market-based economics," declared the former treasury secretary Robert Rubin in the *Economist*'s millennial issue, "have replaced *dirigiste* economics. . . ."

So in a special issue predicting events in 2000, he shot down the dirigi-ble. (That is an arcane allusion to the midair explosion of the airship Hindenburg, tearfully described by a reporter in one of old-time radio's most thrilling moments. The Latin *dirigere* means "to direct," and a balloon capable of being directed by a pilot was dubbed a *dirigible* in 1885.)

"What are *dirigiste* economics?" asks Susan Neisuler of Newton, MA. (*MA* is the Postal Service's arbitrary abbreviation for *Massachusetts,* not *Maine;* my style follows the more sensible *New York Times* style, which abbreviates *Massachusetts* as *Mass. Maine* is *ME* at the Postal Service and *Me.* at the *Times;* I write out the whole word.) "Should I be afraid of them?" Ms. Neisuler wonders, construing *economics* incorrectly as plural. "Is Robert Rubin making it up?"

No, Mr. Rubin was not making it up. Back in 1989 *Barron's* was writing about the "French, who left to their own devices, would fashion Brussels into the capital of *dirigiste* economics." *Dirigiste* is also used with things other than economics. At the end of January this year, Federal Reserve Chairman Alan Greenspan told the Senate Banking Committee he was encouraged by "forces emerging in Europe which will gradually bring down a lot of the *dirigiste* attitudes."

If you're a capitalist, or if you have no capital but believe in the creative force of untrammeled free enterprise, then you will be glad that the *dirigistes* are on the run. Their philosophy calls for "direction and control of the economy by the state." The mildly socialistic phrase that preceded it was *central planning,* and the phrase that took it all the way to the Soviet system was *command economy,* the opposite of *market economy.*

The earliest use I can find is in the Nov. 28, 1946, issue of *Le Monde,* when the writer summarized the American attitude toward France as "Be liberal or *dirigiste.* Return to a capitalist or a socialist economy. But take the decision and show us a serious program." The English translation first appeared in *Political Science Quarterly* in September 1947 and soon was taken up on both sides of the Atlantic. The *Economist* in the same month denounced such control as fascistic: "Authoritarianism or stagnation—that is the choice which *dirigisme* thrusts on us." Nor was the word limited to economics: in the earliest entry in the *OED,* from a 1951 *Archivum Linguisticum,* a roundheeled lexicographer sneered at "linguistic *dirigisme,* standards of correctness in a constantly evolving language."

(Now wait a minute: some of us think that kind of *dirigisme* is good.)

Another watcher of Rubinlingo, John Di Clemente of Tinley Park, IL (that's a postocrat's idea of an abbreviation for Illinois; I still write the old-fashioned *Ill.*, which the postocrats think is sick), sends in a clipping from the *Wall Street Journal* quoting Rubin about restrictions on his lobbying the White House from his new banking job: "We'll be *belt and suspenders* with respect to those." Mr. Di Clemente wants to know: "What's the connection between such haberdashery and ethics?"

Earliest use I can find of this locution is in the *Dallas Morning News* in 1987: "To qualify for the Scott Burns *Belt and Suspender* Bank List, a bank had to have primary equity capital amounting to at least 10 percent of its assets." From the context, it appears that (a) this is not the first use of the phrase and (b) it refers to safety. Nor is the metaphor limited to finance: an 11th Circuit U.S. Court of Appeals decision in 1997 described a government motion to compel testimony as "this *belt-and-suspenders* approach," using the phrase as a hyphenated compound adjective.

I called Mr. Rubin at Citigroup, where his trousers are now most securely held up, to ask his definition of the metaphor. "It emphasizes certainty," he says. "When you're wearing both, you're doubly safe." And so it is with stable banks and legal rights and ethical standards. In the lingo of newsies, my *Times* copy desk colleagues inform me, it means "overkill."

I suspect the fairly recent U.S. usage of "belt and suspenders" is merely a transatlantic translation of the English "belt and braces" which I believe I have seen in pre-WWII British fiction (e.g., "I brought a knife as well as a gun because I'm a belt and braces man."). Same range of signification and same register.

Daniel F. Melia
Department of Rhetoric
University of California
Berkeley, California

In Double Indemnity, *the Billy Wilder classic from the late 1940s, Edward G. Robinson plays a crafty insurance manager. He is Fred MacMurray's boss. After Barbara Stanwyck's husband is murdered and dropped from a moving train, there is a witness to the event. He arrives at the insurance office to meet Edward G. Robinson, who is suspicious of the apparent suicide. Robinson calls the witness a cautious man. The witness asks why. Robinson replies that he is a "belt and suspenders man," since he is wearing both.*

Michael McTague
New York, New York

℃

Don't Go There.   After I expressed my intent to explore an area that strikes terror of embarrassment into so many hearts, a colleague warned, "I wouldn't go there if I were you."

Linguistic exploration rejects such faintheartedness. We will now deal forthrightly with the cliché that has been embraced by the squirming squeamish: *Don't go there.*

Its literal sense is of no concern. *There,* meaning "a place," can be construed as an adverb modifying *go* or as a noun in its own right. But the figurative sense—of some undiscover'd country from whose bourn no shamefaced traveler returns—is what has gripped the bromide set.

It can mean "We'd better not talk about that." Or "If our conversation reaches that subject, you will be uncomfortable and I will be chagrined." Or "Now you're getting into a touchy subject." Or more severely, "Beware—you are approaching a taboo zone."

Interviewing Dan Quayle, the former vice president, last spring before he withdrew from the presidential race, the *Times* reporter Melinda Henneberger noted this intelligent man's abiding need to prove he was not stupid. "Waking up from a nap on the campaign plane, he asked what I was reading," she wrote, "and it was *Anna Karenina.* He squeezed his eyes shut, opened them again a second later. 'Russian, right?' Then, a look of relief. Why, oh why, does he *go there*?"

Where is *there* in this figurative sense? It is not uncharted territory; on the contrary, it is a subject area all too well charted or remembered for its embarrassments by the person not eager to get back to that place.

"I suspect this may have had its origin in psychobabble," writes Stephen Rosen of New York. "Where does it come from?"

Let's go there. David Barnhart, editor of the *Dictionary Companion* that bears his name (I like that archaic locution), suggests that the proto-phrase for the expression is "I don't want to *go that route.*" If so, the meaning has changed from "way of getting there" to "being there, unhappily." The first lexicographic listing I can find is in *Da Bomb!*—the March 1997 dictionary of slang compiled by Judi Sanders's intercultural communication class at California State Polytechnic University in Pomona. It defined *Don't even go there* simply as "Do not say that" and the shorter *Don't go there* as "Don't talk about it or mention it." (*That's da bomb,* by the way, is synonymous with the no-longer-so-cool *cool.*)

Tom Dalzell, the California slanguist, has no citation to offer but opines that "*don't go there* started with black drag queens and then found its legs with Ricki Lake," the talk-show host.

Barry Popik of the American Dialect Society found a 1994 usage of the imperative warning by the comic Martin Lawrence, talking to *Entertainment Weekly* about his Fox sitcom. "We started using the expressions 'You go, girl!' and '*Don't go there!*' " Lawrence said, "and no one in television was doing that. No one. Now a lot of Fox shows are using the same stuff."

Now that its roots and overusage have been exposed, we can hope for the early demise of the cliché. As Yogi Berra once put it, "That place is so popular that nobody *goes there* anymore."

Referring to a popular restaurant, Yogi said, "Nobody goes there anymore, it's too crowded." The eloquence is in the phrase, not just the thought.

Richard Schlesinger
New York, New York

Don't Presume.   Asked by one of his fellow candidates if he would commit to choosing a pro-life running mate, George W. Bush replied, "I think it's incredibly *presumptive* for someone who has yet to earn his party's nomination to be picking vice presidents."

The cable commentator Laura Ingraham promptly picked up the error, pointing out that the word Governor Bush had in mind was *presumptuous*.

It's a fairly common error, with both words based on the verb *presume*, from the Latin *præsumere*, "to take in advance." That would now be put as "to take for granted," as in "Dr. Livingstone, I *presume*." (If less certain, the newsman Henry Stanley would have used *assume*, "to suppose." How did I get in darkest Africa?)

Presumptive means "probable," based on a reasonable assumption, as in "Bush and Gore have been, for a year, the *presumptive* standard-bearers." The meaning of *presumptuous* departs sharply from that, to "arrogant, assuming the unwarranted"—the presuming in that formulation to be unreasonable, not to mention uppity and pushy.

Few suffixes split the meaning so drastically from the root word. A subtler difference was examined some years ago, when a State Department spokesman denounced as *contemptible* an article of mine sneering at some feckless action of the then secretary. An alert reporter followed up with "Don't you mean *contemptuous*?" To which the quick-thinking diplomat replied, "That, too."

Doofusism.   "Bush has been minimized and diminished by Hollywood liberals," said Lionel Chetwynd, a Hollywood conservative, about the new president, "and it's reflected in all those *Saturday Night Live* sketches, which depict him as a *doofus*."

The derogation *doofus* popped up in the '60s and is usually thought to be an alteration of *goofus*, the noun form of *goofy*. However, the German *doof* means "dull-witted," and there is this file entry in the *Dictionary of American Regional English*, harking to the '50s: "As a boy growing up around adults who used German words, I heard '*doofus*' a lot . . . to mean something like 'you dumbass.' "

The synonym *dumb-ass* made its third appearance in the *New York Times* two months ago when President Clinton was reported to have told *Rolling Stone* interviewer Jann Wenner, "And it was only then that I worked out with Colin Powell this *dumb-ass* 'don't ask, don't tell' thing."

The magazine immediately issued a correction, saying that its stenographer had erred in transcribing *don't ask* as *dumb-ass,* which suggested that the president had repeated the phrase. The White House's recording of the interview had been taped over, perhaps in a fit of frugality, and a Clinton spokesman was pleased to accept *Rolling Stone*'s apology.

Apparently the sensitivity to the possible use of the term stemmed from a notion that *dumb-ass* is a mild vulgarism referring to the posterior. More likely, it is a variant of *jackass,* the name of an innocent animal that bears the burden of frequent disparagement for stubbornness or stupidity.

Both as a modifier and as a noun, *dumb-ass* should be hyphenated as an aid to avert pronunciation of the silent *b.* Caution should be exercised in applying *dumb* to a person who is mute, because of the second sense of the word, meaning "unintelligent," but as a noun, *dumb-ass* can be used without shame as a suitable synonym for *doofus.*

Duckmanship.   There should be no debate over the meaning of *weaponized:* a biological or chemical agent "put in a form that can be used effectively in a weapon."

Asked about "weapons grade" anthrax, Dr. Anthony Fauci, director of the National Institute for Allergy and Infectious Diseases, replied: "You can call it whatever you want to call it with regard to grade and size or *weaponized* or not *weaponized.* The fact is, it is acting like a highly efficient bioterrorist agent." The scientist added, "If it walks like a duck and quacks like a duck, then it is a duck."

Not quite. Coinage of this political aphorism is attributed to the labor leader Walter Reuther in the late 1930s, on how to identify a Communist: "If it walks like a duck and quacks like a duck, then it just may be a duck."

If it sounds like an old aphorism and works like an old aphorism . . .

Enchiladaville.   The governor of California, Gray Davis, after meeting with President Bush about the energy shortage causing rolling blackouts in the Golden State, said, "The *big enchilada,* the thing that really matters, above all else, is temporary price relief."

The governor is wandering in a no-man's-land between a *whole enchilada* and the *big enchilada.* A *whole enchilada* means "the entirety of a thing," its synonyms "the whole ball of wax," "whole nine yards," "whole schmear" and the etymologically mysterious "whole shebang." After Jimmy Carter won the presidency in 1976, the former California governor Ronald Reagan said that Democrats, long the majority party in Congress, could no longer claim that divided government impeded progress. "The Democrats cannot fuzz up the issue by blaming the White House," he said. "They've got the *whole enchilada* now."

The *big enchilada* is not a situation but a person. It is "the boss, the person of undoubted authority and influence, the one on top," and from a law officer's point of view, "the main target." In a taped Watergate conversation in 1973, Bob Haldeman says of John Mitchell, the former attorney general, "He is as high up as they've got." John Ehrlichman concurs, "He's the *big enchilada.*" Queried about the coinage of this variant, Ehrlichman wrote me from jail a few years later: "I coined the phrase. I've cooked my own enchiladas for years. My California upbringing. Could have said 'big fish' or 'top dog' or 'big cheese,' I guess."

Governor Davis has been using *big enchilada* to mean, as he defines it himself, "the thing that really matters above all else"—the *ne plus ultra,* the "acme, ultimate" or "most profound degree." In my view it confuses two distinct slang terms.

An *enchilada* is a tortilla into which is rolled a mixture of meat or beans and seasoned with a sauce made of chili, a hot red pepper (the *chil* in *enchilada*). The entire thing can be eaten by a person of great influence in the dark.

Your discussion of the whole enchilada *included practically every variant. In fact, it might be said that you gave your readers the whole* kit and caboodle. *My immigrant mother loved this expression and made it her own, by combining Yiddish and English into* de gantze caboodle.

Sam Unterricht
Hewlett, New York

The End of Minority.   The San Diego City Council last month voted to strike the word *minority* from official use.

Ordinarily, I resist *diktats* about language from politicians (in which I am in a you-know-what), but in California, no racial or ethnic or linguistic group is in the majority. Does that make everybody a *minority?* Only to statisticians and demographers. First, a *minority* is a group, not an individual; you can say, "I am a member of a *minority,*" but you strain the bounds of good usage when you say, "I am a *minority.*" This bound is strained frequently.

Second, *minority* in the past half-century has taken on a meaning of "nonwhite." Though white Jews, Muslims and Buddhists are also self-identified as *minorities,* the primary sense is clear: say, "I'm a *minority* American," and everyone knows you mean you are black, Hispanic, Asian, American Indian or whatever combination you told the census taker.

The word gained that sense, says Fred R. Shapiro, who is editing the *Yale Dictionary of Quotations,* when the Supreme Court in the 1938 *United States v. Carolene Products Co.* referred in a footnote to religious, ethnic, national and racial groups as "discrete and insular *minorities*." In 1949, the *Journal of Negro Education* first used the noun as an adjective in writing of "*minority* workers."

A turning point came when the *Washington Post* in 1977 reported, "Washington, the nation's premier black city, with a *minority* population of more than 70 percent . . . " The newspaper then asked itself, "A 'minority' population of more than 70 percent?" That it characterized as "racial math" and editorialized that it preferred the old, realistic math.

In one of his final-week farewells, President Bill Clinton posed the profound question, "What will the terms *majority* and *minority* mean when there is no *majority* race in America?"

He did not stay for an answer, but mine would be, Drop the racial sense of *minority*. They're not crazy in San Diego.

In the United States, non-Hispanic whites still make up the national majority. But more than half of the one hundred most populous cities have a nonwhite majority, which makes many whites a minority in their hometowns. That new *minority* is learning not to get waspish.

Enjoy!   A lissome Japanese waitress at the Yosaku restaurant in Bethesda, Maryland, presented me with a bowl of *Nabayaki Udon*—thick noodles in broth with bits of chicken and shrimp—and then smiled and said, "Enjoy."

That is not a Japanese word. Indeed, that invitation to pleasure in eating is not an Asian attitude. According to my *Times* colleague Nicholas D. Kristof, author with his wife, Sheryl WuDunn, of *Thunder From the East: Portrait of a Rising Asia,* servers of food in Japan are likely to say *honno okuchi yogoshi de gozaimasuga,* "here's a little something that will make your mouth dirty." The idea is to apologize for the meal and to suggest humbly that it will not be enjoyable at all to the honored guest. The Chinese equivalent, as a mouthwatering repast is placed before the eater, is *meishemma cai,* or "this food is nothing much."

In American eateries, however, and in restaurants around the world that cater to English-speaking patrons, the new server's imperative—*Enjoy!*—

can be heard. The mock-stern but cheerful command is spreading like the Asian leguminous vine kudzu, rivaling the readily understood *OK* and the widely accepted *no problem* as a major American contribution to a universal language.

Waiters (or servers, as the unisexy prefer to be called) in every culture have their national phrases to accompany the placement of a plate. *Bon appétit,* say the French, and the wish for a hearty appetite is expressed in Greek as *kali orexi,* in Spanish as *buen provecho* and in German as *guten Appetit.*

A German waiter is as likely to say simply *bitte,* which usually means "please," and the same idea is expressed in New York's Russian Tea Room as *pozhaluista.* The closest translation of these would be the neutral comment of American hash slingers as they plonk down the plate: "There you go."

A British butler is likely to warn, "The plate is hot, Madam." Until a decade or so ago, the Yiddish term was *es gezunterheyt,* "eat in good health"; the Gaelic equivalent is *sláinte,* "health."

But then along came the imperative, intransitive *Enjoy!* That exhortation has become so ubiquitous that in a Diner's Bill of Rights concocted recently by Zagat's restaurant survey, one of the inalienable rights of patrons was "for the waiter NOT to say *'enjoy'* after the food is served."

How did it all begin? In his 1958 book, *For 2 Cents Plain,* Harry Golden wrote: "When my mother served our meals . . . she would always say, *'Enjoy, enjoy.'* . . . The word *enjoy* was seldom used by itself. It was always repeated." Accordingly, Golden's next best seller was titled *Enjoy, Enjoy!* In 1968, the *New York Times* reporter Marylin Bender quoted the furrier Jacques Kaplan on the effects of inflation: "Whenever they felt money would lose its value, people would gorge themselves. It's a dancing over the volcano attitude, an *enjoy-enjoy* philosophy."

Even as the dialectically duplicated verb lost its duplication on its journey to general usage, lexicographers noticed the way the hortatory *Enjoy!* did not transmit action to an object. Lillian Feinsilver wrote in her Yiddish dictionary in 1970 that *enjoy* as an intransitive verb "has become fairly common in recent years. . . . *'Enjoy* yourself' was abbreviated to the simple *'Enjoy'* by the solicitous Jewish mother." She noted the oddly intransitive usage by the violinist Mischa Elman: "I get a great kick out of life. I know how to *enjoy*."

Now, as a service to philological scholars, we examine the grammatical puzzlement contained in this seemingly simple food fiat. *Enjoy yourself,* meaning "have a good time," is clearly reflexive, turning the verb's action back on *you,* the understood subject. But the simple and now far more common *Enjoy!* poses the question: *Enjoy* what? The food? Yourself gorging the food? The object is indeterminate; the verb's action does not know where to go.

"When used solely in the imperative mood," says Mike Agnes, editor in chief of Webster's New World Dictionaries, "the intransitive verb *'enjoy'* may well qualify as a 'defective paradigm,' whereby a word fails to exhibit the full range of expected inflections. How odd that a word of such felicitous intent seems to reveal itself only in the stern imperative."

Jeffrey McQuain, the new editor of the newsletter *Copy Editor,* calls the new use of *Enjoy!* "the implied intransitive" because it has no direct object but implies there should be one. He tracks the construction back to the ancient *Eat!* or the Italian *Mangia! Mangia!*

"The implied intransitive is especially popular in sports shorthand," McQuain says. "Coaches and fans yell their advice in the imperative mood without the subject (you) and without the object." Thus, *Bunt!* could mean either "Bunt the ball" or "Bunt, you miserable hitter."

Beware the loss of clarity in the defective paradigm or the implied intransitive. Until recently, verbs could be transitive (I *love* you) or intransitive (I *love*). Ron Meyers of New York deplores the de-transitivizing trend, using as his examples "please wait while your credit card is *authorizing*" and "this book usually *ships* in three days." What subject of the sentence is doing the authorizing or shipping? What object is the verb's action being done to?

Grammarians, lexicographers and all those living in syntax will find delectation in plunging into a deep, delicious analysis of this emerging phenomenon. And to those happy linguists we can only say . . .

There are a lot of intransitive verbs in the language, and, when somebody tells you "Get lost!" you probably don't wonder where *you should get lost (since, of course, if everyone knew where, you wouldn't be lost). What is wrong with* enjoy, *intransitive verb, meaning simply, "enjoy yourself; indulge in enjoyment"? There is nothing defective about a paradigm of a verb that, among many that have, has shifted from transitive to transitive/intransitive or even just intransitive.*

Laurence Urdang

Old Lyme, Connecticut

Your column leads in with a comment about how Japanese waitresses, uh, servers would never make a comment analogous to "enjoy" because it is non-Asian, but instead would make some kind of self-deprecating remark that is comical to Western ears. Westerners love to trot out the whole Asian self-abnegation bit, but it is overblown.

Sometimes one does encounter an echo of that self-deprecatory remark, but more likely your waitron will say something like "go-yukkuri dozo" (go ahead, relax, take your time) or just "dozo" (go ahead).

Adam Rice

Austin, Texas

In your learned paper on the Rise of the Intransitive, you do not mention some of the predecessors of enjoy. *By recent I mean of course those I have seen born and taking hold.* Identify *is one of them. One used to "identify oneself" with Dracula or some other favorite character. Again, to say he "converted to Catholicism" would have seemed strange before our blessed day. One said: "he was converted," or "he converted himself," or "became a convert." I suspect that the intransitive grew out of "he converted to oil," when "his furnace" is understood by the context. During the protests here against apartheid, universities and other philanthropies were urged "to divest," that is, get rid of South African securities. "Divest!" sounds to me like the motto of the Strip-Tease Defense League.*

Matching the change in verb use is the reverse twist, as in rankle *and* boggle, *now made transitive. It's a pity in both cases. We need it* rankles *for the festering thought of a slight or an insult, and the other for resisting, being reluctant, hesitating as the result of a shock. We have plenty of other words for the current* boggle *glued to "the mind" in the sense of discomfiting, bewildering, confusing.*

Jacques Barzun
San Antonio, Texas

℃

Enroned.   "I don't want to *Enron* the American people," said the Democrat Tom Daschle, defining the new verb in his next sentence. "I don't want to see them holding the bag at the end of the day just like Enron employees have held the bag."

The workers who have been *enroned* (if we're going to use the name as a general verb meaning "cheated," drop the eponym's initial capital, as we did with *boycott* and *bork*) are called *Enronites*. (This specific group of cheatees takes a capital.)

Other energy-related companies, wrote Bethany McLean in *Fortune,* "disclaimed any sort of *Enronesque* behavior." In forming an adjective, *-esque* strikes me as a more elegant suffix than *-ish,* as in *enronish* or the less critical *enronlike.* (*Child-ish* is "puerile, immature," always with a pejorative connotation, while *child-like* is "innocent," always endearing.)

Michael Wolff, a columnist for *New York* magazine, committed a late hit on Tina Brown when her *Talk* magazine folded, describing the buzzworthily glamorous editor as "a little *enronish.*" This caused the linguistically savvy Jim Sullivan of the *Boston Globe* to note that the adjective "*enronish* captures the spirit of the big magazine cannonball but not its style. It is clunky. *Enronian* rolls off the tongue. Someone responsible for large-scale destruction is then an '*enronista.*' The process of destruction: *enronism.* The verb is simply the name, as in 'He got *enroned* last Thursday.' "

Note the general agreement about the spelling of the verb. The *o* in *Enron* is pronounced *ah,* as in "on," and not *oh,* as in "throne." When adding *-ed* after the single *n,* however, the word appears to invite the pronunciation rhyming with "enthroned." Should we, then, double the *n* to produce *enronned*? No. If this has been worrying you, stop worrying. The analogy to follow is that of *environ,* as in Lincoln's "I am *environed* with difficulties"—one *n,* pronounced *ah,* not *oh.* To *enron* has a lot more snap than the unimaginative to *enronize.*

The suffix *-on* is considered by corporate image makers in the energy and technology fields to be a futuristic syllable—hence Exxon and Chevron, Raytheon and Micron. In the naming of the merged Houston Natural Gas and InterNorth companies in 1986, the consultants Lippincott & Margulies suggested *Enteron,* of Greek origin, which began with the first syllable of *energy* and concluded with the slick, with-it *on.* What's more, a specialized industrial sense of *enteron* was reported to be "a pipeline system transmitting nourishment."

However, when it was pointed out to the directors that the common medical meaning of *enteron* was "alimentary canal, intestines, guts," company officials hastily demanded that a new name be found evocative of energy and the future but with no suggestion of upset stomach or bowel movement. I confirmed this history of corporate nomenclature in a call to Mark Palmer, a spokesman for the bankrupt company. "Legend has it," he added, "that they told the naming firm that they had twenty-four hours to come up with something else or they wouldn't pay them a plug nickel—and they came up with *Enron.*" Palmer seemed relieved that was all he was being asked about.

The namers did not worry about the association with football's *end run* or the possible play on "take the money *enron.*" In future corporate naming, *en-* is very likely to be avoided as a prefix, and the suffix *-on* is off.

Er, um (ahem).   A well-watched Russian newscast called *Naked Truth* is anchored by a woman with a serious expression who slowly strips as she recounts the major events of the day. The weather forecaster is topless. Above the AP article about this news uncoverage, the *Seattle Times* carried the headline "Russian Anchorwomen Do the Nudes, *er,* News."

At about the same time last year, the *New York Times* headlined an article about Hillary Clinton's campaign for the Senate using that same representation of a verbal delay: "The Wonk, *er,* Woman Behind Mrs. Clinton."

These are examples in headlines of the arch pause. In olden times, writers drew attention to puns, nice turns of phrase or metaphors that the inattentive reader might otherwise miss with *so to speak, as it were* or *if you will.* Now the preferred little alarm to awake the sleepy is the written *er, um, uh, ah, well* or, for extreme throat-clearing, *ahem.*

The signification of the arch pause with an *er* or an *um* is rampant in journalese. It says, "Here comes a little witticism, you ninny," as in this usage by Al Kamen in the *Washington Post:* "Loop fans will recall Tuesday's item on Monica S. Lewinsky preparing to field questions from law students in Manhattan that night as part of an upcoming HBO special. It was quite an, *um,* affair." That meaning of the pause—"Gee, but I'm being naughty here"—recently extended to the gardening pages of the *New York Times:* "The spring peeper, Pseudacris crucifer," croaked Anne Raver in a delightful piece about frogs, "is one of the chorus frogs, so-called because of its joyful song heralding warmer weather and, *ahem,* the joys of mating."

Sometimes the arch pause says, "I am understating," as in the *Times* columnist Gail Collins's "The wounds of the primary campaign have, *um,* not exactly healed." At other times, the writer, as if wondering, "Do I dare to eat a peach?" asks the reader's pardon for having the audacity to wax metaphoric, as in my colleague Paul Krugman's reference to "the renewed enthusiasm of Americans for huge, gas-guzzling vehicles—an enthusiasm, *er,* fueled by cheap gas." In the same way, Andrew Coyne of Canada's *National Post* wrote last month that an energy report's "call for increasing capacity on interstate transmission lines is, *er,* well grounded."

Writing about the movie *The Mummy Returns,* the UPI Hollywood reporter Vernon Scott pulled out all the lingual stops: "While plots for mummy movies thicken and special effects provide more gaudy mayhem, the deep, primeval horror of the walking dead has been *well, er, ah,* deadened, so to speak." The reader who did not appreciate that metaphoric play must be wrapped in gauze.

The publication that led the way in the use of the arch pause is the *Econ-*

omist. In 1975, it wrote of the lawyers in the offices of Arab nations participating in the economic boycott of Israel: "Each office has the task of seeing that its country's trade relations are strictly, *er,* kosher." A year later, it wrote that "for Westminster to interfere with Edinburgh would be like, *er,* the House of Lords rejecting Commons legislation." And in the same month, an article on industrial success was headlined, "Take a Bow, Britain (*er,* Wales)."

In British English, the self-deprecating hesitation or Churchillian stutter is often used to draw attention to what follows; Rudyard Kipling in 1913 described life in smoking rooms as seen "through clouds of '*Ers*' and '*Ums*.'" Americans tend to see it as expressive of indecision. I put that to Johnny Grimond, editor of the *Economist*'s style guide: "Probably when we've resorted to *er* or *um,* it's not so much an indication of indecision," he replied with authority, "but when one is led inexorably to a conclusion that is embarrassing or awkward or obvious."

Geoffrey Nunberg, who does a regular language feature on NPR's *Fresh Air,* says he thinks that the use of the written *er, um, uh,* is an articulation of the dash, with which writers like Thackeray and Trollope indicated a rethinking of what went before. "In theory, in writing there should never be any false starts and pauses. When you use *er* or *um,* you are reproducing in a fictitious way the process of communication. It's a specious sense of the writer letting you in on the business of composition." Nunberg fears, as I do, that we'll see much more of this reconstruction of the writer's thought process in e-mail, which usually revels in the conversational and prefers the appearance of a work in progress.

If the goal of the writer is to reflect a character's sloppy spoken language or to set on paper some revealing oral self-correction, then the pauses signified by *er* and its ilk serve a communicative purpose. We all make sounds that show we are thinking before we speak, and a writer's recording of them, though sometimes annoying, adds verisimilitude to dialogue.

But that's not the arch pause in narrative or commentary. My target today is not just the signifier for "Here comes one of my best zingers" but the one that says, "I ostentatiously hesitate to say this." A good example of the latter is in a note that President George Bush the elder wrote to his wife, Barbara, after being told that his opponent, Michael Dukakis, was scoring points with voters by showing public affection for his wife, Kitty. "Sweetsie, please look at how Mike and Kitty do it," Bush wrote. "Try to be closer in, more—*well, er* romantic—on camera."

I inveigh against the use of the written grunt because either it assumes the reader is an ignoramus or it needlessly apologizes for a writer's attempt at wit. Do not presume that your reader is moving his lips as he reads your prose. Do not be afraid to deliver the nudes.

Euphemism Watch.   In Shakespeare's time, they were called *gravedig- gers*. Then they got organized, raised prices and named themselves *under- takers*. When that acquired a too-gloomy connotation, they changed it to *morticians*. But now that caretakers have given way to caregivers, and even *sharing* has been overtaken by *caring* as the most pious participle, we have—trumpeted in a reverential, hushed *ta-dah!*—the *deathcare industry*.

The other major euphemism to burst forth this year is the diplomatic replacement for *rogue state*. The earliest use I can find of this phrase was in a 1983 *Wall Street Journal* story noting that smokestack industries have "won Ohio a largely deserved reputation as a *rogue state* on the environ- ment." Two years later, the columnist William Pfaff first applied it in its current sense: "The Soviet Union had deliberately isolated itself. Its role was that of a *rogue state,* a revolutionary power that challenged all the others."

In recent years, the phrase has been applied to states like Libya, Iran, Iraq, Serbia, Sudan, Syria and North Korea that supported or condoned the presence of terrorists. Last month, however, on National Public Radio's *Diane Rehm Show,* Secretary of State Madeleine Albright revealed an offi- cial smoothing-over: "We are now calling these states *states of concern*." Asked about this new locution, State spokesman Richard Boucher said of Iraq, a hard-core *rogue state* in the earlier formulation, that it had become "a state previously known as *rogue*."

Problem solved; worry removed. Of course, if one of those *states of con-*

cern gets hold of a nuclear or biological missile, it could be a bonanza for the *deathcare industry*.

Eviscerate.   A word with a fearsome and odious primary meaning has been adopted by our military to describe the effect of our air power on the enemy in Afghanistan.

At a Pentagon briefing, Lt. Gen. Gregory Newbold informed reporters that "the combat power of the Taliban has been *eviscerated*." The vivid verb became the basis of a front-page headline in the *Washington Post:* "Pentagon: Taliban Forces '*Eviscerated*.' "

Eviscerate has to do with the removal of the *viscera*, or "internal organs." A *visceral* reaction is also called a *gut* reaction, because the noun *gut* means "intestine, entrails." (Only in the plural, *guts*, does that word gain the meaning of "courage," or "intestinal fortitude.") Thus, the literal meaning of the verb *eviscerate* is "disembowel, gut." It evokes the image of medieval combat with swords.

But it gave rise to a figurative sense, less bloody-minded: "to deprive of essential parts, to remove the essence of." Interviewed by Fox News the day after the Pentagon briefing, Benjamin Netanyahu, the former prime minister of Israel, said that in considering the possibility of a Palestinian state, air and water rights would have to be restricted: "You'll *eviscerate* a lot of those powers that are normally associated with sovereignty." Also using that figurative sense, Seth Waxman, solicitor general in the Clinton administration, wrote in the *Boston Globe*, "Statutory provisions that permit information-sharing relating to terrorism do not *eviscerate* constitutional freedom."

Headline writers have to be careful to apply the verb to a power, using the figurative sense, and not to military forces made up of people, seeming to take the original sense. Such disempowering, rather than disemboweling, is what the Pentagon general surely had in mind.

Eviscerate is the removal of contents of a multiple-layered cavity or organ, according to our terminology. As an ophthalmologist, when I eviscerate an eye I remove its contents without removing the eyeball itself (i.e., the scleral shell).

Heskel Haddad, MD
New York, New York

Eviscerate *is the term preferred by feminists and other right-minded people to* emasculate, *as it is gender neutral and has the added advantage of not insulting those of us who are non-masculine by nature.*

Beverly S. Cohen
New York, New York

Fall Fashionese.   "For Fall," headlined the *Times'* fashion page, "Some Swash, Some Buckle and a Tougher Look."

To *swash*, as every swordsman knows, is to swing your blade violently so as to make a great clanging sound on the *buckler*, or shield, of your opponent. Your noisy blustering does not hurt anybody, but such intimidating braggadocio satisfies your urge to swagger, especially when it is difficult to see anything through your iron visor. Hence, the 1560 word *swashbuckler*, "a swaggering ruffian," defined now as the 2001 woman with the tough high-fashion attitude.

Vogue magazine's September 2001 issue featured ten pages of a hard-eyed supermodel in thigh-high, flat-heeled boots wearing what appeared to me to be a chef's hat made of fur, as if created by a cook about to visit a walk-in meat refrigerator. One caption under a threatening pose by the usually delectable Nadja Auermann read, "She'll lead you on with *toques* to die for."

Toque is a French word for "cap," most famous as *toque blanche*, the tall white hat originally worn by chefs in monasteries and now the phrase that adorns a thousand bistros. The word appeared early in English spelled *toockes;* perhaps because this might cause confusion among Seventh Avenue designers with its homonym in Yiddish, the French spelling and pronunciation are preferred. When trimmed with fox to go with the leathery equestrian dominatrix look, the *toque* has a Russian air. (If the czar only knew . . .)

"So what gives with all this hard extravagance with the economy in a soft slump?" wrote my colleague Cathy Horyn in her sparkling analysis of the new toughness. (The phrase *What gives?*, first cited in John O'Hara's 1940 novel, *Pal Joey,* is a direct translation of the German *Was gibt's?*, an idiom meaning "What is happening?" Editors permit such informal, with-it usage on fashion, op-ed and sports pages, where au courant prose is encouraged.)

I prevailed on Horyn to translate some of the words in her article. It seems that the peasant look adopted in Tom Ford's collection for Yves Saint Laurent "consists of nothing more than a *ruched* blouse" with "nicely done *ruching*."

"*Ruching,* pronounced *rooshing,* is a common technique in dressmaking and curtain making for gathering fabric and making it pucker," she informed me. "It is looser looking than *smocking*. Picture the neckline of a peasant blouse that might be worn off the shoulders. That look has turned up a lot in fashion for this fall." (Further etymology takes the French word *ruche* to "beehive," an allusion to the frills and plaits of a straw hive.)

She wrote of women wearing "distressed leather or roughed-up shearling . . . jodhpurs and a blanket cape closed with a *snaffle-bit* buckle." That compound adjective, more than four centuries old, describes a gentle form of bridle bit. "It's a bit for a horse's mouth, made up of two metal bars joined by a circular piece of metal," Horyn said. "It's a bit, typically for English-style riding, not western, and has long been a fashion detail. Gucci put a small *snaffle bit* on his loafer, and it's been widely copied." (This is useful information for Washington pundits: when I see a lobbyist on K Street's "Gucci Gulch," I'll look down at his shoes and say, "Nice *snaffle-bit* buckle.")

"It remains to be seen," goes the fashion forecast, "how many soufflé-size *toques* and capacious *Elmer Fudd trapper hats* will be worn." What kind of hat? "It's like a trapper hat with flaps on the ears—same idea but more generous in shape. The *toque* has always been a sort of elegant shape in fashion, but not the Elmer Fudd, which is now just everywhere."

Fudd is not a competitor of L.L. Bean. Further investigation reveals him to be the animated cartoon character created by Tex Avery and Chuck Jones in 1939 who quickly became the dupe of Bugs Bunny. "The root word for *'befuddled'* is *fudd,*" goes facetious ad copy on the Warner Brothers Web site, "and the prefix for *fudd* is Elmer."

He wears a tall cap without earflaps but with a distinctive visor, and when you see one on a glowering glamour girl or atop a mannequin in Bergdorf's window, you'll know what's up, Doc. And *was gibt's,* too.

Toque is not French for cap, which is casquette. *A toque is a type of hat that is cylindrical in shape and of which the top is several inches about the top of the head. It is worn by judges and tall toques by chefs.*

Toqué is colloquial for crazy—hence toquade, *an infatuation with someone or something.*

> Jacques Barzun
> San Antonio, Texas

I have always heard that the term "Gucci Gulch" refers not to K Street, but to the hallway outside the Ways and Means Committee room in the Longworth Building.

> Roger M. Schwartz
> Princeton, New Jersey

Farewell My Lovely Miss/Ms./Mrs.   The Associated Press, reflecting the desire of the great majority of its newspaper members, has just dropped the use of the courtesy titles *Miss, Mrs.* and *Ms.* in its news reports.

That means that the first reference to Emily Jones is her full name, and the second reference is merely Jones, the same way men are treated. Gee; after all the battling that went on years ago in this space to get the *New York Times* to adopt *Ms.,* out it goes.

Not completely; the *Times,* in the main news sections, will continue to use courtesy titles on second reference for both men and women. But, according to the stylebook, "The *Times Magazine* and the *Book Review,* edited in the more literary style of a weekend periodical, omit all courtesy titles." I suppose it all has to do with the appearance of sexual equality. If you don't use the *Mr.* instead of repeating the first name for men, equality demands the same treatment for women. And who would be so boldly old-fashioned and out of joint as to stand up for any form of inequality?

Here goes. It's not such a hot idea because it needlessly conceals information useful to the reader—specifically, the sex of the person being written about. I could understand the change if first names reflected sex as in olden times: "Emily Jones today was appointed commandant of the Marine Corps. Jones, who is 19, said . . ." In that article, the reader knows that a woman was appointed and needs no courtesy title in front of the second reference unless interested in the commandant's marital status, which the reader knows is none of his or her business, and do you have a problem with that?

The problem I have with that is that you can no longer tell the boys from the girls by their given names. A lineup of Alex, Chris, Pat, Brett, Ashley, Cameron, Meredith, Adrian and Leslie could be a bearded baseball team or a Miss America pageant (soon to be the America pageant, skip the honorific). Here's the story: "Cameron Jones today bench-pressed 300 pounds in the Olympic trials. Jones, not even out of breath, said . . ." Is that a normal weight lifter's story, or a breakthrough for the human spirit? How does an editor know, from the copy, whether to bury it or call for a picture to be emblazoned across the front page?

Maybe the new AP rule is a space saver and will boost journalism's profits. It doesn't strike me as helpful to the reader, and in my nonliterary style I will resolutely continue to use the *Ms.* I fought for, but sometimes I feel as lonely as the guy who played the harp in Phil Spitalny's All-Girl Orchestra.

Federalism.   Janus, the Roman god who was guardian of gates and doors, is depicted with his bearded face looking forward and backward at the same time; this helped him watch everybody. It is the metaphoric source of "Janus words," those confusing terms that mean both one thing and its opposite, like *cleave* ("to split" and "to cling") or *sanction* ("to approve" and "to punish"). Janus has now taken over the central word defining the American system of government. *Federalism* is suffering through a semantic crisis and needs our help.

A headline in the *New York Times* over an article about a case that pitched states' rights against the authority of the national government read: "Supreme Court, in Blow to Federalism, Shields States From Age Discrimination Suits." Linda Greenhouse reported that the court, "continuing its march in the direction of states' rights, ruled today that Congress lacked the authority to bind state governments to the federal law that bars discrimination against older workers."

That was surely a blow to the *federal* (by which we mean "national") government in Washington, but was it a blow to *federalism*? The founding fathers (a paternalistic but accurate alliteration coined in 1918 by Senator Warren G. Harding) would say no. Not if you take the *Oxford English Dictionary*'s first definition of that word (coined in 1788 by Patrick Henry with his irate question, "Is this *federalism*?"). The *OED* answers his query with "that form of government in which two or more states constitute a political unity while remaining more or less independent with regard to their internal affairs."

Other lexicographers agree about the essence of the *federalist* idea, which is to divide power between a central authority and its constituent political units. But right from the start two centuries ago, confusion was built in; to George Washington, John Adams and Alexander Hamilton, *federalism* accentuated the unity that only a strong central government could provide. To Thomas Jefferson and James Madison, who formed a faction they called "republican" but that was promptly labeled Anti-Federalist, *federalism* emphasized the diffusion of power to levels of government closest to the people and furthest from *royalism*—at that time, the states.

When Jefferson defeated the Hamilton-Adams *Federalists* to become president, he famously said, "We are all *Federalists*," to absorb the defeated party. But the word's meaning was no longer just "a power-sharing arrangement among national and regional sovereignties"; its primary sense had become "a strong central government." These meanings, if not antithetical, are at least Janus-like in their difference.

Some political scientists today are reverting to the power-sharing meaning. "While Federalists in 1787 advocated creation of a powerful central government," reports Warren Richey in the *Christian Science Monitor,* "those advocating *federalism* today are seeking a resurgence of a federal-state balance as mandated in the Constitution."

This linguistic case is ripe for semantic decision; certiorari accepted. *Federal* (from *fœdus,* "league") is an adjective that has come to mean "characteristic of a national union" and not "of a confederation"; *federalize,* despite the powers denied the national government and reserved for the states and the people in the Tenth Amendment, is a verb meaning "to bring under central control."

However, the Supreme Court, even as it has recently been devolving power from the central government to the states, *cleaves* to the earliest meaning: Chief Justice Rehnquist, in a decision this month briefly departing from that decentralizing trend, said that a federal law protecting drivers' privacy over South Carolina's objections "did not run afoul of the *federalism* principles." He was using *federalism* as Patrick Henry did, in the sense of "sharing power."

I care not what semantic course others may take; as for me, give me current meaning or give me death. Time for the Supremes to bow to the inexorability of common usage, a kind of Tenth Amendment of language change. Most people take *federalism* to mean "dominated by the federal government," much as the empire-building Hamilton intended. In this, Chief Justice Rehnquist is behind the times.

Thus, the headline words "in Blow to *Federalism,*" which meant "anti-central government," were correctly up to date; it would have been even better stated as "in Blow to *Federalizing.*" Norma Loquendi's final decision is remanded to the court for reversal.

You used the phrase, "certiorari accepted," in apparent mimicry of the Supreme Court's exercise of its discretionary jurisdiction to review lower-

court decisions. In asking the Court to consider a case, a lawyer files a petition for a writ of certiorari; such a writ would direct a lower court to certify the record of a case for review (certiorari = that it be certified). If four members of the Court vote in favor of the petition, the Court "grants" a writ of certiorari, an action often shortened to "cert. granted." Thus, certiorari is not accepted or rejected, it is granted or denied.

Again in apparent imitation of judicial locutions, you declare that "Norma Loquendi's final decision is remanded to the court for reversal." When the Supreme Court decides against a lower-court decision, it does not send the case back for reversal; it reverses the decision itself and then remands the case to the inferior court. A common formulation would be that "the decision below is reversed and the case remanded for further proceedings not inconsistent with this opinion"; this diplomatic form of words leaves the lower court with a measure of latitude in deciding how to deal with the reversal.

J. William Doolittle
Washington, D.C.

You assert that the word "federalism" was "coined in 1788 by Patrick Henry." This appears to be a well-researched assertion, perhaps derived from a search in the American Memory database, pointing to Henry's usage of "federalism" on June 6, 1788. The citation improves upon the Oxford English Dictionary's *1793 dating and the June 14, 1788, first use in the* Dictionary of Americanisms.

A search in the Accessible Archives database, however, yields an earlier example of this word. A December 26, 1787, "letter from a gentleman in Salem" quoted in the January 16, 1788, issue of the Pennsylvania Gazette, *includes the following sentence: "For before the federalism of a HANCOCK, a BOWDOIN, a DANA, a KING, and many other illustrious characters, who are members of the convention, anti-federalism must droop, and recoil in silent shame."*

Fred R. Shapiro
Editor, *The Yale Dictionary of Quotations*
New Haven, Connecticut

Finagle.   Reporting from the recent Arab summit meeting in Beirut, Neil MacFarquhar of the *New York Times* wrote that some participants could be found wandering through the smoke-filled hotel lobby talking to "reporters who *finagle* their way through dragnet security."

The use of that apparent Yiddishism in covering an Arab event struck me as amusing. I turned to Leo Rosten's *Joys of Yiddish* for a rundown on *finagle*—and could not find it.

That's because it is not a Yiddishism. (Funny, you don't look English.) Like *mishmash*, which dates to 15th-century English, the verb *finagle* is a word that sounds Germanic. It rhymes with *bagel,* from the Old High German verb *boug,* "to bend." (A store in Boston calls itself Finagle a Bagel.)

The verb appears occasionally in the *Times,* especially in the entertainment sections, not in quotation marks. Describing the movie *Family Man:* "the plot allows him to *finagle* his way back to Wall Street." Describing Richard Wagner's *Ring* operas: "You cannot pursue power without sabotaging love; you cannot have love without relinquishing power. Wotan tries to *finagle* this."

That's because it is not slang, but a once-special term now in such general use that it has shed its dialect status. One proposed origin is in the southwest English shires: *fainaigue,* "to cheat; to renege on a debt; to deceive by flattery," perhaps associated with the Old French *fornier,* "to deny."

However, the *Dictionary of American Regional English* speculates that it may be an eponym from Gregor von Feinaigle, a "German proponent of mnemonics who lectured (and was often ridiculed) in England and France." (It's an easy way to remember his name.)

Finagler first appeared in the United States in 1922. In current use, the element of outright cheating has faded; its primary sense is no longer "to obtain by trickery or dishonest means." Deft deception now dominates: *finagle,* as we use it today, is "to slyly gain entry or advantage; skillfully to employ a devious scheme to achieve one's ends." A *finagler* is one who knows the ins and outs of power brokerage and favor exchange, who finds ways to exploit the weaknesses of others, who knows how to use indirection to gain leverage and win some small but useful advantage.

A crook he's not; a devious schemer the *finagler* remains, drawing minor opprobrium for his methods as well as a tut-tutting admiration for his ability to deliver results.

In chemistry at Brooklyn College in the fifties, to use "Finagle's Constant" was to create data to support a predetermined result. It's also interesting that "finagle" rhymes with "inveigle," which has meanings, or at least connotations, that overlap "finagle." See if you can finagle to inveigle Hegel out of his bagel.

Martin Smith
Ypsilanti, Michigan

Fire That Wall.   The hot new word in primary politics this season is *firewall*.

Karl Rove, George W. Bush's chief strategist, told the Gannett News Service that in thirteen state contests after the New Hampshire primary, "virtually every one of those states presents the possibility of a *firewall*." (In a parody in the *Weekly Standard,* Rove was shown to be conducting "Operation *Firewall*.")

"In the past week," said Dan Schnur, John McCain's communications director, "you've started to see the Bush people talk about Michigan as a *firewall*."

The word clearly has a Bush connotation. In a United Press International dispatch in 1989 about the political genius of the GOP's Lee Atwater, it was noted that "what clinched the nomination was a political *firewall* Atwater constructed with the pack of Southern primaries on Super Tuesday." Jeffrey Birnbaum wrote in the *Wall Street Journal* just after that 1988 campaign that Bush's strategy "was to lock into place a political *firewall* in the Midwest to prevent any late surge by Democrat Michael Dukakis."

In political parlance, the word means "an unassailable political barrier; a front-running state campaign denying a creditable showing to a challenger who must do well in that area for his or her underdog campaign to survive."

The word is also used more generally. The Alliance for Worker Retirement Security accused President Clinton of trying to "break the traditional *firewall* between Social Security and income taxes." The *Washington Post* noted in 1987 that Reagan officials said they were "committed to nurturing the contras as a *firewall* against Communism." The word is stronger than *bulwark* and not as rickety as *rampart;* it has replaced the earlier *seawall.*

In his 1951 *Dictionary of Americanisms,* Mitford Mathews cited a 1759 transaction of the Moravian Historical Society regarding the proper way to build a house: "the chimney and *firewall* shall be made strictly according to the draft." The wall built to prevent the spread of fire was extended metaphorically to a barrier against anything harmful. More recently, in computer lingo, a *firewall* is a security system set up to protect a network from direct attack by hackers through the Internet; in politics, it is now the preventive preferred by strategists who, if the *firewall* fails, turn to *damage control.*

In an aircraft with the engine in front, the firewall *is the fireproof barrier between the engine compartment and the crew/passenger compartment. In flying, it is sometimes urgently necessary to go to full power, which is done by pushing the throttle(s) all the way in (or forward), i.e. towards the firewall, hence the verb "to firewall" the engines.*

Professor Steven H. Weintraub

Louisiana State University

Baton Rouge, Louisiana

Fog of War.   "The early days of any battle introduce what's called the *fog of war,*" said Andrew Card, White House chief of staff, "and we're still looking through that fog to find the truth." Senator Hillary Clinton used the same military metaphor: "We need to cut through the bureaucratic and turf battles. . . . We need to cut through the *fog of war* here at home."

They were speaking of the frustrating investigation into the source of anthrax in the mail. This picked up on the repeated uses of the phrase at the embattled Defense Department regarding the air campaign in Afghanistan. Asked if he could be sure that Osama bin Laden would not try to escape to another country, Secretary of Defense Donald Rumsfeld replied: "I can't be sure of anything in life. In the *fog of war,* it is a confused picture on the ground. Half of the 24 hours is darkness, there's a bit of a problem with dust in that region and weather's going to get bad soon. You can't be sure of anything." General Richard Myers, chairman of the Joint Chiefs, later chimed in with "In the *fog of war,* things happen that you don't expect." Twelve years before, a predecessor of his at that job, Admiral William Crowe, extended that uncertainty principle; he said that his Pentagon officers "hear a lot about the *fog of war,* but they've also learned that the fog of peacetime is rather mind-boggling as well."

This fog originally crept in on the little cat feet of Carl von Clausewitz, the Prussian strategist whose 1832 book, *On War,* guided generals of many nations through the wars of the 20th century. Using the direct literal translation of the 19th century, his words were "The great uncertainty of all data in war is a peculiar difficulty, because all action must, to a certain extent, be planned in a mere twilight, which in addition not unfrequently—like the effect of a fog or moonshine—gives to things exaggerated dimension and an unnatural appearance." (In the same book, *Vom Kriege* in German, published one year after his death, Clausewitz wrote, "War is nothing more than the continuation of politics by other means." Few books are immortal-quotation twofers.)

In a two-front war such as we are now experiencing, the phrase is also used to recall past periods of confusion and apprehension and to offer perspective: "Right after Pearl Harbor," said Representative Lindsey Graham of South Carolina after the anthrax scare forced the House of Representatives into recess, "this country was in a bit of a *fog of war.* It took us a while to get up and running. But over time, we got our footing."

My colleague in columny down the hall, Maureen Dowd, found a way to turn the phrase around. She evoked the terrorist danger from spores and viruses sprayed in a fine mist: "We know about the *fog of war*. Now we learn about the *war of fog*."

Foot/Hoof in/and Mouth.   We need a cure for the confusion surrounding the common name for *aftosa*.

"In Britain today," reported Peter Jennings on ABC six weeks ago, "the government has now confirmed twelve separate cases of *hoof-and-mouth* disease." For his American audience, he explained, "We call it *foot-and-mouth* disease here."

He may have it turned around; for example, in a 1978 Supreme Court decision about waste disposal, Justice Rehnquist, not yet chief justice, wrote in dissent that New Jersey must "treat New Jersey cattle suffering from *hoof-and-mouth* disease." Noting that, Timothy Crowley of Tulane Law School adds, "I have never seen a hoofed animal with a foot."

The confusion extends further. A year earlier, a dispatch from the *Wall Street Journal*'s Marcus Brauchli in Shanghai gave the two terms a different differentiation, noting that the fast-spreading disease was "known as *hoof-and-mouth* in cattle and *foot-and-mouth* in hogs." That may not be correct, either.

To the origin: the earliest citation in the *OED* is from an 1862 *Edinburgh Veterinary Review:* "Cows affected with the *foot-and-mouth* disease." When that nomenclature crossed the Atlantic to the United States in 1869, *Harper's Weekly* put it that Liverpool was informing the State Department that "a contagion called murrain, or *hoof-and-mouth* disease, has broken out." The *Dictionary of Americanisms* lists *hoof-and-mouth* as an Americanism, citing an 1884 use here and defining it as "the *foot-and-mouth* disease."

As *foot* predominated in Britain, *hoof* had the usage edge in the U.S. In the 1963 western movie *Hud,* starring Paul Newman as a cattle rancher, *hoof* was the word employed, causing Bill Cosby to do a comedy routine he called "Hoof and Mouth," reviewing the movie from a cow's point of view.

But the U.S. Department of Agriculture has always resolutely followed the British Ministry of Agriculture's preference for *foot,* and leading American dictionaries have gone along. The *New York Times Manual of Style and Usage* directs us unequivocally to use the *foot,* sternly warning "not *hoof-and-mouth.*" (The *Times* also prefers the plural *hooves,* but it behooves me to use *hoofs.*)

I'm sorry about those lexicographical and official *diktats* about striking *hoof,* because further confusion is caused by the shortening of *and* after *foot,* which is often heard as *in.* We never hear *ham 'n' eggs* as *ham in eggs,* but we do hear *foot 'n' mouth* as *foot in mouth.* That's because of a similar expression, *to put your foot in your mouth,* defined as "to commit a gaffe" or by the bureaucratic locution "to misspeak." The expression is rooted in Jonathan Swift's 1738 "The bishop has put his foot in it" and was carried forward when a 1984 collection of stories by Saul Bellow was titled *Him with His Foot in His Mouth.*

In the early '50s, when Eisenhower Defense Secretary "Engine Charlie" Wilson showed a lack of sympathy for the unemployed by saying he preferred bird dogs to kennel dogs, he admitted that some of his cabinet colleagues "seem to think I have *foot-in-mouth* disease."

That play on words has since been used often to deride the tendency of politicians to commit verbal blunders. In 2001 at the Gridiron Dinner, where political figures and journalists poke fun at themselves and one another, President George W. Bush acknowledged his habit of tripping over his tongue with the line "You know that *foot 'n' mouth* disease rampant in Europe? I've got it." Such wordplay will become muted as concern rises about the possible spread to the U.S. of the real cattle, sheep and swine disease.

Relatedly, another cattle affliction is raising even greater worries: bovine spongiform encephalopathy, known formally by its initials BSE and more widely as *mad cow* disease. Unlike *foot-and-mouth* disease (which the French call *la fièvre aphteuse* after its virus and the Germans call *Maul- und Klauenseuche,* "jaws, muzzle or snout and claw, paw or hoof"), BSE can be transmitted to humans, in rare cases.

Mad cow, probably bottomed on *mad dog,* was coined or first used in 1988 by David Brown, then agricultural correspondent for the *Sunday Telegraph* and now editor of the *Daily Telegraph*. He chose *mad* because "the cattle went from being very placid and calm to raging beasts, suddenly berserk." He recalls that the name "took off very slowly" but then "just cranked itself up."

I have been told, no reference, that the change in the nomenclature occurred because horses have hooves but do not get the disease.

Bernadine Z. Paulshock, MD
Wilmington, Delaware

Forward, Lean!   In Warsaw, George W. Bush used a vivid figure of speech in responding to a question about European reaction to his plans for an American missile defense: "I was very pleased to see how *forward-leaning* many nations were during our discussion." A week later, he repeated the compound adjective in answering a question from Peggy Noonan of the *Wall Street Journal* about global warming: Bush found a "different attitude" among European Union leaders, who were "a little more *forward-leaning*" about it.

That word-picture of a crouch of cooperation, or a tilt toward tomorrow, appeals to him. On the eve of his second mission to Europe, asked about his desire to include in NATO the democratic countries nearest Russia, the president said, "We ought to be very *forward-leaning* toward those countries."

What does this fast-spreading trope mean? Ari Fleischer, Bush's press secretary, uses it in the sense of "premature": "I think it's just a tad *forward-leaning* to call that quite a 'proposal' at this time." George Tenet, the director of Central Intelligence, uses it to mean "open," as in his core dump of five million pages of old classified documents: "It reflects my commitment to be as *forward-leaning* as possible in releasing information that with the passage of time no longer needs to be protected."

A quite different sense is "aggressive": a former Justice Department prosecutor, asked by two *Times* reporters about the present reluctance to bring charges against Iranian officials in a major terrorist bombing case, demanded to know, "Why haven't we been more *forward-leaning* on Iran?" This picks up on an early definition by Morton Kondracke in a 1987 *New Republic*, holding that the Reagan National Security Council staff was peopled with hyperactivists: "subordinates who were '*forward-leaning*'—bold, imaginative and aggressive."

Yet another meaning is "advanced," as in Governor Tom Ridge of Pennsylvania's applause for the Bush administration's "*forward-leaning* 21st-century energy plan." Vice President Dick Cheney gave it a sense of "eager" when asked about his boss's appearance of remoteness from the press when relaxing on his ranch: "We've been criticized for being too *forward-leaning*. Now you suggest maybe we're too laid-back." I have been bending over backward here to permit the reported usage to determine the hot modifier's primary meaning. Time now for a semantic judgment.

The most widely understood sense of this compound adjective is the new sense of *forthcoming*. That old word's early definition as "soon to appear" has been largely eclipsed by *upcoming*, and a new meaning of *forthcoming* has emerged of "responsive, open, outgoing, cooperative," even "a pleasure to do business with." For some reason, that happy extension of *forthcoming* is losing favor under the vogue onslaught of *forward-leaning*.

Thus, the forthcoming (in the old sense) meaning of *forthcoming* (in the new sense) is "forward-leaning." The fresh figure of speech racing through the lingo of the edge-cutting calls up the image of a runner straining ahead, the tilt of the body throwing weight forward to aid acceleration. That fine image will have its moment of popularity but contains the seed of its metaphoric destruction: if you lean forward far enough, you fall on your face.

You left out the most interesting question: why are people (and ideologies) leaning? And what happens if they lean too far; fall on their faces and their behinds respectively? And what about the left and right leaners? Do the for-

mer become Maoists and the latter paleoconservatives or just right-wing cra-zies. And why aren't centrists leaning?

Herbert J. Gans
Department of Sociology
Columbia University
New York, New York

Ɛ

Franken–.   The hottest combining form in populist suspicion of science was coined in a letter to the *New York Times* on June 2, 1992, from Paul Lewis, professor of English at Boston College.

Commenting on an op-ed column criticizing the Food and Drug Administration's decision to exempt genetically engineered crops from case-by-case review, Professor Lewis held, "Ever since Mary Shelley's baron rolled his improved human flesh out of the lab, scientists have been bringing such good things to life." After this reference to Dr. Victor Frankenstein, who created the monster in Ms. Shelley's 1818 novel, the academic letter writer shot a bolt of juice into the lifeless coinage dodge with "If they want to sell us *Frankenfood,* perhaps it's time to gather the villagers, light some torches and head to the castle."

And that's what they did! "Genetic engineering" was not then a scary enough phrase. The science of making foods more productive or resistant to disease had noncontroversial roots in hybrid corn pioneered in 1923, but ethical concerns about cloning merged with worries about mad-cow disease and suited the promotion of "organic" foods. A frightening metaphor was needed, and the *Franken-* prefix did the trick.

A *Boston Globe* reporter wrote in 1992 that *Frankenfood* "summed up nicely the monstrous unnaturalness of such controversial new products as genetically enhanced tomatoes and chromosome-tinkered cows," and quoted the delighted Lewis, today chairman of the English Department, saying: "It has a phonetic rhythm, it's pithy and you can use the *Franken-* prefix on anything: *Frankenfruit . . . Frankenair . . . Frankenwater.* It's a *Frankenworld.*"

Since then, biotechnophobes and other members of the antigenetic movement have denounced *Frankenseeds, Frankenveggies, Frankenfish, Frankenpigs* and *Frankenchicken,* lumping them together as fearsome *Frankenscience.* In the *Chicago Tribune,* David Greising wrote in 1999 of *Frankenfarmers* supported by *Frankenfans* arguing with *Frankenprotesters* about unfounded *Frankenfears.*

Frankly, there's no telling when or how it will end. It has enhanced the sales of the metaphysical novel that Ms. Shelley's husband, the poet Percy Bysshe Shelley, encouraged her to write, and has not harmed sales at "Frank 'n' stein," the fast-food chain whose hot dogs and beer I find delectably inorganic.

At the American Dialect Society, Laurence Horn says: "I was hoping somebody might have coined *Frankensense* by now. This would be sort of the opposite of common sense, maybe as a description of politicians' motivations for a creatively stupid piece of legislation."

But this play on *frankincense,* an aromatic gum resin used in religious ceremonies, has not caught on. "Alas," says the dialectologist Horn, "all the Web site usages I can find for *Frankensense* seem to be unintended misspellings of the traditional Christmas gift. You can tell because there's an equally orthographically challenged rendering of *myrrh.*"

If you enjoy Frank 'n' Stein, let me recommend a few other eateries that may have escaped your notice.

There is Health's Angels, a natural food restaurant for bikers; Howe's Bayou, for kosher Cajun cuisine; and finally (one I am sorry to say may shortly go belly-up) Pieces of Ate, which specializes in used food.

Harvey Fried
New York, New York

Fulminations.   The specialists are in open rebellion at the theft of their vocabularies. Egged on by sly agitation in this space to fulminate about raids by the general public on their fields' linguistic larders, the specialists have at last found an outlet for their ire at the twisting of their favorite terms.

"I cannot resist the invitation to rail against the boneheaded misuse of *organic*," fulminates Stephen Slatin, at the Department of Physiology and Biophysics of the Albert Einstein College of Medicine in the Bronx. "It does not, or certainly should not, mean 'vegetables grown without fertilizers' or 'fruit produced without pesticides.' "

Right on, says Richard Fireman of Chicago: "*Organic* used to mean 'carbon based.' An 'inorganic food' would be an oxymoron"—prescriptive usagists would insist on the more specific "contradiction in terms"—"unless someone knows a way to get nourishment from stones."

Chemists think of an "organized body" as an animal or plant containing compounds derived from hydrocarbons; they call that kind of chemistry *organic* and bristle at the "unscientific" extension of meaning into food "grown without chemical additives or genetic manipulation."

Geologists, too, excoriate lay writers with rocks in their heads. When I wrote that San Jose was the *epicenter* of the California computer industry's power consumption, Julian Stone of Rumson, New Jersey, noted: "*Epicenter* is a scientific term referring to the point on the surface of the earth above the underground focus of an earthquake. Do you mean that the center of power consumption in California is underground?"

The geophysicist Joseph D. Sides adds, "Writers should be advised that *epi-* no more intensifies the meaning of *center* than does *pen-* intensify the meaning of *ultimate*." (The prefix *epi-* most often means "on" or "over"; *pen,* not a prefix, is from the Latin *pæne,* "almost.") Sides defines *epicenter* as "the point on the surface of the earth vertically above the center of an earthquake, the quake's 'hypocenter.' " It is also, he says, "the point on the earth's surface vertically below the atmospheric detonation of a bomb, the 'hypercenter' of the explosion." He finds "misuse of the offending term attributable to spurious erudition on the part of the writers combined with scientific illiteracy on the part of copy editors."

Is your understanding of these terms growing exponentially? No! thunders a totality of mathematicians. "I'm vexed to hear some trend described as 'growing *exponentially*' when the writer means it is growing rapidly," writes Maurice Fox of Arlington, Virginia. "*Exponential* growth is not necessarily rapid. The mathematical term merely describes something whose rate of growth is proportional to its size. My savings account grows *exponentially* but not rapidly."

Geometric, or compound, growth can be fast or slow; if our economy grows by 0.1 percent a year, that's *exponential*, but the stock market tanks. A professor of physics at Tufts University, Roger Tobin, is equally annoyed at the lay misuse of *exponential* to mean "a whole lot," referring to quantity rather than rate of growth, "but to say my annoyance is *exponentially* greater today than yesterday is gibberish."

Tobin is not offended, however, by a general use of *quantum* to mean "sudden," provided we don't use it to mean "huge": "The crucial characteristic of a *quantum jump* isn't its size but its abruptness—something goes from one state to another without passing through any intermediate states in between." That's one of the "stolen meanings" that started this specialist agitation, which is growing fast if not exponentially.

Those intellectuals who name their companion animals Peeve (to be able to say "This is my pet, Peeve") have as their ally Jacques Barzun, America's only best-selling nonagenarian. "A couple of misplaced technicalities," he writes from San Antonio. "*Synergy*, which belongs to physiology and relates to the working together of muscles, etc. Applied to the merger of two clothing firms (actual), it is ridiculous, especially since technically the meaning is 'greater effect than the sum of the efforts.'"

A semantic theft by educators is *module*, which Professor Barzun says "is used ambiguously to mean 'a class period' and 'a portion of program.' (Years ago, it was 'nucleus.') A *module* in architecture or building generally is a part that does not change size, character or function and thus serves as a measure of a larger whole. In a column, it is the measurement itself—half the diameter of the base."

Architects, too, have their linguistic bêtes noires. ("Peeve, meet my *bête*, Noire.") "I am very annoyed at the current usage of the term *architect*," writes Fran Read, who is one. "Examples include '*architect* of the peace plan,' 'software *architect*' and in the phrase spoken by several CEO's and commentators on CNBC, 'We *rearchitected* the software.'"

Read's pique is superstructured by Tim Groninger, a project engineer. "Word thievery in engineering has become especially acute," he seethes, "due to the ever-growing hunger for words in the world of computers. I can no longer use the word *architecture* in the traditional sense. The word now implies the design and construction of computer networks, not buildings."

The architect Edwin Elias-Narvaez piles on with "It is particularly galling to perform an Internet search for *architect* only to find thousands of references having nothing to do with the traditional meaning of the word."

(The magazine *Architectural Record* recently interviewed Richard Saul Wurman, who said: "I invented the term *information architect* in 1975, when I was national chairman of the AIA [American Institute of Architects] convention in Philadelphia. It was called 'The *Architecture of Information.*' Now I would say that somewhere between 20,000 and 100,000 people in the U.S. have *information architect* on their business cards.")

Fulminations from other fields are still coming in. Ophthalmologists narrow their eyes at the nearsighted semantic theft of their *myopic*. Yoga practitioners in rooster position cock-a-doodle mellowly but firmly about the extension of *guru* from "revered teacher and spiritual leader" to a sarcastic "self-appointed cult figure." And most of all, logicians everywhere pose the query, What are the philistines doing to our *beg the question*?

The specialists are not going to take it anymore.

Stephen Slatin, you report, "rail[s] against boneheaded misuse of 'organic' thus: 'It does not, or certainly should not, mean "vegetables grown without fertilizers" or "fruit produced without pesticides."'" Perhaps Mr. Slatin should see a phrenologist. On one point he is simply mistaken: organic does mean "grown without fertilizers" and "produced without pesticides." Just ask your specialist in the produce section of your supermarket or their patrons. As to whether it "certainly should not" mean this, does Mr. Slatin mean an a priori certainty deducible from the deep structure of the language itself or an observational certainty based on universally accepted, peer-reviewed, repro-

ducible results obtained under controlled conditions? Perhaps Mr. Slatin intends the conditional meaning of should *as in it "certainly should not mean" this (were I to become the final arbiter of English usage). Or perhaps he means "certainly" only as an intensifier and not to mean irrefutable. I hate it when folks do that.*

And why do physicists refer to the likeliest location of an electron in an atom as an orbital *despite the obsolescence of the planetary model of the atom? They also refer to the elliptical paths of celestial bodies as "orbits." Orbs are spheres. They're round, you blockheads.*

And why do doctors insist on perpetuating their arcane Greek and Latin anatomical nomenclature when universally understood and unambiguous substitutes are available? (Or one might say, "Why do doctors still use fancy words for parts of the body when simple ones would do as well?") Is anterior *superior to* front? *Is* rear *inferior to* posterior? *Does* upper arm bone *sound any funnier than* humerus?

Barry Brown
Nashua, New Hampshire

Ballistic may well sound impressive but is totally wrong (just as a measure of distance—the light year—is wrongly used to describe a long period of time). Moving under the force of gravity only, thus an intercontinental ballistic missile is fired (under rocket power) into the heavens and when the rocket cuts out or whatever, it continues on its way where its course is determined by gravity and the momentum imparted by the prior rocket power. Thus an ICBM may well explode upon impact with its target (because it contains an explosive warhead) but to go ballistic *is not to explode—it is to coast after an initial boost ceases. Similarly, as the bullet leaves the barrel of a gun the explosive force that propels the bullet has been exhausted and the trajectory is determined by gravity and the previously imparted momentum—the bullet is coasting—& this is why the '60s TV cop shows I grew up with always had investigations by the "guys from ballistics."*

Malcolm Park
University of Melbourne
Melbourne, Australia

Your last column was turned into a soapbox for a bunch of language cur-
mudgeons. It seems only fair that you give some equal box time to some
looser linguistic thinkers.

Words get reused in different disciplines and words become trendy and
overused, but neither of these things makes a word usage incorrect or inap-
propriate. If the curmudgeons had their way, every word would have a fixed
definition and there would be no poetry. (For what is poetry but a play on
words?) Where would our language be if it wasn't allowed to move, stretch
and dance? Oh wait, language cannot dance, dancing applies only to physi-
cal objects, right?

It is fair to criticize a true misuse (like penultimate *or* literally, *both of*
which are misused all the time), but these people seem to have no love of lan-
guage, only a bean counter's love of organization and rules.

I suggest that these people just need to pull their collective noses out of
their professional journals and pick up a good work of fiction or poetry. Or
even a bad one for that matter—anything to get them out of their literal
heads for a moment.

Ben Gold
New York, New York

I think one must include "periodically." The term has come to be used to
mean "occasionally" or "infrequently" when, in fact, it means "regularly," re-
gardless of what frequency is being described. An item, as I am sure I do not
have to explain to you, is periodic if it occurs annually, monthly, weekly or
each second. The period of a pendulum is the time it takes for it to complete
a sweep of its arc, to and then fro. Periodicals arrive daily, semi-annually, et
cetera. "Periodicity" refers to "frequency" in a number of scientific applica-
tions including chemistry, physics and, more specifically, electricity.

But of course, many folks use "periodically" in everyday speech to indicate
that they do or experience something only once in a while. They may, in fact,
experience it periodically—but likely not. Probably, they experience it occa-
sionally, and at irregular intervals, and believe that suffices it to be periodic.

Mark Foggin
New York, New York

The chemists should talk! They themselves have hijacked the word "organic" which simply means, "of use, useful," especially in reference to the body (obviously from the Greek organikos*). But when science hijacks something, that's called a definition.*

John Hymers
Universiteit Leuven
Leuven, Belgium

I enjoyed your recent article on "penultimate" and its Latin origins. I was a little surprised that you didn't use my favorite Latin example, peninsula (pæne, "almost" + insula, "island").

My little rural Indian school in Indiana didn't offer French, Spanish or German, but some of us took four years of Latin.

Jack E. Garrett
Monroe Township, New Jersey

Tim Groninger makes a classic error when he writes, "word thievery . . . has become especially acute," suggesting that the problem has reached pandemic proportions. Acute, as in "acute appendicitis," refers to suddenness of onset, not severity. We doctors note that word appropriation from medicine is a chronic condition.

Eric Flisser, MD
New York, New York

Your lead sentence should have read, "The specialists have been in open rebellion at the theft of their vocabularies."

In his monumental American Language, *Mencken, in Supplement One, cited the misappropriation of the word "engineer" by Engineering News-Record, as follows: "The* Engineering News-Record, *the organ of the engineers, used to devote a column every week to uninvited invaders of the craft . . . One of its favorite exhibits was a bedding manufacturer who became the first mattress-engineer and then promoted himself to the lofty dignity of sleep-engineer. The hatching of bogus engineers still goes on."*

Displaying its sense of humor at the theft of its craft, Mencken offered this:

The rat, cockroach and bedbug eradicators of the country had for years an organization called the American Society of Exterminating Engineers. On November 8, 1923, the News-Record *reported that one of its members followed the sideline of mortician in Bristol, PA, and suggested sportively: "That's service for you. Kill 'em and bury 'em for the same fee."*

EN-R's umbrage is not quite on the target of your fulminators, but close enough.

Dick McQuillen
New York, New York

Is it okay with paleontologists if language evolves?

Fred Rosenthal
Marblehead, Massachusetts

*The term "lesion" is rarely used by lay people, but I've seen it used often by science writers. It is almost universally used incorrectly. As an example, in an article on foot-and-mouth disease this sentence appears: "Foot and mouth disease is a viral infection that causes fever, blisters and lesions, and results in weight loss and a reduction in milk production" (*The New York Times Magazine, *April 6). The word* lesion, *from the Latin for "injury," is used very generally by physicians. It is used to refer to any abnormal condition of the body. Thus a blister is often a lesion, but so is weight loss, and so is reduction in milk production. Because it is a general term, it is often used to refer to an abnormality that has been described but does not fit a defined category. In the phrase I quote, the implication is that a lesion is a clearly defined entity like a blister. It is an impressive-sounding word, but it seems to carry no meaning when used by science writers.*

Paul Cunningham, MD
Tacoma, Washington

Please tell your editors that "methodology" is not a fancy word for method, nor is it a word for fancy method. To quote Evans and Evans, "The use of the word 'methodology' for 'method' is common among social scientists, many of whom seem to have a great love for redundant syllables."

And please tell them that the misuse of "parameter" is simply a display of ignorance of mathematics.

David Fax
Canton, Massachusetts

Chemists think of an "organized body" as an animal or a plant containing compounds derived from hydrocarbons. Hah, hah, hah!!! The word "organized" has no relationship to "organic" as used in "organic chemistry." Bill, you don't make me fulminate, you make me laugh. By the way, fulmination *is an example of a word derived from a scientific word and now perfectly accepted in non-scientific discourse (without objections from chemists, purists and non-purists). Often, technicians working with scientists will initiate "corruptions" of the original word.*

Jock Nicholson
San Diego, California

Should meteorologists fulminate? Fulmen is, after all, a visual rather than sonic display, and experts who study atmospheric conditions in order to forecast the weather are not often concerned with meteors. When did those usages become acceptable?

I especially appreciate your mentioning my pet peeve, popular misuse of the term "exponential." Without fulminating, I try to point out that the exponential function can take a zero, negative, or even imaginary, argument: radioactive decay, which models "shrinkage," is a valid instance of a rate of change proportional to size.

Noel M. Edelson
New Rochelle, New York

You do exactly what you were writing about regarding stolen meanings. Yoga is a Sanskrit word meaning union, from which the English word yoke *is derived. Yoga, or more properly, Raja Yoga is a spiritual path toward enlightenment. Yoga refers to union with all, in the sense of the Divine or Universe or some equivalent.*

One of the many steps is named Asana, meaning posture. This is what you and most people think is yoga. It is not. Please call it Asana Yoga, although what you describe as a rooster position is very far removed from Yoga.

The so-called Yoga classes offered in the U.S. and elsewhere are physical exercise classes—nothing more. Another case of stolen meaning.

Gerry Dorman
Lindenhurst, New York

Scientists themselves are the guiltiest of "word robbery." They typically assign very specific meanings to such common, broad terms as "frequency," "wave," "tolerance," "elastic" and "resonance," thus confusing the heck out of the rest of us.

If they pay attention to CONTEXT, these erudite complainers will find that their understanding of everyday English will grow exponentially.

Peggy Troupin, PhD
New York, New York

You report that Prof. Tobin of Tufts University (where I once was an under-graduate) is not offended by the use of "quantum" to mean "sudden," provided we don't use it to mean "huge." But of course that is what is usually implied by the term in general parlance. Prof. Tobin knows how very small a quantum is; it equals the frequency of radiant energy multiplied by Planck's constant, which is 6.25×10^{-27}, or 0.00000000000000000000000000625, that's 26 zeros after the decimal point. Used correctly, a quantum leap is a change SO tiny as to be undetected by unaided human senses.

Curt W. Beck
Professor of Chemistry
Vassar College
Pleasant Valley, New York

One of the most flagrant thefts from specialists' vocabularies is orchestration. I am a composer and I actually have orchestrated a quantity of music, some of which has been performed by major orchestras.

But over the past twenty years or so I have heard the word used in absurd contexts such as: this or that CEO "splendidly orchestrated an international trade agreement with China." Or, a U.S. secretary of state "has made great strides in orchestrating peace in the Middle East." Or a university president "orchestrated an effective fund drive for the endowment."

Usually it is an authority figure who orchestrates and I think this comes from the mistaken idea that the supreme authority figure of the symphony orchestra, the conductor, is "orchestrating" when he or she conducts a work —pointing commandingly to this or that instrument or section of the orchestra. Often conducting from memory, he is viewed as a genius and a great leader. From this comes the metaphor of a great leader (of anything) "orchestrating" rather than simply planning.

But it is a bad metaphor, for in most cases the conductor is leading the orchestra in a work that has been orchestrated by someone else, usually the composer. The exceptions are composer/conductors such as Gustav Mahler, who conducted many of his own symphonies with the New York Philharmonic, or film composers such as John Williams who frequently conduct their own film scores.

Ravel really did orchestrate Mussorgsky's Pictures at an Exhibition, *but as far as I know, Henry Kissinger, William Silber or Bill Gates never orchestrated a thing.*

John D. White
Evergreen, Colorado

Exponential growth refers to growth conforming to an exponent, e.g., the accumulation achieved by squaring the number 2, then squaring that accumulation, etc. If the exponent is a positive number above 1, the rate of rise of the accumulation does indeed become rapid in time. Plotted out on semi-logarithmic graph paper, exponential growth results in a straight line. Plotted out on graph paper, exponential growth is parabolic.

Your savings account grows arithmetically, unless your bank is unique, as does our economy when growing at 0.1 percent a year.

Kai Kristensen, MA
La Jolla, California

❦

Fulminations II.   When a word with a clear meaning in a specialized field like science, math or music crosses over into the general language, its meaning can get twisted. This infuriates the specialists, who see it not merely as a form of linguistic corruption but also as highway robbery from their vocabulary. Examples:

Physicists cannot string together a theory to explain why *quantum jump*, which in their world means "a sudden alteration in an atom's energy," and is therefore exceedingly small, has leapt into general public usage with the meaning of "huge change."

Psychiatrists can be seen to approach hysteria when *schizophrenia*, a psychosis often characterized by withdrawal and hallucinations, is bandied about by a public that thinks it means "split personality" and uses *schizoid* to describe any duality.

Neuroscientists wince at the way *congenital*, which to them means "inborn; existing at birth," is stretched by vituperative columnists to a more general "habitual, chronic."

Mathematicians cannot calculate why their *parameter*, "a variable constant used to determine other variables," is confused by laypeople with the quite different *perimeter* and has now adopted the second word's meaning of "limits" or "characteristics."

And musicians note the way *crescendo*, which to them means "a gradual increase in volume," has been seized by nonmusicians to mean "climax"—not the reaching but the reached.

A "crescendo" is not a peak of sound, or a sudden outburst, but a gradual increase in volume. Loudness is not even necessarily implied; Tchaikovsky, for example, goes so far as to indicate a crescendo from ppppp to pppp. Also, "staccato" does not mean rapid, cf. the opening of In the Hall of the Mountain King *from Grieg's music to* Peer Gynt.

Worse, though, is the appropriation of "orchestration," to mean any kind of arrangement or planning. I've done orchestration and taught it, and I know it to be a complex technical subject. I don't mind so much hearing about Presi-

dent Bush "orchestrating" a deal with Senate Democrats, but when Dr. Laura Schlessinger thanks her DJ for "orchestrating our music," I experience a crescendo in my blood pressure and accelerando in my heart rate.

James Redding
Granville, New York

Fulminations III.   If the issue I raise today cries out for an answer, if the point of this article invites close cross-examination, am I *begging the question*?

No. Though my trickle-down convictions may beggar my neighbor, I will not *beg the question*, because I am not in the fallacy dodge. Of the many fulminations from specialists about the distortions of their vocabularies by the lay public, this mendicant phrase leads all the rest.

Here's how it is mistakenly used: Tom Daschle, the Senate Democratic leader, noted that a downturn in the economy would reduce tax revenues and said: "So it *begs the question*, how large the tax cut? And it *begs the question*, how long the tax cut?"

"As a retired teacher of logic," writes Daniel Merrill, who taught philosophy at Oberlin College, "I implore you: give the technical use of *beg the question* back to the logicians!"

A Rutgers University philosophy professor, Tim Mauldin, agrees: "Let's stomp out this abuse!" He explains: "If the defender of the thesis asks ('begs') that his interlocutor accept as a premise of the argument the very issue in dispute ('the question'), then he or she has *begged the question*. This error is sometimes called 'circular reasoning.' "

Example of circular question-begging: "Parallel lines never meet because they are parallel." That takes you right around the barn and back where you started.

Example of linear question-begging: "Anything Safire says about anything is suspect because you can't believe what you read in the newspapers." All the people who fervently believe that to be true make no legitimate argument because they take for granted a premise that is unproven. Their solution to that would be to offer proof: "Safire is suspect because he misspelled the name of James Madison's wife (Hello, Dolley!)." That causes me to beg pardon, not question.

Schoolteachers should petition their principals to stop taking for granted this abuse of fair argument. Let us now turn to the second most constant gripe of ophthalmologists (the first is the tendency of linguistic Magoos to pronounce the first syllable of their profession with a "p" rather than the correct "f").

"*Myopic*, in ophthalmological practice," writes Heskel Haddad, MD, "is a person with sharp vision at near. However, it is often used to connote someone as 'narrow-minded.' "

That's the meaning Ralph Nader had in mind at the Detroit Economic Club last year, when he called the assembled auto executives who opposed tighter fuel economy standards "craven and *myopic*."

The Greek *myops* means "shortsighted." Distant objects cannot be seen sharply because light entering the eye is focused in front of the retina.

Shortsighted and *nearsighted* are interchangeable, according to the ophthalmologist Malvin Krinn, MD, of Washington. "But *nearsighted* may sound a little more sophisticated."

The word *myopia* was coined in 1693, and the meaning was soon extended. In 1801, the poet and novelist Charlotte Smith wrote of "the *myopia* of the mind," and in 1891 Oliver Wendell Holmes, the poet of the breakfast table, referred to "the kind of partial blindness which belongs to intellectual *myopia*."

Because their word's meaning was stolen so long ago, eye doctors should blink away their tears at the loss. Besides, the general sense has a nice metaphoric connection to the eye: "lack of foresight."

Ecologists, however, have a more legitimate beef. "One of my many pet peeves," notes Terence Ball of Phoenix, "concerns people who speak of President Bush and others 'hurting the *ecology*.' What they mean is 'hurting the natural environment.' " Nancy Eldblom, a field botanist in Potsdam, New York, says, "Here's an example of 'stealing' an entire branch of science: using *ecology*, the life science 'concerned with the interrelationship of organisms and their environments,' to mean the environment generally."

My call: if you're discussing that branch of biology dealing with the way living organisms relate to their surroundings, use *ecology,* rooted in the Greek for "dwelling." If you're talking about air or water pollution or global warming (now renamed "global climate change"), use *environment,* from the Latin *viron,* "circle." (Lincoln: "I am environed with difficulties.") If you just want to apply a political label, *green* will do fine.

"Equating *theory* with *hypothesis* is the booboo that boils the blood," fulminates Joe Rosen of Bethesda, Maryland. Judith Weis, president of the American Institute of Biological Sciences, agrees: "In science, the word *theory* refers to an underlying principle of observed phenomena that has been tested and verified. However, in common usage, it has come to mean 'hunch' or 'speculation' (what the word *hypothesis* means in science)."

While scientists who admire precision often treat the word *theory* as "a confirmed hypothesis," lexicographers since 1706 have defined it as "a supposition" far from proven. I recall sitting in a box with Henry Kissinger at a Washington football game; when the referee outrageously penalized the Redskins for pass interference, Henry rose to his feet, shook his fists and shouted, "On vot *theory*?" Strictly speaking, he meant *hypothesis,* but "only a *theory*"—as against demonstrated fact—is a longtime sense of the term.

Sports enthusiasts as well as scientists defend their linguistic turf. "Railbirds bristle at the misuse of *track record*," vents Dan Hely of Carlisle, Pennsylvania, who reminds us that the track record for the mile and a half at Belmont is 2 minutes, 24 seconds, held by Secretariat since 1973. Yeah, adds David Hawkins of Brooklyn: "As a former horseplayer, I get exercised at the use of *track record* as in 'the track record shows that he'll make a good president.' A track record is the fastest time ever recorded for a specific distance at a given track. The racing term that should be used is *past performance*."

All this raises, not begs, the question: are specialists understandably miffed at the expropriation of their precise vocabulary by the generalist "meaning thieves"? Sure; but they don't own the words and should stop being so myopic.

When Dr. Kissinger questioned the referee's call with the phrase, "on vot theory?" his intended meaning may have been closer to "theorem" than either "theory" or "hypothesis."

The rules of a game are axioms in a system of logic, and the decisions as to whether a violation has occurred, and if so, the penalty, are theorems derived by deduction from the rules. If the facts of the incident were in question, then the scientific terminology would be appropriate, but if it were a matter of the interpretation of the rules, then the language of logic would apply.

Andrew Raybould
Irvington, New York

It is indeed good to petition principals because school administrators need to be asked to do this kind of thing. Or am I committing petitio principii?

Edward M. Young
Pasadena, California

I became a bit concerned at your final sentence where you pointed out that specialists "don't own the words and should stop being so myopic." Apparently you felt that it doesn't matter if the public takes a specialist's term and uses it in a different way. Well, I'll give you one example of how it can matter enormously.

Although we know for a fact that biological evolution occurs—it's observed to occur both in the lab and in the field—many people don't believe it and go so far as to insist that it not be taught in public schools without some disclaimer or suggested alternative. Any of these doubters like to say that evolution is "only a theory," not realizing that, in science, the term theory *has a very specific meaning and implies a large amount of supporting evidence (as you recently explained in your column).*

When I lecture about this, I always have to point out that scientific theory is not merely speculation and, many times, is a confirmed fact. (An example of this is the "theory of flight," about which all aviation students must learn. Although we use the word theory *here, there is, of course, no doubt that airplanes can fly.)*

So, in the case of evolution and the push to cast doubt on it in public schools, the public's misuse of the specialist's term is creating a situation in which large numbers of people are at risk of becoming, to varying degrees, scientifically illiterate. That's not merely myopia; that's outright blindness to mankind's impressive scientific progress, the methods we use to achieve that progress, and the folly of impeding that progress in the future!

Matthew Bobrowsky, PhD

Challenger Center for Space Science Education

Alexandria, Virginia

Galumphers.   In a review of the latest work of the modern dancer Mark Morris, Anna Kisselgoff, the *New York Times* dance critic, used a verb of great piquancy: "Mr. Morris *galumphs* with charm."

Alice Cheang, writing in the *Harvard Journal of Asiatic Studies,* used it to describe a belly-rubbing self-caricature by the poet Su Shih: "This leisurely rambler *galumphs* merrily through the woods in pursuit of a view of the 'tall bamboo.' " In the *Los Angeles Times,* Susan Spano reported from Costa Rica about a sea turtle: "It's a big black blur in the shallows that starts to take shape as it *galumphs* up the beach on powerful front fins ill suited to terrestrial locomotion."

The verb began as a concoction of Lewis Carroll in his *Through the Looking Glass.* The beamish boy slew the burbling jabberwock with his vorpal blade, which went snicker-snack: "He left it dead, and with its head / He went *galumphing* back."

Most scholarly speculation about what was going on in Carroll's mind as he coined the word suggests *galumph* is an amalgam of *gallop* and *triumphant.* The coinage applies nicely to sea turtles, happy yogic exercisers and expressive dancers, not to mention a parade of journalists traipsing after candidates through the primaries.

Gentile-American Person's Guide.　"What disturbs me," writes Jack Tucker from somewhere in cyberspace, "is the politically correct way that Senator Joseph Lieberman has to be referred to on television: 'a Jewish person.' The media don't want to say he is a 'Jew' because the word sounds so harsh."

Not only is Mr. Tucker correct in construing *media* as plural, he is also sensitive to the oversensitivity of some newscasters. He was not the only one to notice the lengthy terminology: in a related vein, a call came from Gerald Rafshoon, the documentary producer who was a Carter White House aide, to ask, "How come I never hear 'Episcopalian-American'?"

The use of the word *Jew* is not a problem in print journalism; both the *New York Times* and the *Washington Post* headlined "First *Jew* on Major U.S. Ticket." One reason is to save space, a consideration of all headline writers; another is that speaking—even in quick news flashes—differs from writing. Speaking is more personal. That's why many in broadcast and cable news preferred *first Jewish person* or *first Jewish-American* or even *first person of the Hebrew faith* to be so named. They had the vague feeling that the monosyllabic word might be taken as offensive—as it is when delivered with a curled lip—and went out of their way not to offend.

No Jew would say, "I am a Jewish person" or, except in the most formal circumstances, "Mine is the Hebrew faith." Jews are comfortable with the adjective, "I'm Jewish," or the noun, "I'm a Jew." The reluctance of non-Jews to use the "harsh" word is well intentioned, but such overly sensitive shying-away from the J-noun draws a sardonic smile from some Jews.

Formerly, when many whites referred to blacks in their speech, they hesitated to apply the noun to a person; instead of saying, "He's a black," they would say, "He's a black guy," as if the use of *black* as an adjective to modify *guy* somehow removed it from any interpretation as derogation. This awkwardness was removed by the adoption of *African-American;* that compound noun is not as stark as *black.*

Nouns often sound harsher than the adjectives on which they are based; thus *Jew* is felt to be stronger than *Jewish,* which could also be taken to mean "like a Jew." Take *blond/blonde*: "She's *blond*" is acceptable as a description of hair color, but *she's a blonde,* using the noun form to impute fun-loving characteristics, could be taken by some to be the newly dread lookism.

What about *Jewish-American;* is it any different from *American Jew*? Yes; the difference is context. When I am in a voting booth, I can fairly be counted by demographers to be *Jewish-American,* and when I am in a synagogue, I can be identified as an *American Jew.*

Back to Senator Lieberman. He is undeniably a person and a member of a religious faith, but the quick identification is best: *Joe's a Jew.* So is his wife, Hadassah, whose name is the Hebrew equivalent of Esther. The feminine form *Jewess,* popularized in Sir Walter Scott's *Ivanhoe* (1820), has long been considered sexist, like *actress.*

"Jew" is a perfectly good, and short, word and I resent and resist efforts to expunge it because bigots over the centuries have used it as pejorative. Doth a Jew not bleed? I am neither orthodox nor observant but proud to be, and be called, a Jew.

> Jack Rosenthal
> The New York Times Company Foundation
> New York, New York

The day after Lieberman was chosen, I was listening to the Today *show and everybody down to Al Roker was calling him a "Jewish-American." It sounded odd to me, like Irish-American or Italo-American. I was chatting later with Tim Russert, who had been one of the talking heads, and he thought about it and agreed, and then suggested to his colleagues that they drop the phrase. Then Lieberman went on* Meet the Press *and used the term repeatedly, hisownself.*

> Adam Clymer
> *The New York Times*
> Washington, D.C.

Kenneth Tynan dreamt that Harold Pinter and Lady Antonia Fraser are living in Sam Spiegel's New York penthouse, a garish leather-padded pleasure dome full of marble grilles and priceless art work. (He had gone to Sam's house-warming party there and when he was asked what he thought of the place, said: "It looks like the men's room at the Taj Mahal.")

Q: Lady Antonia, can you confirm that you are a convert to Judaism?

Antonia: Yes, but as Dr. Jonathan Miller once said, "I'm not a Jew. I'm Jew-ish."

Q: Mr. Pinter, are you aware that this apartment was once likened to the men's room at the Taj Mahal?

Pinter: Yes, but it's not a lav. It's lav-ish.

Paul Streeten
Spencertown, New York

Hadassah.   I erred in writing that the first name of Senator Lieberman's wife, *Hadassah,* was "the Hebrew equivalent of Esther." I was misled by every translation I can find of the Old Testament passage Esther 2:7, which reads, "And he brought up *Hadassah,* that is, Esther." In that passage, *that is* is confusing.

The Hebrew word *hadas* means "myrtle." It does not mean, nor is it the equivalent of, *Esther,* which may be the Hebraized form of *Ishtar,* a Persian goddess. In the Bible, the beautiful Jewish girl *Hadassah* took the name of *Esther* to better fit in with Persian society, where she became the queen of Xerxes and was able to save her people from annihilation.

Whoever next translates the Bible would do political pundits a favor by changing "Hadassah, that is, Esther" to "Hadassah, *also known as* Esther."

Gig a Bite.   After taking criticism for the cost of his government-subsidized office rental in New York, former President Bill Clinton announced that his foundation would pick up part of the cost of the park-view space. "I'm not going to let the taxpayer get *gigged* on this," he assured reporters, and subsequently moved his office quest to Harlem.

Clinton has used that term before. He was asked by CNN's Larry King in 1995 if he was likely to appear on David Letterman's show, in light of the CBS late-night host's caustic joking about the prices that the government paid for goods and services. "Since we got this procurement reform passed," Clinton replied, "there are no more of those ten-dollar ashtrays and five-hundred-dollar hammers. So he's got no *gig* anymore."

In Clinton's usage, the noun *gig* seems to be a pointed complaint. A century ago, George Ade, in his *Modern Fables,* wrote: "The Old Gentleman was very rough on Wallie. He gave him the *Gig* at every opportunity." In army use, a *gig* was a demerit, and if you were *gigged* often enough, you would be expelled from West Point.

The noun has a second meaning, which originated in jazz lingo: "an engagement to perform, usually for a single evening." In black talk, to work a series of short-term jobs is to *gig around*. But that's not what we're talking about here.

The slang verb to *gig,* as in "let the taxpayer get *gigged,*" primarily means "to cheat." Earlier recorded use was in a *Dialect Notes* in 1914: "Say, didn't you *gig* me a little on the price of that room?"

The word comes from fishing. A *fishgig* is a spear. "At each End of the Canoe stands an Indian," noted a history of Virginia in 1722, "with a *Gig,* or pointed Spear . . . stealing upon the Fish, without any Noise." Thus, to *gig* the taxpayer is "to stick it to him."

Go, To!   When you're in trouble; when you need someone to pull you out of a hole; when your desperate circumstance cries out for a reliable partner, a trustworthy executor, a situational savior—to whom do you go?

At that brink of disaster, you do not go to your spiritual adviser or your spouse, nor your lawyer or broker. You go to your *go-to* guy.

"Cheney . . . Carves Out Role as *Go-To* Guy," headlined the *Boston Globe.* Howard Kurtz of the *Washington Post* called the frequently quoted think-tank analyst Marshall Wittmann, a master of sound bites, "the *go-to* guy for legions of journalists."

The phrase *go to* was used in medieval times to dismiss with contempt, a brushoff currently expressed as *g'wan* or *geddoutaheah.* However, the origin of the alliterative encomium "*go-to* guy" is in football. A *go-to* receiver, the fourth edition of the *American Heritage Dictionary* alertly notes, is a player "relied upon to make important plays, especially in clutch situations." While a body man is useful, a *go-to* guy is essential.

Goodness, Gracious.   Donald Rumsfeld is what used to be called a "man's man." He is tough-minded, direct, virile, authoritative and sure of himself. As head of the Cost of Living Council in the early '70s, the designated inflation fighter kept a tight lid on wages and prices and taught his deputy, a kid named Dick Cheney, how to crack the whip. He ran a tight White House as President Ford's chief of staff and later, in the business world, was named one of the ten toughest executives by *Fortune* magazine. He is again secretary of defense, and woe betide the brass hat who tries an end run to lobby for a favored weapon.

If he's so macho, then how come the phrase that comes most frequently to his lips—the words heard most often at his high-powered news conferences—is the sort of exclamation heard on *The Golden Girls*? In the height of dudgeon, professing shock just short of horror, Rumsfeld can be heard with his grandmotherly trademark: "My *goodness gracious!*"

To NBC's Tom Brokaw, who asked about the pace of the attack on Afghanistan, the square-jawed SecDef retorted, "To hear your question and the urgency and 'Don't you need quick success?'—my *goodness gracious!* go back to World War II." (Brokaw has done very well going back to World War II.) This was using the phrase as a straight interjection. Rumsfeld also uses it in an adverbial form modifying an affirmative. Asked if he wanted Osama bin Laden dead, he answered, "Oh, my *goodness gracious,* yes, after what he's done?" adding for emphasis, "You bet your life."

According to the spouse of a senior administration official, speaking at poolside on condition of anonymity, Rummy began using "my *goodness gracious*" at New Trier High School in Winnetka, Illinois, where he first met his wife, Joyce, and continues to use it in expostulations at home.

What does it mean? What did Charles Dickens have in mind when he had a character in his 1841 novel *Barnaby Rudge* exclaim, "*Goodness gracious me!*"?

Goodness is a frequent euphemism for *God,* a name that many believe should not be taken in vain. Shakespeare used it that way in *Henry VIII,* and the capitalization is the clue to the substitution: "For *Goodnesse* sake, consider what you do, / How you may hurt your selfe." The phrase, with *gracious* added, I conjecture, is based on "by the grace of God." It also appears as *gracious sakes alive* and *goodness gracious, Agnes,* the latter partly drawn from the Latin words in the Mass, *Agnus Dei . . . miserere nobis,* "lamb of God . . . have mercy on us," referring in that case to Jesus as sacrificial lamb.

By the mid 19th century, the vehement exclamation had acquired a connotation of archness associated with elitist gentlewomen. Under "Gossip," the *New York Times* reported in 1855 in trochaic measure: "*Goodness gracious!* Mrs. Davis, / Have you heard how Mrs. Thompson / Spoilt her new broche this morning?"

Another substitute word for *God* is *gee,* though *gee whiz* and *gee whillikers!* are ways of not quite saying "Jesus." *Gosh* led to *land o' Goshen!* This was a favorite usage of the cartoon character Loweezy, wife of Snuffy Smith, in Billy DeBeck's comic strip *Barney Google.* DeBeck was also responsible for popularizing the expression "tetched in the haid." Many hear the phrase *land o' Goshen* as "Atlantic Ocean." That confusion is known as a "mondegreen," from the misheard line of poetry that goes "laid him on the green." Another example of this phenomenon, expressed by many young children parroting the Pledge of Allegiance, is "I led the pigeons to the flag." Currently, *ohmygosh* and *omigod* are often expressed in writing as a single word, thereby avoiding the appearance of blasphemy.

The alliteration of *goodness gracious* has been matched in recent years by *good grief,* popularized by the *Peanuts* cartoonist, Charles M. Schulz. According to Joan Hall, editor of the *Dictionary of American Regional English* at the University of Wisconsin, the frequency of use of *good grief* and *goodness gracious* is running neck and neck, with *good Lord* and *good gracious* off the pace by half.

Exclamations beginning with *great* are holding their own. You can still hear *great Caesar's ghost!* rendered half as often as *great God!* and *great Scott!* while *great day in the mornin'* has gained a rural connotation, and a jocular quality has overtaken *great balls of fire!*

With unbowed head, we approach the secular use of *holy*. In *DARE*'s survey, *holy cow!* is the most commonly used, followed by *mackerel, smoke, Moses* and *cats*. (Don't e-mail me another; we are dealing here with exclamations neither profane nor obscene, not popular expletives.)

Have you noticed, from many of the ejaculations cited above, how religious allusions dominate the world of exclamation?

Examples: from *ye gods and little fishes* and *heavenly days* to *hell's bells* and *mercy me,* the lexicon of astonishment is rooted in the wonderment at the eternal. *Well, I swan* is a way of ostentatiously not swearing, and the *Pete* in *for the love of Pete* and *for Pete's sake* is Simon Peter the apostle. *My stars!* (originally *my stars alive!*) is thought by the lexicographer Sol Steinmetz to be an alteration of *myst (all) crity,* a transposition of *Christ almighty! Heavens to Betsy* is a mystery, however; Steinmetz speculates that it might be an alteration of the obsolete *bedad!* a euphemism for *by Dad!* itself a euphemism for *by Gad!* and alteration of *by God!* but that's a long stretch. The archaic *zounds!* is known to come from "God's wounds."

Not all interjections of mock horror or other jowl-shaking expostulation have biblical roots. Don't forget *fiddlesticks!* and *get off my back.* And, *for crying out loud,* you can still stamp your foot and explode with *botheration!* Come to think of it, that last is probably a euphemism for *damnation!*

After these explanations, will Secretary Rumsfeld—when seemingly taken aback or ostensibly outraged by a question, and with the chairman of the Joint Chiefs sternly at his side—continue to let off steam with the use of his quaint, old-fashioned, grandmotherly *goodness gracious!*?

Son of a gun! I hope so. *Jumpin' Jehoshaphat!* I'd hate to see him change.

Gotcha.   "A president can help purge the system of this kind of *gotcha* politics," George W. Bush told Larry King late last year, defining the term as "pile-on politics."

This month, Bush inaugural parade organizers gave prominent position to the University of Tennessee marching band, from the home state of Al

Gore, in what the *Washington Post* called "a particularly galling case of political *gotcha.*"

This was a variation of *gotcha journalism,* a phrase defined by the *Time* magazine columnist Calvin Trillin in 1999 as "campaign coverage dominated by attempts to reveal youthful misbehavior." Bush's first choice for secretary of labor, Linda Chavez, described the firestorm that followed revelation of her sheltering of an illegal immigrant as "a game being played by the media, a kind of *gotcha*-game, where it's a never-ending dribble of one story after another."

Gotcha, the noun, has now been entered in the latest printing of *Merriam-Webster's Tenth Collegiate Dictionary,* defined as "an unexpected, usually disconcerting challenge, revelation or catch," its etymology "an alteration of '*got you.*' " I would add that the original verb phrase carried a second sense, "understood," as in the exchange: "Capish?" "I *gotcha.*"

Longtime readers of "On Language" are familiar with, or are members of, the *Gotcha!* Gang, described here decades ago as "shock troops of the Nitpicker's League" (the sort who insist that it be written "Nitpickers' League" and have their own rump faction who demand hyphenation as *nit-pickers*). The GG takes particular delight in correcting the resident grammarian in mock-furious letters directed to "you, of all people."

F. Scott Fitzgerald used the term in its original, simple "*got you*" meaning in *This Side of Paradise,* his 1920 novel: "Ole zebra *gotcha,* Amory?" In 1974, an informal group of New Jersey state troopers called the "I *Gotcha* Squad" was accused of harassing and intimidating Camden County politicians.

In its current usage, the elided word *gotcha* is an attributive noun modifying *journalism* or *politics* or, alliteratively, *gang.* When did it first become a noun? Dealing with its derivation as that nominative part of speech, we enter delicate slang territory.

"A sudden discomfiture or humiliation" is the definition given in the *Random House Historical Dictionary of American Slang,* "or that which causes it." Getting specific about student use in the early '60s in the phrase "throwing a *gotcha,*" the noun *gotcha* means "the act of suddenly exposing one's buttocks or genitals as a crude prank." You thought the phrase had no salacious root? I can say only [insert here word under discussion]. There is no need to moon over this, because that sense of "flashing" is in decline. In a 1984 citation from the *Knoxville Journal,* the television interviewer Mike Wallace was quoted using the term in its current sense: "Wallace called that a '*gotcha* question.' "

Ground Zero.   Three days after the World Trade Center's twin towers were brought down, Peter Jennings told ABC-TV viewers of the emotional impact on those who had the chance "to go down to what we all call *ground zero* and see the work effort that is there and see the destruction up close." A few days later, Bill Hemmer of CNN reviewed the alternative names of the site: "We're going to take you now to the area known as the zone. Some people are calling it the pile, others *ground zero.*"

Though many of the workers clearing away the tons of debris still refer to the pile, the more formal designation of the place of the cataclysm has emerged—by usage, not proclamation—in the phrase that recalls nuclear devastation.

Governor George Pataki began a statement in the aftermath with "As you tour what is called *ground zero.* . . . " President George Bush saluted "citizens near *ground zero* in New York" who rose to the occasion. Vice President Dick Cheney said: "This afternoon I was at *ground zero,* and I saw the damage at close range. It is staggering."

The phrase had its genesis in an account of the "Trinity Test" of an atomic device on July 16, 1945, near Alamogordo, New Mexico. Philip Morrison, a physicist who worked on the Manhattan Project, wrote, "I observed the Trinity shot looking toward *Zero* from a position on the south bank of the base camp reservoir." On July 7 of the following year, in a *New York Times* article by Hanson W. Baldwin, we have the earliest citation of the whole phrase: "The intense heat of the blast started fires as far as 3,500 feet from '*ground zero*' (the point on the ground directly under the bomb's explosion in the air)."

Several dictionaries define it as "the surface directly above or below the point at which a nuclear explosion takes place." The location below the center of a nuclear detonation is, strictly speaking, the *hypocenter*, with the Greek *hypo-* meaning "under"; that word was soon overtaken by *epicenter* (the Greek prefix *epi-* means "on, over"), the outbreaking point on the earth's surface above the focus of an earthquake. More dramatic than *epicenter*, still most often associated with quakes, is *ground zero*, evoking the image of a huge explosion.

In the past half-century, the meaning was extended to "the center of violent activity or sudden change," and even to "the ultimate origin, very beginning," as a near-synonym to the informal board-game phrase *square one*; as such, *ground zero* is lowercase. In its present, specific sense, as the name of the site of New York City's terrorist attack, it means "the place where terrorists killed thousands of people working in the buildings that symbolized trade in the modern world." That is a proper noun, to be capitalized; in this instance, I dissent from the style preferred by three major dictionaries as well as by the *Times*.

Gumming the Bullet.   As political bromides pile up, a salute to Jim Hoagland, associate editor and chief foreign correspondent of the *Washington Post*, for picking up on a little-used play on an overused metaphor—*biting the bullet*—stemming from Civil War pre-anesthetic field-hospital use, now meaning "facing up to a painful decision."

Hoagland described the U.S. government's reluctant toleration of the development of Iraqi weapons as "gumming the bullet," a variation first noted by Nick Poulos in the *Atlanta Journal-Constitution*. That's how to *galumph* through the thicket of clichés.

You wrote that "biting the bullet" stemmed "from Civil War pre-anesthetic field-hospital use, now meaning 'facing up to a painful decision.'"

I believe you are wrong. The term is British and goes back to the 1850s when the British armies were issued new Enfield rifles. These rifles used a new invention—a paper cartridge that contained both the ball and the powder charge. To load the rifle for firing, the soldier would bite the bullet, *tear-*

ing off the top of the cartridge. He would then jam the torn end of the car-
tridge down the barrel, exposing the powder for easy ignition.

So, what biting the bullet *really means is "to prepare to take decisive ac-*
tion"—as in making ready to fire one's rifle with serious intent.

M. Gregg Smith
Salem, Oregon

Gunman.   "President Boris Trajkovski," reported the *Guardian* correspondent in Skopje, Macedonia, "vowed to continue the fight against the
gunmen of the National Liberation Army."

In Belfast, the Associated Press reported that "two *gunmen* fired shots at
Catholic men smoking outside a community center."

"Three Palestinian militants were killed" in an Israeli helicopter attack,
reported ABC News. "In apparent retaliation, Palestinian *gunmen* killed an
Israeli yesterday and set off two car bombs."

Words have connotations. In the disputed territory known as the West
Bank, an Israeli village is called a *settlement,* implying fresh intrusion; a
small Palestinian town, even one recently settled, is called a *village,* implying permanence.

A word that terrifies many fair-minded editors is *terrorist;* it connotes
criminality. Because it is said that one man's terrorist is another man's
"freedom fighter," journalists have reached out for other nouns, like *guer-*
rilla, militant or *paramilitary.*

The latest rush from judgment is *gunman.* In 1999, that word appeared
once in the database I checked for every five uses of *terrorist* in connection
with Israel; now it's running about one in two.

Because the Associated Press stylebook has no specific entries on *terror-*
ist or *gunman,* I asked its editor, Norm Goldstein, about what went into the
choice. "Words like *gunmen, separatist* and *rebel* are often more precise
than *terrorist* and less likely to be viewed as judgmental," he notes. "We often prefer the more specific words for that reason." Nor does the *Times*
stylebook have a guideline; its editors tell reporters to use "the most accu-

rate and impartial term, especially in cases where the political merits are disputed."

The United States Department of State has a guideline in Title 22 of the United States Code, Section 2656f(d): "The term 'terrorism' means premeditated, politically motivated violence perpetrated against noncombatant targets"—that means civilian or unarmed military—"by subnational groups or clandestine agents, usually intended to influence an audience."

Gunman may be a useful catchall for journalists who do not want to appear less than objective by applying that standard of political intent and noncombatant victim. But in avoiding one problem, it engenders another: "Why do you suppose this gender-biased word is still in use?" asks Isaac Moses of Cambridge, Massachusetts. "Perhaps the lesson that violence is a particularly male occupation is not one that we want to impart to our little boys."

In every other walk of linguistic life, sexism is being rooted out. Firemen are *firefighters,* policemen *police officers,* postmen *mail carriers.* But in current ultra-nonjudgmental parlance, there are neither *terrorists* nor *gunwomen.* A female terrorist using a gun goes by the name of *gunman.*

Doesn't "gunman" go back in its terrorist usage to the Irish Troubles of 1916 and thereafter?

I think it was also used in frontier days—the kind James Fenimore Cooper wrote about, not the kind with cowboys—to refer to the number of military effectives an Indian tribe could muster, but I'm rusty on this one. (As in, "the Suwannee had 100 gunmen.")

Somebody is sure to suggest gunsel *as a potential gender-neutral term. You will recall, of course, that that is a misinterpretation of a line from* The Maltese Falcon. *"Keep that* gunsel *away from me," Spade says to Gutman, referring to Wilmer, using a Yiddish pejorative for a homosexual. People of small Yiddish thought Spade was using a slang term for gunman, since Wilmer fancied himself one. The line was thus (gleefully, I'm sure) slipped past the Hays office for the Bogart movie.**

Thaddeus Holt
Point Clear, Alabama

*See also "Carvilification."—W.S.

Hark the Dark. "*Darkly* nasty" is the blurb selected from *People* magazine in a Warner Brothers ad for *Death to Smoochy*. It quotes other major media outlets (the closely followed Westwood One Radio, not to mention Sixty Second Preview and the trendsetting KCAL-TV) calling the comedy "*dark,* demented and hysterical," the "*darkest* movie ever" and "deliciously *dark.*"

Dark is in the limelight because advertisers believe the deliciously moody description sells. *Bright* is eclipsed, though it lingers in toothpaste ads. Not since the poet Matthew Arnold wrote of "a *darkling* plain . . . where ignorant armies clash by night" and the novelist Joseph Conrad "penetrated deeper and deeper into the heart of *darkness*" has this ancient adjective enjoyed such a revival.

The movies did it. Not the current Robin Williams–Danny DeVito epic, in which "Smoochy" is a fuchsia rhinoceros (the name derived from the German dialect verb *schmutzen,* "to kiss"; in American slang, the noun *smooch* now refers to any good-humored, occasionally wet expression of affection). The new look of *dark* springs from its use in the film criticism of the 1940s: the *film noir.* Lexicographic Irregulars will vividly recall a column five years ago on the renaissance of hip cynicism, moral ambiguity and sharply shadowed fatalism ("Film Noir Is My Bête Noire"), in which I argued that if a film was not *noir,* it was nowhere. However, the earliest citation of the phrase I could find in the databases was from 1958, and a call was put out for etymological assistance. The dossier on *dark* has slowly ripened to provide background to the word's current, dazzling adjectival vogue.

Cast your mind back to the late 1930s and early '40s hard-guy detective novels—Dashiell Hammett's *Maltese Falcon,* Raymond Chandler's *Farewell, My Lovely*—and the bleak, menacing camera work of such directors as Fritz Lang in *Scarlet Street* and Billy Wilder in James M. Cain's *Double Indemnity.*

"Some people connect the term *film noir,*" writes Kenneth Turan, film critic for the *Los Angeles Times,* "to the famous yellow-and-black *Série Noire* series of translations of American writers like Chandler and Hammett published by Gallimard."

The film historian Marshall Deutelbaum of West Lafayette, Indiana, picks up that thread: "Following the end of World War II, French audiences discovered all at once what Hollywood filmmaking had been like during the war years, when no Hollywood films could be exhibited." In a review by Nino Frank in *L'Écran Français* dated Aug. 28, 1946, the French critic wrote, "These *noir* films no longer have any common ground with run-of-the-mill police dramas." In the same year, the critic Jean Pierre Chartier titled an article in *La Revue du Cinéma* "Americans Also Make 'Noir' Films."

The *Time* film critic Richard Schickel wrote me in 1997: "Obviously the term made its way into English via the work of French movie critics whose regard for American genre films of all kinds influenced some of their American counterparts to start taking seriously a body of work that most middlebrow critics had previously dismissed as being impossibly lowbrow.

"Be that as it may," Schickel added in this correspondence he must think was lost or ignored, "I join you in deploring the vague and trendy application of the term to other modes of expression. When I use it, I have a very specific movie style and attitude in mind."

The new, extended *noir* (it means "black" but carries the connotation of "dark") has shed its previous image of "somber, wicked, foul" even to the point of evil, exemplified by Satan, "Prince of Darkness." In modern journalism, the columnist Robert Novak was given that sobriquet; he recalls being so dubbed in his 20s, when he was "very pessimistic about the state of the world," but has lately been cheering up a little. (To go over the cliff on this tangent, Satan's other name, *Lucifer,* is rooted in the Latin *lucem ferre,* "bearer of light"; go figure.)

As the copywriters for *Death to Smoochy* demonstrate, the new *noir* not only has a romantic, severely fashionable sense but an antic noncoloration as well.

A word of caution: the French treat the English word *film* as masculine, like *cinéma,* which takes the masculine adjective *noir,* not the feminine *noire.* In a parallel journalistic universe, a vituperative right-wing journalist wrote about a *film blanche;* this elicited a torrent of e-mail messages from multilingual readers of the *International Herald Tribune* correcting it to *film blanc.*

Having It All.   "Bush Will Tell Americans They Can Have It All" was the *Washington Times* headline about the presidential budget for 2001. A grumpy right-wing pundit followed a few days later with the phrase in participial or gerund form: "Having It All." In both cases, the meaning was that the president's message contained not merely something for everybody, but everything for everybody—tax cuts, debt reduction, increased spending, the works.

That all-at-once sense, particularly regarding material things, was the original meaning of the phrase. "She desired high rank and great wealth," wrote the novelist Anthony Trollope in 1880. "With him she might have *had it all.*" Forty years later, Edith Wharton, in her *Age of Innocence,* wrote: "Pictures, priceless furniture, music, brilliant conversation.... And she *had it all.*"

Then "career women" adopted the phrase. In 1980, Joyce Gabriel titled a book *Having It All: A Practical Guide to Overcoming the Career Woman's Blues.* Helen Gurley Brown, two years later, used the same title, defining it in the subtitle: *Love, Success, Sex, Money.* The phrase then meant "having a wonderful life that you create for yourself," Brown recalls. "Later it came to mean the three big component parts for women—having a job, a man, children."

The phrase underwent a semantic shift. "Twenty years ago, it was a triumphant phrase and also a demand—women were not going to be limited to a circumscribed set of rules," says Patricia Ireland, president of the National Organization for Women. "By *having it all,* we were talking about doing all the traditional things, and on top of that a job in the waged work force, and for many of us, on top of all that political activism."

Back then, the full feminine life was defined in Wendy Wasserstein's play *Isn't It Romantic* when a young woman asks her mother, "Do you think it's possible to be married, or living with a man, have a good relationship and children that you share equal responsibility for, and a career, and still read novels, play the piano, have women friends and swim twice a week?" The mother replies: "You mean what the women's magazines call *'having it all'*? Harriet, that's just your generation's fantasy."

Harriet's mother was on to something. "About 15 years ago, I started hearing fewer women concerned with *having it all* and more concerned with having to do it all without help," Ireland says. "The phrase has come to carry with it a sense of being overwhelmed, as you see on the T-shirt in the NOW store that says: 'I am woman. I am invincible. I am exhausted.' Today, we realize you can have it all, but in sequence. There's been a kind of evolution in the meaning of the phrase."

Not everyone accepts that evolved, sequential meaning. When the Bush White House passed the word that officials would make time for their families—even if it meant going home at 5:30—Marjorie Williams of the *Washington Post* called that "one of the capital's sunniest self-delusions." In the real world, she wrote, "official Washington is implacably, impartially hostile to family life. . . . To pretend otherwise is just to write one more chapter in the big book of lies titled *'Having It All.'* "

Thus, the phrase now has a split meaning. To many feminists, *having it all* suggests varied experience in stages: no longer supermom doing all at once, but first a career, then a family, or vice versa. But to those in or covering political life, the phrase retains its earlier connotation, whether about working women with families or about presidential budgets: "everything at once." I would like to offer greater lexical clarity, but you know what you cannot have.

Homeland.   "I was wondering if you know the origin of the word *homeland*," asked Brian Reich, a student at Columbia University, "as in '*Homeland Defense*' and '*Homeland Security*.'"

That zeroes in on a word with a history that rivals any for resonance in the realm of politics. Its origin in English comes quickly to hand: in 1670, Richard Blome wrote in his geographical treatise, *Travel and Traffick*, of merchants plying their trade between Scotland and Ireland as "Homeland-Traders." The *OED*'s definition makes a nice distinction between senses— "the land which is one's home or where one's home is"—before settling on the more general "one's native land."

But that's the easy part. Now to the deliciously complex geopolitical connotations and semantic shadings of the word.

The first Zionist Congress, meeting in Basel, Switzerland, in 1897, set the goal "to establish for the Jewish people a publicly and legally assured home in Palestine." Twenty years later, Foreign Secretary Arthur James Balfour of Britain, eager to enlist the support of Jews for the Allies in World War I, wrote a letter to the Jewish leader Lord Rothschild that said, "His Majesty's Government view with favor the establishment in Palestine of a national home for the Jewish people." In recording this in September 1918, an anonymous writer for the *British Political Science Quarterly* made the leap to today's word when he noted Balfour's "declaration, made Nov. 6 [1917], and since officially endorsed by France and Italy, in favor of the establishment of a Jewish homeland in Palestine." When David Ben-Gurion and his fellow Zionists signed the declaration establishing the state of Israel on May 14, 1948, the Hebrew word *moledet*—translated as *homeland*—appeared four times.

In the meantime, the homely word *home*—in German, *Heim*—gained a more sinister connotation when it became a favorite of Fascists. In Austria and Germany in the late 1920s, the *home guard,* or *homeland defense forces,* were known as the *Heimwehr* or *Heimatschutz.*

During that war, *homeland* was applied to the islands of Japan, as distinct from the territory conquered by the Japanese in their quest for empire. Winston Churchill wrote in 1941 that "we should therefore face now the problems . . . of driving Japan back to her *homelands* and regaining undisputed mastery in the Pacific." Harry Truman, in a diary entry dated July 18, 1945, referred to the Manhattan Project producing an atomic bomb: "Believe Japs will fold up before Russia comes in. I am sure they will when Manhattan appears over their *homeland.*" One week later, at the Potsdam conference, the word appeared in an official diplomatic document: "The full application of our military power," the Big Three warned, would lead to "the utter devastation of the Japanese *homeland.*"

The word surfaced in South Africa in 1962 amid the controversy about apartheid. R. F. Botha, then South Africa's foreign minister, introduced the "Bantu *Homelands* Citizenship Bill" in 1969 linking blacks to tribal sites of origin, or "Bantustans," in an effort thereby to separate the races permanently. This was denounced as evidence that white supremacists in South Africa regarded black Africans as aliens.

A kind of linguistic full circle was reached when Arabs in the Middle East sought to reject the Jewish state in their midst by evoking the word so long associated with Israel: the PLO, in Article 1 of its national charter of 1968, stated, "Palestine is the national *homeland* of the Arab Palestinian people; it is an indivisible part of the Arab *homeland.*" (Later, a spokesman appropriated another Israeli phrase in demanding "a right of return.")

Then, in 1997, the U.S. government got into the *homeland* act. In the Quadrennial Defense Review mandated by Congress, a defense panel was set up to rethink military strategy up to 2020. The panel foresaw a need to counter potential terrorism and other "transnational threats to the sovereign territory of the nation." Its recommendation of an "increased emphasis on *homeland* defense" did not get much attention.

Almost one month after the Sept. 11, 2001, attack on the United States, the Bush administration established an Office of *Homeland* Security. Why was *security* substituted for *defense*? A rationale was set forward that security was the umbrella term, incorporating local and national public-health preparedness for attack, the defense of the nation offered by the armed services, plus the intelligence and internal security activities of the CIA, FBI and local police. (In fact, I'm told by secret nomenclature sources, *security* was chosen because the Defense Department did not want any jurisdictional confusion with the new White House organization.)

Americans have adopted *homeland* much as Russians chose *motherland* and Germans *fatherland*. An association exists with the World War II phrase the *home front,* which was a metaphor then (as opposed to *war front*) but is a reality now in light of September 11.

The British are different. "*Home* on the range, *home* of the brave, *hometown* boy," wrote John Mullan in Britain's *Guardian.* "Perhaps '*home*' is an easier word for patriotic Americans than it would be for us. *Homeliness* is at a premium in such anxious times . . . a word was wanted that sounded reassuring but unaggressive. Americans have become more sensitive or more wary about the *homeliness* of their geopolitical talk." In referring to their place of origin, speakers of British English prefer *this country* to *homeland*.

Mullan's usage brings up a tangential point: Britons use *homeliness* for what we would call *homeyness*. To Americans, *homely* has unfortunately come to mean "almost ugly." We still use the compound adjective *downhome* to mean "unpretentious, devoid of affectation," and *homeboy* is black slang for a friend in or from the neighborhood, but the lovely *homely* is an insult. This shows a lack of appreciation for the boy or girl next door.

Contrariwise, the Yiddish *haimish* means "homely" but is a compliment, suggesting home cooking for food and a homebody for a person who does not long for dancing in nightclubs or trips to spas. Few Americans use *homelike,* which I apply warmly to residents of my *homeland*.

Hooking Up.   "Only yesterday," notes the copywriter for the Farrar, Straus & Giroux fall catalog, "boys and girls spoke of embracing and kissing (necking) as getting to first base. Second base was deep kissing, plus groping and fondling this and that." No longer; first base is today deep kissing, also known as *tonsil hockey*. The writer then speeds up to date in orally touching second and rounding third base, which is now "going all the way," and slides home with a surprise twist of the old sex-as-baseball metaphor: "Home plate is being introduced by name."

The occasion for this recollection and updating of antediluvian teenage lingo is the promotion of a new book of essays and short fiction by Tom Wolfe titled *Hooking Up*. "How rarely our *hooked-up* boys and girls are introduced by name!" laments the promotion copy, which goes on to promise a chronicle of "everything from the sexual manners and mores of teenagers to fundamental changes in the way human beings now regard themselves, thanks to the new fields of genetics and neuroscience."

Wolfe has a sensitivity to *le mot juste* in describing social phenomena. The title of his *Right Stuff*, a book about the early astronauts, has now become part of the language, as is his popularization of the mathematicians' *pushing the envelope*. In selecting *Hooking Up* as his title, he is again on the cusp of usage.

When we hear a sultry seductress say to an aging Lothario, "We'll *hook up* one of these days," what does her promise mean? (A Lothario is a male deceiver, from a character in Nicholas Rowe's 1703 play, *The Fair Penitent*. My need to point this out is what philologists call "coinage compulsion.")

The compound noun *hook-up* (which the *Times* no longer hyphenates) was born in a political context in 1903, as "a *hook-up* with the reform bunch," and meant a general linkage. In 1930, the term became specific, as "a national *hook-up*" came to denote a radio network.

As a verb, to *hook up* has for a century also meant "to marry," a synonym of "to get hitched," as a horse is to a wagon. But not until the 1980s did the meaning change to a less formal sexual involvement. It was first defined as "to pick someone up at a party" and then progressed to "become sexually involved with; to make out."

The swinging sense mainstreamed in 1995. "A few women insist," wrote *USA Today*, "they never go out with the intention of '*hooking up*' or having sex," while a CNN commentator noted, "The kids see shacking up and *hooking up* as the equivalent of marriage." In 1997, the *Cleveland Plain*

Dealer quoted a Brown University student as saying, "In a normal Brown relationship, you meet, get drunk, *hook up* and then either avoid eye contact the next day or find yourself in a relationship." The scholarly reporter noted, "Depending on the context, a *hook-up* can mean anything from 20 minutes of strenuous kissing to spending the night together fully clothed to sexual intercourse."

To *be hooked,* taken from the fishing vocabulary, is to be addicted to drugs; however, with the addition of *up* to make the compound, the term has no sinister narcotics meaning. In current usage, which may not last long and is probably already fading, it most often means "have a sexual relationship." Nor is the "linking" verb limited to American English. An exasperated Liz Jones, editor of *Marie Claire,* wrote in the *Sunday Times of London* this year about men who are habitual sexual deceivers (Lotharios), "Are all men like this or is it just the ones I *hook up* with?"

Let's go back to first base. *Tonsil hockey,* as used at Farrar, Straus & Giroux to mean "deep kissing," is at least a decade old, having replaced *tonsil boxing.* A more recent variation is *tongue sushi,* which shows some metaphoric imagination: the Japanese sushi—cold rice rolled up with bits of raw fish and vegetables—is evoked to describe the mutual rolling-up of teenage linguae engaged in lubricious osculation.

Tonsil hockey goalies have, in a spasm of good taste, rejected the phrase, popular in the '80s, to *suck face.* That undeniably vivid but odious locution seems to have been replaced in some localities with the almost euphemistic *mess around.* Its variants include *mashing, macking* (from *smack,* the sound of a kiss) and *mugging,* the senses of which run the semantic gamut from "flirting" to "foreplay with no intention of intercourse." Those familiar with Old Slang would call it "taking a long lead off first base."

Though *hooking up* seems a mediumistic metaphor for what used to be euphemized as "sleeping together," it is more romantic than the phrase in current use on college campuses: *parallel parking.*

"Hooked up" and "hook up" have at least two meanings in auto racing. In drag racing or acceleration testing, a car hooks up when, after initial wheelspin (one word in car magazines), the tires finally grab the pavement and the

car takes off. In track racing, particularly but not exclusively NASCAR stock car racing, a car is said to be hooked up when it is handling ideally well and not incidentally is easy to drive fast enough to be a winner.

John Strother

Princeton, New Jersey

Hurr I.   Your eyeglasses have been specked with dust or speckled with stains. Or, as in my case, a new Bernese Mountain puppy has besmeared my spectacles with the saliva dog lovers call "puppy lick."

No source of moisture is near with which to clean the glasses. What do you do? The answer is easy: you breathe heavily on the lenses to form a vapor on them, which you wipe off with a tissue.

Question: What is the verb to describe the action you take to moisturize the lens? There is no single correct answer, but in regional-dialect coinage, there are always some answers. Sitting next to me in our car with our puppy, Geneva, wriggling on her lap, my wife, Helene, said, "You'd better *hurr* on your glasses if you expect to see the road."

That was onomatopoeia in action. The sound of deliberately expelling breath is *hurr* or *huh* or, in cases involving irate discovery, *hah!* In this instance, the sound created the verb first cited in a 1947 *American Speech* quarterly as "*Huh-ing* your glasses."

I believe the new member of your household belongs to a breed properly known as the Bernese Mountain Dog. That makes her a Bernese Mountain Dog puppy. A Bernese Mountain puppy is a Swiss hill.

Patricia M. Sherwood

Editor, *The Quotable Dog Lover*

Windham, Connecticut

Hurr II.   You want to clean your glasses. You are in the middle of a desert and no water is handy, so you breathe heavily on your spectacles to form a vapor on them. The question was posed here to the Lexicographic Irregulars: what is the verb to describe the action you take to moisturize the lenses?

The purpose of this scholarly endeavor is not merely to survey the different locutions for the same action in regional English ("different strokes for different folks," as painters, lovers and the cardiologists say). More to the pedagogical point, this snapshot of varied usage is to illuminate the competition that precedes the acceptance of a neologism in the general language.

We began with *hurr:* "You'd better *hurr* on your glasses if you expect to see the road" was the sentence used to stimulate discussion, backed up with a 1947 citation for *huh,* sometimes pronounced *hunh.* "One of my daily chores when I was commissioned in the RAF during World War II," writes Horace Hone of Palm Coast, Florida, "was to polish the brass buttons on my tunic. Occasionally we would pass muster by breathing on them and giving a brisk rub. This was known as *huhing* and preceded your citation by half a decade."

Thirty-five percent of the innumerable participants in the survey chose some form of this onomatopoeic verb, from *haar* and *haw* to *harf* and *hauch.* The *hauch* form, three readers noted, is from the German *hauchen,* "to exhale." (A related verb for the same action, according to Hans Van Wouw-Koeleman of Old Bennington, Vermont, is the Dutch *ademen,* derived from the Sanskrit *atma,* "spirit, breath." People everywhere have been blowing on glass for a long time.)

An important subsection of the aspirate-*h* category is *huff.* The most famous use of this verb is in Joseph Jacobs's 1890 *English Fairy Tales,* perhaps using the great 19th-century lexicographer James Halliwell as the source, when a wolf seeks to intimidate three little pigs with "Then I'll *huff,* and I'll puff, and I'll blow your house in."

The wolf was a fox in an 1813 version, whose house-blowing was foiled by three little goslings, and is not to be confused with an unrelated story about three little kittens who lost their mittens. The wolf was not characterized as big, bad until 1933. In a Disney *Silly Symphony* animated cartoon, the songwriters Frank Churchill and Ann Ronell enlivened the tale of the three little pigs with the song "Who's Afraid of the Big Bad Wolf?" To many Depression-era moviegoers, the wolf symbolized hard times, and the piglets' triumphant defiance of the huffing and puffing was taken as an expression of resolute optimism, similar to "Happy Days Are Here Again." (Even today, when stock market bears *huff* and puff their pessimism, some analysts reply, "Not by the hair of my chinny-chin-chin.")

The fairy-tale marriage of *huff* and *puff* followed the pairing of the two rhyming verbs in John Phillips's 1678 parody of Virgil's *Aeneid:* "And *puff* and *huff* and toyl and moyl." (I refrain from citing an earlier scatological pairing; the coolest guess at the origin of *huff* is the *OED*'s "imitative of the sound of a blast of air through an orifice.")

Controversy rages among etymologists over the meaning of *huff.* "I believe the big, bad wolf *huffed* when he was inhaling," e-mails Tim Gaston. This is based on logic; how can one *puff* out without first having *huffed* in? The century-old *Century Dictionary* defines the verb *huff* as "to swell; puff; distend," but adds that *puff* does not mean "blow"; rather, it means "to puff up, inflate."

Inhalation is also suggested by the phrase *to be in a huff,* or to be *huffy;* that is, to be swelled up with anger or arrogance. Many years ago, when I was building model airplanes with my cousin Bobby Siegmeister, we became happily cross-eyed from the smell of the glue; today, sniffing glue or aerosol gas, a dangerous activity, is known as *huffing.*

Therefore, I reject to *huff* as the preferred verb meaning "to blow on one's glasses to moisten them with vapor." Actors and orators will dispute this rejection, arguing heatedly that making the sound of the aspirate *h,* as in *ha-ha-ha,* engages the diaphragm and should be associated only with exhaling. Let 'em; prescriptive usagists ain't cream puffs.

Other entries in the moisturization derby included *blow, breathe, mist, steam, expire, phumph, yawn, whoo* and *pft-too.*

And the winner is . . . (A digression. In the Academy Award presentations, we never heard the familiar phrase "And the winner is." Instead, every celebrated presenter, marching in linguistic lockstep, said, "And the award goes to." That is because the academy, ever sensitive to hurt feelings, decreed that there were to be no *winners.* Why? Because, as the MC, Steve Martin, noted, "God forbid anyone should think of this as a competition.")

Use of *winner* would suggest that those nominees who did not receive the award were *losers,* and in Hollywood nobody is to be more reviled than a *loser.* In the enforced absence of the word *winner,* the tight-lipped or sobbing stars who were not called up to the stage are supposed to be considered *nonawardees.* They're *losers,* he said huffily.)

And in the usage contest for "verb to describe the way water-deprived Magoos clean our glasses," the winner is—

Hurr III. "The best way to clean a lens," advised *Time-Life*'s 1970 *Photographer's Handbook,* "is to blow away dust, then '*fog*' the glass with your breath." John P. Knight of Seattle sends that citation with "I remember my father showing me how to *fog up* my glasses when I was 11." Jonathan Carleton of Santa Fe, New Mexico, thinks it is "on the analogy of physicians of a former day passing mirrors under comatose patients' noses to see whether they '*fogged* the mirror,' that is, were breathing."

Fully 45 percent of the votes, or hotly aspirated assertions, were for *fog* or *befog.* Those of us who *hurr, huh, breathe* and *spit* are in a vanishing minority, but at least we can all see where we're going.

Fog *is fine, but I would put* fog up *into the same unnecessary pigeon-hole as* listen up.

> Victoria Matthews
> Denver, Colorado

Hyper. Forget *cyber;* Norbert Wiener's once-modernistic combining form is passé. And *super* is positively archaic, no longer the "soupa" used by teenagers munching subs. Get with the hot prefix of our times: *hyper.*

This El Supremo of prefixes has in the past generation become a term in itself: we have clipped *hyperactive* to the simple *hyper,* its meaning ranging from "excitable" to "keyed up" to "frantic." More recently, this Greek word for "over, above, beyond" has gained mastery in the worlds of diplomacy and communication.

Though the United States seemed content with being the world's only superpower, that word did not have a pejorative enough connotation for the French. In February 1999, France's foreign minister, Hubert Védrine, called the U.S. a *hyperpower,* which he defined as "a country that is dominant or predominant in all categories . . . attitudes, concepts, language and modes of life." He elaborated later that "the word superpower is no longer sufficient to describe the United States. That's why I use the term *hyperpower,* which American media think is aggressive. . . . We cannot accept a politically unipolar world, nor a culturally uniform world, nor the unilateralism of a single *hyperpower.*"

The diplomat probably bottomed his coinage on *hypermarché,* in English *hypermarket,* which means "a large supermarket." The French president, Jacques Chirac, aware that Védrine's term implied American arrogance, assured Craig Whitney of the *New York Times* in December 1999 that "when Védrine said America was a *hyperpower* there was nothing pejorative about it." Whitney noted that this was because Chirac "knew it sent American officials into overdrive."

After Secretary of State Madeleine Albright began introducing herself to him as "hyperMadeleine," Védrine adopted Chirac's amelioration, insisting, "*En français,* 'hyper' *n'est pas péjoratif.*" The opposite is true; it is an accusation of hegemony, carrying what he admits is "*la connotation pathologique.*" Why did Védrine make it the essence of France's attitude toward the U.S.? Only because, he claims, it's a more original word than *superpower:* "*Superpuissance, c'est banal.*"

The old word *text* is apparently also considered banal or hackneyed in a world where the written word is only one part of the vast communications scheme. Hence the rise of *hypertext.*

Most of us think of a *hypertext* link as the letters that come up in blue on your computer screen, often preceded by www. (Whoops! As I just typed the three *w*'s followed by the instruction to the copy editor "unitalics," the letters turned blue, as if suddenly deprived of oxygen. Why do I have to wrestle with my word-processing program for control of the color of my own text? Who owns which?) You click on the *hypertext* link and get shot to someplace else, which often offers other links inviting you to get lost in hyperspace.

Through the good e-offices of William O. Goggins, deputy editor of *Wired* magazine, I tracked down Ted Nelson, the coiner of *hypertext,* now a visiting professor at the University of Southampton in Britain. Though some trace his idea to a 1945 work by Vannevar Bush, the coinage was in an August 1965 paper by Nelson titled "A File Structure for the Complex, the Changing and the Indeterminate."

Warming up before coming across with his definition, Nelson tells me he doesn't like the use of *intelligent* as a combining form, "which generally means 'stupid'—as in *'intelligent* cars,' where the lights stay on after you leave to show your possessions to thieves, or *'intelligent* agents,' which means remote programs that will be even less controllable than the ones you now buy." (Yeah, like letters on my screen that turn blue, unasked. This is my kind of guy.)

Nelson considers *hypertext* to be "the manifest destiny of literature— breaking out of the imprisoning four walls of paper." By "literature" he means "media that we contemplate and keep," including recordings, movies, sheet music and whatnot, "which can be nonsequential and parallel."

In the old-fashioned written texts, Nelson writes, "thoughts have always tried to wriggle free, escaping through every possible loophole—into parentheses, footnotes, marginal glosses, headlines and subheads, headings and captions and parallelism of layout and structure—perhaps most magnificently in the Talmud, but effusively and gloriously in the last century's books and magazines, dust jackets and medical texts with celluloid overlays."

He deplores the way "the tekkies want to colonize this as their own fiefdom, claiming these literary, artistic and cognitive realms as 'technology,' and the result is the broken and clumsy formats of the Web, with only one-way links, no version management, no principled reuse and no copyright solution."

Just as I was about to tap him on the shoulder to get to my question, he e-mailed, "OK, the definition already." It is "nonsequential writing with free user movement." Let's figure that out: "nonsequential" means not along a time line or insistent that *b* follow *a,* but allowing the reader to use many different branches and explore alternatives along other pathways. You don't like a happy ending? Veer off to one where heroes die of heartbreak. In Nelson's definition, "free user movement" means "not constrained by forms like adventure games and computer-assisted instruction, where the writing may be nonlinear but the user has little or no explicit freedom."

That's clear enough; my own prose about language is crisscrossed with parenthetical tangents that reflect the maze in a maven's mind. But why call it *hyper,* which in medicine can mean "pathologically excessive"? (To *hypertext* at this point, that was what the Frenchman was indicating.) "Because *hyper* in mathematics means approximately 'extended, generalized and multidimensional,' " answers Nelson. "*Hyperspace* means a space with more than three dimensions, and a *hypercube* is a cube in more than three dimensions. Nothing wrong with that!"

Thus, Americans accused of being an arrogant *hyperpower* can, by means of *hypertext,* access the pejorative comments and contemptuous cartoons in all the nations of the *tiers monde* following France's anti-unipolar lead and thereby get thoroughly *hyper.*

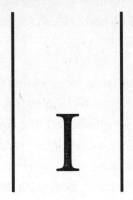

In a Persian Mirror. "With words we govern men," said Benjamin Disraeli. To which we have a corollary: by proverbs we enliven copy. Adages never age.

The insightful and gutsy reporting from Iran of Elaine Sciolino of the *New York Times* has led to a book, *Persian Mirrors: The Elusive Face of Iran.* Seemingly in passing, but actually to illuminate culture, she tosses in local proverbs.

For decades, adage-trackers have sought the origin of what John F. Kennedy described only as an old saying: "Victory has a thousand fathers, but defeat is an orphan." The earliest pre-Kennedy use we have found so far is in a 1951 film, *The Desert Fox,* spoken by a German general. But Sciolino cites a Persian proverb that suggests its source may be in folk wisdom from another land and an ancient time: "Winners have large families, but losers are orphans."

She learned another saying from a filmmaker willing to discuss censorship while inside Iran, but never while abroad. Why, if Persians have the courage to complain of repression at home, are they reluctant to criticize the regime when abroad? "As my father used to say, 'If your head breaks, it is better that it breaks in your own hat.'"

A third proverb strikes the Western ear as arcane, referring as it does to a flaky confection of crushed sesame seeds in honey, but might be the sort of wisdom to impart to political candidates lagging in public-opinion polls: "Have patience, and I'll make halvah for you from unripe grapes."

In Word Heaven.　In his youth, your leering great-grandfather dated a *chorus girl*. Your grandfather, his leer slightly modified in the 1930s, dated a *chorine*. And what did your father call the dancer he dated, after both *chorus girl* and *chorine* gained a ditzy or lascivious connotation?

If he was in showbiz, he called her a *terp* (from Terpsichore, the muse of dance) or a *gypsy,* and was invited, along with the cast's families, to the rehearsal called "the gypsy run-through." If he was a stage-door Johnny, Pops called the object of his affection what we call her today: a *dancer.*

That's because the choreographer Agnes de Mille changed the nature of the chorus in the 1943 musical play *Oklahoma!* The stereotype of the bored, gum-chewing, leg-pumping *chorine* was transformed into the reality of dancing actors and singers. Even the performers in *A Chorus Line* in 1975 were not labeled *chorines* or *chorus boys;* they were identified as *members of the troupe* or *ensemble* or just *dancers* and *principal dancers.*

This raises the question (no, not *begs the question,* which has to do with circular obfuscation): where do words like *chorine* go when they fall into what Grover Cleveland called "innocuous desuetude"? We remember them; we know what they mean; but not even old fogies use them anymore. What happens to these ghostly darlings?

"Whenever we edit a new edition of one of our dictionaries," says Joe Pickett, executive editor of American Heritage, "we consider which words we should delete." He's like a cowboy forced to shoot a favorite old horse. "We have to be careful about what we consider to be a 'dead word.'" People still find obsolete terms in old books and turn to the dictionary expecting to find their meanings.

In 1998, Pickett was on the verge of eliminating *chad* to make room for one of the many new words rushing into the language: "What could be more insignificant than those little bits of paper punched out from cards used in an obsolete computing technology?" But because there was still occasional use involving elections, his lexicographers left it in—"and are we glad we did." It became the hottest word of the year 2000.*

What became of the noun *motorcar,* or the verb *motoring*? Roadkill, both of them, along with dreams of leggy *chorines* who were the bee's knees in the rumble seat. And where is *centigrade* today, now that Anders Celsius's last name has replaced it? *Centi-* became ambiguous when the metric system came along: did it mean *one hundred* or *one-hundredth*? And the last syllable—*grade*—could mean *step* or *degree*.

Language mavens no longer use *tautology;* it has been thrust aside by *redundancy* (and when I am caught out erring along those lines, the Squad Squad has a pleonasm).

Dictionaries have no labels for words that are still in use but seem to be breathing their last. When no use is recorded after 1755 (when Samuel Johnson published his dictionary), most lexicographers mark it "obsolete"; if the word is only occasionally used after that glorious watershed date, it's marked "archaic." But how are we to warn those who turn to dictionaries for guidance that *industrialist* is passé and *financier* hopelessly out of it?

Whole phrases die, too. When I chastised the FBI recently for denying the existence of what every crime reporter knows is called the Cold Case squad, an e-mail message came in asking about another cold case: the Dead Letter Office. I called the Postal Service to see if the phrase was still in use and was told by its forthright spokesman, Gerry Kreienkamp, that "we no longer have a 'Dead Letter Office.' We stopped using those words in 1994. There are three *Mail Recovery Centers,* in Atlanta, St. Paul and San Francisco, where letters with no discernible address for either the recipient or the sender are sent." What if I mailed a letter addressed to the Dead Letter Office with no return address? Where would it be delivered? Long pause. "To one of our three *Mail Recovery Centers,* I suppose."

I like to think of these words and phrases as unforgotten angels in a Word Heaven, ready to revisit the language when the need for them arises. *Hussy,* for example, was originally a phonetic reduction of *housewife* and

*See also "Chad."

came to mean "a mischievous, ill-behaved woman." As it faded from memory, Alan Herbert rose in Parliament to deliver his first, or "maiden," speech to the House of Commons, by tradition a mild and deferential effort. When it came across as fiery and substantive, Winston Churchill promptly denounced this "maiden" as "a brazen *hussy* of a speech." And so a delicious old word was saved; no such luck for *chorine*.

The distinction that I—and, I believe, many of my colleagues—make between Obsolete and Archaic is that the former means that the word, expression, or sense is no longer in use, and the latter refers to a word that is essentially obsolete but is used occasionally to evoke a sense of times gone by. Words like pantywaist *I should probably label as obsolete; a word like* yclept, *which crops up either facetiously or evocatively in speech and writing now and then, I should label as archaic.*

Laurence Urdang
Old Lyme, Connecticut

The phrase "brazen hussy" has been immortalized in the name of a variant of a common European plant, the Lesser Celandine (Ranunculus ficaria). Some years ago the renowned English garden writer and plantsman, Christopher Lloyd, noticed plants with chocolate brown to bronze leaves. He christened them "Brazen Hussy" and they are now cultivated on both sides of the Atlantic. In the USA, the name "Brazen Hussy" has also been applied to a cultivar of the Plantain Lily (Hosta) that has bright yellow leaves.

Victoria Matthews
Denver, Colorado

Infamy.   The first draft of President Franklin Roosevelt's request to Congress for a declaration of war began, "Yesterday, December 7, 1941, a date which will live in world history." In his second draft, he crossed out "world history" and substituted a condemnatory word that was far more memorable: *infamy*.

Though its adjective, *infamous,* was frequently used, the noun *infamy* was less familiar. It means "evil fame, shameful repute, notorious disgrace" and befitted the nation's shock at the bloody destruction at Pearl Harbor, a successful surprise blow that was instantly characterized by the victim nation as a "sneak attack."

The word, with its connotation of wartime shock and horror, was chosen by headline writers to label the terrorist attack on New York and Washington that demolished the twin towers of the World Trade Center and a portion of the Pentagon. In newspapers and on television, the historical *day of infamy* was the label chosen, along with the more general "attack on America."

The killers were *hijackers*. This Americanism, origin unknown, was first cited in 1912 as to *kick up high jack,* which *Dialect Notes* defined as "to cause a disturbance"; ten years later, a book about hobos noted "*hi-jacking,* or robbing men at night when sleeping in the jungles." In the 1960s, as terrorists began seizing control of airliners, the verb *skyjack* was coined, but it has since fallen into disuse.

The suicidal hijackers were able to slip a new weapon through the metal detectors: a *box cutter,* defined in the on-top-of-the-news *New Oxford American Dictionary* as "a thin, inexpensive razor-blade knife designed to open cardboard boxes." Barbara Olson, a passenger aboard the airliner doomed to be crashed into the Pentagon, was able to telephone her husband, Solicitor General Ted Olson; she told him that the hijackers were armed with knives and what she called a *cardboard cutter.*

These terrorists were *suicide bombers,* a phrase used in a 1981 Associated Press dispatch by Tom Baldwin in Lebanon about the driving of an explosives-laden car into the Iraqi Embassy. In 1983, *Newsweek* reported that "the winds of fanaticism have blown up a merciless throng of killers: the assassins, thugs, kamikazes—and now the *suicide bombers.*"

Kamikaze is Japanese for "divine wind," a reference to a storm in the 13th century that blew away a fleet of invading Mongols. In World War II, the word described suicidal pilots who dived their planes into enemy ships. English has now absorbed the word: Al Hunt of the *Wall Street Journal* wrote last week that airline policy "was turned upside down by these *kamikaze* fanatics."

Hunt, like President Bush and many others, called these acts of murder-suicide *cowardly*. That is not a modifier I would use, nor would I employ its synonym *dastardly* (though FDR did), which also means "shrinking from danger." If anything, the suicide bomber or suicide hijacker is mania-cally fearless, the normal human survival instinct overwhelmed by hatred or brainwashed fervor. *Senseless* and *mindless* are other mistaken modifiers of these killings: the sense, or evil purpose, of modern barbaric murder is to carry out a blindly worshipped leader's desire to shock, horrify and ulti-mately intimidate the target's civilized compatriots.

Another word that deserves a second look is *justice*. Both Senator John McCain and Bush adviser Karen Hughes called for "swift *justice*" to be meted out to the perpetrators, ordinarily a sentiment widely shared. But the columnist Charles Krauthammer wrote: "There should be no talk of bringing these people to 'swift *justice*.' . . . An open act of war demands a military response, not a judicial one."

The leading suspect at the center of the terror campaign is Osama bin Laden. The *bin,* meaning "son of," is not capped; Westerners have chosen not to capitalize the Arabic just as they have often chosen to capitalize the Hebrew *Ben,* which has the same meaning. This has nothing to do with correctness; it is strictly idiosyncratic convention, varying among regions and stylists. (When starting a sentence with bin Laden's name, *Times* style calls for capitalizing it, which then looks like a mistake.) Bin Laden has been given a shorthand, bogus title, much like *vice overlord, fugitive financier* and *drug kingpin:* his is *terrorist mastermind.*

The name of his organization, *Al Qaeda,* means "the base," in looser modern Arabic, "the military headquarters." His host in Afghanistan is the *Taliban,* a religio-political group whose name means "those who seek." The Arab word *talib,* "student," has been given a Persian suffix, *-an,* which is an unusual amalgam or was a mistake.

The Taliban (proper noun construed as plural) *harbor* bin Laden and the base of his organization. That is now becoming a political verb with a vengeance.

"We will make no distinction," President Bush said, "between the terror-ists who committed these acts and those who *harbor* them." A key sense of the verb *harbor* is "to give shelter and concealment to wrongdoers." The next day, Bush used the noun form creatively: "This is an enemy that thinks its *harbors* are safe, but they won't be safe forever." That was an extension of the noun's present meaning of "place of shelter, haven, port" to "place where evildoers think they are out of reach of punishment."

Finally, the word *terrorist*. It is rooted in the Latin *terrere*, "to frighten," and the *-ist* was coined in France to castigate the perpetrators of the Reign of Terror. Edmund Burke in 1795 defined the word in English: "Those hell-hounds called *terrorists* . . . are let loose on the people."

The sternly judgmental word should not be avoided or euphemized. Nobody can accurately call those who plotted, financed and carried out the infamous mass slaughter of September 11 *militants, resistance fighters, gunmen, partisans* or *guerrillas*. The most precise word to describe a person or group who murders even one innocent civilian to send a political message is *terrorist*.

I can explain where the -an in Talib-an *came from: -an is the regular animate masculine plural ending in Pashto, the native language of the vast majority of the Taliban. The close relationship between Persian and Pashto accounts for their having identical plural markers.*

Barbara Robson, PhD

Arlington, Virginia

Invest.   "The Northern Alliance does not want to physically enter Kabul," said Secretary of State Colin Powell on the Nov. 11, 2001, *Meet the Press,* expressing more of a diplomat's hope than stating a fact. "So we think it'd be better if they were to *invest*—if I can pull an old military term out of my background—*invest* the city, make it untenable for the Taliban to continue to occupy Kabul, and then we'll see where we are."

In the *Weekly Standard,* Robert Kagan and William Kristol saw in Powell's use of that military sense of the verb the essence of two different strategies that had riven the State and Defense departments in the first two months of war in Afghanistan. "The key word was '*invest*,'" they wrote, "by which Powell meant surround but not enter." State's priority was to create a new coalition government; Defense's priority was to help the anti-Taliban fighters take the city. The Pentagon's view prevailed, and the city was entered rather than *invested*.

It was not Powell's first use of the verb in its military sense, cautioning the northern fighters. He told *India Today* two weeks before that "they want to at least *invest* Kabul. Whether they go into Kabul or not, or whether that's the best thing to do or not, remains to be seen."

The verb's original meaning is rooted in the Latin *vestire*, "to dress, clothe." A *vestment* is a ceremonial robe; a *vest* is a sleeveless garment now worn more by stylish women than by male business executives.

Now comes the connection with Powell's meaning. The transitive verb to *vest* has since 1583 meant "to envelop a person with an article of clothing." A couple of months ago, when the newspaper publisher Conrad Black became a member of Britain's House of Lords, his induction was called an *investiture* as well as an *ennoblement*. Jonathan Swift, in his 1704 *Tale of a Tub*, extended the meaning with a metaphor: "They held the Universe to be a large suit of clothes which *invests* every thing." This sense of the verb is defined by "to cover, to surround with a garment."

It was also applied to the surrounding movement of an army: "No wearisomnesse of long siege & assault," goes the translation of the Roman Titus Livius by Philemon Holland in 1600, "is able to raise the Roman armie from any towne once by them *invested*." We are now into the siege mentality. To a military strategist, *invest* means "to surround, to besiege, to cut off escape"—but not to invade or occupy. That's what Powell had in mind, giving him time to build an internal government, but—if all the scuttlebutt about the inner workings of the National Security Council is true—not what the Pentagon's Donald Rumsfeld had in mind.

What about *investigate*? No etymological connection with "cover up," except in its most modern sense. The ultimate Latin root is *vestigium*, "footprint," which investigators track. Forget about it here; it will only lead to confusion. But the verb *invest* has also long meant "to employ for profitable use," or at least does mean that in those times when the market has not fallen out of bed.

Those looking glumly at retirement investments know what *vested* means: "having a consummated right." Those of us with a quarter-century at the *Times* are popping our *vested* buttons. The pejorative phrase *vested interest*, in regard to the privileged class, was coined by the economist Henry George, who died of a stroke while running for mayor of New York in 1897. In that regard, Aloysius (Just Call Me Vic) Meyers, lieutenant governor of the state of Washington a half-century ago, told voters, "Habitually I go without a *vest* so that I can't be accused of standing for the *vested* interests." Few caught his play on the original clothing sense of *habitually*.

In 1948 I covered the investiture *of Queen Juliana in Amsterdam, and then the* coronation *of King Baudouin in Belgium. The Dutch explained to me that investiture is more democratic. The Dutch word, if I can remember some fifty years later, is* Inhuldiging, *which means something like ennoblement.*

> Daniel Schorr
> National Public Radio
> Washington, D.C.

Iron Fist.   "They wanted this *iron fist* to command them." That was the statement of Arthur Wellesley, the Duke of Wellington, about the need for discipline among the English troops sent to the Canadian frontier in the 1812 war with the United States. The victor over Napoleon at Waterloo became known as "the Iron Duke."

Iron is hard. An *iron hand* is rule that is rigid, stubborn, severe, even cruel; *iron-fisted* has an additional connotation of "parsimonious, close-fisted, niggardly."

Thus it was surprising to read in several articles that an *iron fist* was in control of the Republican convention in Philadelphia in August 2000. The attribution, though not in direct quotation of a full sentence, was to George W. Bush himself in the week before he became his party's nominee. In the *New York Times,* the prescient R. W. Apple Jr. wrote, "If there are abortion rights supporters at the podium this week, for example, they will talk about something else, thanks to what Mr. Bush calls his *'iron fist'* control of the proceedings."

That's a curious phrase from a candidate who popularized the marriage of the adjective *compassionate* with the noun *conservative*. The decidedly noncompassionate phrase *iron fist* has not even the smooth qualifier that Thomas Carlyle reported in 1850 was used by the Iron Duke's defeated rival: "Soft of speech and manner, yet with an inflexible rigour of command . . . *'iron hand* in a velvet glove,' as Napoleon defined it."

Strange that Bush should adopt that phrase; perhaps it was a slip under stress. Political figures from Austin are sensitive to the political meanings of words.

For example, Karl Rove (invariably described as "Bush's chief strategist"; there is apparently nobody with the title "deputy strategist") demonstrated a grasp of nuance in an interview on the *New York Times*/ABC News Webcast at the GOP convention. His questioner had asked about the gap between the convention's "moderate, inclusive message" of those chosen to speak and the notably conservative views of the delegates shown in polls.

"Let me correct," Rove responded quickly. "You said *'inclusive* and *moderate.'* What we're saying is, it's 'inclusive and *compassionately conservative.'* "

What was the chief strategist's chief strategy, while accepting the adjective *inclusive,* in going out of his way to reject the nearly synonymous adjective *moderate*?

Rove knew that *moderate,* when used as a noun, causes political reverberations. From a conservative's point of view, a *moderate* is the liberal's way of avoiding the pejorative tag of *liberal*. From a liberal's point of view, *moderate* is not only self-applicable but also a friendly way of describing a Republican who is not a hard-core, reactionary, troglodyte kook.

The word's political sense was born in the Eisenhower administration. Minutes of the Nov. 4, 1954, cabinet meeting reported the president using the phrase "a policy of *moderation*." Adlai Stevenson, a year later, told a fund-raising audience: "*Moderation,* yes! Stagnation, no!" At the same dinner, Averell Harriman, a potential opponent for the 1956 Democratic nomination, disagreed: "There is no such word as *moderation* in the Democratic vocabulary."

The conservative columnist William F. Buckley wrote at that time, "I resist *moderate* because it is a base-stealing word for the benefit of GOP liberals." The Nelson Rockefeller wing of the party at first accepted it in the early '60s, but then supporters of Barry Goldwater used it in derision, to catch the centrist minority off the Republican political base. On July 14, 1963, Rockefeller denounced Goldwater "extremists" for a philosophy "wholly alien to the broad middle course that accommodates the mainstream of Republican principle."

I recall dragging a large banner across the San Francisco Cow Palace floor at the 1964 convention that read "Stay in the Mainstream!" But as Francis Bacon pointed out in "On Faction," written in 1597, "a few who are stiff do tire out a great number that are more *moderate*." The Goldwaterite true believers scorned the electoral *mainstream* and lost in a landslide; four years later, Nixon steered toward it and narrowly won.

In 1968, Nixon and his writers shied from the noun *moderate*, still inflammatory to "real" Republicans, but embraced its euphemism *mainstream*. President Gerald Ford, after his 1976 defeat, called a meeting of the Republicans Ronald Reagan, John Connally and Nelson Rockefeller and used an older metaphor: "The Republican tent is big enough to encompass the four individuals who are here today." As the *big tent* was replaced by *mainstream*, both were supplanted by "the politics of *inclusion*" in the 1980s.

That's why the *iron-fisted* Bush chief strategist Karl Rove accepted *inclusive* and rejected *moderate*. General Colin Powell followed up with a convention speech hailing George W. Bush's "passion for *inclusion*."

In his acceptance speech to the GOP convention in Philadelphia, Governor Bush repeated *compassionate conservatism*, defining it in a plain sentence: "It is to put conservative values and conservative ideas into the thick of the fight for justice and opportunity."

Where and when did the phrase (akin to Jack Kemp's *bleeding-heart conservative*) originate? In his book, *Compassionate Conservatism*, Marvin Olasky, professor of journalism at the University of Texas at Austin (and the Bush adviser who suggested the phrase to the Bush campaign), provides a lead. Olasky suggests coinage by Vernon Jordan, then head of the National Urban League, who said on July 22, 1981, in criticism of the Reagan administration, "I do challenge its failure to exhibit a *compassionate conservatism.*"

However, four months earlier—on March 13, 1981—in an article by Judith Miller of the *New York Times,* Senator Orrin Hatch, Republican of Utah, said: "I'm a conservative, and proud of it, but I'm a *compassionate conservative.* I'm not some kind of ultra-right-wing maniac, despite some portrayals in the press." That remains the current political sense of the phrase.

Iron Triangle.   On the eve of his victory in the South Carolina primary, recalling his stunning defeat in New Hampshire, George W. Bush said: "People may not think I'm tough enough, but I am. This is a process of *steeling* me to become president."

Newsweek, reporting on the "hardening" of the candidate during the rough tactics of that southern campaign, commented, "Consider him *steeled.*"

The verb, in its sense of "to make hard or strong as steel," is used in Shakespeare's poem *Venus and Adonis,* as Venus says: "Give me my heart ... O give it me, lest thy hard heart do *steel* it, / And being *steeled,* soft sighs can never grave it." Governor Bush, in subsequent interviews, repeated the verb; he evidently felt that being *steeled* is an admirable development in a candidate.

Senator John McCain is also partial to a metallic metaphor. "I've taken on the *iron triangle:* special interests, campaign finance and lobbying," he said in mid-February 2000. A few weeks earlier, his definition was formulated slightly differently: "The establishment obviously is in a state of extreme distress, if not panic, because they know I have taken on the *iron triangle* of money, lobbyists and legislation."

The origin is military. On United States Army maps during the Korean conflict of 1950–53, an area about thirty miles north of the 38th parallel with its apex at Pyonggang and its corners at Chorwon and Kumhwa was marked the *Iron Triangle*. This was the center anchor of the North Korean defense line and the hub of a communication and supply network. During the Vietnam War, an area of 125 square miles northwest of Saigon was called by the same name. Then the phrase was transferred to Europe and used for nations rather than small areas: in 1977, an editorial in the *New York Times* called East Germany, Poland and Czechoslovakia "the USSR's *iron triangle*."

Meanwhile, the military phrase was being used as a synonym for what Dwight Eisenhower, in his 1961 farewell, called "the military-industrial complex"—that is, the military services, defense contractors and members of Congress busy at the pork barrel. In the '70s, the term spread beyond the military to include the cozy relationship among federal agencies, congressional committees and lobbyists.

Ronald Reagan, as he was leaving office, substituted the media for the military in his triangulation. "A *triangle* of institutions—parts of Congress, the media and special-interest groups—is transforming and placing out of focus our constitutional balance," Reagan warned. Modestly, he did not claim credit for the phrase: "Some have used the term *iron triangle* to describe what I'm talking about."

McCain left the media out of his *iron triangle,* substituting "money," so that his three corners are now "money, lobbyists and legislation."

How did his opponent deal with the three-sided ferrous metaphor? George W. Bush's department of figure-of-speech ripostes did fairly well. Another sense of *triangle* is "an iron rod bent in a triangle with one angle open, used as a percussion instrument or bell when struck with another iron rod."

After being asked frequently about McCain's symbol, he was readied with a colorful reply. "If a man says, for example," said Bush, undoubtedly alluding to the man as McCain, "that there's an *iron triangle* in Washington, D.C., of lobbyists and special interests, and he's ringing it like a dinner bell to raise money for his campaign, I think that I have a right to point out that he says one thing and does another."

Although Bush's *triangle* had only two sides, his word-image nicely brought to mind a picture of an *iron triangle* used sometimes on Texas ranches to call cowhands to dinner.

What is it about iron that attracts phrase makers? John C. Calhoun, vice president under Andrew Jackson, was nicknamed "the *cast-iron man*" by the English economist Harriet Martineau because he "looks as if he had never been born, and could never be extinguished." Lou Gehrig, the "*iron horse*" (originally referring to the railroads), was followed by Cal Ripken, the "*iron man*," who broke Gehrig's endurance record of 2,130 consecutive games in 1995.

But there is a cruel connotation to the word-image. *Blood and iron*, in German *Blut und Eisen*, meant "military force as distinguished from diplomacy" and was associated in the 1870s with Prince Bismarck, "the *iron chancellor*." Autocratic rule was governance with an *iron hand*. Churchill famously called the Soviet separation of the tyrannized East and the free West the *iron curtain*, after a fireproof curtain used in French and English theaters as early as the 18th century. (The Viscountess Snowden, after a visit to Russia soon after World War I, wrote, "We were behind the '*iron curtain*' at last!") In the United States, the undemonstrative first lady Rosalynn Carter was derogated (unfairly, in retrospect) as "the *steel magnolia*." The *iron rice bowl* was Mao Zedong's guarantee to China's workers of a job for life under the Communist system, with cradle-to-grave benefits. President Bill Clinton, celebrating what he believed was the emergence of capitalism in China, said in 1998 that "restructuring state enterprises is critical to building a modern economy, but it is also disrupting settled patterns of life and work, cracking the *iron rice bowl*."

Thus, McCain's *iron triangle* has a built-in pejorative connotation. Even the triangle has dark memories, as its evocation in necromancy and in the military usages above indicates. There's also the *Bermuda Triangle*, where boats disappear mysteriously, as well as the *golden triangle*, the area of Southeast Asia—Myanmar, Laos and Thailand—where opium is cultivated. (On the other hand, people in rejuvenated downtown Pittsburgh, and Texans in the Beaumont–Orange–Port Arthur area, are happy to call their neighborhoods the *golden triangle*.)

J

Judge Fights. "*'Borking'* is out. *'Court packing'* is in." So wrote E. J. Dionne Jr. in the *Washington Post,* using two of the great politico-judicial attack phrases in rapid succession. Comes now the etymology to help readers rap their gavels when slanted words joust with each other.

The notion of *court packing* can be traced to Lincoln, who wanted a tenth justice on the Supreme Court, and before that to John Adams, whose nominations of "midnight judges" just before he left office caused a ruckus with his successor, Thomas Jefferson, who refused to swear them in.

The phrase *packing the Court*—always pejorative, imputing one-sidedness—burst on the scene in 1936 in criticism of President Franklin Roosevelt's plan to appoint a new Supreme Court justice every time one of the "nine old men" (a phrase coined by the columnists Drew Pearson and Robert S. Allen) reached the age of seventy and refused to step down.

But the president was seen to have overreached, and his plan backfired; even on the verge of a landslide reelection, FDR was put on the defensive. "If by that phrase *'packing the Court'* it is charged," he said, "that I wish to place on the bench spineless puppets who would disregard the law and would decide specific cases as I wished them to be decided, I make this answer: that no president fit for his office would appoint, and no Senate of honorable men fit for their office would confirm, that kind of appointee to the Supreme Court."

FDR's proposal, universally denounced as *court packing,* died in com-

173

mittee; however, the balance of power on the Court soon shifted to the liberals, causing one wag to note, "A switch in time saved nine."

Turnabout is fair play. The phrase is now the rallying cry of Democrats worried that Bush nominees to the federal bench at all levels will make the court system more conservative. Said Senator Pat Leahy of Vermont, ranking Democrat on the Judiciary Committee, "It sure looks like they are intent on building an ideologically driven *court-packing machine*." Bruce Ackerman, a professor of law at Yale, writing in the *Los Angeles Times*, added a note of breathlessness: "We are on the brink of a *court-packing crisis*."

Republicans are countering with the eponymous verb possibly first used in the *Atlanta Journal-Constitution* on Aug. 20, 1987: "Let's just hope something enduring results for the justice-to-be, like a new verb: *Borked*. Dictionaries will say it's synonymous with 'maligned.' " This referred to the way Democrats savaged Ronald Reagan's nominee, the Appeals Court judge Robert H. Bork, the year before.

"A concerted effort to '*Bork*' John Ashcroft would not be well received," said Senator Trent Lott, the majority leader, about George W. Bush's nomination for attorney general. The newly nonconfrontational Ashcroft was not *borked*. (I use the lowercase *b* now that the verb is established, but then I lowercase *draconian* and *stentorian*, over the objections of the strict solon Draco and the Greek herald with the booming voice, Stentor.)

The columnist Fred Barnes went to the eponym himself for a definition. "What it means is to be attacked with a series of—not to put it too strongly—a series of lies and mischaracterizations," Bork said. "And it is an effort at the politics of personal destruction."

Debate rages over whether the confirmation criteria should be character and merit, or whether an otherwise estimable nominee should be rejected for holding views that some activists believe are outside the ideological mainstream. It may be that senators will vote on the basis of ideology without getting personal. But in coming months, Democrats will charge Bush with *court packing*; returning the fire, Bush will deplore *borking*.

Keep It Short.   "The use of short words is an art," writes Nat Bodian in the winter issue of *Publishing Research Quarterly,* published at Rutgers. "It takes a bit of time to think them up," he tells us, "but once you learn how to make your thoughts known in short words and to write with them, you will find that they work well and, as a whole, they tend to make good sense."

Why? "Short words are sharp, clear and to the point," notes Nat. "They spark the thoughts of those who read them, and they urge them to read on. They let you say what you want, and they leave no doubt as to what you mean. So try to find ways to write in short words when you speak of or deal with books."

His pick of best names for books? *Gone With the Wind, The Joy of Sex, Live and Let Die, A House Is Not a Home, The Prince of Tides, The Way Things Ought to Be, The Cat in the Hat.*

Do you go for that as I do? Let us pledge, then, to swap long words for short ones. At first, you may find it hard to join this cause, but it is not as hard as you may think to pick nouns that shine, to choose verbs that stun and to use fresh tropes that sing. The need is real and the good it will do will make your spouse proud and your work sell. No, the trend toward a taut style should not be scoffed at as just a blip—you can bet your life it will last for years. Think of it: crisp talk warms hearts, and prose packed with punch is sure to make you stand out in a crowd. Give it a shot.

I share your liking for short words. Nothing raises the goose bumps like Lady Macbeth's: "Who would have thought the old man had so much blood in him?" or Churchill's: "Blood, toil, tears and sweat."

However, there is another factor that affects length of words: short words are generally of Anglo-Saxon origin, while longer words tend to come from Norman-French. In your last monosyllabic paragraph of about 130 words only eight are clearly of Latin, Greek or French origin; the rest are Anglo-Saxon.

This wonderful concoction called the English language is still an imperfect blend of the two main linguistic strains. If you closed your eyes and listened to the conversation in any barrack room on either side of the Atlantic, you could be excused for wondering if the Norman Conquest had ever taken place.

John Binsted

San Mateo, California

Kibosh.   In denying a newspaper report that the United States had ordered a halt to accepting the surrender of Al Qaeda terrorists, Defense Secretary Rumsfeld said, "To my knowledge, the U.S. did not nix, stop or put the *kibosh* on anything."

Nix is "to refuse, deny," from the German negative *nichts*. And the meaning of to *put the kibosh on* is widely understood: "to forbid, with unmistakable conclusiveness." But what's a *kibosh*?

Nobody knows. It has been attributed to Yiddish and Gaelic, but with no citation. H. L. Mencken thought it was an Americanism, but irate British etymologists shot that down with an 1836 use by Charles Dickens in his *Sketches by Boz* spelled *kye-bosk*. Its origin remains one of the great mysteries of slang.

Let me suggest the Hebrew word kavash *as a possible origin of the slang word* kibosh. A Hebrew and English Lexicon of the Old Testament, *by Brown,*

Driver and Briggs, offers as its primary meanings to "subdue, bring into bondage." I hope this puts the kibosh on the mystery.

Rabbi Ira J. Schiffer
Associate Chaplain
Middlebury College
Middlebury, Vermont

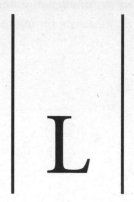

Language on Demand.   Two new ways to deliver books are upon us. One is the e-book, which you can download from the Internet and squint at on your screen or print out on your printer. The other is the print-on-demand book, which you order over the Web or from a traditional bookstore and get a bound copy of in the mail.

This will mean that just about any literate person can become a "published" author. Online services already exist that—for a few hundred dollars—will take your digital manuscript and pictures and make them available to buyers for roughly the same price as bookstore books.

The Internet publishers turn down porn, hate stuff and guides to building H-bombs. However, they do not judge content for quality and cannot, for such a low publishing fee, edit copy. What will the coming wave of amateur authors do to the language? Will we be inundated with vanities in gibberish?

Maybe not. I punched up iuniverse.com and ordered *Blow the House Down: The Story of My Double Lung Transplant,* by Charles Tolchin.* I've known Charley since he was a kid with cystic fibrosis given little chance to live. His book is a stunning, moving, personal account of a young man's

*Charles P. Tolchin, avatar of optimism, died from complications of his cystic fibrosis on Aug. 7, 2003. I miss him.

bravery in action. Tolchin's unprofessional writing is straightforward, colloquial and frill-free. He has produced an intimate memoir that grabs you and has found a new way to distribute it that reaches you.

Will such disintermediated prose encourage new authors or discourage writing discipline? We'll see. Worth watching.

Laydown Dates.   The book-publishing industry has its own new term for a variation of a release date: *laydown*. "This review copy is being sent to you," Knopf Publicity notifies me, "with the understanding that you will not run your review before Tuesday, July 18—which is the National *Laydown* Date for bookstores all across the country. (Official Publication Date is July 25.)"

A vision came to me of the National *Laydown* Date, a date that would live in the annals of relaxation. Hammocks would be handed out, busy intersections closed for pedestrians to stretch out and take a nap, yoga teachers enlisted for supervision of supine and prone meditators, all putting out of their slackened and refreshed minds the dread prospect of the inevitable National Standup Date.

Belay that dream: a *laydown date* is the day that a book officially goes on sale. It is used especially when the publisher wants to restrict any sale or revelation of the news in a book before it leaks. The publication date is a week or month after that, giving reviewers time to noodle the book around and buyers the feeling that they are getting the jump on their neighbors. *Laydown* without the date means "distribution": *Publishers Weekly* (where's the apostrophe?) wrote recently about a Beatles book that "hits the stores with a worldwide *laydown* of 1.5 million copies."

The reclining noun has a sinister use among arms merchants (an obliterating strike is a *nuclear laydown*) and can also be found in the lexicon of graphic artists, construction workers and railroaders. But its most prevalent use is in gambling, as the adjective in a *laydown hand*.

In poker, it's the "showdown," when all hands are laid open for all players to determine the winner. In bridge, a *laydown hand* is a winning hand placed faceup on the table all at once, rather than being played out. This bridge meaning has been extended to a general "sure thing." A Boston economist told the *Times*, "The Fed has more reason to tighten than not— but it's not a *laydown*."

Some of us who respect reasonable embargoes resist marketing manipulation. Let's say I go to a bookstore, the bookseller sells me a book and I spot a news story in it. Would I feel free to use it in a column no matter what its *laydown date* or publication date? You bet I would; that's a *laydown*.

In the world of salesmen, laydown *has a far different meaning from those mentioned in your column.*

It is usually used in the sense of, "That deal was a laydown; *the guy answered the door with his checkbook in hand!" or "What a* laydown! *The first unit I showed them, they said, 'We'll take it!'"*

As such, it is not really describing the "win-win" situation that a sale ideally should be; rather, it's alluding to the prospect "laying down" (yes, it SHOULD be "lying down") and submitting, i.e., letting the salesman "have his way" (I'm trying to be delicate here!). But it certainly indicates a deal that the salesman didn't have to struggle to close.

Stuart Tarlowe
Rosedale, Kansas

You asked where the apostrophe is in Publishers Weekly. *I suppose it's in the same place the apostrophe is in the Screen Actors Guild, the Writers Guild, the Authors Guild, etc. I suggest that in each instance the members of the group making use of the organization do not own it but are members of it. Buy that?*

Frank O'Donnell
Rockville Centre, New York

Left Coast. "If she was wearing a revealing top," wrote the *Los Angeles Times* in a guide to the geographic origins of guests at a Conga Room party during the Democratic National Convention, "a short, tight micro-mini and strappy stilettos, if she had that come-hither look, she was definitely *Left Coast.*"

When did the West Coast of the United States become the *Left Coast,* and why?

The East Coast is rarely called the Right Coast; its only synonym is the Eastern Seaboard, as in "We ought to saw off the Eastern Seaboard and float it out to sea," 1960s hyperbole attributed to Senator Barry Goldwater of Arizona, who considered the Rockefeller-Dewey Northeast to be a hotbed of liberalism. (*Seaboard* means "land bordering a seacoast," though "Western Seaboard" is an unfamiliar term.)

The earliest *Left Coast* citation I can find, with the help of Fred Shapiro of Yale, is in the title of a 1977 *Rolling Stone* record review: "Wet Willie *Left Coast* Live." Three years later, a *New York Times* writer put it in context: "If you're standing in Texas looking north, as Texans frequently do, the *Left Coast* is where Hollywood is." These usages had no political connotation.

In the mid '90s, however, a liberal coloration emerged. The *Denver Post* noted that President Clinton "swayed to the *left coast* and invited gays into the military." The combination of geographical and political direction was irresistible. "The Pacific Northwest was a center of so much outcry against the Reagan administration in the 1980s," wrote Joel Connelly in the *Seattle Post-Intelligencer,* "that conservative pundits referred to the region by a derisive nickname—the '*left coast* of America.' "

As California has become more solidly Democratic, the name—with its political connotation—is most closely associated with that state. (Oregon and Washington are still up for linguistic grabs.)

Other nicknames for Los Angeles and Hollywood, home of the *glitterati* (an amalgam of "glitter" and "literati"), seem to be fading. "*Tinseltown,* with its reference to the silver screen and the glamour surrounding it, is at least mildly positive," says Arnold Zwicky, visiting professor of linguistics at Stanford. "*La-La Land,* with its suggestion of kookiness, is (mildly, jokingly) deprecatory, and I don't think I've heard Angelenos use it except in explicit self-mockery."

La-La Land is a play on the initials LA, perhaps influenced by *Lotos-land* in "The Lotos-Eaters," a poem by Tennyson: "In the hollow *Lotos-land* to live and lie reclined / On the hills like Gods together." In his posthumous 1941 novel, *The Last Tycoon,* F. Scott Fitzgerald had a character describe Hollywood as "a mining town in *lotus land.*"

Jack Smith of the *Los Angeles Times* tracked *La-La Land* back to a 1985 recording, "Land of La-La," by Stevie Wonder, the pop-soul music star, with backup singers chanting *el-lay* every few bars. The only uses found before that were a 1979 *Los Angeles Times* lead, "Monday night in *Lalaland* is not like Monday night in, say, Washington," and a 1984 reference in the *Washington Post* by the fashion columnist Nina Hyde, reporting on a bar that "encourages the cocktail waitresses to pour themselves into black super-clingy spandex pants, very *LA-LA land,* very Cher of a couple of years ago, very roller disco." A second sense exists, only tangentially related to the city: a state of unreality, induced by drink, drugs or congenital dreaminess.

Whether used derisively by unappreciative visitors to the Golden State or used self-mockingly by residents, when the nicknames refer to a specific place, they are proper nouns to be properly capitalized: *Tinseltown, La-La Land* and now the *Left Coast.*

Legacy.　Certain words and phrases become taboo in the White House. *Out of the loop, amiable dunce, malaise* and *crook* come to mind.

The Clinton White House, we are told by Glenn Burkins of the *Wall Street Journal,* is eager to make clear that it is "not being driven by a quest to establish" Clinton's *legacy.* The interviewer reports that John Podesta, the chief of staff, "has banned the use of that word in the White House."

That's because the word, in its political sense, is most often being used in derision. "The Clintons' *legacy,*" wrote the *St. Petersburg Times* as far back as 1996, "will be the attack and invasion of our justice system by social entrepreneurs." Two years later, the columnist Stephen Chapman pronounced, "Clinton's *legacy* is likely to be the enduring diminution of the office he holds." In that year, the *New York Times* columnist Maureen Dowd suggested that "Bill Clinton's biggest *legacy* may not be in politics, but in letters. . . . He has inspired one entirely new and remarkable genre: feminist erotic journalism."

More charitably, Governor Jeb Bush of Florida recently said that free trade "is a place where Clinton can legitimately say that he has a *legacy*." And when asked by a reporter, "How much of the president's *legacy* is dependent on peace in Ireland and in the Middle East?" the White House spokesman Joe Lockhart replied, "His *legacy* will be decided, thankfully, not by us and not by any of the people who are scribbling in notebooks."

That official rejection of *legacy*-itis may have led to the banning of the word itself in White House usage. Podesta probably winced when President Clinton, at a recent fund-raising gathering of American Indians, deplored United States negligence of their rights, adding, "This is the part of the historical *legacy* we want to be proud of." However, it was not in the context of Clinton's own historical bequest to the American people and could thus not be construed as a violation of the ban.

The Latin *legare* means "to dispute" and "to bequeath," which is fitting when you consider how many bequests are disputed. Not in dispute, however, is the 1460 coinage by Robert Henryson, who writes of a widow's "*legacy* and lamentation."

Despite its ban, watch for what is sure to be the most overused word of the coming interregnum. An unwanted gift from a predecessor, parent or older sibling is derogated as a hand-me-down; a happier, lasting bequest is called a *legacy* with legs.

Legit.   "*Legitimacy* is a word that we've tossed around an awful lot in the last few weeks," Cokie Roberts said on ABC during the uncertain interregnum.

True, but the problem we've been having is with the verb form: is it *legitimate*, with the last syllable pronounced "mate," as distinct from the adjective ending "mit"? Or is the verb *legitimatize*, as Secretary of State Madeleine Albright uses it? Or should the word meaning "to make lawful" be shortened to *legitimize*, which my copy editor suggested I use in a recent column instead of *legitimate*?

"The oldest form is *legitimate*," says Mike Agnes, editor in chief of *Webster's New World Dictionary,* "which tends to be used in the historical sense of 'to make a bastard child *legitimate.*' " This is not the specific sense that television's talking heads use in discussing George W. Bush's forthcoming presidency. For them, the sense is "to become widely recognized as being legal," and the preferred form is the one used by Al Gore during the contested count: "The next president should be *legitimized* in an election in which every vote that is legally cast is counted."

When Andrew Card, Bush's designated chief of staff, said, "The Supreme Court ruling *legitimizes* many of our concerns" about other, adverse judicial decisions, he was in the mainstream of usage. How can we be sure? A search on the Westlaw database shows *legitimized* running ahead of *legitimated* by six to one, with *legitimatized* with its extra syllable trailing far behind, and you can do your own recount.

Relatedly, Brian Williams of MSNBC sent me a message over the air recently: "If you're listening, do a Sunday column on *disenfranchised* that's being used incorrectly by both sides."

I was listening and heard that question raised by other logic-obsessed colleagues in the news business: shouldn't the opposite of *enfranchise* be *disfranchise,* which the Merriam-Webster dictionary likes, and not the unnecessarily longer *disenfranchise*? If common usage knocks a syllable out of *legitimatize,* why doesn't it do the same to *disenfranchise*?

It does not because language is not neat and tidy. The Old French *enfranchir,* its meaning originally "to make free," which we now take to mean "to enable to vote," is one word, despite Samuel Johnson's dubious derivation two centuries ago. To show its opposite, the *dis-* goes in front of the whole word, on the analogy of *disenthrall* and *disenchant.* Loosen up, Brian and Merriam-Webster; go with the flow.

Ligging.   Amorous Brits not yet ready to *hook up* traditionally get their kicks by *snogging,* their word for "smooching." But they have another word for the lifestyle of the freeloader: *ligging.*

"The Cannes Film Festival may or may not be a shrine to cinema," wrote Frederic Peugeot of Agence France-Presse last month, "but one thing it certainly is: an adventure playground for *liggers*." He defined the noun as "the camp followers who have developed the skills of freeloading and gate-crashing to a fine art."

The *Daily Mail* defines it as "being on the list of every P.R. company, leading to a multitude of party invites. This results in the *ligger* existing on a diet that consists solely of free canapes and Champagne." The *Times of London* derided "a lifetime of limelight *ligging*."

Lig is a dialect variation of *lie*. *Ligging* was first spotted by the *Oxford English Dictionary* in 1960—"the mere *'ligging'* layabout." The definition: "to idle or lie about; also, (slang) to sponge, to 'freeload,' to gate-crash or attend parties."

This is a word from the mother country that zings home, and should be adopted in the colonies.

Livid. "One longtime friend of the president," wrote Neil A. Lewis of the *New York Times*, "said Mr. Clinton was *'livid*, off-the-wall angry' about the disbarment proceedings."

Off the wall, hyphenated as above when used as a compound modifier of the word it precedes, is a figure of speech that shows staying power. It can mean "bizarre," with a second sense of "being a few apples short of a picnic." It should not be confused with an earlier phrase, *up the wall*, "into a fury," now fallen into desuetude. Evidently *off the wall*, as used above, carries with it some of the fury associated with *up the wall*.

Less easy to figure out is the meaning of *livid*. It is a word that President Clinton used recently in response to a question put to him by a Justice Department counsel seeking his knowledge of illegal campaign contributions: "All I can tell you," said Clinton, "is that I was *livid* about it."

What color do you turn when you turn *livid*? Red with anger? Purple with rage? White with fury?

The Latin *livere* means "to be blue." The Old Slavic *sliva* is "plum." (A few shots of the liquor called *slivovitz* will make you either flushed or ashen-faced.) This is cognate with the Old English *sloe*, a reddish-purple blackthorn berry that gives a sloe gin fizz its color. Whash neksht?

Early usage: a writer named Henry de Knyghton used *livid* in 1258 to describe corpses. Thomas Norton in his 1477 incunabula best seller, *The Ordinall of Alchimy*, wrote of "This Waun Colour called *Lividitie*, In Envious Men useth much to be." That *waun* suggests the modern *wan*, "pale." James Fenimore Cooper, in his 1841 *Deerslayer*, had a character "almost *livid* with emotion," but never said what color that was; however, Walter Scott's 1814 use of the word as a modifier of a color—"his trembling lips are *livid* blue"—suggests to me that the meaning was "pallid, ashen, leaden."

The lexicographer Frank Abate, former editor in chief of American dictionaries for Oxford University Press, disagrees: "The idea of 'pale' in the *OED* seems to me to be misleading. The image I have is that of a violently angry person, with eyes bulging and a deep reddish color in the face—such a deep color that it suggests bluishness." There are usages that treat the word as meaning "black and blue, the color of bruises," and a furious person has long been said to get "blue in the face."

Fred Shapiro of Yale reports that "the contexts of the many early uses I have examined make it clear that the color associated with the state of *livid* anger is a pale one." His citation of Arthur Conan Doyle's 1890 "His swarthy features blanched to a *livid* gray"—with *blanched* meaning "turned white"—clinches the primary meaning for me: "pale, drained of color."

This just in: it may not be a color, or lack of color, at all. The word *livid* has so long been associated with anger that it has lost its coloration and now means "infuriated."

While we're hopping mad, turn to another recent statement of President Clinton that in its expression of irritation touches three dialect bases. Addressing the way the media bash candidates in the current campaign, he observed testily: "I think it's a bunch of *bull*. . . . I do not think America is very well served by all this *rigamarole*. . . . That's a bunch of *hooey*."

Bull, a truncated form of what used to be called "a barnyard epithet," is no longer considered a vulgarism. The animal itself is the acceptable euphemism for its manure. (This has not happened with *chicken* in a similar barnyardism because the name of the animal already has a slang meaning of "cowardly.")

Rigamarole, which added a syllable to the 1736 *rigmarole,* means "incoherent harangue; a lengthy, meaningless procedure or tale." It is derived from *rig-my-role,* which some etymologists say is derived from a *ragman's roll* or backpack containing a variety of unrelated items.

Hooey is a mystery. The synonym for "nonsense, baloney, hogwash" is cited in the *OED* as coined in 1924 in *Plastic Age,* by Percy Marks: "My prof's full of *hooey*. He doesn't know a C theme from an A one." The poet W. H. Auden derided "Lip-smacking Imps of mawk and *hooey,*" and the feminist author Germaine Greer in her 1970 *Female Eunuch* rescued equestrian interests of women from psychological leers with "The horse between a girl's legs is supposed to be a gigantic penis. What *hooey!*"

Clinton's usage echoed that of Harry Truman, who told a 1948 news conference that unless it could be adopted on a national scale, "daylight saving is a lot of *hooey*." Origin obscure. My speculation: *hoo* is a sound made with an exhalation of breath that expresses wonderment or disdain. *Hoo-boy!* Don't make such a *hoo-hah*. (This speculation could be a blinding flash of insight, or . . .)

"Hooey" is a vulgar Russian term for the male member: "Na hooey"— meaning, "screw it." "Ne sooey hooey v chai"—loosely meaning "don't screw around"—literally "don't stir the tea with your [male member]."

I especially enjoyed your mention of Germaine Greer's unintentionally ironic, "The horse between a girl's legs is supposed to be a gigantic penis. What hooey!" Because . . . it is!

Dick Wallingford
Napa, California

Coincidentally or not, "hooey" bears a strong resemblance to a Russian vulgarism for the penis, which in Cyrillic would resemble something like хуй *and is transliterated approximately as "khuy." It is used in much the same way as we use "hooey" and worse, as in "nyekhuya nye znayet," which translates quite literally as "He don't know dick."*

Annie Gottlieb
New York, New York

Lockboxing Day.   If any issue dominated the 2000 campaign, it was Social Security; if any cliché dominated, it was "the third rail of American politics"; and if any word was given the glow of energy from that power source, it was *lockbox*.

It landed in the political lexicon in 1995, as House Speaker Newt Gingrich promised that a spending bill would be amended to include what he called "a *lockbox* provision" stipulating that no spending cuts would be used to offset tax reductions. This was purely symbolic because government funds are fungible.

Bill Archer, chairman of the House Ways and Means Committee, used the *lockbox* in 1999: "We created the Social Security *lockbox* to lock that money up so it cannot be spent for anything else." GOP leaders actually used a strongbox as a prop for television coverage.

Bill Clinton promptly adopted the metaphor, leaving the Republicans sputtering. In the 2000 campaign, Al Gore made it central to his stump speech and debate appearances: "I think we need to put Medicare and Social Security in a *lockbox*. The governor"— Bush—"will not put Medicare in a *lockbox*."

The meaning was taken to be "a box with a lock on it; a small safe." The more specific definition is "a safe-deposit box in a bank." Especially in the central states, *lockbox* is an old-fashioned word for "safe-deposit box." A *lockbox* is to a safe-deposit box what an icebox is to a refrigerator.

The origin is "a postal box with a window requiring a key for the postal customer to open." In 1906, Mary E. W. Freeman, in her novel *By the Light of the Soul,* wrote: "She saw one letter slanted across the dusty glass of the box. It was not a *lock box,* and she had to ask the postmaster for the letter."

That is, it was a box unlocked to the postal worker, as distinct from a locked box rented by the customer.

Now, it means, generally, "strongbox," or more specifically, "a political metaphor for a trust fund that cannot be spent for purposes other than specified in the politician's promise."

Lookism.   Communism is all but dead, and socialism is passé. Capitalism is doing fine, but as an attack word it has been replaced by *market economy*. Has the suffix *-ism* lost its sting?

In politics, *ism-itis* is receding, but in reference to forms of discrimination, the beatism goes on. On the analogy of *racism,* a term that began as *racialism* in 1907 but dropped the second syllable in 1935, we have *sexism* (1968) and *ageism* (1969). And now a relatively new entry:

"We face a world," says Nancy Etcoff, a psychologist at Massachusetts General Hospital, "where *lookism* is one of the most pervasive but denied prejudices." She is author of *Survival of the Prettiest;* though her title is Darwinian, her message bewails the evolution of the power of beauty.

Oxford's 1999 *20th Century Words,* by John Ayto, defines *lookism* as "prejudice or discrimination on the grounds of appearance (i.e., uglies are done down and the beautiful people get all the breaks)." The lexicographer's earliest citation was from 1978 in the *Washington Post Magazine,* which reported that fat people coined a defensive word: "*lookism*— discrimination based on looks."

When the GOP candidate George W. Bush flashed a half-smile that struck some as a smirk, he was widely derided for this facial expression. "Bush isn't the only presidential candidate to suffer from this elaborately sanctioned *lookism,*" wrote Julia Keller in the *Chicago Tribune.* "Former Republican hopeful Steve Forbes endured numerous remarks about his blinkless stare . . . while Al Gore has been called 'wooden' so often that he probably measures himself by the board foot."

The word's usage is transatlantic. "*Lookism* is a crime," a writer in London's *Daily Telegraph* observed in 1991, "on the same level as racism, sexism, ageism, heterosexism, classism, etc." In Barre, Maine, last year, a workshop was held on the topic "Today's Pressures: Drugs, Alcohol, Sex and *Lookism.*"

A Reuters reviewer of the new *Oxford Compact English Dictionary* had a bright lead: "So there you are, all decked out in chuddies, carpenters and a shrug with a brand-new buzz cut, and for some reason your best friend refuses to talk to you. It is probably a serious case of *lookism.*"

OK: *chuddies* are underpants, *carpenters* are pants with loops for tools, a *shrug* is a tight-fitting cardigan and a *buzz cut* is a close crew cut. I'll also pass along the OCED's *screenager,* "Internet- or computer-addicted teenager."

The extension of *lookism* is already in circulation: if you call out to someone you consider in any way attractive, "Hey, good-lookin'," you are a *lookist.*

There is no Barre, Maine. There is a Barre, Vermont, a lovely town near Montpelier, a likely site for a drug workshop. Or, there is a Barre, Massachusetts, a village near Worcester. No powwow here.

I'd guess you meant Barre, Vermont!

Dickson Scott
Wallingford, Connecticut

I've always thought that the correct term should be looksism, *since the offense is invidious discrimination on the basis of looks. It was as* looksism *that I first encountered the concept, during the mid-'70s, in the form of a wisecrack by my then wife, Michele Slung, who was doing a "where-will-it-all-end" riff inspired by the proliferation of racism-based grievance words such as "ageism."*

Lookism, strictly speaking, should refer to invidious discrimination on the basis of a look on a person's face. Negative responses to Bush's alleged smirk, Cheney's alleged sneer, Clinton's alleged pout, and Quayle's alleged deer-in-headlights expression would, thus, all fall into the category of lookism. *On the other hand, disliking Lieberman because he's kind of funny-looking, or liking John Kerry because of his Dudley Do-right chin, would be* looksism. *But I guess I'm fighting a losing battle on this one.*

Hendrik Hertzberg

Editor in Chief, *The New Yorker*

New York, New York

You identified blond/blonde *as a potentially new lookism, declaring that* blond *is used "to impute fun-loving characteristics." It is my understanding that* blond/blonde *is the only term in the English language taken directly from the French,* blond *being the masculine,* blonde *the feminine.*

I have several blonde daughters none of whom embody the flightiness implied in your use of the word.

Frank O'Donnell

Rockville Centre, New York

An inveterate ogler is a lookist. *A man who hires a woman because she is pretty should be called a* looksist.

Professor Morton G. Wurtele

Berkeley, California

The suffix "itis" always refers to the presence of an inflammatory condition (e.g., appendicitis: inflammation of the appendix; tonsillitis: inflammation of the tonsil, etc.).

The suffix "osis," on the other hand, merely denotes the presence of a condition (e.g., thyrotoxicosis: the presence of a toxic condition of the thyroid gland; diverticulosis: the presence of pouches known as diverticula in the wall of the intestine . . . if, however, the diverticula become inflamed, we then have diverticulitis).

In your second paragraph, therefore, we should be referring to ism-osis, although I must admit that it can be inflammatory in another sense!

Noel H. Seicol, MD

Rye, New York

Lounge Act.   The opening salvo at the phrase *foreign service* was fired by
Secretary of State Colin Powell. He proposed to strike those words from
the medal established by Congress in 1999 to honor federal employees
killed or injured while serving under chiefs of mission abroad. It was Powell's plan to change the name of "the Foreign Service Star" to "the Thomas
Jefferson Star."

That triggered a protest to the secretary from Marshall P. Adair, president of the outfit that still calls itself the American Foreign Service Association. "I write to express AFSA's strong disagreement," he began, "with
plans . . . to strip the words 'Foreign Service' from the Foreign Service Star."
Like a good diplomat, he suggested a compromise: "The Thomas Jefferson
Star for Foreign Service."

Powell went along with this suggested fallback position, but grudgingly:
in reply, he wanted foreign service officers to know that the medal, a kind
of civilian Purple Heart, was for "recognizing the risks and dangers to *all*
United States government civilians assigned to our embassies and con-
sulates" and not just FSOs alone. That playing down of the phrase *foreign
service* was what civil service employees wanted. (Everybody denies it, but
many civil servants, derogated as bureaucrats by the elite *foreign service*
corps, still refer to the diplomats as *cookie pushers.*)

But in his campaign to expunge *foreign service* from the Foggy Bottom
vocabulary, Powell then went a couple of bridges too far. After seventy-
seven years of referring to "Foreign Service and Civil Service employees" in
official documents, State Department testimony began substituting the
phrase "International Affairs Officer," lumping the two groups together.
And "Foreign Service Day" was mysteriously postponed for renaming.

The spark that ignited the fury of our diplomatic corps—and enlisted
the support of the American Academy of Diplomacy as well as the Council
of American Ambassadors—was an act that offended the dignity and ruf-
fled the feathers of everyone with a pair of striped pants in the closet. The
State Department, protested Adair of the AFS in a follow-up letter to Pow-

ell, "has removed the name '*Foreign Service Lounge*' from that facility (after a half-century of usage)."

And what was the former *Foreign Service Lounge*, whose name recalls the camaraderie and easing of tensions of generations of diplomats, to be called? It would be rechristened the *Employee Service Center*.

"Some foreign service officers believe the new name has the charm of an auto repair shop," wrote Steven Mufson of the *Washington Post*, who broke the story and fingered Patrick Kennedy, assistant secretary for administration, as the perpetrator of the name change. Others did not like the implicit put-down in *employee*; I am told that others hypersensitive to harassment found a barnyard allusion to the verb meaning of *service* in the new title.

With his left flank crumbling, Powell pulled back. He explained that his onetime use of "international affairs officers" was merely "to shorten the sentence in which the phrase appeared" and denied that he was trying to merge the two services. As for the former *Foreign Service Day*, he thought it would "enhance teamwork" to be more inclusive and invite the civil servants.

"Assistant Secretary Kennedy did change the name from '*Foreign Service Lounge*' to '*Employee Service Center*,' " he confirmed. "His motive was to update the name from something that connotes a bar or rest area to an accurate reflection of what the area truly is—i.e., a center that provides services for all employees."

Now to the crux of the controversy, in which lexicologists can elbow aside diplomatists: Is the noun *lounge* taken to mean *cocktail lounge*, denoting "bar"—that is, a place where alcoholic beverages are served, life histories are recounted to bartenders and singles mingle and tingle? Does it also connote, in Powell's genteel usage, "rest area" (derived from *restroom*, euphemism for "toilet, loo, lavatory" or "baby changing-room")? Or is it just a place in which to sit around, to loll about dreamily or, in more up-to-date parlance, to hang out?

In the language of languor, *lounge* leads all the lollygagging. The intransitive (very inactive) verb is from the 15th-century Scottish dialect noun *lungis,* meaning "laggard, lingerer," rooted in the Latin *Longinus,* the apocryphal name of the soldier who lanced Jesus in the side, and was influenced by *longus,* "long," associated with "slow." The easygoing verb is defined in the *OED* as "to move indolently, resting between-whiles or leaning on something for support," which grew out of an earlier meaning, "to skulk, to slouch."

The noun has come to be the place (or piece of furniture) in which this sort of leaning or reclining position is taken. In Richard Brinsley Sheridan's 1775 play *The Rivals,* Mr. Fag describes the city of Bath as "a good *lounge.*" In 1927, Ernest Hemingway noted "the cocktail hour," which Graham Greene in 1939 placed in a "cocktail *lounge.*" A decade later, *Time* magazine reported the "metamorphosis of the old-fashioned corner saloon into the modern, glittering cocktail *lounge.*"

Thus, Powell's concern for the controversial connotation of conspicuous conviviality is correct. The noun *lounge* reeks of booze, as any visitor to the United Nations Delegates' *Lounge* in New York can testify. Less justifiable for the name change at Foggy Bottom is the connotation of "toilet." To call a restroom a *lounge* is to euphemize euphemism, to touch up the painting of the lily. Few people ask, "Which way to the *lounge?*" They prefer, "Is there somewhere I can wash my hands?" or "Whereza john?"

You don't hear about *lounge lizards* anymore. That was a World War I derogation of lizard-lidded gigolos who hung about chichi bars and nightclubs in search of rich women to seduce and bilk. The phrase had a nice alliterative ring to it. Its nearest replacement today is directed to the position rather than the purpose of the lounging: *couch potatoes.* At the Department of State, they can be found staring at the screen in the Employee Service Center.

Have you observed yet another use of the word "lounge"? It is incorrectly, though appropriately, used to name the piece of furniture, the seat of which extends several feet. Thus, chaise longue *has become, except for the very few purists,* chaise lounge.

Madeline Hamermesh
Minneapolis, Minnesota

I was in the automobile business (sales) for several years. Anyone who would drive onto the new or used car lot and cruise around without getting out of their car, just to check what was for sale without daring to make an overture of any kind of interest by setting foot on the ground, was known as a lot lizard *(the bane of all car salesmen).*

John S. Wilkins
Rosepine, Louisiana

M-commerce.　Lord knows, this department tries to keep up. But no sooner is the letter *e* fixed firmly in my mind in all its permutations as the key to the new electronic world (*e-commerce, e-mail, e-whatever*) than along come the jargoneers of digitese with another letter to thrust it aside. Here comes *m-commerce*.

M is not for the million things your mother gave you, as the old song went. Rather, it stands for *mobile;* as the Internet speeds up transactions, mobility is where it's at. (And *where it's at* is no longer where it's at, either; I am on the lookout for the latest phrase for what the French still call *au courant*.)

"*M-commerce* is *e-commerce* that's done over mobile phones and other hand-held digital devices like personal digital assistants," writes the *Business Times of Singapore*. "It covers buying and selling everything from stocks to flowers, using handphones and PDA's." (Just be careful of chewing gum while *m-commercing* on Lee Kwan Yew's tight little island—you could wind up running from a cane.)

Though a British outfit named Logica claims coinage in 1997, the locution is now coming on stream. "Just when the language has begun to absorb the letter 'e' as a prefix," notes Katie Hafner in the *New York Times*, "comes the latest twist on electronic money and the language of the digital age: mobile commerce, or *m-commerce*, which promises to turn your cell phone or hand-held organizer into an electronic wallet." She quotes Richard Siber of Andersen Consulting as foreseeing the day when "*m-commerce* will be bigger than *e-commerce.*"

Dunno 'bout that. (That's how impatient e-mail writers, rat-tat-tat just-like-that, express "I am not so sure that linguistic prediction is well founded." That may bring in a lot of *m-mail,* a locution coined right here and now.) Both phrases use *commerce* as the suffix; *electronic,* the source for the *e*-prefix, is a more general term than *mobile* and may subsume it. Thus we would have "mobile electronic commerce" as against stationary electronic commerce (the sort you're involved with when ordering kiwiburgers while parked), but that would bring us *m-e commerce,* too late for the "me generation."

The key to mobile electronic commerce, as I get it, is the ability to peddle while pedaling, or to buy on the fly. "Rather than stand in front of a soda machine fishing for a dollar bill that is neither too faded nor too wrinkled," writes Hafner, "you may someday simply dial the phone number posted on the machine."

Here my with-it colleague has lapsed into an archaism. *Dial,* the noun, originally meant "the graduated face of a timepiece," as in a sundial, rooted in the Latin for "day." Some of us can remember when the verb to *dial* meant "to turn a disk with numbered finger holes." This verb was generalized, as linguists like Sol Steinmetz say, into touching the numbers on a touch-tone phone that has no dial. (Another such new generalization is to *bookmark,* which meant "to place a marker in a book" but which has a newer sense of "to mark the address of a Web site.")

Will the archaism to *dial* persevere in a dial-free age? Will we long refer to digits on the broadcast spectrum as "on your radio dial"? Will marketers of the deodorant soap have to rename their product? My guess is the verb will be replaced not by *punch, poke* or *jab,* which suggest dialing in anger, but by *key, press* or *tip,* as in "fingertip." We are likely to *tip in* rather than dial the numbers. (Where am I? Back to the future.)

In a recent conversation in advanced digit-English with the *Times'* new-media guru, Martin Nisenholtz, CEO of Times Company Digital, I was told that my column might someday, in audio or video form, be part of *streaming media.* That was satisfying; I like my prose to go with the flow. Writing in a 1995 *Interactive Age* (you were expecting maybe Intrapassive Era?), Richard Karpinski defined *streaming media* as delivering "audio and video on demand, rather than requiring a user to download a file off the Web and play it back from a local drive." In that way, the simultaneous display and transfer of sound and image can be watched and heard as the data flows in.

And now for some *shovelware.* A word association with *streaming media* leaps to mind: *screaming meemies.* This expression, origin obscure, was first defined in the *New Republic* in 1927 as a synonym for *drunkenness.* It soon came to mean "hysterics" like those in subsequent DTs, or delirium tremens. In World War II, allied soldiers applied it to the *Nebelwerfer,* a German multibarreled rocket mortar that went off with a series of high-pitched sounds.

Shovelware, according to Eric Raymond's Jargon File, is "a slipshod compilation of software dumped onto a CD-ROM without much care for organization or even usability." Its source, I recall vividly, is the newspaper term "editing with a shovel," applied to editors who fail to trim copy of extraneous paragraphs used by lazy writers who have a certain space to fill. It's nice to see that the old "slug it 'Slay' " lingo has found a place in the streaming, screaming media-meemie language of technology.

Your poor old mother probably worked hard enough trying to make a nice person out of you already, without adding to her burden.

If you are going to quote old tunes, get 'em right.

"M" is for the many things she gave you. Not "million." How busy could she have been? Nit nit nit nit nit nit nit nit nit nit. (Choose one.)

Bill Richards
Queensbury, New York

Millenarian.   On the subject of Greek coinage and the Espy playfulness: what shall we call a person who has lived in the second millennium?

"*Duomillenarian* has wrong connotations," replies Frederic G. Cassidy,* chief editor of the *Dictionary of American Regional English*, and "Greek is better in any case as more classical." So with *DARE*'s classicist, George Goebel, the great lexicographer turned from Latin to Greek: *deutero* means "second" and *chiliast* refers to the biblical "kingdom of a thousand years."

Thus, *deuterochiliast*, "a person of, or anything characteristic of, the second millennium." Drop this coinage in a conversation; see if it clanks.

Mine Run.   Writing for the majority in a Supreme Court decision early this year, Justice Ruth Bader Ginsburg used a phrase about a Missouri judicial rule dealing with continuances: "like the *mine run* of procedural rules." Steve Allen of Jersey City notes that *mine run* was used four times in recent years, three by Ginsburg, one by Chief Justice Rehnquist, and wonders, What does it mean?

The lexicographer David Barnhart spotted a 1994 use in the American Lawyer Newspapers Group—"in the '*mine run*' of cases"—and James A. Landau, a computer engineer who lives in Linwood, New Jersey, finds a recent citation of "ordinary, *mine-run* politicians" and adds, "You really ought to look up Robert E. Lee's celebrated victory over the Union on Dec. 2, 1863."

This variant of *run of the mill* and *run of the kiln* came out of the bituminous coal industry. *Mine run*, like its cousins, is an extraordinary way of saying "ordinary." The *run* means "normal course," a metaphoric extension of "stream, running brook," like *Bull Run*, or the stream west of Chancellorsville, Virginia, that is a tributary of the Rapidan, where Union forces under Maj. Gen. George Meade took a long look across *Mine Run* and decided not to launch an attack against the Confederates. Northerners characterize the "battle of *Mine Run*" as "inconclusive"; Southerners treat it as a victory.

*Frederic Cassidy, *DARE*'s magnificent dialectologist and lexicographer, died June 14, 2000.

I suspect that *mine run* has gripped the legal profession because it is not as drearily ordinary as *run of the mill.*

Mole.   In pursuit of the nuances of spookspeak, the arcane language of the intelligence "community," I have been in correspondence with Aldrich Ames. He was the classic *mole:* a CIA employee secretly in the pay of the Soviet Union. His spying for cash led to Moscow Central's execution of a dozen American sources.

"*Mole* is the best example of jargon created by literary or journalistic use," Ames writes from his cell in the Allenwood Federal Penitentiary in White Deer, Pennsylvania. "Whether or not SIS [the Senior Intelligence Service] ever used it, it gradually entered use in the American community from John le Carré's novels."

A few weeks ago, the FBI arrested another American espionage official and accused him of serving for nine years as a KGB *mole* in its ranks. In an affidavit supporting the arrest warrant for Robert Hanssen, the Feds included a glossary of intelligence terms; though the government lexicographers did not dare to deal with terms as colorful as *mole,* they subtly corrected a recent error in this space. I had defined SCIF as an acronym for "secret compartmented information facility," a room sealed and secured from prying eyes and ears. Got the *S* wrong; change that "secret" to "sensitive."

An *agent in place* or *recruitment in place,* swears the FBI (an affidavit is, by definition, sworn; I swear by my definitions, too), is "a person who remains in a position while acting under the direction of a hostile intelligence service, so as to obtain current intelligence information." The glossary differentiates this from an *illegal,* "who operates in a foreign country in the guise of a private person and is often present under false identity."

Hanssen is accused of being an *agent in place,* as Ames was, who utilized a *dead drop,* defined by the FBI as "a prearranged hidden location used for the clandestine exchange . . . which avoids the necessity of an intelligence officer and an agent being present at the same time." (A *dead drop* is a noun phrase; *drop-dead* is a compound adjective and is not spookspeak unless in a formulation like "Mata Hari took the SCI document to her *dead drop* in a *drop-dead* dress.") When the location is marked by a chalk mark or piece of tape, it is considered "loaded" with stolen data or payment for same and becomes a *signal site*.

A double agent is said by the FBI to be an agent "engaged in clandestine activity for two or more intelligence services who provides information about one service to another." In his letter from Allenwood, Rick Ames offered a subtler definition: "A double agent may be of two sorts: one who was a bona fide agent of an espionage service but who was *turned, tumbled* or recruited by another without the first service's knowledge or one who falsely gains the trust of an espionage service in order to serve another. A *dangle* would be of the latter sort, one who volunteers, walks in or brings himself attractively to the attention of the target service."

I had asked Ames for the etymology of *wet work*. "This is a literal translation of the GRU/NKVD [former Soviet intelligence agencies] jargon for 'killing'—assassination or elimination of people by murder. It's never been used as CIA jargon, since no comparable operational programs existed. The closest to it would be *executive action*, under which assassination, physical violence of some sort or other extreme (and highly compartmented) action could be carried out."

What about the fearsome euphemism *termination with extreme prejudice*? "The phrase *termination with prejudice* has nothing to do with extreme actions (ditto for *extreme prejudice*)," he notes, "but merely with the discharge of an agent and a notation not to rehire."

There goes a nicely sinister phrase back into bureaucratic limbo.

What about *traces*? "The idea here is the product of an inquiry to a database," Ames writes, "traditionally a card index in which the cards contain information on persons or things and usually a cross-reference to documents and files from which the index cards were prepared. *Trace* as espionage jargon surely was adapted from similar usages in the wider world: *skip trace*, or lest we forget Mr. Keene, tracer of lost persons."

(*Skip trace* is the method of tracking down a missing person—one who has "skipped," or run away—by checking credit-card and hotel-registration records, as in "the girl in the *drop-dead* dress at the *dead drop* hired Mr. Keene to put in a *skip trace* to find the deadbeat dad." My age group shares with Ames the memory of Mr. Keene, a radio character in the '40s who came on between *Jack Armstrong, the All-American Boy* and *The Green Hornet.*)

And what of the linguistic workings of Hanssen's mind, beyond the confines of spookspeak? If the file of correspondence between accused spy and Kremlin control is authentic, we have Hanssen writing to the KGB, "I have proven *inveterately* loyal."

Inveterate, its root the same as *veteran*'s, has a historical sense of "long-standing" but with a sinister connotation: Shakespeare's Richard II was assured of "no *inveterate* malice," and John Milton in 1645 questioned those who "grow *inveterately* wicked." Even today, the synonyms are "obstinate, habitual, malignant, hardened." Unless Hanssen was being exquisitely subtle about the evil empire for which he is charged with spying, he should not have modified *loyal* with *inveterately*.

Worse, the accused spy is an *inveterate* mixer of metaphor. "So far," reads his purported letter to the KGB, "my ship has successfully navigated the slings and arrows of outrageous fortune." The last seven words are from Hamlet's "To be or not to be" soliloquy, wholly out of sync with the navigation of a ship. Literate spooks saw a sea of troubles in that; Hanssen would more suitably have navigated Scylla and Charybdis.

However, in sending a warning to his Moscow handlers about the FBI's closing in on Felix Bloch, an American diplomat suspected of somewhat clumsily spying for the Russians, Hanssen wrote with dialectical accuracy, "Bloch was such a *shnook*. . . . I almost hated protecting him."

Synonymous with *jerk* or the more recent *nerd, shnook* is an Americanized Yiddishism probably derived from the German *Schnucke,* "a small or weak sheep." (Hanssen, Leo Rosten and I all spell it without the *c.*)

Shnook is not proper spookspeak and surely confused the KGB control in charge of the *mole.* Unless, of course, some skilled dialectologist in the KGB concocted the file in order to place Hanssen in our hands as a grand *dangle,* but that is what spookspeak calls *sickthink.*

I do not believe you are correct in placing Mr. Keene between Jack Armstrong and the Green Hornet. When I grew up in the thirties, it was Jack Armstrong, Little Orphan Annie, and Superman that I listened to. Mr. Keene was for adults, and would have been post-dinner fare. However, since by the forties I was into baseball and disdaining of those kids' shows and Mr. Keene, I have no proof you are wrong (hence my use of the word "believe" above).

I also believe that you were stretching in describing Mata Hari as "going to a dead drop in a drop-dead dress." Why would she want to attract the attention of every slobbering agent in the country while she was doing her dirty work? Ordinary clothing would have been far more effective.

George Gerson
Westfield, New Jersey

"SIS," as used by Aldrich Ames and quoted in your column, does not stand for "Senior Intelligence Service." It stands for "Secret Intelligence Service," the British agency more widely known as "MI6."

In spook history, it also stands for (a) the Special Intelligence Service of the FBI, the WWII American overseas intelligence service in the Western Hemisphere; (b) the Signal Intelligence Service, the communications intelligence service of the United States Army; (c) Servizio Informazioni Segrete, the intelligence service of the Italian Navy.

Thaddeus Holt
Former Undersecretary of the Army
Point Clear, Alabama

A second column on spookspeak, and I'm happy to see my rather gray comments were of some use to you. And I'm sure you're accustomed to your correspondents' endless follow-ups!

I didn't spell out SIS, unfortunately, it's Secret Intelligence Service. Over there, the "Senior Service" is the Royal Navy (and I can't resist the echo of "Silent Service" for the submariners in the U.S. Navy).

My handwriting is at fault at another point. You quote me on a double agent as "one who was turned, tumbled or recruited." I meant my scribble to read "doubled." But "tumbled" is very nice, indeed, a serendipitous discovery which would be a lively addition to the jargon. If you're working on another spy novel, maybe you can help it along.

Secret, special and sensitive are adjectives beloved of espionage bureau-crats. They allow boxes of organizational charts representing unmentionable functions to be given names. (Angleton's CI staff [James J. Angleton and CIA counterintelligence] was a prolific user.) So when you see the "S," be careful.

As I re-read my comments on "wet work," I wonder if you've already heard protests about my phrase, "since no comparable operations [CIA] pro-grams existed." It's my belief that the agency's assassinations have always been ad hoc efforts, organized usually at the behest of policymakers above the agency—and usually unsuccessful. I suppose I would be a bit less shocked to-day were we to learn otherwise, than I was in the early '70s by the ad hoc op-erations. I had been assured for years, secretly and solemnly by senior and working-level agency officers, that while accidents and violent political events can kill, the agency had not and would not embark on an assassina-tion.

The "in place" term is rather old-fashioned; we must remember that the FBI is a counterespionage service, and picks up espionage jargon only at sec-ond hand and often not quite with the same understanding (I should say that the FBI has a really fine and vivid jargon of its own). "In place" origi-nated as a way of contrasting an agent with a defector. "Defector in place" or even "to defeat someone in place" was common usage in the late '50s and into the '60s, but is pretty much dead today. But the "in place" was attractive because it suggested that the agent was where the action was, inside an insti-tutional target. "Penetration agent" is a good variant on this idea. But at this point I am trying your patience, so will close.

Aldrich Ames
White Deer, Pennsylvania

The Yiddishism shnook is not derived from German Schnucke, "a small or weak sheep." This derivation, from Rosten's The Joys of Yiddish, is wrong, as Rosten himself acknowledged in his later book, Hooray for Yiddish! Yiddish

shnuk means, "an elephant's trunk, a snout." And the transferred sense of
"jerk" is a slangy American innovation.

Sol Steinmetz
New Rochelle, New York

Moral Clarity.   "No great nation can abandon the obligations of *moral clarity*," said Senator John McCain last month, "for the convenience of situational ethics." In his speech to the American Israeli Political Action Committee, he repeated the phrase *moral clarity* three times. (McCain's speech led with "There'll always be an Israel," a paraphrase of the 1939 song by Ross Parker and Hugh Charles, "There'll Always Be an England.")

This followed some 1,100 hits on *moral clarity* in the Dow Jones database over the past twenty-two years, almost 550 since September 11. On the morning after the Qaeda attacks, the phrase appeared in the monthly column written by Robert Kagan, the hard-liner at the Carnegie Endowment for International Peace, in the *Washington Post*. Kagan said he hoped that Americans would respond to the attacks "with the same *moral clarity* and courage as our grandfathers did."

Later that day, William Bennett, conservative author of *The Death of Outrage*, used the phrase five times in an interview with Chris Matthews on MSNBC's *Hardball*, beginning with "This is a moment for *moral clarity*." (Six months later, it appeared as the subtitle of Bennett's new book, *Why We Fight: Moral Clarity and the War on Terrorism*.) Charles Krauthammer's column in the *Washington Post* the week after the attacks was headlined "We Need *Moral Clarity*" because, he wrote, "we are already beginning to hear the voices of moral obtuseness." The voice he had in mind was Susan Sontag's in the *New Yorker*, where Sontag denounced those writers outraged by the terrorist attack for what she called their "self-righteous drivel."

As these usages show, the ringing phrase *moral clarity* has a clearly conservative political coloration. The *Chicago Tribune* noted that White House officials saw President George W. Bush's plain talk about "evildoers" as a virtue: "He is bringing '*moral clarity*' to a convoluted world, aides said, just as President Ronald Reagan did when he declared the Soviet Union an 'evil empire.' "

Democratic Senator Joe Lieberman agreed last month that Bush "has brought a *moral clarity* to the conflict we are in." However, by pressuring Israel "not to do exactly what we ourselves have done to fight terror in Afghanistan, . . . I'm sorry to say the Bush administration has recently muddied our *moral clarity*."

(A tangent: Lieberman's prepared text reads *muddied;* many newspaper accounts of the speech reported his verb as *muddled*. He may have used both, at different times. To *muddy*, from the metaphor of beclouding clear water with earth, thereby to make turbid and obscure vision, now has the extended sense of "to confuse." To *muddle*, with the same origin, has a more Mr. Magoo-like quality, defined in the *Oxford English Dictionary* as "to busy oneself in a confused, unmethodical and ineffective manner." End tangent.)

The earliest use of the phrase *moral clarity* I can find is by the University of Chicago philosophy professor James Hayden Tufts, who said in a 1934 speech to the American Philosophical Association that "the law is often thought to be the most conservative of institutions. It is necessarily conservative, for it uses compulsion and therefore may well hesitate to move in advance of general *moral clarity*." The phrase was picked up in the '80s and increased in usage in the next decade. The *Times* columnist Maureen Dowd, describing the pope's meeting in 1999 with President Clinton, observed that the pontiff may have received a public-opinion boost from the president: "*Moral clarity* is all well and good, but you've got to keep those poll numbers up."

Bennett defined the phrase to a pro-Israel crowd in Washington as "seeing things for what they truly are. It requires the understanding of distinctions . . . between a democracy fighting for its survival and its opponents fighting to push that democracy into the sea. . . . It means the time for *moral equivocation* and *moral equivalence* should be over."

Just as Krauthammer used *moral obtuseness* as the direct opposite of today's phrase under study, Bennett used *moral equivalence* scornfully, dismissing the term as an obfuscator of clarity. This phrase originated in

William James's 1906 speech about the need to find what he titled "The *Moral Equivalent* of War." His point was that mankind needed a new outlet for combat, and he suggested an "equivalent discipline"— conscription of men into universal nonmilitary service to "coal and iron mines, to freight trains, to fishing fleets in December, to dishwashing"—to "get the childishness knocked out of them, and to come back into society with healthier and soberer ideas." James's purpose, as he wrote to H. G. Wells that year, was to cure "the *moral flabbiness* born of the exclusive worship of the bitch-goddess success. That—with the squalid cash interpretation put on the word *success*—is our national disease."

Since then, James's idealistic phrase has pejorated to mean "with no distinction between right and wrong, between the unpleasant and the horrific or between aggressor and victim," and as such has become a favorite whipping-phrase of the political right.

I checked with William F. Buckley, who helped popularize the current sense of the phrase, and the inventor of modern conservatism reports: "*Moral equivalence* is a handy imposture by which behavior and misbehavior are equated. Some years ago I made the point after an 'antiwar' demonstration by the American left. The demonstrators were arguing that Ronald Reagan's defense budget was the equivalent of Mikhail Gorbachev's. I said that that was like saying that the man who pushed old ladies out of the way of an oncoming bus is like the man who pushes old ladies into the way of an oncoming bus. Both push old ladies around."

Then there is *moral relativism*. Its advocates describe it as a view that moral standards are grounded in social custom, varying from culture to culture, while its critics call it loosey-goosey moralism incapable of deciding that such institutions as slavery are wrong.

A *moral certainty* has nothing to do with morality; it means "high probability." To use it in a sentence: The continued clash between *moral clarity* and its antonyms—*moral relativity* and *moral equivalency*—is a *moral certainty*.

We certainly enjoyed your piece on equivalence and relative-ness. The subject can certainly stand more clarity and you did it proud with all the refer-

ences to the clarity and mud of Lieberman, Kagan, Bush, Krauthammer, Clinton and William James.

But we do wonder whether you clarified or muddied the waters with your use of an unknown form of "pejorative"—pejorated. Since Merriam-Webster does not provide any verbal form of pejorative—or are you now manufacturing for us a new verbal form to demoralize the right/wrong distinction we conservatives demand? Maybe you have to get Bill Buckley's acquiescence before we start pejorating?*

> Ben and Doris Haskel
> Chevy Chase, Maryland

❦

McCain the Antonymist.   Who wins the language maven's award for the most effective use of semi-antonymy in the primary campaign to date? Push the envelope, please.

The winner is Senator John McCain, for an apparently offhand statement made aboard his campaign bus, the Straight Talk Express, rolling through South Carolina. According to Edward Walsh of the *Washington Post,* McCain said that among Republicans, he is "not trying to appeal to the *disaffected.* I'm trying to appeal to the *disenchanted.*"

What's the difference? Plenty.

Disaffected means "ill disposed, unfriendly, inimical." The core of the word is *affect,* same as in *affection;* the usual sense is "to lose affection for."

A more extreme sense, used more in law and politics, is "estranged; alienated; resentful; disloyal." Judge Learned Hand, speaking to educators in 1952, deplored an atmosphere "where nonconformity with the accepted creed, political as well as religious, is a mark of *disaffection.*" At a time when charges of Communism were being made, that word was carefully chosen to denote a state just one step short of "disloyalty."

Disenchanted, though not the opposite, is markedly different. It evokes the ancient breaking of a magical spell, and is a calibration stronger than

---

*Buckley and I stick together.—W.S.

"disillusioned." In its verb form, to *disenchant* means "to free from an often false belief."

Thus, McCain rejected any characterization of those Republicans to whom he was appealing as "unfriendly" or "disloyal" to the GOP; on the contrary, he saw these potential supporters as people disillusioned with the current leadership—let down by political dealing—but whom he could bring back into the fold, their faith restored. A key meaning of *disenchant* is "to restore to reality."

This careful contradistinction of *disaffected* and *disenchanted* could not have been conceived by McCain off the cuff. I suspect a skillful speech-writer at work and hereby put my dibs on the first interview if he or she makes it to the White House.

There's a related word for that mystery ghost to think about: *disenthrall*. That poetic verb has a more active and positive connotation than *disenchant* and has historic resonance; it was last used in politics with great effect by Abraham Lincoln: "As our case is new, so we must think anew, and act anew. We must *disenthrall* ourselves, and then we shall save our country."

What you say about the meaning of enchanted *is etymologically true, but the element of magic spell and illusion that you stress has pretty well sunk out of sight in common use of the term. When one is enchanted one is not deceived. An enchanting person, landscape, work of art radiates true delight. On being introduced to someone in France, one says "Enchanté," which implies no witchcraft on the other's part; it means "delighted."*

The question is whether disenchanted *does imply having been fooled. In some cases it probably does, but it also suggests mere weariness or boredom with the once pleasurable object—or more mature tastes. Besides, the object itself may have changed: a friend behaves badly and one is disenchanted. But that does not mean that the previous enchantment was not based on genuine qualities of mind and heart.*

Jacques Barzun
San Antonio, Texas

The words enthrall *and* disenthrall *have metamorphosed since Lincoln's time. When one now says, "I am enthralled," upon first look at the Acropolis or during a new performance by Alvin Ailey, the meaning is what? Awestruck? Overcome with admiration? The first entry in my dictionary is "captivated; charmed." To be enthralled these days is a good thing.*

In antebellum, enthralled *meant "enslaved." Indeed, a thrall was a person in bondage to another. Lincoln's use of* disenthrall *was dual. Here is a more complete look at the quote:*

> *The dogmas of the past are inadequate to the stormy present. The occasion is piled high with difficulty, and we must rise with the occasion. As our case is new, so we must think anew, and act anew. We must disenthrall ourselves, and then we shall save our country.*

Not only did the president refer to abolition of slavery, but also to the liberation of American social and political thought. Disenthrall *was a perfect choice of words.*

A word with similar changes is captivate. *If you are willing to have a new department for anachronisms, why not one for metamorphisms?* Fabulous *and* fantastic *and* terrific *are all expressions now of satisfaction. Nothing like their original meanings. And my favorite,* hysterical, *used so loosely today as the harmless equivalent of* hilarious.

T. J. Harvey
Huntington Station, New York

Movable Modifier.   Word mavens get a linguistic thrill when a skillful politician manipulates the language with great deftness and an alert reporter catches him at it.

British Prime Minister Tony Blair, maneuvering his way through the sticky wicket of the Middle East, wanted to stress the need to maintain an international coalition, including Arab states, when talking to Israel's Ariel Sharon—while getting an antiterrorism message across to the Palestinians' Yasir Arafat.

Accordingly, he spoke in Jerusalem to Sharon of an "international coalition against terrorism in all its forms" and later the same day, with Arafat in Gaza, spoke of "a coalition against international terrorism." He switched the placement of the adjective *international* from modifying *coalition* (acceptable to the Israelis) to modifying *terrorism* (acceptable to the Palestinians).

"It is a distinction with a difference here," wrote the *New York Times'* Jerusalem bureau chief, James Bennet. "Mr. Sharon and other Israeli officials like to identify their efforts against Palestinians with the American attack on the Taliban," he noted, "and they reject as hair-splitting any distinctions between 'international' terrorism and Palestinian attacks on Israelis. Palestinian officials, of course, prefer not to be lumped in with the Taliban."

Thus, merely by moving his modifier, Blair pleased both camps. To Israelis, his *international* modifying *coalition* included them in, while to Palestinians, his *international* modifying *terrorism* was taken as differentiating their local warfare from the global terrorism of Al Qaeda. Subtle move by the politician, intended not to be noticed; good catch by the reporter.

Mujahedeen.   An Arabic noun that has been bandied about on the front pages in recent years has a meaning and a spelling that often wanders. Who are the *mujahedeen*?

First use I can find in English: "When the question of disbanding the *mujahidin* or 'warriors of the Holy War' arose," noted the *Encyclopædia Britannica* in 1922 in an article about Persia (now Iran), "these soldiers of fortune, for the most part, assumed a menacing attitude and threatened to mutiny unless their exorbitant demands for pay were granted." Fifty years later, greeting President Nixon on a visit to Tehran, the shah of Iran dismissed the noise of demonstrators as "just the shouting of the *mujahadin*"; guided by Muslim clerics, they deposed the shah in 1979.

A *mujahid* is a fundamentalist Muslim fighting what he considers to be a *jihad,* or "holy war," literally "struggle." Why is a *jahid* fighting a *jihad?*

The reason the vowels are transposed is based upon what is called, in Semitic languages, the tri-consonantal root. According to Patrick Clawson of the Washington Institute for Near East Policy, "You take three consonants"—like the *j, h* and *d*—"and play with them. It's like a Latin declension, but with a vengeance."

By the 1950s, the word was used mainly as a collective plural, *mujahedeen*, applied to guerrilla fighters and later to terrorists throughout the Middle East. "To the east of Kabul," wrote the *Observer* in 1979, "the rebel *mujahideen*, or 'holy warriors,' effectively control all but the provincial capital and the major towns."

Nationality is not part of the definition. There were Iraqi *mujahids* fighting in Syria against the Damascus regime, and Iranians who call themselves by that name who shouldered aside the secular Marxist fedayeen; later ejected by Tehran's ayatollahs, some of these Iranian *mujahadin* are now under the protection of Saddam Hussein in Iraq. In 1980, Saddam, not then assuming a religious pose, said: "Those are the ones whom Khomeini calls *mujahadin*. Those so-called *mujahadin* are traitors."

Because it is a transliteration of the Arabic, the various local assemblages of what some of us call terrorists are spelled *mujahadeen/mujahadin /mujahideen/mujahadein/mujahedeen/mujahidin*. All are correct. The Library of Congress likes *mujahidin;* the *Times* prefers *mujahedeen*.

Mushy.   With Valentine's Day bearing down on us, you need to know the difference between the pronunciation of *mushy* as *mooshy* (with the first syllable rhyming with *whoosh*) and *mushy* (with the first syllable rhyming with *hush*).

The *mooshy* locution does not concern lovers. In current usage, the adjective means "pulpy, mealy," an onomatopoeic alteration of the noun *mash*, a thick, boiled cereal. Mark Twain, in his 1880 *A Tramp Abroad*, used that *mooshy* sense in writing of "*mushy*, slushy early spring roads."

That meaning, metaphorically extended, landed—plop!—in the middle of political terminology as a derogation of moderation. Theodore Roosevelt in 1900 derided "the *mushy* class" with its "wild and crude plans of social reformations." Nearly a century later, Governor George W. Bush said, "I'm skeptical about a national test which the federal government could use to promote a feel-good curriculum or *mushy* curriculum."

Senator Chuck (what kind of name is that for a serious senator?) Hagel said approvingly of Senator Joe Lieberman's partisan oratory in the 2000 campaign that his was "not a faint-of-heart, kind of *mushy* middle role." Afterward, Senator John Kyl predicted that the Bush cabinet would include "a lot of nominees from the *mushy* middle."

That's how *mushy* as *mooshy* developed from "a soft mass" to "soft on the masses"—undefined, imprecise, fuzzy-edged.

On the other hand, *mushy*, pronounced with an *uh*, is back in vogue among lovers. It means "romantic, sentimental, tender." After an explosion that introduces potential lovers in the 1994 movie *Speed*, the female character says: "You're not going to get *mushy* on me, are you? . . . Relationships that start under intense circumstances, they never last." In 1998 grand jury testimony, Monica Lewinsky said that she gave an antique book to the president along with "an embarrassing, *mushy* note." Last year, David Brooks of the *Weekly Standard* described the conclave that nominated George W. Bush as "a lovey-dovey, *mushy* convention." *Time* magazine writes that in the current movie *What Women Want*, Mel Gibson, a star who often plays tough-guy roles, "learns to get *mushy*."

The romantic sense of the word can cross the border into sloppy sentimentality. The novelist Henry Miller wrote in 1927 of "*mushing* it up in a corner," and a character in Saul Bellow's 1952 *The Adventures of Augie March* spoke of "the kind who'd never . . . let you stick around till 1 a.m. *mushing* with them on the steps." Rob Long, a screenwriter, reviewed a Fox Television "reality" series last month and asked, "How gooey-*mushy* could they really be, deep down, if they're willing to head off to Temptation Island to test-drive their monogamy?"

One who overdoes tenderness is called a *mushball*, which has replaced the earlier *mushhead*. In the Arctic, husky sled dogs that hear their drivers urge them on with a shout of "*Mush!*" know that the command is not an endearment but a corruption of the French "*Marche!*"—meaning "Move on!"

Those poets and pundits tiring of the voguish *mushy* in its meaning of "excessively sentimental" might try the Briticism *soppy,* which means "dreamily silly" or "emotionally overboard," as in this recent *Times of London* assessment of "canine and feline transition" in Washington: "Mr. Bush genuinely seems to be as *soppy* about animals as any of his predecessors."

The synonymy of such lovesick sappiness: *mawkish* is unpleasantly insipid; *maudlin* is teary (an alteration of the weeping penitent Mary Magdalene); *gushy* is prone to pour out torrents of flattery; *schmaltzy* is cornball; *gooey* implies a substance or emotion both sticky and slithery; *squishy-soft* is moistly weak; *bathetic,* from the Greek *bathos* ("depth"), coined on the analogy of *pathos* to *pathetic,* connotes both triteness and insincerity.

Does this mean we should treat the sweetly sentimental *mushy* with scorn or cynicism? Of course not; we should never forget the gentle quality of romance long attached to the word, at least when pronounced with an *uh.* But let's not overdo the sentiment; a touch of tartness helps the saccharine go down. As Al Capone's men said to the members of Bugs Moran's gang before lining them up and letting them have it in a Chicago garage, a Happy St. Valentine's Day to all.

Another mush with political overtones is polenta, *which is how Mario Cuomo described Walter Mondale. The* American Heritage Dictionary, *3rd edition notes the word* polenta *as being of Italian origin and defines it as "a thick mush made of cornmeal and boiled in water or stock." Cuomo, as I recall, went to his ethnic roots to describe Mondale's blandness.*

Gary Muldoon
Rochester, New York

My . . . What?   How do you start a speech if you're president?

My countrymen was the standard opening of a presidential address for generations. But that was back in the days when *men* were men—that is, when *man* embraced womankind and before both mankind and womankind became *humankind.*

Some speakers chose *My fellow countrymen,* even though John Witherspoon in 1781 denounced that as "an evident tautology" and advised, "You may say fellow citizens, fellow soldiers, fellow subjects, fellow Christians, but not *fellow countrymen.*" If a member of the Judson Welliver Society of former White House speechwriters were writing an opening for Mark Antony today, it would have to be "Friends, Romans, fellow citizens"— perhaps followed by the nonmetaphoric "lend me your auditory facility."

My friends was a salutation that got Horatio Seymour, governor of New York, into trouble when he used it to address draft rioters in 1863. But when Franklin D. Roosevelt began using it in 1910, in a campaign for the New York State Senate, it became his signature opening and is still closely associated with him as a verbal handshake at the start of his series of radio "fireside chats." (FDR did not, as legend has it, use *My fellow immigrants* in addressing the Daughters of the American Revolution.)

Abraham Lincoln also used *My friends* in saying farewell to his neighbors in Springfield but used no salutation at the dedication of the cemetery at Gettysburg; that decision was appropriate to the occasion's solemnity. In his second Inaugural Address, Lincoln used *Fellow countrymen,* the anti-redundancy Witherspoon to the contrary notwithstanding.

In his farewell address, President Clinton saluted his audience with *My fellow citizens,* his most frequently chosen salutation, consciously following the one chosen by Thomas Jefferson in his first Inaugural Address. Clinton also often used *My fellow Americans,* but that, like *fellow citizens,* seems to ignore the global audience. John Kennedy handled that problem nicely in his Inaugural Address with *"My fellow citizens of the world,* ask not what America will do for you. . . ."

Moving past the salutation, the farewell addresser must pass two tests: first, to exhibit none of the bitterness he feels toward his carping critics, and second, to say good-bye. George Washington almost failed the first; Bill Clinton finessed the second.

In the first draft of his farewell in 1796, written in his own hand on May 15 and sent to Alexander Hamilton for his review, President Washington gave vent to his feelings about the Anti-Federalist press: "As some of the Gazettes of the United States have teemed with all the Invective that disappointment, ignorance of facts and malicious falsehoods could invent," wrote our nation's preeminent founding father, "to misrepresent my politics and affections; to wound my reputation and feelings; and to weaken, if not entirely to destroy the confidence you had been pleased to repose in me; it might be expected at the parting scene of my public life that I should take some notice of such virulent abuse. But, as heretofore, I shall pass them over in utter silence."

That is an example of *paraleipsis,* the rhetorical technique of pointing something out by asserting you will not point it out, often preceded by the phrase "not to mention." Critics like the pamphleteer James Thomson Callender (secretly subsidized by the Anti-Federalist Thomas Jefferson) evidently infuriated Washington.

Hamilton, who had been G.W.'s wartime aide-de-camp and later his treasury secretary, reacted as a faithful speechwriter should. He sent a fresh draft of a farewell address back to Washington, leaving out the anti-press diatribe. The president, with his true feelings off his chest, agreed to the excision and is not remembered for what he did not say.

Washington's contribution to presidential inaugurals came after the oath itself: the emphatic "so help me God." That is not in the oath prescribed in the Constitution; it was added by Washington. Ever since that first inauguration, the chief justice doing the swearing-in has had to ask the president-elect beforehand if he wanted to repeat Washington's addition. All have, with the possible exception of Franklin Pierce.

Clinton's farewell had none of G.W.'s first-draft bitterness, though the forty-second president surely felt that there were some vituperative right-wing columnists out, in the framer's phrase, "to wound my reputation and feelings." Even now, in the nostalgic glow of nonpartisanship, I am tempted to point out that, in his otherwise carefully composed self-encomium, Clinton's "working together, America has done well" is a prime example of a dangling modifier. It could be corrected by changing the subject "America" to "Americans" or "the American people," which would be a plural subject that could be "working together." But in the father of our country's para-leiptic tradition, I will pass over this grammatical lapse in utter silence.

In farewell, Washington's draft took his leave with "I leave you with un-defiled hands—an uncorrupted heart—and with ardent vows to heaven." Lincoln, departing Springfield to take up leadership of a country coming apart, more personally noted: "Here my children have been born, and one is buried. I now leave, not knowing when, or whether ever, I may return, with a task before me greater than that which rested upon Washington. Without the assistance of that Divine Being, who ever attended him, I can-not succeed. . . . To His care commending you, as I hope in your prayers you will commend me, I bid you an affectionate farewell." Clinton did not say good-bye at all.

What phrase does a president use to best conclude any speech to the na-tion? "Good night and God bless you" now seems to be the preferred leave-taking, though some might take it as a response to the sneezing of an entire people. Lately, we have been hearing more "God bless you and God bless America," which suggests to some a plug for an Irving Berlin song.

Most Americans take a presidential blessing in stride, but some wonder, What credentials does a secular figure have to give a benediction? Con-trariwise, in any absence of an evocation of the deity at the speech's con-clusion, the more reverent members of the audience may wonder, Why was the blessing left out? What's next—will he strike "In God We Trust" from the nation's coinage?

"Thanks for listening" is not quite right for viewers, and "Thanks for watching" leaves out the radio audience. "Keep those cards and letters coming" is outmoded in an e-mail generation.

How best for a president to wrap up and let the screens go to black? I don't have that answer. Thank you and good night.

Name That Enemy. "Osama bin Laden's organization is called Al-Quaeda," e-mails Michael Klein of New York, "also spelled as Al-Quaida. President Bush pronounces it 'al-KYDE-a'; others pronounce it 'al-KADE-a'; still others pronounce it in four syllables: 'al-ka-EE-da.' Which is correct?"

Al Qaeda (no hyphen, and meaning "the base," or of late, "the headquarters") should be spelled without the *u* after the *q*, thereby giving it a fricative *kh* sound. (We went through this with Ayatollah Khomeini.) The pronunciation bruited about the *New York Times* is "al CAW-id-ah," with a *k* sound, though correspondents who have worked in Arabic-speaking countries use the palate-clearing sound of *kh*.

And while we're at it, the Persian suffix -*stan* in Afghanistan, Pakistan, Uzbekistan, Tajikistan and de facto Kurdistan means "country," from the Indo-Iranian *stanam,* "place" or "where one stands."

A person from Pakistan is called a *Pakistani* and takes umbrage at being called a *Pak* or *Paki*. A person from Afghanistan, however, is called an *Afghan* and would look at you funny if called an *Afghani* or *Afghanistani*.

That is partly because *afghani* is the name of the currency: about 5,000 *afghanis* are worth one dollar, while *Afghan* has the high value placed on any human being (unless you are referring to the rug or the hound). The same shortening—no *i* or *istani*—is OK with Uzbeks, Tajiks and Kurds.

The Pakistanis prefer the long form for the reason usually expressed in the punch line of a joke as "that's the Middle East."

Nameless Event.   The surprise attack on the U.S. fleet in 1941 is remembered by the name of the place where it happened: Pearl Harbor. The bloodiest day in all our wars is also identified by its locale: Antietam creek (though southerners often identify that battle by the nearby town, Sharpsburg, Maryland). The shocking murder of a president is known by its victim: the *Kennedy assassination*.

But what label is applied to the horrific (more horrid than *horrible*, perhaps because of its less frequent use and similarity in emphasis to *terrific*) events of Sept. 11, 2001?

Because the calamities occurred almost simultaneously in two cities, they could not adopt the name of one locality or single structure: taken together, they are not written about in shorthand as the *twin towers destruction* or the *bombing of the Pentagon*. (And *bombing* is a misnomer, since no bomb was dropped.) *Attack* (or *Assault*) *on America* has been a frequent usage, but it seems too general, since Pearl Harbor was also an attack on the United States.

Terrorist massacre is accurate, since *massacre* means "indiscriminate killing of large numbers," but that phrase has not been widely adopted. The *recent tragic events* is euphemistic and antiseptic, and the *catastrophe in New York and Washington* too long.

We may settle on using the date. Just as FDR vividly identified Dec. 7, 1941, as "a date which will live in infamy," many journalists use "ever since Sept. 11" as shorthand for this new date of infamy. (A further shortening is *9/11*, as in "The *New York Times* 9/11 Neediest Fund," which is also a play on the number punched on a telephone keyboard for emergencies.) In time, however, the nation's choice of the date of December 7 was replaced by the location of the disaster, as Americans "remember Pearl Harbor." On that analogy, perhaps a new designation will appear for the disaster that struck an unsuspecting nation now seeking a return to normalcy.

❦

Needing To.   "You *need to* shut up and follow when an order is lawful," said Lt. Col. Martha McSally as she sued the Defense Department for requiring a female fighter pilot to wear a head-to-toe gown off-base in Saudi Arabia. "You *need to* step out when it's unlawful."

Washington's health commissioner felt strongly that it was time to let the public know the degree of ignorance about anthrax: "It's time for us to stop *needing to* say we know," said Dr. Ivan Walker, "and let the people know what we don't know."

And President Bush made official the growing use of this semimodal auxiliary verb with his answer in a news conference: "Anybody who harbors terrorists *needs to* fear the United States."

What's with the new *need* for *need*? We're not talking about the noun, of Teutonic origin associated in Welsh with "starvation"; today, the noun *need* means "a lack of something essential, a desire for a missing necessity." Nor is it the simple transitive verb *need,* as in "I *need* help," that concerns us— that meaning of "have the desire to get what is urgently lacking" is clear enough.

It's the semimodal verb that's on the rise in usage and requires our help. The language has a bunch of short verbs that help determine the timing or character of the action-oriented verbs that follow. These affect the "mode," sometimes confusingly called "mood," of the verb that follows—coloring it as a fact, a possibility or a command. These auxiliary verbs that extend the meaning of the main verbs include *can, may, must, shall* and *will.* (In "I *may* bollix up this explanation," *may* is the modal auxiliary that sets the conditional mode, sometimes called "subjunctive mood," of the verb *bollix,* a verb whose ancient nautical coinage has its genesis in genitals. The other moods are "indicative" for a statement of fact and "imperative" for an order. In grammar, "melancholy" is not a mood.)

But sometimes those out-and-out modals don't quite do the job to clarify or color the meaning of the verb that follows. In "I can see," the modal *can* is ambiguous: it doesn't mean the same in "I *can* see a steeple" as in "I *can* see deficits as far as the eye can see." That's why speakers who want to emphasize *can*'s sense of "ability" choose to substitute the semimodal verb phrase *am able to*. It won't be confused with "know how to" or "is likely to" or "is permitted to"—all different senses in "*Can* I?"

Same with *must,* a modal verb that doesn't always do for *do* what it used to do when bosses were tough: "I must do my homework." In written form, it can be ambiguous: either a firm decision or a wishy-washy "if I don't, I could flunk." That possible misinterpretation of emphasis led to the semimodal *have got to:* there is no mistaking the meaning of "I *have got to* do my homework" (or be expelled, ruined, spat upon and subsequently spend my life miserably flipping burgers).

We're now ready to deal with the semimodal *need to*. "This *need to* is felt to be a stronger, more literal expression of necessity than *must,* which is felt to express less need than strict obligation," says Sol Steinmetz, the great lexicographer and my modal mentor.

But what do people mean when they use the semimodal *need to* today? "Be required to, obligated to"? Or something quite different—"want to, desire to"? Sol says, "One could indeed say 'I *need* to mail this letter' instead of 'I *want* to mail this letter' when the emphasis is on necessity rather than desire."

What with the explosion of semimodal usage, I needed to get this off my chest (in the sense of "wanted to," because I like to flush out vogue uses). Now I need to turn to another subject (in the sense of "am required to," as in "or else this will be followed by white space, apoplectic editors and a new career flipping burgers").

This usage of "need" has long irritated me. It seemed to have flourished in Washington during the Clinton years. Remember him telling the country, after distancing himself from "that woman," "I need to get back to work"?

John J. Sheehy
New York, New York

I wish you had included an analysis of the neologism I need you to (as in "I need you to sign your name, or roll up your sleeve, or take off your bra"), a recent successor to the equally inane for me (as in "make a tight fist for me"). *Where do these (faintly belittling) locutions come from—and how do they spread so fast?*

Maria Pelikan
New York, New York

Negative Pregnant.   One advantage of being a card-carrying language maven is that you suffer no compunctions about asking, "What does that mean?" (Or, in colloquial conversation, "Whassat?") Your interlocutor rejects the possibility of your being ignorant, which you may well be, and instead thinks: "This is a test. He knows and is trying to trap me."

In an interview with Richard Danzig, a former secretary of the navy, about the bioterrorism threat, we came to an arcane point of military strategy. When he said, "That's an example of the *negative pregnant*," I perked up with my usual shucks-that's-beyond-me question, which he countered with "You'd better look it up. It's a fascinating legal term."

I have and it is. It means "a negative implying an affirmative," and understanding it is a way of stopping the slippery.

Pregnant (from the Latin *præ*, "before," and *nasci*, "to be born") is most commonly taken to mean "with child in the womb." But there is a figurative sense of "filled with," "fertile," "big with consequences," which appears in our *pregnant pause*. Grammarians have the phrase "pregnant construction" to denote a phrase that implies more than it expresses and is thus a favorite with poets. The *Century Dictionary*'s example is "The beasts trembled forth [that is, came forth trembling] from their dens."

It was the Augustinian logicians who adopted the *negative pregnant*. Paul of Venice, working in the 14th century, came up with *propositio categorica negativa prægnans*. The lexicographer John Cowell in 1607 gave an example of a negative implying also an affirmative, which I will put in updated English: "As if a man, asked if he did a thing upon such a day, or in such a place, deny that he did it in some specific manner, he implies an admission that nevertheless in some form or other he did it."

If an inexperienced prosecutor asks, "Did you kill your husband on March 15 of last year?" and the witness replies, "I didn't kill him on March

15," she is trying to be evasive; to the alert, this implies that she killed him on some other date. That denial of a partial qualification of a charge is a *negative pregnant*. It's a sneaky way of wriggling away from an honest answer, and political observers will be glad to learn its name.

Netenclature.   Let's say you wanted to set up a Web site containing the complete works of William Shakespeare, or commenting on the use of bawdy language in his plays, or selling your closetfuls of souvenir Shakespeare busts.

What would you name it? How about something simple and direct, like *shakespeare.com*? First you have to see if it has already been taken. Every name has to be registered with the Domain Name System, which translates names into the Internet protocol numbers that route all the computers in the world to a chosen address.

You start by checking with Network Solutions Inc., registrar of more than eight million domain names, or one of its ninety or so rivals that have sprung up since competition was permitted in the past year. You discover that your proposed *shakespeare.com* is already taken by a dreary wordplay gamester and *shakespeare.org* is the site of a nice company of thespians in Lenox, Massachusetts. Also taken are *thebard.org* and *stratford-upon-avon.com*.

Some seeming Shakespearean sites are not Bard-related: *soundfury.com* lays not on *Macbeth* but on music, and *killalllawyers.com* is not an analysis of a slanderous crack by a villain in *Henry VI* but a compilation of lawyer jokes. (Lawyers sensitive to this relentless spoofing find fun being made of other people on *hardyharhar.com*.)

You will find that almost all famous names are already taken by people who were quicker than you. These name claimants either conduct business or educate the world under that domain name, unless they are cybersquatters, grabbing the most salable words and well-known names for sale to the highest bidder.

One enterprising outfit, claiming it was merely protecting me from predatory types warehousing names for sale, "owned" *williamsafire.com*, and I had to pay to reclaim my identity. (Few others wanted my name, which was somewhat deflating but lucky for me.) Indeed, some 90 percent of the most common words in English are already claimed by the fast operators of "netenclature," my unregistered appellation for the Internet-naming business or racket. For details on the way the naming system works, click on *ICANNWatch.org*, a private organization that keeps an eye on the government-sanctioned Internet Corporation for Assigned Names and Numbers. (A domain name for fed-up television viewers or opponents of voyeurism would be *ICANTwatch*, surely not registered yet.)

What's in a name? As Shakespeare's Juliet discovered, plenty. This department's interest is in the more creative names now dotting the linguistic landscape. Some are thoughtful: a site dealing with general semantics, often illustrating the differentiation of words, is *thisisnotthat.com*. Others compress a readily understandable message into a new compound: *bibliofind.com*, for example, uses the Greek *biblion*, "book," which bibliophiles know, with the English verb to *find*—you use this Web site to find old books.

Most people who want access to official White House transcripts and pictures of the first family do not use the correct "top domain" (the suffix-like three letters after the dot). Instead of punching in *whitehouse.gov*, which would get them a smiling face of President Clinton, they mistakenly use *whitehouse.com*. This takes them to a site that a pornography distributor shrewdly glommed on to. (It was a commercial trick, not a GOP plot.)

I have not checked this out because I am writing this on a *New York Times* computer at the office and can envision the oh-yeah smirk on the face of systems support when I sputter out an explanation that this search lasting several hours was only in furtherance of my scholarly duty.

But Web criticism, especially self-criticism, is clearly labeled. *Worstoftheweb.com* competes with the more informal *webpagesthatsuck.com*. License-plate messaging has been adopted by domain namers: *Ubid.com* is an auction site; *4800numbers.com* helps you find an 800-number; *uexpress.com* leads you to the free expressions of some columnists.

Some names are registered by groups that want to protect their members from offense. There is a *nigger.com* registered, property of the NAACP, to keep the slur from being used by racists. In the same way, the Anti-

Defamation League owns *kike.com,* as well as other top-domain endings. That shows foresight by organizations fighting bigotry. Taking a leaf from their book, political candidates this year have been preempting the names of sites that might be used to embarrass them. Though *buddhisttemple* is taken, *bobjonesu* remains available.

Some names are inexplicable: *amazon.com,* originally a bookseller, has nothing directly to do with the South American river or the legendary tribe of dominatrixes. Jeff Bezos, creator of that successful site, named it after the river because it carries more water than any other. (The Nile, though longer, carries less water.) *Monster.com* is an employment finder, so named for no reason I can ascertain other than that is the way some people characterize bosses.

Many of the best names are those that succinctly describe products. For example, *johnnyglow.com* sells fluorescent adhesive strips to put on the inside of toilet bowls to aid men who can't find the light switch in the dark. (The slang term *john* is applied to men's lavatories because it was once the most common male first name. I thought I would name my Web site *tangent.com,* but somebody with a wandering mind already did.)

Names make not only news but also profits; and as Amelia Bloomer and Captain Boycott taught us, names also make words. We will watch the coming Internet battles over trademark and copyrights in its nomenclature, but just as important, we will keep our sticky eyeballs on the creativity that labels the most eminent domains.

I enjoyed your reference to amazon.com. You may know this, but Jeff Bezos had originally decided to name his company cadabra.com (as in abra cadabra, it's magic, I assume) but apparently, when he went to incorporate it, his lawyer pal said it would sound too much like "cadaver.com" and thus turn people off. So he opted for amazon instead.

Sam Verhovek
The New York Times
New York, New York

Netspionage.   *E-fraud* solicitor is how Steven Philippsohn, a lawyer in London, describes his line of work. In a recent article in *Communications World,* he used a word that fills a void (once pronounced in Brooklyn as "a woid that fills a verd"): "*Netspionage* is already affecting computer contractors."

Netspionage is a blendword. (That is usually written as *blend word,* but in my view, its meaning of "mingling" all but forces the two words together.) It uses the *net* of *Internet* as a prefix, following *Netiquette* (for "Internet etiquette"), *Netsploitation* movies (which exploit fears of the Internet) and *Netspertise* (which I don't have).

You'll see plenty of other blendwords created with the *net* prefix. Forget *cyber,* from Norbert Wiener's *cybernetics:* that was the last decade's hot combining form. It's now almost as outdated in the neologism dodge as the suffixes *-arama* and *-aholic.*

Because *inter-* begins so many words, it is not a popular new combining form. *Internesia* means "inability to remember where on the Web you saw a particular bit of information," and I presume a lesson plan to overcome this mental lapse is called an *intercourse.*

But let us return to the subject of *Netspionage.* What new words are the real spooks speaking out there in the cold? A cleaning out of the usual dead drops takes us beyond the computer world and *elint* (electronic intelligence) into *humint*—a blendword formed by *human* and *intelligence.*

Here's one I heard rather than read: *skiff,* as in the sentence "Is there a *skiff* where we can talk?" At first, I thought it was a small boat, the word *skiff* derived from the Germanic *schif,* akin to *ship.* But it has nothing to do with naval information; thanks to Thomas Powers, author of *Heisenberg's War,* I am informed that it is the sound of an acronym—SCIF—secret compartmented intelligence facility.

"Secret compartmented intelligence," says Powers, "is a level of classification for a class of intelligence that's above top secret. A SCIF is a room that has been secured and sealed under very tight regulations, where classified information can be safely discussed, read and handled."

We used to call that a "clean room." At Spaso House, our embassy in Moscow, I recall meeting other presidential aides in a soundproof, penetration-proof room built inside another, less secure room, whose walls were suspected to have ears. Now such a room within a room is called a SCIF.

Another relatively new term of the clandestine arts is *perception management*. David Wise, in his book *Cassidy's Run: The Secret Spy War Over Nerve Gas,* notes that this phrase means "the manipulation of the perceptions of the target country. But the latest term of art, like its predecessors, boiled down to the same thing—tricking an adversary into believing false information by persuading it that a source, actually under U.S. control, was selling America's secrets."

I asked Wise if he had picked up any of the latest spookspeak from Yasenovo, the suburban Moscow headquarters of the KGB. (That agency now calls itself the SVR, but Americans still refer to it with the name by which it came to be known and feared.) Just as the CIA calls itself "the Company," Wise reports, the KGB now refers to Yasenovo as *Kontora*, "the Office." Fake passports are called, in Russian, "shoes" because the passport forgers are called "cobblers." What we call a *dead drop*—often a tree in which secrets are left to be picked up by another agent—is *dubok,* or "little oak."

Because United States policy frowns on assassinations, the intelligence community needed a phrase to cover the idea of bombing the general area in which an unfriendly dictator or terrorist is likely to be resident. Such attacks are now enshrined in bureaucratese as *regime lethal. U.S. News & World Report* spotted the usage regarding Saddam Hussein in November 1998, defining it as "targeting the dictator and the powerful Revolutionary Guard units that keep him in power."

Ed Epstein, author of *Dossier: The Secret Life of Armand Hammer,* reports that *mole hunt* now has a pejorative connotation, bottomed as it is on *witch hunt.* In that regard, *sickthink,* coined on the analogy of *doublethink* and *groupthink,* means "a predisposition to believe one's own agents are controlled by the other side." *Sickthink* is usually accompanied by intimations of paranoia and mutterings about counterspies who grow orchids.

Deer park is defined by Epstein as "a diplomatic area, like the U.N., in which headhunters recruit agents." (I am informed by the novelist Norman Mailer, who titled a 1955 book about a decadent Hollywood *The Deer Park,* that he dimly recollects taking that title from a passage in *The Private Life of Louis XV* in which Mouffle d'Angerville described *le parc aux cerfs* as a wooded area near the court of Versailles where *stags*—male courtiers— would seek out the *does,* courtesans selling sexual favors. Spymasters like such literary conceits.)

In examining the new words of espionage, let us not neglect the secrets of an old word about secret dealings. *Surreptitious* means "taken by stealth; unauthorized; clandestine." It comes from the Latin *surreptitius,* "obtained by surreption," with the *rep* from *rapere,* "to quickly seize or snatch," also the root of *rapid* and *rape.*

You never heard the word *surreption*? Neither did I; the form the word takes is always the adjective, never the noun. But the *Oxford English Dictionary* says the obsolete term means "suppression of truth or fact for the purpose of obtaining something; fraudulent misrepresentation." I'll find a use for it when some politician clams up.

Now about *clam up,* a 1916 Americanism that describes what a good spy does when caught. But how did a clam, known for its ability to shut itself tightly, clamping its shell, get its name? From the Teutonic *klamb,* "to press or squeeze together." Before that, and perhaps unrelatedly, we have the Latin *clam,* "secretly, in private"; the *m* changed to *n,* which led to *clandestinus,* "secret, hidden"—and to the work of those who practice legal surreption in the clandestine service.

Never Said It.   "Let them eat cake." Those words have come ringing down the centuries as the height of hauteur. Marie Antoinette was never able to live them down, even after the queen followed her husband, Louis XVI, to the guillotine after the French Revolution. To this day, whenever a hard-hearted trickle-downer suggests that a rising tide lifts all the boats, he or she is denounced for having "an arrogant let-them-eat-cake attitude," unconcerned with the needs of the common people.

She never said it. The source of this canard is the sixth book of *The Confessions of Jean-Jacques Rousseau:* "At length I recollected the thoughtless saying of a great princess, who, on being informed that the country people had no bread, replied, 'Let them eat cake.' " (The words, in French, read "*Qu'ils mangent de la brioche.*")

However, these words were written in or about 1770, the same year the daughter of the emperor of the Holy Roman Empire arrived in France to marry its crown prince. Rousseau was attributing that saying to some other "great princess." The truth about Marie was just the opposite: she recognized the need for austerity at court and reduced the royal household staff, but in so doing offended snooty nobles, who proceeded to down-mouth her for posterity. I get incensed at this historical linguistic injustice every time I look up the phrase.

Nor is that the only never-said-it. Who can forget "The Guard dies, but never surrenders" ("*Le Garde meurt, mais ne se rend pas*")? The Count Cambronne, the head of Napoleon's most loyal troops at the battle of Waterloo, and to whom it was attributed, went to his grave wishing we would forget it, because he insisted that he never said it. A half-century after the battle, the writer Edouard Fournier credited a reporter named Rougemont with the creation of the ringing phrase. It may be counter-apocryphal, but some say the count's battlefield response to a demand for surrender was the expletive "*merde!*"—a favorite Hemingway word for excrement and sometimes referred to in France as "*le mot de Cambronne.*"

These belated corrections are made here today because of a response received after a correction of a more recent misconception: Richard Nixon's never-said "I have a secret plan to end the war." I challenged anyone to come up with a contemporary citation directly quoting the 1968 candidate saying it; nobody ever has.

Because word got around the White House that great misattributions were being straightened out in this space, the following handwritten note came in from Samuel R. Berger, national security adviser: "Bill—Since you have asserted frequently that Bill Clinton is the 'architect of the strategic partnership' with Beijing, and because you are a stickler for the facts, I would like you to show me one instance in which the President describes the relationship as a *strategic partnership.*"

Gee, could it be that Clinton is being unjustly saddled with a never-said-it? You can get hundreds of citation hits on the databases when you type in "*strategic partnership*" and "Clinton." An article in Japan's daily *Yomiuri Shimbun* in 1998: "Last year, Chinese President Jiang Zemin visited the United States, and this year, U.S. President Bill Clinton returned the visit. On both occasions, the two countries began using the term '*strategic partnership*' between the two powers to describe their relationship." Robyn Lim wrote recently in the *International Herald Tribune,* "Two years ago, Mr. Clinton announced a '*strategic partnership*' with China." And a vituperative right-wing *New York Times* columnist (albeit a stickler for the facts) has been writing frequently of "Clinton, architect of the discredited '*strategic partnership*' with Beijing." Could we all be wrong?

Berger goes on: "On many occasions we have said that we would hope to develop a *strategic partnership,* i.e., described it as an aspirational goal. But there is a big difference between describing an objective for the future and what exists today. I can provide you what the President actually *said* in Beijing."

And so, upon my eager request, he did. On July 3, 1998, the president (*Times* style, unlike White House style, is to lowercase the name of the office) said in Hong Kong, "My view is that the potential we have for a *strategic partnership* is quite strong." This followed by five days Jiang Zemin's usage: "progress in the direction of building a constructive *strategic partnership.*"

In each case, and in a dozen other citations provided by the White House, the Clinton context is, as Berger asserts, "aspirational"—a hope for the future. If the future were the only context for the Clinton use of the phrase, then all of us who have been deriding the president as "architect of the discredited policy of a *strategic partnership*"—as if it signified his notion of a present state of affairs—would surely owe him and his advisers abject apologies.

And yet there is the problem of the Clinton statement to business leaders in Shanghai on July 1, 1998, dutifully provided by the White House. Discussing normal trade treatment for China, an issue then known as MFN (for "most favored nation"), Clinton warned what would happen if Congress did not respond to his plea to vote to renew the normal treatment.

"Failure to renew that would sever our economic ties," he said, "denying us the benefits of China's growth, endangering the *strategic partnership*, turning our back on the world's largest nation at a time when cooperation for peace and stability is more important and more productive than ever."

When Berger saw that citation, he must have uttered an American translation of *le mot de Cambronne,* but to his credit he did not remove it from the file. A close analysis of the structure of that sentence, especially its concluding "at a time" clause, indicates clearly that the president was speaking of the *strategic partnership* as something now in existence— a current relationship that would be endangered if Congress failed to act as he wished. Had he only put *prospective, potential* or *hoped-for* in front of the key phrase, the Berger hypothesis would have been unchallengeable.

You could say in Clinton's defense that he was ad-libbing and intended to follow the agreed-upon future formulation but just slipped into the present tense on a single occasion. And it is undeniable that the other Clinton and Jiang citations follow the prospective-relationship formula.

What's fair? We should recall the raw deals that loose historians have given the brioche-free Marie Antoinette, the die-hard count and the secret-plan-less Nixon. Unless other usages surface, accuracy-stickling Sinophobes should limit themselves to castigating "the '*strategic partnership*' that Clinton frequently hoped for and in one instance suggested his policy produced."

No Child Behind.   Democrats are somewhat irked at the adoption by President Bush of a phrase that belonged to education reformers: to *leave no child behind.*

"If schools do not teach and will not change," he told a campaign rally in October 2000, "instead of accepting the status quo, we will give parents better options, different choices. We'll *leave no child behind* in America."

When President Bush's first budget proposed reductions in some child-care programs, the *New York Times* columnist Bob Herbert wrote: "He hijacked the copyrighted slogan of the liberal Children's Defense Fund and then repeated the slogan like a mantra, telling anyone who would listen that his administration would *'leave no child behind.'* Mr. Bush has only been president two months, and already he's leaving the children behind."

Who coined the powerful phrase? Marian Wright Edelman, president of the Children's Defense Fund, in 1993 credited "the black community," but further research tracked it more specifically to Barbara Sabol, in November 1991 a member of the CDF's Black Community Crusade for Children. One year earlier, on Nov. 15, 1990, the *Courier-Journal* in Louisville, Kentucky, reported that Dave Armstrong, a Jefferson County judge, in asking a juvenile-justice commission for better community care for children, said, "We can *leave no child behind.*"

Seven years before that, at a White House reception on July 28, 1983, President Ronald Reagan told the National Council of Negro Women that he had "begun to outline an agenda for excellence in education that will *leave no child behind.*" Mari Maseng Will, who worked on that speech, says, "President Reagan has not, to my knowledge, been credited with the phrase."

Until now. And until someone comes up with an earlier citation, the Gipper's the coiner.

Nomenclature Wars.   When did the *inheritance tax* (a pro-taxing term) become the *estate tax* (a neutral term)? And who changed it to the *death tax,* which has a built-in anti-tax message?

In the same way, who abolished *most favored nation*? MFN, as it used to be initialized, was a trade status equal to that of the *most favored nation—* which was denied to certain countries, often for human rights reasons. But the phrase made it seem as if China, for example, would become the most favored nation—and most people did not favor that. So the name was changed to *nondiscriminatory trade practices*—and who was in favor of discrimination? The name was changed further to *normal trade relations,* leaving opponents to espouse *abnormal relations,* a loser. The name changes helped change the policy.

The classic example was *pro-life,* adopted by those who were *anti-*

abortion. This not only put the case in positive terms (which *anti-abortion* did not) but also suggested that the opposition was *pro-death*. In their defense, people who opposed restrictions on abortion adopted the term *pro-choice*. Thus a right to abort was presented in the more favorable light of a right to choose.

In the war of words in the Middle East, the Palestinians won. Israel referred to the land gained after it repelled invasions as *Judea and Samaria*, the ancient names of the land. The Arab world preferred the *West Bank*, situated on the west bank of the Jordan River in what had been Transjordan. For a time, the Israelis fell back to the *administered territories* and later to the *disputed territories*, but almost all the media adopted *West Bank* as distinct from Israel proper, and any traditionalist reference to *Judea and Samaria* is now considered quaint or slanted.

Remember when *global warming* was a hotly disputed phrase? At the sudden order of the Great Namechanger, *global warming* was iced and *global climate change* took its place. No explanation; no argument; the order came down, and multitudes on both sides of that argument marched off in lockstep.

"The latest semantic fashion in Congress," reports the *Hill*, Martin Tolchin's lively Washington weekly, "is renaming *fast track trade authority* as *trade promotion authority*, or TPA." *Fast track* apparently reminds too many Republicans of the Clinton era.

Representative David Dreier, a California Republican, requires his staff to put a dollar in a jar every time one of them uses the taboo term *fast track*. It's the same jar he used to coerce his minions into using *normal trade relations* when they blurted out *most favored nation*.

No More Patients.   How do you get rid of mental patients in one fell swoop? Put in a more caring way, how do you make the mentally ill feel better about whatever ails them? Call them *mental-health consumers*.

Here's the idea: A *patient* is one being cared for; in a "doctor-*patient* relationship," the doctor has the power. But in a "merchant-*consumer* relationship," the *consumer* is supposedly king. When you think of health care as a commodity, to be sold by medical professionals and bought by ailing purchasers of such therapies, then the patient is a *consumer,* the boss.

"It's a respect thing," says Frank McMyne, a board member of the Pennsylvania affiliate of the National Alliance for the Mentally Ill. "It changes the relationship. If we are merely *patients,* it diminishes our ability to question the kind of treatment we are receiving."

Dr. Karen Shore, president of the Coalition of Mental Health Professionals and Consumers, is more conflicted. "I call my patients *patients.* But to a lot of people who are consumer advocates, *patient* sounds pejorative." Her associate Sheri Laribee adds: "What *consumer* stands for is 'someone on a health care plan.' If I am paying for the managed health care plan, I am the *consumer* buying insurance. The managed-care organizations call people *consumers* so that they don't have to think of them as *patients.*"

I have a quibble or two with your use of the phrase, in one fell swoop.

Quibble one: The phrase is from Shakespeare and is actually "at one fell swoop," although the corrupted form does appear quite frequently these days. It is uttered when Macduff has been told that his wife and his children have all been murdered at Macbeth's command, and is an analogy to a hawk striking its prey.

Quibble two: The phrase has a literal connotation of both suddenness— which you wanted to convey—and evil—which I presume you didn't. I recognize that many people use the phrase simply to mean accomplishing something swiftly and completely, whether the object was good or bad. However, this often leads to unintentionally humorous statements such as, "After years of suffering, the medicine cured her in one fell swoop."

You might be interested in what [Bergen] Evans & [Cornelia] Evans had to say about it in A Dictionary of Contemporary American Usage *([Random House] 1957):*

The word fell *in the phrase means fierce, savage, cruel and ruthless. It is akin not to the past of* fall *but to* felon *and has connotations of wickedness and bitter savagery. It is, plainly, exactly the word that Macduff wanted and, fortunately, Shakespeare was right there to provide it to him.*

But the phrase is now worn smooth of meaning and feeling. Anyone who uses it deserves to be required to explain publicly just what he thinks it means.

Gil Haselberger
Bellevue, Washington

Normalcy.   "I was taught that *normalcy* was a nonword," writes Floyd Norris, chief financial correspondent of the *New York Times,* "a poor substitute for *normality* invented by one of our worst presidents, and that educated people avoided the word. So I have been surprised to see it used so frequently in the *Times* since the September 11 attack. When did President Harding win the language battle? Or were my mother and my teachers wrong all along?"

They were. Norris is a colleague whose sober market advice we all should have taken throughout the recent irrational exuberance, but he was swept up by a previous generation's Harding-hooting. Last week the economics columnist of the *Washington Post,* Robert J. Samuelson, used the word that is out-usaging *normality* 3 to 1: "We are now slowly returning to '*normalcy,*' though we don't know what that means—and can't know."

I know. It means the same as *normality,* coined by Edgar Allan Poe in 1848. Nine years later a couple of mathematicians used an equally logical extension of *normal,* preferring *-cy* to *-ity.* The two forms competed, *normality* in the lead, until Harding made the alliterator's hall of fame in 1920 with "not heroics but healing, not nostrums but *normalcy,* not revolution but restoration, not agitation but adjustment" and (my favorite) "not experiment but equipoise."

When mocked by users of *-ity,* the president told his critics to look it up in the dictionary—and there it was, in Merriam-Webster's. The populace was bullish on *normalcy.* Which leads to another miscorrection:

The Defense Department junked the name *Operation Infinite Justice* for its campaign against terrorism. New title: *Operation Enduring Freedom.*

"*Enduring* suggests that this is not a quick fix," said Defense Secretary Donald Rumsfeld. President Bush embraced the phrase in a pep talk to the CIA: "We are on a mission to make sure that freedom is enduring."

"There is a double meaning to '*Enduring Freedom*,' " objected Franz Allina of the Bronx in a letter to the *Times*. "*Enduring* means 'tolerating' as well as 'persevering.' " Other e-mail and faxes flew in to make the same point.

Not so. "He's taking the root meaning of the verb," replies Fred Mish, editor in chief of *Merriam-Webster's Tenth Collegiate*, "and transferring it to the participial adjective. A verb can have many meanings, but they don't all carry over to the adjective." The intransitive verb *endure*, rooted in the Latin *durus*, "hard," has many senses: "to last," or "to remain firm under adversity," but a different meaning when transferring action: "to suffer, tolerate, countenance."

Does that difference carry over when the verb *endure* adds an *-ing* and becomes a participial adjective? No. *Enduring* is almost always used to mean "lasting, permanent," as in "*enduring* friendship"; occasionally it means "durable," as in "an *enduring* substance"; only once in a blue moon does it mean "tolerating," as in "*enduring* personal attacks, he carried on."

"The meaning that comes to mind with most people," says the lexicographer Mish, "is the meaning Rumsfeld probably meant." That meaning is "lasting," using *enduring* as a modifier. The other meaning would be close to an *abnormality*. (*Abnormalcy*? No such word.)

No Sentence Fragments.   Jim Nicholson, the GOP chairman, sent out a release under a header encapsulating his party's message for the current campaign: "Renewing America's Purpose. Together."

This raises the issue of sentence fragments. Slogans—from the Gaelic *sluagh-* (army) *gairm* (yell), or "battle cry"—need not be complete sentences. A Republican slogan in the 1928 campaign was "Hoover and Happiness, or Smith and Soup Houses," which contained no verb. (The Democratic response four years later, "In Hoover We Trusted, Now We Are Busted," was a comma splice of two complete sentences and helped elect

FDR.) Some facetious slogans of the '70s were sentences ("Support Mental Health or I'll Kill You") and some were not ("Dog Litter—An Issue You Can't Sidestep").

I have long rallied to battle cries containing verbs. "Keep Cool with Coolidge" strikes me as more forceful than "Rum, Romanism and Rebellion," the ill-chosen phrase that sank James Blaine's campaign against Grover Cleveland, though both phrases were alliterative gems. "Vote As You Shot," with its two verbs, stirred Ulysses Grant's followers, while "Elect a Leader Not a Lover" savaged Nelson Rockefeller, and "Make Love Not War" signs danced at demonstrations in the 1960s. All these were short sentences studded with the action of verbs and not passive sentence fragments.

What is a sentence fragment? A decade ago, I collected a bunch of "fumblerules" that demonstrated the errors they intended to correct. These ranged from "Don't Use No Double Negatives" to "Avoid Clichés Like the Plague," and included "No Sentence Fragments." I confidently passed along the conventional pop-grammarian wisdom that a sentence should contain a complete thought and thus requires a verb.

Not so fast (as sentence-fragmenters say). James McCawley, the late linguistics master at the University of Chicago, took issue with my knee-jerk pedagogy. First, he noted that a sentence should *express*, rather than *be*, a complete thought. This was no nitpick; the example he gave was the answer to "What did he buy?" "A hatrack." McCawley wrote that "*A hatrack* expresses exactly the same thought as *He bought a hatrack* and hence doesn't express any less complete a thought: the difference between the full sentence and the sentence fragment is not in the completeness of the thought expressed but in the completeness of the form in which it is expressed."

Furthermore, McCawley instructed me that "for something that occupies the position of a sentence to be a 'sentence fragment,' it is *not* necessary that it *not* contain a verb." The fragment of an expressed thought—not a complete sentence—can indeed contain a verb: Lincoln's anguished "And the war came" is an example.

Seized of the great grammarian's clarifying subtlety, and willing after ten years to rethink my pronouncement (and allowing for sloganeering license), I cannot now denounce the current Republican slogan as blatantly incorrect.

That slogan—"Renewing America's Purpose. Together."—may be choppy prose and less than catchy or rousing. And putting *together* at the end, freestanding, rather than at the beginning as "Together Renewing America's Purpose," seems to make the unity pitch appear to be an afterthought. But the two expressed thoughts cannot be easily denounced as an offense to good grammar. Just awkward.

No Way. A decade ago, the youngest editor at Merriam-Webster, who was fresh out of college, noted to his boss at the *Collegiate Dictionary* offices that the system of dating senses of words was "way cool."

That snapped Fred Mish's head around. "It was really so striking when I first heard it," the lexicographer recalls. "*Way* was being used as an adverb to modify the kind of adjective or adverb that it did not traditionally modify."

In olden times, the adverb *way* was a shortening of *far away,* as in this 1868 praise of the mail service by General George Armstrong Custer: "They had braved the perils . . . in order to bring us, *way* out here, news from our loved ones." (Contrary to popular belief, the last-standing Custer did not then say, "Those look like friendly Indians.") The same sense of distance existed in the 19th century in phrases like *way off, way up* and *way over yonder.*

But in the middle of the 20th century, adverbial *way* took a sharp turn: *way-out* was a compound adjective in this 1954 Merriam-Webster citation from a toast recorded in Sing Sing prison: "I'll make a whole lot of money for you, 'cause hustling's in my blood, / And because I go for you and think you're a *way-out* stud." A drug connotation was added with a 1958 "I turn on a little, and I get *way out*"—that is, removed from reality—and was soon accompanied by a sense of avant-garde, as in Norman Mailer's description of a favored hypothesis of his as *way out.*

Way was long an intensifier of distance but through the popularity of *way-out* became an intensifier of anything. In 1985, *People* magazine surveyed contemporary slang and classified as admiring value judgments terms like *neato, superpeachy, awesome, intense, funky fresh, totally hot* and *way cool.*

Two years later, Marla Donato wrote in the *Chicago Tribune,* "No matter how cool you are . . . there is always somebody even cooler than you— somebody who is *way cool.*" She defined *way cool* as "being rich enough to hire bodyguards to create your own constant, mobile, limited-access V.I.P. space." A few years later, as we have seen, the usage cruised up to the offices of Merriam-Webster.

And, in due course, to network television. Katie Couric, on NBC's *Today* show, said in 1999, "I recently spent some time talking to President Clinton in the Oval Office at the White House, which, I have to say, was *way cool.*" To which her cohost, Ann Curry, responded, "*Way, way cool,*" twice using the adverb *way* to modify the adjective *cool.* This exemplified the adverbial use of *way* as a general intensifier like *profoundly, indubitably, very* or *damn.*

A quick database scan shows a rush of usages in the past couple of years, from *way serious, way bad* to *way cute, way fun.* Last month, *Time* magazine, straining to be as with-it as *People*'s 1985 glossary, subheadlined, "The latest trendy drugs are . . . *chic, mellowing* and *way addictive.*" I spotted a billboard on the way (in its original noun sense of "path," from the Latin *via*) to La Guardia Airport. Its only message: "*Way Fast.*" (At the bottom of the billboard is the word *Informix,* presumably the name of a software company or a dot-com shop or a new movie about the Irish troubles starring Victor McLaglen. Way soft-sell.)

We now have *way* as the intensifier of choice in the vogue-word set. It has grown steadily for nearly a generation, has separated itself from any hint of distance and is now *way, way* with-it. Will it replace *very,* as in the Johnny Mercer lyric "You're much too much, and just too *very very*"? Hard to tell. But a copy editor long ago had this advice for writers who tried to strengthen feeble adjectives with *very:* "Change the *very* to *damn,* and somebody will surely cut out the *damn*." Apply the same treatment to *way*.

You refer to Custer being a general in 1868; he was not. At the end of the Civil War, he was a major general of volunteers, but his rank in the regular army was much lower: at the time of his death in 1876 he was a lieutenant colonel. That he wanted people to call him general doesn't change things.

David Hawkins
Brooklyn, New York

As a Germanophile, I must dispute your etymology of "way," that it developed "from its original noun sense of 'path,' from the Latin via.*" "Way" is the modern English descendant of the good, old Anglo-Saxon* weg, *an immediate cognate of the German* Weg, *and only related at the* Centum *level to the Latin* vehere. *Gnarly, isn't it?*

Brad James
Quakertown, Pennsylvania

Although I live in California (a linguistic researcher's paradise in itself), I would say that the majority of people my age use "very," "incredibly," or "really" as a modifier twenty times for every "way" they use, and most likely if they say "way cool" it's in an ironic sense. The more common slang version (probably used more on the West coast) would be "super," "hella," and "uber," all prefixed to words. While "super" and "hella" mean approximately the same thing (equivalent to "very"), "uber," which is mostly used by those from Los Angeles, is only used in situations of grand importance: "That guy is the hottest guy I've ever seen; he is an uber-hottie!" Additionally, there is a usage I've heard in conversation where people use hella *to modify nouns to mean "a lot of." For instance, when responding to "How are your finals going?" one might answer with, "Dude, I have* hella-work *to do tonight. I'll be up until 3 a.m."*

Ryan Blitstein
Stanford, California

℃

Nuance.   After George W. Bush said, "I do believe Ariel Sharon is a man of peace," the Associated Press White House correspondent Ron Fournier noted that this was "widely viewed as a sign that he was endorsing Israel's military action and backing off demands for an Israeli withdrawal. White House aides scoffed at those interpretations."

"I think things can be *overnuanced*," responded the president's press secretary, Ari Fleischer. The AP reporter countered in his story, "But *nuance* is the lifeblood of diplomacy."

If not the lifeblood of diplomacy, *nuance* is its mother's milk. (The difference between lifeblood and mother's milk is *nuanced;* the adjective form that Al Haig, Reagan's secretary of state, preferred was *nuancal,* but that delicate variation never made it into the dictionaries.)

The noun *nuance* started in the Latin *nubes,* "cloud," which led to the French verb *nuer,* "to shade," and then to the noun *nuance,* "a shade of color or variation in tone." The essayist Horace Walpole captured the beautiful word for English in 1781, writing awkwardly, "The more expert one were at *nuances,* the more poetic one should be." In today's diplolingo, it means "a delicate distinction; a subtle shading or veiled variation that gives a hint of a shift in tone."

President Bush has been castigated by reporters for not being *nuancal* enough. "In the diplomatic *nuance* of Mideast policy," wrote Dana Milbank of the *Washington Post,* "Bush has really proved himself a geek." (Merriam-Webster defines the origin of *geek* as "a carnival performer often billed as a wild man whose act usually includes biting the head off a live chicken or snake." In current use, the slang term often refers to a computer whiz absorbed in technical arcana. It is unclear which meaning the reporter had in mind.)

Bush has shown himself to be aware of the meaning of the word *nuance* and applies it to diplomatic jargon. After this column reported *forward-leaning,* meaning "progressive" or "helpful," to be in vogue at Foggy Bottom, Bush said of a meeting with Russian President Vladimir Putin, "I thought he was very *forward-leaning,* as they say in diplomatic *nuanced* circles." And after saying in plain words, "The policy of my government is the removal of Saddam," he added, "maybe I should be a little less direct and more *nuanced* and say we support *regime change.*"

Nudge That Noodge.   A political divide has opened into a cultural chasm between two old friends. "Al [Gore] and I have tremendous regard for this industry," Senator Joseph Lieberman told entertainment moguls at a star-studded fund-raising event. "It's true from time to time we will have been, will be, critics or *noodges.*" Having used the Yiddishism *noodge,* a noun meaning "pest, annoying nag, persistent complainer," Lieberman went on to confuse the assembled glitterati by using the English verb *nudge* as if it were interchangeable with the Yiddish noun: "We will *nudge* you, but we will never become censors."

To *nudge* is "to push mildly or poke gently in the ribs, especially with the elbow." One who *nudges* in that manner—"to alert, remind, or mildly warn another"—is a far *geshrei* from a *noodge* with his incessant, bothersome whining.

Lieberman's use of both the Yiddish noun and the English verb in the same paragraph, suggesting wrongly that they meant the same, resulted in the compounding of the error in a statement by his longtime across-the-lines soulmate, William J. Bennett.

"I did not realize that when Joe Lieberman and I," stormed the author of *A Book of Virtues* and other best sellers, "were denouncing the filth, sewage and mindless bloodletting of the popular entertainment industry, calling it what it is—degrading and dehumanizing—we were just being '*nudges.*' I am a virtual absolutist on the First Amendment, but Senator Lieberman and I were doing more than '*nudging*' the entertainment industry; we were trying to shame them."

Set aside the rights and wrongs, the hypocrisy or hyperbole, in this lusty exchange during the heat of a campaign. Consider only its demeaning of meaning.

From here in Semantic Damage Control Headquarters, cool heads are obliged to issue this advisory: *noodge* is primarily a Yiddish dialect noun that risks confusion with the English *nudge* when used as a verb. The meaning of *noodge* is not merely "a critic" but "a habitual, pesky critic." The Yiddish noun *noodge* signifies a person, one who can sometimes prove useful but who is also not the sort you want around all the time. The English noun *nudge* is not a person but an action, often of the elbow to another's ribs and frequently accompanied by a wink or a leer.

The Yiddish noun is only a noun; when the action of a verb is wanted, the phrase is to *give a noodge*. The English *nudge* is both a noun and a verb, first used in verb form by Thomas Hobbes in 1675 in his translation of the *Odyssey*: "I *nudg'd* Ulysses, who did next me lie."

The pronunciation is different. Though some *noodges* will dispute this, in the Yiddishism the *oo* is pronounced as in *look* rather than the *oo* in *stooge*. Not in dispute is the English pronunciation of *nudge*, rhyming with *judge* and never even close to the Dickensian *Scrooge*.

You got that, Bennett? *Du herst,* Lieberman? Now shake hands and come out fighting.

The actual Yiddish for "bore, pest," is, of course, nudnik. *The verb is* nudyen, *and that, you'll see right away, easily evolves to "noodgen," hence, "noodge."*

Israel Wilenitz
East Setauket, New York

Nukes Again.   George W. Bush has a nuclear problem. Like Presidents Eisenhower, Carter and Clinton before him, he mispronounces the word *nuclear*. At the Naval War College earlier this month, he tripped over the word a dozen times with great authority, pronouncing it somewhere between Carter's "nuke-ular" and Clinton's "nu-ky-ler."

The confusion is in the middle syllable of the three-syllable word. Instead of separating them as *nu, clee, er,* many who reach the Oval Office treat the first syllable as *nuke,* perhaps influenced by the bellicose verb in "We'll *nuke* 'em back to the Stone Age."

A helpful speechwriter would write the word in the presidential reading copy as if there were only two syllables: "*new-clear.*" After all, *clear,* which some pronounce with two syllables, as *klee-uh,* often sounds close to a single-syllabled *cleer.*

This persnickety presidential pronunciation problem can be solved. Forget *nuke.* Think *nu.* Clear?

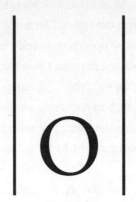

O Beautiful.   Returning in 1894 from an inspiring trip to Pikes Peak in Colorado, a minor New England poet named Katharine Lee Bates wrote a verse she titled "America." It was printed the following year in a church publication in Boston to commemorate the Fourth of July.

Lynn Sherr, the ABC News correspondent, has written a timely and deliciously researched book about how that verse was written and edited and how it was fitted to a hymn called "Materna," written about the same time by Samuel Augustus Ward, whom the poet never met. In *America the Beautiful: The Stirring True Story Behind Our Nation's Favorite Song*, Sherr reveals rewriting by Bates that shows the value of working over a lyric.

"O beautiful for *halcyon* skies," the poem began. *Halcyon* is a beautiful word, based on the Greek name for the bird, probably a kingfisher, that ancient legend had nesting in the sea during the winter solstice and calming the waves. It means "calm, peaceful" and all those happy things, but the word is unfamiliar and does not evoke the West. *Spacious,* however, not only describes Big Sky country but also alliterates with *skies,* so Bates changed it.

The often-unsung third stanza contained a zinger at the acquisition of wealth: "America! America! / God shed his grace on thee / Till selfish gain no longer stain / The banner of the free!" Sherr writes that Bates, disillusioned with the Gilded Age's excesses, "wanted to purify America's great wealth, to channel what she had originally called 'selfish gain' into more noble causes." The poet took another crack at the line that derogated the profit motive, and the stanza now goes: "America! America! / May God thy gold refine / Till all success be nobleness / And every gain divine!"

The line that needed editing the most was the flat and dispiriting conclusion: "God shed his grace on thee / Till nobler men keep once again / Thy whiter jubilee!" That cast an aspersion on the current generation, including whoever was singing the lyric. The wish for "nobler men" to come in the future ended the song, about to be set to Ward's hymn, on a self-deprecating note.

In 1904, ten years after her first draft, Katharine Lee Bates revised the imperfect last lines of the final stanza. The new image called up at the end not only reminds the singers of the "spacious skies" that began the song but also elevates the final theme to one of unity and tolerance. Her improvement makes all the difference, especially in times like these:

> *America! America!*
> *God shed his grace on thee*
> *And crown thy good with brotherhood*
> *From sea to shining sea!*

Oh Oh.   A satirical form of intellectual sabotage took place at the *Boston Globe* twenty years ago. An editorial about President Carter's economic plan was scheduled to be headlined "All Must Share the Burden." This is one of the dullest, most hackneyed clichés in journalism, always followed by a mournful paean to responsibility.

Either a printer-prankster or an editorial writer who could not stand it any longer changed the headline at the last minute to "Mush From the Wimp." This could have been a derogation of the president's policy or of the chief editorial writer's prose. The underground dissident was never caught, but editorialists ever since have been on the alert to this form of internal sabotage.

(I remember this vividly because it triggered a column about the origin of *wimp,* defined as "a person weepy as a drip and listless as a nebbish," derived from *whimper* and influenced by the name *Wimpy,* for a sleepy-eyed lover of hamburgers in the comic strip featuring Popeye the sailor. *Wimp,* a derogation dreaded more by politicians than "ax murderer," has since been edged out by *wuss,* a rhyming form of unprintable etymology. But I digress.)

Last month, in an editorial in the *Washington Post* supporting the Justice Department's raid on a Miami home to seize Elian Gonzalez, the headline remained as intended: "The Elian Operation." But the key line read: "Eight agents were in and out of the house in three minutes, carrying the boy in a blanket. *ohhoh.*"

When I asked Fred Hiatt, editor of the *Post*'s editorial page, about this strange insertion of *ohhoh* into the editorial, he muttered, "We think it was a mechanical error."

I am prepared to accept this explanation from an embarrassed fellow opinionmonger, but am inclined to wonder: could *ohhoh* have been a prankster's surreptitious editorial comment on editorial comment? If so, what does it mean?

The exclamation or interjection *oho* is defined in the *Oxford English Dictionary* as "an exclamation expressing surprise, taunting, exultation." Its first recorded use was in 1369 as a shout to arouse a sleeper (some readers of editorials need this sort of antisoporific) in a passage by Chaucer: "This messenger . . . cried *O how,* a-wake anoon." Shakespeare changed the spelling when he picked it up in his 1601 *Twelfth Night,* with Malvolio telling himself, "*Oh ho,* do you come neere me now."

Chaucer, in his 1386 *Canterbury Tales,* also spelled the exclamation differently: "*A ha* the fox! and after him they ran." This sense of the sound as "lo and behold" was taken up in the 1611 King James Bible thrice in Ezekiel, transliterated from the Hebrew *heach,* later translated by some as indicating "malicious joy."

In current use, *oh-hoh* has been overtaken by *aha!*—its sense a "triumphantly derisive discovery of a minor subterfuge." I asked the playwright Neil Simon about this a few years ago, and he came up with several meanings, from "a response when you know something but find it unnecessary to share" to "the first half of an uncompleted sneeze." His most apt usage: "*Aha!* is said sarcastically to your daughter when she says she came home at 11 last night when you know it was 12:15."

Now let's take a different tack. What if the mechanical errorist at the *Washington Post* meant to represent typographically a sound of wry derision, as if to say, "Sure, that's what you say"? That would be spelled *uh-huh*. (That meaning is also expressed in what Edward Bleier of Time Warner has termed the "double positive," which turns the sense of the word around, as in "*yeah-yeah*.") *Uh-huh* is also the sound of "I hear you, I understand" or the slightly more affirmative "Yeah, I guess so." The earliest recorded uses of *uh-huh* were in the late 19th century by magazine fiction writers transcribing Negro dialect, more as exclamation than affirmation.

In contradistinction to that positive, if sometimes mocking, *uh-huh* is the clearly negative *uh-uh*. The first literary citation for this negation is in Dashiell Hammett's 1930 *Maltese Falcon:* "Do you know who he is?" asks Effie Perine, and Sam Spade replies, "*Uh-uh,* but I'd guess he was Captain Jacobi."

Now for a final run at the possible meaning of the mysterious *ohhoh* in the *Post* editorial.

Dictionaries that have an entry for *oh* as "an expression of wonderment" fail to carry a definition of *oh-oh,* or the more staccato *uh-oh.* But almost every native speaker of American English knows *oh-oh* to mean "watch out" or "trouble ahead"; when our leading lexicographers read this, they will utter *uh-oh* and hasten to include the commonly exclaimed warning in their next revisions.

Could the phantom of the pressroom have meant "Watch out—the preceding opinion will draw a lot of mail"? Perhaps; we'll never know unless somebody confesses. But a new generation of proofreaders is now alerted to avert mush from the wimp.

On the university campus where I found myself in the summer of 1946, one of the many clichés constantly bandied by veterans was uh-oh. *It was al-*

ways an underplayed warning that danger (at least of a sort) was immedi-
ately at hand. Thus an ex-B-17 pilot who two years earlier had looked out
to see that a wing had fallen off would now utter uh-oh *when a spigot at-*
tached to a beer keg produced a dry hiss instead of a rush of suds. Or an
erstwhile infantryman who had recently seen enemy mortar fire walking its
way in his direction, would now mouth uh-oh *when a professor wrote an*
exam question on the board which bore no resemblance whatsoever to what
had been in his lectures. By no means all veterans had faced such dangers,
but all adopted uh-oh *as a way of saying that they too had taken part in the*
great experience. Along with the Britishism, "I've had it" or "we've had it,"
uh-oh *was the big code word that summer and into the following fall.*

Richard M. Wight

Ponte Vedra Beach, Florida

Of Wimps and Mush.   In an aside (watch out for those asides) in an article, I recalled a 1980 headline over an editorial in the *Boston Globe* that
read "Mush From the Wimp," which I presumed a prankster substituted
for the cliché "All Must Share the Burden." I am now informed by David
Greenway, who retired last month as editor of the *Globe*'s editorial page,
that it was not sabotage but a self-inflicted wound.

"It was the late Kirk Scharfenberg, editorial writer and later editor of the
page," writes Greenway, "who wrote 'Mush From the Wimp' over his editorial on President Carter's economic plan. He wrote it as a joke, never thinking that the headline would ever see print.

"As you know, the copy editors write the headlines," continues my colleague Greenway, "but in this case the copy editors let it through. The night
editor caught it in midrun, and the headline was hastily changed to the
clichéd 'All Must Share the Burden' as a last-minute sub for the rest of the
run."

Many years later, when Greenway became editor of the *Globe*'s editorial
page, the paper criticized animal rights advocates who wanted to close
down dogsled racing in Alaska. The headline chosen for its historic resonance: "More Wimps for the Mush."

On the Hook.   In a parallel universe, I write a didactic political column. Recently, I sternly directed the president to get *on the hook* to Prime Minister Blair to coordinate positions on United Nations inspections of Iraq. John Strother of Princeton, New Jersey, shot back, "Did you substitute *on the hook* for *on the horn*?" Kevin McNulty of Newark agrees: "A phone can be *on the hook,* but it must be *off the hook* to be used. Shouldn't that be *on the horn*?"

On the hook is military usage for "on a radiotelephone hookup." In his 1976 *Grunts,* C. R. Anderson wrote, "Six *on the hook,* Sir." (*Six* is a frequent radio call sign for the unit commanding officer.) An easier-to-understand term is *on the horn,* as all who remember yelling "Hello Central!" into the speaker of the telephone hanging on the wall fondly recall. The other term —and one I should have used—is *on the blower,* which has a nicely archaic feel.

Dial into this: all the metaphors for telephonic communication are direly in need of updating. Dials are gone (have you seen *Punch M for Murder?*). Because of wireless cell phones, a line now requires a retronym: *landline.* (If you're calling from a cave, use the *landline.*) Use e-mail; stay off the dog. (That's Cockney rhyming slang of the second order: the dog, which chews a *bone,* rhymes with *phone.* That's a little out of date, too.)

In my opinion, on the blower *originated as a nautical/naval expression referring to a ship's speaking tube connecting (especially) the bridge with the engine room. To signal the person at the other end that one wanted to talk to, one blew into the tube, which created a whistle-like signal at the other end, prompting the other person to pick up the tube.*

Laurence Urdang
Old Lyme, Connecticut

Old Guard.   "Let others argue the case for the *old guard,*" Al Gore said in his Los Angeles acceptance speech. "We're the *new guard.*"

In Michigan two days earlier, the vice president scorned "the failed ways of the *old guard*," and one night before, his choice for vice president, Joseph Lieberman, asked the Democratic convention, "Are we going to elect the *old guard* that created the problems or a *new guard* that will continue to work solving them?"

From this we can safely assume that Democrats have formulated a rhetorical strategy to get around the In party's traditional "time for a change" problem. "My goodness," exclaimed the CNN analyst William Schneider as the slogan was repeated, "they've been in for eight years—how can they be the *new guard*?"

As the old song goes, wishing will make it so. The daring idea is to take the "new" out of *newcomer* and the "in" out of *incumbent*. How? By hanging the *old guard* label on the challengers, those who have been the Ins for the past two terms cast themselves as the contrasting *new guard*. No such audacious reversal has been suggested since Adlai Stevenson countered the charges of a "mess in Washington" by saying that the GOP slogan in 1952 should be "Throw the rascals in."

As the fair-minded reader will note, the scholarly function of this linguistic column during a presidential campaign is to examine, with scrupulous nonpartisanship, the roots of its catchphrases.

"The Guard dies, but never surrenders" (*"La Garde meurt, mais ne se rend pas"*) was supposed to have been said by Count Cambronne on June 18, 1815, rejecting the Duke of Wellington's call for Napoleon's surrender after the battle of Waterloo. He did not say "the *old* Guard"; indeed, Cambronne went to his grave denying that he ever said anything of the sort, which was one of the last times anybody denied making a historic utterance. (I erred recently in attributing the wrong gender to *La Garde. J'en suis désolé.*)

Others suggested that the count had said, simply and forcefully, *merde!*—an expletive of excrement, which sounds like *meurt*, the French for "dies." General Anthony McAuliffe of the United States, rejecting surrender at Bastogne in the World War II Battle of the Bulge, is also suspected of having used a more forceful expression than his recorded "*Nuts!*" But I digress.

Even if Cambronne did say, "The Guard dies," etc., whence comes the *old* Guard? Evidently this was the familiar name of the Imperial Guard of Napoleon I, cited in an 1809 message to the emperor as *la vieille Garde* and repeated by him in his final adieu in 1814: "Soldiers of my *Old Guard:* I bid you farewell."

The phrase was not extended beyond the specific Napoleonic troops until applied to "grim sea grenadiers" by the American novelist Herman Melville, in *White-Jacket* in 1850, who called them "hearty old members of the *Old Guard.*" The phrase continued to have an affectionate, loyal-veteran connotation until 1880, when supporters of a third term for President Ulysses S. Grant wore medallions proclaiming "*Old Guard*" on them; Democrats reacted by using the phrase as a description of Republican reactionaries.

That is the current sense. Aware of this, a conservative Republican group in the 1970s, the Young Americans for Freedom, named its publication the *New Guard.* But in political terminology, anything can be freely swiped. In this case, that is what the creative Gore word-slingers seeking to keep the Democrats in office have done in their coordinated effort to derogate the freshness of the Bush challenge.

On the Right's Words.   William F. Buckley announced last month that he has decided to give up public speaking; in its stead, this pioneering practitioner of self-mocking rodomontade has endowed his conservative followers with *Let Us Talk of Many Things,* a high-stylish compilation of fifty years of piquant and literate comment.

His speeches show his easy way of teaching as if in passing. "I shall not introduce—the rhetoricians call this *paraleipsis*—the wonderful woman sitting, appropriately, on my left, Mrs. Robert Kennedy." This is a device of emphasis by pretending to omit (the old "to say nothing of" and "not to mention" trick). When you *paralep* like that, but then call attention to your own emphasis-by-omission, you're subtly instructing.

He also provokes you to teach yourself. Buckley is known for his delight in using unfamiliar words. He referred to Henry Kissinger and "one truth no one can challenge: the *petrology* of our association." I had to look it up: *petrology* is the study of the structure of rocks. So why not say "the rock-solid quality of our association"? Because the speaker sometimes wants to push his audience a little. He is saying, Go look up the word—work on it a little—and then you won't forget it or my point.

He's made those of us in the word trade stretch. "There is pleasure in even a little progress," he said in tribute to the conservative thinker James Burnham, "even among those of us taught, at our mother's knee, not to seek to *immanentize the eschaton.*"

Eschatology is the study of ultimate destiny, the purpose of life reckoned at the last accounting. The *eschaton* is its Greek root: the last thing, the divinely ordained climax of history, with its present sense of a final judgment that should inform our lives. That's the easy part.

But *immanentize*? The Latin *immanere,* "to remain in," leads us to *immanent,* "inherent, intrinsic," with a special philosophical sense of "confined to the mind." It's not a word I would use because *inherent* does the job and *immanent* is too easily confused with *imminent,* "about to take place," with a connotation of danger.

So I admitted defeat and called Buckley.

"The source of *immanentize the eschaton* is the 1952 *New Science of Politics,* by Eric Voegelin," he explained. "It's a warning against taking ultimate reality and treating it pantheistically, rather than as an objective philosophical phenomenon." The conservative pioneer added: "It was turned into a bumper sticker by the Young Americans for Freedom. Delicious, don't you think?"

"The petrology of our association," my foot! Buckley has over-reached with that figment of speech. Petrology is not the structure of rocks. It is the study of rocks, and in the science of the Earth it is generally taken to mean the origin of rocks—how they got that way. I am a petrologist. I know from petrology.

Buckley no doubt came at this private and irreproducible meaning through his biblical understanding. This is the way I used to introduce my subject at the start of a course in petrology. This is not about petroleum, I used to say; oil from rocks. This is from petrus, *rock and* logos, *word. It means this is The Word about Rocks. (If you want the full discourse on* logos, *read Tolstoy's translation and extended commentary on the gospel of John. If you get past* logos, *let me know.) This word* petrology *should be understood not from the more familiar oil of rocks but from what is in English an apparent pun by Jesus in the New Testament.*

When Simon Bar-Joan proclaims the Christ, Jesus responds: "Thou art Peter, and upon the rock *I will build my church, and the gates of hell shall not prevail against it. And I will give unto thee the keys of the kingdom of heaven." (Matthew 16:18-19)*

This powerful statement is taken by the Buckley faithful to be prophetic of the founding of the Christian church in Rome by the apostle Peter. I am told by Jesuits that this is not an actual pun in the original Greek.

S. A. Morse
Research Professor of Petrology
University of Massachusetts
Amherst, Massachusetts

Your piece on Buckley reminded me of my latest memorable encounter with him. He murmured something nice about my book, identifying himself as a member of that generation and then said, "So thank you for enhancing my already exaggerated sense of self-importance."

Tom Brokaw
NBC News
New York, New York

Operation Proceed.   When the governor of Massachusetts, Paul Cellucci, is confirmed as our ambassador to Canada, Lt. Gov. Jane Swift will become our first pregnant acting governor. "And although no governor has ever given birth before," wrote the *New York Times* columnist Gail Collins, "plenty of them take to their beds for one reason or another. Mr. Cellucci himself underwent heart surgery while in office. 'We like to call it a *proce-*

dure,' said an aide." Ms. Collins noted wryly that Jane Swift "is expecting a *procedure* in June."

That spotted and skewered a rising euphemism. When do you have an *operation,* when a *procedure,* and how is each different from having *surgery*?

LaSalle Leffall Jr., MD, professor of surgery at Howard University Hospital, says: "Every *operation* is a *procedure,* but not every *procedure* is an *operation.* A *colonoscopy,* for example, is a *procedure* and not an *operation.*

"You can say 'a surgical *procedure,*' " Dr. Leffall continues, "but it would be redundant to say 'a surgical *operation.*' But *surgery* is a discipline of using manual means for diagnosis and treatment. I'd never say, 'He had *surgery.*' "

Claude H. Organ Jr., MD, a surgeon and editor of the AMA's *Archives of Surgery,* agrees that "the word that a lot of people are using today that is not appropriate is *surgeries.*" But he uses *operation* and *procedure* interchangeably, as does George McGee, MD, who adds, "in general, if it requires an incision, then it would be called an *operation.*"

Eric Rose, MD, chairman of surgery at Columbia Presbyterian Medical Center in New York, uses a nice metaphor to illustrate the difference: "If a *procedure* is a melody, then an *operation* is a symphony. A lot of component *procedures* make up an *operation.*"

An *operation* is a surgical procedure. Patients who call operations *procedures* without the *surgical* modifying it are the sort who sit up in bed afterward and ask for a dish of stewed dried plums.

Surgery *also means a physician's, dentist's or veterinarian's office (in the U.K.).*

Herbert S. Saffir, PE, Hon. M. ASCE

Coral Gables, Florida

. . . Or Shut Up.   "The time for generalities without specifics," said candidate Al Gore, "I think is just about over. . . . It's kind of *put up or shut up* time."

His opponent promptly complained about the "tone" of this remark. Amid the general fear of being counterpunched with a charge of negativity, politicians shy from any locution that can be construed as harsh. Evidently Gore was concerned about his use of the directly challenging *put up or shut up,* because he preceded it with the ameliorating *kind of* and followed it with *time.*

The *time* combining form was pioneered in *party time* and was popularized by TV's Bob Smith in the late 1940s with "Hi, kids—it's Howdy Doody *time!*" The *time* turns the preceding word or phrase into a modifier, thereby weakening *put up or shut up.*

The substance of the charge has no place in this resolutely nonpolitical column. To philologists, however, the use of the Americanism *put up or shut up* poses a question: from what metaphor is it derived?

The earliest recorded use is in Fred H. Hart's 1878 collection of stories, *The Sazerac Lying Club.* (This may have been a dialectical source of the poet Mary Karr's recent memoir of her childhood, *The Liar's Club;* that best seller is soon to be followed by the avidly awaited memoir of her adolescence, *Cherry,* a slang reference to virginity. I enjoy digressions.) In a Hart story, the initialese *PU or SU* appears, explained by a character saying, "*PU or SU* means *put up or shut up,* doesn't it?" The caption to a cartoon in an 1884 *Police Gazette* was "*Put up, shut up* or get!" (presumably, "get out" or "git"), and the Americanism was locked into language by Mark Twain in his 1889 *Connecticut Yankee in King Arthur's Court* with "This was a plain case of '*put up, or shut up.*'"

Put up what? If the metaphor is from fisticuffs, the figure of speech is one of a fighter putting up his dukes, or fists, and telling his opponent to be quiet or prepare to put up his own dukes to defend himself.

A different possibility: the phrase could come from card playing, a rich source of phrases used in politics. Samples: FDR's *New Deal,* Truman's *the buck stops here,* with the buck, often a silver dollar, used to mark the position of the dealer, and *stand pat,* a poker locution used once by Richard Nixon as "America cannot *stand pat,*" and struck by his speechwriter from subsequent speeches after it drew a sharp glance from the candidate's wife.

Card playing is a strong possibility for the root because of the first verb, *put,* which is also used in *put your money where your mouth is.* To *put up* is synonymous with *ante up,* a call to place money in the ante, or "pot." (*Ante* means "before," and could allude to the stake that must be placed "before the draw." In 1882, Charles Welsh wrote in his poker guide about the "eldest hand" in the game: "Before the dealer begins to deal the cards, the player next to his left, who is called the *ante-man,* or *age,* must deposit in the pool an *ante* not exceeding one-half the limit previously agreed upon.")

Did dealer Gore obliquely demand that the ante-man put up or quietly fold? Or did he make a veiled dialect reference to the stance of a pugilist? It's a down-and-dirty dialectical mystery.

"The buck stops here" is a Navy term. In an officers' mess or wardroom a small object—a silver dollar would do—is placed at the table setting of the person who is to be served first that day. It is then moved to the adjoining seat, and that person is served first and his seatmate last. The term does not denote responsibility, but rather fleeting privilege. Truman was an excellent man in many ways, but alas, he was an officer in the Army, which evidently has no such sociable practice.

Senator Daniel Patrick Moynihan*
United States Senate
Washington, D.C.

There are two howlers in your article. (1) The stake is placed before the "deal" not the "draw" (draw is taking new cards after the deal); (2) logically the "ante-man" could never "put up or quietly fold" (fold is not meeting someone else's bet); how could the first to bet be in that position? He could either "ante" or "pass." Not "fold."

Thomas R. Moore
New York, New York

*Daniel Patrick Moynihan died on March 26, 2003.

P

Package Deal. In the Left Coast convention speech introducing himself to the nation, Senator Joseph Lieberman said: "My dad lived in an orphanage when he was a child. He went to work in a bakery truck and then owned a *package store* in Stamford, Connecticut."

The week before, however, in a speech to the AFL-CIO convention in Hartford, Lieberman used the phrase *liquor store*. Crawford Lincoln of Brimfield, Massachusetts, asks, "Was this a gentler locution to soften the image of his family's business for a national audience?"

I'd say yes, and thereby hangs a euphemism. A *package store* is a store, not a bar, where liquor is sold by the bottle and not by the drink and where the contents of the "package" are consumed off premises.

In 1880, *Bradstreet's* reported active trade in *package houses*. In 1890, the *London Daily News* reported that "Judge Foster recently decided that liquor could only be sold in 'original packages,' which is construed as meaning one or more bottles of beer or whisky. The merchants . . . are not allowed to sell beer or whisky by the glass."

Our earliest evidence for the phrase *package store,* I am informed by Joanne Despres at Merriam-Webster, "is an entry in the 1918 Addenda to the *New International Dictionary* (originally published in 1909), where it is labeled 'cant, U.S.' " (*Cant* means "jargon," and business euphemisms fall into that category.)

Let's face it: what the seller is selling is not a package but what is contained in the package, which is liquor. Why the squeamishness about that word? After Prohibition was repealed in 1933, state legislatures had the opportunity to license booze shops and saloons but did not want to upset the many "drys." That led to the linguistic prettification of *saloons* as *taverns* and of shops purveying the mother's milk of John Barleycorn as *package stores*.

Maybe the senator uses the terms interchangeably. But I have a hunch that some politically sensitive soul remembered that "drys" still exist and vote and changed the candidate for vice president's word from *liquor* to *package*. It shows a sandpapered-fingertip sensitivity to the shades of meaning of words.

Pashmina.   Do advertising tricks—those hidden persuasions of the huckster class—get your goat? If so, consider what has been done to the *Capra hircus*, a hairy wild goat that likes to graze along the mountainsides of the Himalayas.

For generations until 1684, the maharajah of Kashmir had exclusive rights to the underfur combed from the throat and belly of this cold old goat. The maharajah's domain was spelled *Kashmir*, a land that remains in dispute even today between India and Pakistan, but the wool was spelled *cashmere*.

Though sometimes challenged by exotic fabrics like vicuna (who now remembers what kind of coat Bernard Goldfine gave Sherman Adams?), cashmere has long been known as the finest wool that money can buy. That meant, of course, that it had to be topped by a wool even more rare, available at a higher price, to warm the skin of those late-arriving *arrivistes* who could learn to scorn the harsh feel of the cashmere worn by the riffraff.

Shahtoosh is a no-no; that "king of wool" comes from the Tibetan antelope, an endangered species. Enter *pashmina*, pronounced "pash-MEE-nah," a new name to create the illusion of a new goat with softer fur. The linguistic trick is to use the Persian word for the mountain goat's fur and to ignore the name of the place—*Kashmir,* pronounced "cashmere"—where the weaving into wool is done.

Pashm is the Persian word for "wool," or more specifically, "soft wool from under the throat of sheep or goats." In 1880, Mrs. A.G.F. Eliot James in *Indian Industries* wrote, "The *pashm,* or shawl-wool, is a downy substance, growing next to the skin and under the thick hair of those goats found in Thibet and in the elevated lands north of the Himalayas." Thirteen years later, a British natural history magazine explained, "It is this *pashm* of the goat of these regions which affords the materials for the celebrated Kashmir shawls."

Pashmina is the Persian word for "woolen," with a feminine ending. A couple of years ago, the *pashmina* push began. "Finer than cashmere," touted one catalog, "extraordinarily soft, warm and lightweight." Scarce; higher-priced; a gift even more eagerly sought after by the uxorious luxurious.

In the *Wall Street Journal* in November, Lauren Lipton shot it down: "Sit down, fashionistas: *Pashmina,* this most hyped of fabrics, is not a particularly premium kind of cashmere." She quoted textile-science sources scoffing at the promotion and cashmere industry sources saying: "Cashmere is the hair of the cashmere goat. *Pashmina* is the same goat."

Pashmina marketers were quick to bleat that cashmere fibers were usually fifteen microns thick while *pashmina*'s were a few microns thinner, and their product was woven on a warp of spun silk. You can believe that if you're a Big Spender. A company calling itself Nepal *Pashmina* Industry, in Katmandu, honestly begins its product profile with "*pashmina* (better known as cashmere)."

The source of the expression "to pull the wool over one's eyes" is a mystery. It was first seen in a *Jamestown* (N.Y.) *Journal* in 1839, at about the same time the term *OK* appeared: "That lawyer has been trying to spread the wool over your eyes." The allusion seems to be to spread a blanket over the head to obstruct one's figurative sight, similar to the origin of *hoodwink;* other speculation goes as far as to suggest pulling a person's hairpiece over his face. But no etymologist has yet come up with the specific item made of wool, or fine goat's hair, on which the expression is based.

❦

Perils of Parlous.   These are *parlous* times. Make that observation in a speech, and each member of your audience will frown and nod, joining in the general worriment. One or two misfits will be wondering, "Does the speaker mean *parlous* or *perilous*?"

In the *International Herald Tribune,* the historian Roger Buckley writes darkly about "the *parlous* prospects for the economy." Bloomberg News was told by a spokesman for Cathay Pacific Airways that the airline industry "is in a *parlous* state worldwide." The ABC anchor Peter Jennings was quoted by Mark Jurkowitz of the *Boston Globe* as saying, "We are in *parlous* economic times."

The word is not related to *parley;* it has nothing to do with the French *parler,* "to talk." *Parlous* has the same meaning as the word it sounds like: *perilous.* The Latin *periculum,* akin to *peritus,* "experiment," means "risk." But *perilous* is beyond "risky," scarier than the general "dangerous" or the unavoidable "hazardous"; it is "fraught (meaning 'full of, laden') with peril."

If *parlous* means *perilous,* who needs both? The two forms of the same word have been battling it out for seven centuries, and today we're going to declare a winner.

Parlous is a delicious example of linguistic syncopation. Every ragtime or jazz enthusiast knows that when you *syncopate* (from the Greek for "cut short"), you begin a note on a weak beat in the bar, sustaining it into the accented part, thereby shifting the accent. In grammar, you *syncopate* by snipping a word short or by skipping one or two syllables in the middle. Examples: *fo'c'sle* for *forecastle,* and *Chumley* for *Cholmondelay.* They don't order *Worcestershire* sauce in Wooster, Ohio.

Usually the shorter and easier forms win, and *extrality* is likely to overtake *extraterritoriality.* However, *parlous* has an arch, archaic ring and carries a touch of the pompously bookish (like *fraught*), while *perilous* has a straightforward, sailor-take-warning feel. You won't be incorrect if you try to impress your friends with the syncopated form of *perilous,* but if you do, it's at your *parl.*

ℰ

Ping!   From the highest reaches of the *New York Times* comes the query: "What does the verb *ping* mean, as in 'I'll *ping* him and ask'?"

At the same time, Microsoft Windows asked itself this question and sent my computer a copy: "What is the *ping* command and how is it used?"

Both senses are illustrated in this comment in *Internet Magazine* in May 2001: "In some offices, people are even sent to '*ping*' the sales department to see if their figures are ready, just as networked computers '*ping*' one another to see if they're still there."

"The *ping* command," Windows informs my machine, "is used to test whether a network connection is active." You send your *ping* and wait for a response from the *pinged* machine. From this we get a metaphoric extension: to *ping* a person, you send an e-mail message to see if your friend is alive and online.

Do not believe the Internet dictionaries that treat the verb as an acronym for Packet Internet Groper, a Unix utility that accomplishes the above test but sounds to me like an odious new form of sexual harassment. The verb's e-mail meaning lies halfway between "to buzz" and "to noodge."

The origin is not, as commonly believed, in the short, high-pitched pulsing sound emitted by sonar. Before that, *ping* signified the engine sound dreaded by motorists; if your engine *pinged,* you probably had piston problems. Before that, it was the sound of a bullet's ricochet: "If a button was shown," wrote Sir James E. Alexander in 1835, "*ping* went a bullet at it immediately." And before that, in 897, King Ælfred the Great, in his translation of St. Gregory's *Liber pastoralis curae,* wrote in Old English, "He waerlice hine *pynge* mid sumum wordum," which means "Let him prick him very cautiously with some words." And before that, Roman noodges used the Latin *pungere,* "to prick, poke, urge." The same basic meaning echoes through the millennia.

If any deeper etymology is required, Arthur, don't *ping* me; I'll *ping* you.

I strongly believe you are mistaken in writing that the network sense of ping *doesn't derive from analogy (direct equivalent, really) to the sonar ping.*

You send out a signal and pay attention to the response. In sonar or on a network.

All of your examples of earlier uses of ping *don't have a darned thing to do with that sense of the word. They are just other uses, other meanings, of* ping.

Sonar ping may derive, cleanly and directly or obscurely and circuitously, from your referenced uses, but it's absurd and contentious to argue that those who originated the network sense of the word didn't take it directly from the everyday knowledge of sonar. You've outsmarted yourself and gotten lost in your own scholarship.

Peter Horton
Santa Monica, California

Playing Percentages.   President Bush the elder often liked to quote Woody Allen as saying, "Ninety percent of life is just showing up." I checked with Allen, who confirmed his authorship of the line but said the percentage he mentioned was 80. Why 80? "The figure seems high to me today," he replied, "but I know it was more than 60, and the extra syllable in 70 ruins the rhythm of the quote, so I think we should let it stand at 80."

This is a formula for profundity, but presidents keep upping the ante, sometimes ruining the rhythm. On a fund-raising trip to California in the fall, Bill Clinton saw a baby girl reach out to him, her little fingers clutching at his hand. "Look at her," he said. "She's holding on. That's 90 percent of life, just holding on."

Ploy.   "That's nothing but a *ploy*," said Bill Bradley to Al Gore on *Meet the Press* last month.

The two men were locked in TV combat. Gore had just suggested that the two Democratic candidates pledge to shun TV commercials and engage only in debates. The vice president dramatically extended his hand and said: "I'm ready to agree right now. Debates aren't *ploys*."

Bradley looked at his opponent's hand like an uninterested palm reader;

he wasn't having any part of the surprise offer: "No, to come here, shake my hand—that's nothing but a *ploy*." At Gore's repeated use of the word, Bradley edged it with increasing scorn, adding, "I'm not someone who's interested in tactics, Al."

Across America, the question arose: was the no-commercials proposal a sincere suggestion, as Gore maintained, or was it merely a *ploy, tactic, ruse, stratagem* or *trick*, as Bradley insisted? Around the world, viewers asked a more fundamental question: What is a *ploy*, anyway?

The attack word is closely associated with the current campaign. Two months ago, Cragg Hines of the *Houston Chronicle* wrote that "Gore has repeatedly tried the weekly debate *ploy* against Bradley, who has refused to take the bait." A month before that, when Gore relocated his headquarters to Nashville—the better to detach from Washington Beltway associations and reestablish middle-American roots—Tex Austin, a musician and cowboy-boot salesman, was quoted deriding the move in the *Chicago Tribune:* "This is obviously just a political *ploy*." This drew an observation from James Dao, a *New York Times* reporter: "History may someday show that voters viewed Mr. Gore's headquarters shift as a disingenuous *ploy* or, more likely, a move that was forgotten the day after it happened."

The word's origin is shrouded in mysterious Highland vapors. Most etymologists believe it to be the product of aphesis, the process by which we clip unaccented vowel syllables off a word's stem. That is how *alone* becomes *lone* and *around* becomes *round*. ("Is the Lone Ranger *round* here, Tonto?") In this hypothesis regarding the origin of *ploy*, the Scottish dialect clipped the *em* off the verb *employ* to create a noun that meant "activity" and later "an amusing way to pass the time; an escapade, hobby or sport."

In 1950, Stephen Potter, the British author of *Gamesmanship* and *Lifemanship* and the coiner of *one-upmanship*, gave the word a tongue-in-cheek sense of "a maneuver to gain the better of an opponent or co-worker." He wrote, "Each one of us can, by *ploy* or *gambit*, most naturally gain the advantage."

In the following decade, the Potter sense of the word was snatched up into the language of diplomacy. An occasional plot device in the 19th-century novels of Anthony Trollope involved the misheard proposal or the misread caress. A man would say or do something innocuous; a Victorian maiden would interpret that word or gesture romantically and accept what she considered as amounting to a proposal of marriage; and the poor (or lucky) fellow found himself affianced.

Lord Rufford makes such a gesture to the husband-hunting Arabella Trefoil in Trollope's 1875 *American Senator* and finds himself in the center of Trefoil's formidable attempt at landing a proper mate. (Her attempt does not succeed.) Trollope uses the same *ploy* four years later in *John Caldigate,* in which John gets thrown into a linen closet with his cousin Julia and comes out, in Julia's and her mother's minds, engaged.

During the Cuban missile crisis of 1962, President Kennedy received two messages from the Soviet Union's Nikita Khrushchev: one was informal and ambiguous, a later one more official and threatening. He chose to ignore the later one and to interpret the earlier one as an offer to remove Soviet missiles in return for a pledge not to invade Cuba—an inference that left Khrushchev with his non-offer "accepted." This deft maneuver was described, in what some felt was the mythmaking that followed, as "the Trollope *ploy.*"

In current usage, a *ploy* is more cunning than a *subterfuge,* not as overtly false or bookishly old-fashioned as a *ruse* and somewhat more creative than a *tactic.* It is not planned in as much detail as a *stratagem,* is less contrived than an *artifice* and does not have the coquettish quality of a *wile.* A *ploy* is more underhanded than a *maneuver* and not as playful or artful as a *dodge.*

Another synonym is *gambit,* which began as an opening move in chess that sacrifices a pawn to gain position for a more powerful piece. By metaphoric extension, a *gambit* can range from an enticing opening in conversation to a *tactic* in gaining advantage in business.

In the lexicon of trickery, a correct gamesman uses a *gambit* while an engaging rogue employs a *ploy,* and the mildest deceiver trots out a *gimmick.* When Bill Bradley's spokesman, Eric Hauser, followed up his candidate's *ploy* characterization by castigating Gore for "resorting to contrived *gimmicks,*" his use of *contrived* was redundant.

In politics, as we see, a *ploy* is double-edged; accusations of trickiness can get tricky. In dealing with nationalities, Winston Churchill observed in 1906, "Nothing is more fatal than a *dodge*. Wrongs will be forgiven, sufferings and losses will be forgiven or forgotten, battles will be remembered only as they recall the martial virtues of the combatants; but anything like a *trick,* will always rankle."

I think you connived at a crime. (Note first the precise use of connive.*) You inserted* tactic, *in the singular, among synonyms for* ploy: ruse, stratagem, trick. *That use of* tactic *in the singular destroys the root ideas of the proper word* tactics, *also a singular though it looks plural. It means* arrangement, method, system, plan of action. *To reduce it to a detail of the plan is to ignore a difference that runs through all talk about practical matters, the difference between means and their coordination.*

The distinction is embodied in all the words that end in -ics: ethics, politics, esthetics, mathematics. They are collectives and suffer loss when used in the singular. Usage has sanctioned "the Protestant ethic" and "the artist's esthetic," and there is a bare excuse for it, because in these phrases the collective idea is retained. Nobody is tempted to say that Van Gogh's esthetic was thick oil on the brush, any more than with system, *one would say "my system for driving nails is a hammer."*

In short, tactics is a bunch of ploys, and there's an end.

Jacques Barzun
San Antonio, Texas

Plus Which.   As Bill Clinton prepares to leave the White House, constitutionally forbidden to return as its principal occupant, some wonder: what will we miss most about his tenure? The answer to those in the dialect dodge is plain: the Ozarkian's free-and-easy use of the American idiom.

"There are a lot of family-owned businesses," the president said in support of reduction of inheritance taxes, "that people would like to pass down to their family members . . . that would be burdened by the way the estate tax works. *Plus which,* the maximum rate's too high."

Plus which is an intriguing Americanism. Its meaning is not merely "plus, in addition to" or "and." In the context of Clinton's usage, *plus which* means "besides"; its direct synonym is the earlier "besides which," in its adverbial sense of "moreover, furthermore"; these are connecting words that transmit greater emphasis than conjunctions like *and* or the *plus* that is unaccompanied by *which*.

Plus which, first cited by Merriam-Webster in *Down Beat* magazine in 1950, seems to have overtaken *besides which* in recent years. Perhaps this was stimulated by the advertising industry's fascination with *plus* at the beginning of sentences to mean "as an extra added attraction."

The fourth edition of the *American Heritage Dictionary* labels *plus which* "not well established in formal writing"; its editor, Joe Pickett, calls the usage "a bizarre construction that combines two conjunctions and has the force of a conjunctive adverb" (indeed!).

OK; that does it with *plus which*. But in settling that meaning of "furthermore, you ninny," we have just blundered into an area of furious lexicographic controversy: is *plus* a conjunction (which connects) or a preposition (which introduces)?

Should you say, "Two plus two *is* four" or "Two plus two *are* four"? (I'm a preppy, and say *is*.) Should you begin a sentence with *plus*? (I say no, never.) But Fred Mish, editor in chief of *Merriam-Webster's Tenth Collegiate* and now America's Rex of Lex, says, "Nobody should let their drawers get in a twist over this question." (Plus this subtly demonstrates that the plural *their* can refer to the singular *nobody* in an idiom.)

If I had given someone a list of my needs, and suddenly remembered another one, I'd naturally call out plus. *If we didn't use* plus *we'd have to use a long-winded group of words, such as "in addition to all of which," and by the time we'd have said all that we'd have forgotten what we needed to add.*

In its proper place, plus *is a fine word. We couldn't do without it. Please don't abuse it.*

Estelle Gelshenen
Northport, New York

Two CONJUNCTIONS? *I can agree with Mr. Pickett that "plus which" behaves like a conjunctive adverb; but when has "which" ever been defined as a conjunction? The construction is quite straightforward (although—in my opinion—the recent popularity of "plus" as a preposition, or a conjunction, or a conjunctive adverb, is an abomination and ought to be abolished!): it is simply an adverbial prepositional phrase, a preposition plus (!!!) a noun phrase or, in this instance, a pronoun object. The pronoun "which" is used to replace the noun clause(s) "that people . . . too high." An analogue: "I didn't feel like going to the birthday party; in addition to that, I hadn't bought a gift." My own "Sprachgefuehl" would lead me to use "in addition to that" rather than "plus which." It has more euphony and style, at the cost of just four more syllables.*

Robert Frankum
Huntington, New York

As a person who has been a teacher of mathematics for a long time it is clear that "Two plus two is four" is shorter for "The sum of two plus two is four."

Stan Lieberman
Howard Beach, New York

Two plus two equal four. So there.

"Plus" is a perfectly proper word to begin a sentence with. Similarly, "with" is a perfectly proper word to end a sentence with. Additionally, plus can be an adjective as well as a conjunction, as in the following sentences, and there is no rule preventing starting a sentence with an adjective:

"Plus fours are no longer fashionable in golf."
"Plus sizes are hard to find at the mall."

Ralph Kirshner
Center Harbor, New Hampshire

Politics Of.   Think of Ronald Reagan, and his phrases *evil empire* and *there you go again* and *make my day* come to mind, along with the derogations *star wars* and *morning in America.*

Think of George Bush the elder, and you have *a thousand points of light* and *line in the sand* and *kinder and gentler nation,* with his *voodoo economics* and *read my lips, no new taxes* tossed back at him.

Think of Bill Clinton, and—what? In his ascent to power, the vividly Carvillian *it's the economy, stupid* was indelibly associated with Clinton; in his descent, it was the relentlessly replayed sentence accompanied by his wagging finger.

This department seeks memorable Clintonisms from friend and foe, but will begin today with a linguistic sleeper. A phrase coined by candidate Clinton in his campaign for the Democratic nomination has been gaining strength as the years flash by.

His chief rival at the time, Paul Tsongas of Massachusetts, ran a TV spot claiming to be honest, truthful and unpolished—"no Bill Clinton, that's for sure." Asked in an Illinois cheesecake emporium in March 1992 about this and other charges about his character, Clinton replied: "I think that the American people can spot somebody that's on their side. . . . They're tired of *the politics of personal destruction.*"

As president in 1994, Clinton lashed out at Republicans in Congress for blocking his proposals, charging them with "*the politics of personal destruction* and of legislative obstruction." This caused a Georgia member of the House minority, Representative Newt Gingrich, to call his attack "not *the politics of personal destruction;* it's the politics of self-destruction." After the GOP upset that year, establishing itself as the majority in the House, Clinton slammed back with: "My job is not to stand in the way and be an obstructionist force. My job is not to practice *the politics of personal destruction.*"

He continued to use the phrase as an attacking defense, culminating in a short Rose Garden speech after impeachment in 1998: "We must stop *the politics of personal destruction.* We must get rid of the poisonous venom of excessive partisanship, obsessive animosity and uncontrolled anger." Nitpickers who winced at the redundancy of "poisonous venom" were impressed with Clinton's alliteration in his peroration to "rise above the rancor."

The phrase outlived the Clinton presidency. Last month, the *Washington Post* played on it in a headline above a column by George Will about the likely resistance to George W. Bush's proposals by a Senate controlled by Democrats: "The Politics of Personal Obstruction." When a phrase is familiar enough to take such wordplay, that is evidence that it is becoming fixed in the lexicon.

In coining phrases, *the politics of* has long been found useful. In the 1860 edition of his *Leaves of Grass,* Walt Whitman sang of "the politics of Nature"; Upton Sinclair in 1918 excoriated the "politics of hypocrisy"; Aldous Huxley titled a 1963 book *The Politics of Ecology;* and Yippies in 1968 lolled back to enjoy with Timothy Leary "the politics of ecstasy."

In the politics of politics, Arthur Schlesinger Jr. led the way, beginning in 1949 with *The Politics of Freedom,* followed by his *Politics of Upheaval* in 1957 and, five years later, *The Politics of Hope.* This deeply impressed Vice President Hubert Humphrey, who in 1968—not an especially upbeat time in war-torn America—was optimistic enough to hail "the politics of happiness, the politics of purpose and the politics of joy."

Poo-teen.   He may be with us for a while, so let's get his name right: the president of Russia is Vladimir Putin, pronounced "POO-teen." "The stem for Putin's name is derived from *put,* meaning 'path' or 'road,' " notes Albert Weeks, an NYU professor emeritus now living in Sarasota, Florida.

Marat Akchurin of the American Name Society adds: "The meaning of *Putin* was 'the one who was born on the road'; that is, the mother was traveling when the birth took place. So, within the current political context in Russia, Putin could be taken to mean 'transitional.' " Another possible etymology is the verb *putat,* meaning "to swaddle, bind" and, by extension, "to confuse, make ambiguous, entangle."

Can it be connected to *Rasputin,* the derisive name for the swinging Russian monk, Grigory Novykh, who dominated the court of Czar Nicholas II? One meaning of *rasputye* is "debauched," but another is "crossroad"; *putin* without the prefix *ras* could mean "one-track road." Be careful not to read too much into this.

You write that the name of Russian President Putin means in Russian, "born on the road." According to the standard Russian dictionary "Ojegov," the name can be defined three different ways. The first meaning, from the Russian word "Putina" (POOtina), is "fishing season." The second meaning, from the word "Put" (POOT), is a "way" or a road. The third potential meaning—which may be most apropos for Mr. Safire's column—is from the verb "Putats" (Pootats), which means "to make a mess" or "to speak without logical connection."

Boris Zeldin and Damian Schaible

Jersey City, New Jersey

Pop Go the Lyrics.   "Nobody knows what the words mean," goes the Web site advertising for an album titled *All for You,* by the pop singer Diana Krall, "but when Diana sings them, it isn't hard to draw your own conclusions." The album celebrates the songs popularized a half-century ago by Nat King Cole, and the reference is to the song "Frim Fram Sauce."

The lyric reads: "I don't want French fried potatoes, red ripe tomatoes / I'm never satisfied. / I want the frim fram sauce / With ussin-fay, with shafafa on the side."

This is a job for the Deconstruction Workers Union. *Frim fram* is one of the oldest terms surviving as slang, cited in John Heywood's 1546 book of proverbs: "she maketh earnest matters of every *flymflam,*" about a woman easily deceived. *Flimska* is "mockery" in Old Norse and *flim,* "a lampoon"; an attempt to fool the monarch in 1538 was described in England's State Papers as "a *flim flawe* to stoppe the ymagination of the Kynge."

Thus, as sung by Cole and then Krall a half-millennium later, *"frim fram* sauce" is the oleaginous goo of deceit poured over some unsuspecting dupe. (All dupes are unsuspecting, just as all goo is oleaginous; I'll hear from the Squad Squad about those redundancies, but a mouth-filling phrase suspends the rule.)

Next: *Ussin-fay* is pig Latin for *fussin'* (just as *ixnay* conceals *nix*), which in turn has a slang sense of "playing about fretfully"; a whimpering infant is said to be *fussin'*. That locution seems out of place in a menu metaphor, but I can think of no other logical etymology of *ussin-fay*.

Shafafa is a problem; it is too far a stretch from *alfalfa*, and no slang term or Old Norse derivation offers a clue. I called Diana Krall, the singer who resuscitated the word, and asked if she had any idea about what it meant or where it came from.

"It's all about sex," she replied innocently, though in the sultry tone that has become her musical signature.

Oh. That would explain the lyric's "never satisfied," as well as its sauce of deceit, and supply another entendre to the fretful whimpering of *fussin'*.

We have hummed through the hermeneutics of a single lyric to show that in pop music the sophisticated innuendo of the '30s and '40s is being newly appreciated by a generation not then born. That explains the come-back of Cole Porter (whose "Let's Do It" was banned by some radio stations for its suggestiveness), as well as Ira Gershwin, Oscar Hammerstein and Johnny Mercer as interpreted by today's balladeers. The intricate rhyming and occasional character development in their songs is received with respect from enthusiasts of *neo-soul* and *post-grunge* and *house music*. (Definitions for those are vamping until I'm ready.)

"There's a return to personal storytelling," Krall noted. She sang a little of "I've Got You Under My Skin" in the Frank Sinatra style and said: "Then we slowed it down, which made it more tragic. I like messing with tempo because it changes the story."

Story is central in "Contemporary R&B," the designation given the rhythm and blues sung by artists like Alicia Keys and India.Arie. Note the way Arie styles her name: like a dot-com, she uses a period in the middle rather than a space. This playing with normal style was pioneered by the poet Edward Estlin Cummings, who liked to use lowercase initials. It carries forward the corporate mid-capitalization craze begun with "TelePrompTer" in 1950 (a style the *New York Times* resisted) and taken up by "DaimlerChrysler," "WorldCom" and many others. It will soon be followed by other punctuation marks by people and companies following the crowd that is straining to be distinctive. (Should I change my byline to "William!Safire"?)

Dot-Arie sings of an "Acoustic Soul." After the 1950s civil rights revolution, *soul music* enjoyed great popularity. The intense, earthy outgrowth of gospel singing was an expression of black culture; the term took hold about the same time as *soul food* and was followed by political figures who were eager to be said to have *soul*. As the musical style was revived in our time in modified form, a new label was adopted: *neo-soul*.

Time magazine's Christopher John Farley defined the term in 1998 as combining "the classic soul of the 60s and 70s with a healthy appetite for 90s sonic experimentation and boundary crossing . . . lyrics are more oblique and yet more socially and emotionally relevant than those of gangsta rappers." This month, reporting on the sweep of the Grammy awards by Alicia Keys, *U.S. News* said that Keys "sings classic soul-style melodies with a hip-hop flavor. . . . The music biz is praying that Keys . . . and other *neo-soulsters* will revive slumping record sales."

In categories like the chanted patter of *hard-core rap*, the fast-faded, grubby-dingy *grunge*, the anguished, rock-influenced introspection of *post-grunge*, the offbeat, Jamaican *ska-punk* and the *British garage*, violent sex is still a seller. "In terms of language about sex and violence," says Jim Steinblatt of ASCAP, "the gangsta-lifestyle music is still big, but as rap music has become more mainstream, the lyrics are not quite as explicit." Two generations ago, the word *love* was even more frequently used in lyrics than *baby*; in the '90s, as *baby* held its own, the use of *love* declined. But in Keys's "Fallin'," now the "Song of the Year," the word *love* is used no fewer than six times.

Consider the toning-down of the above-mentioned *British garage*—the name taken from the Paradise Garage in New York—also known as *speed garage* and *2-step*. (Strange name for a dance, "two-step"; even I can do it.) Born in the disco music of the '70s and part of the genre labeled *electronica*, this art form combined digital *reggae*, or *ragga*, with "diva vocals"— high-pitched melodies sung at the top of the lungs to a 4-4 beat—and became known in the '80s as *house music*. In the current decade, hoarse voices tell me, the garage outside the house has a quieter, "more soulful, sophisticated and organic feel." *Organic* is a vogue word in modern music criticism, as it is among nutritionists (formerly dietitians) and now automobile advertisers. Its musical meaning varies widely but is never associated with a pipe organ or mouth organ.

The tuned-in reader will have observed the use of *diva* applied to female stars. (*Star* went out with *dietitian*.) This is rooted in the Latin *diva*, "goddess," and until recently has been primarily applied to female opera singers, usually temperamental *prima donnas*. With *star* and even *superstar* passé, and *goddess* limited to "sex goddess," the old *diva* once again took center stage.

Old-time rock is also enjoying a revival, especially as sung by U2. Most of the veteran group's new fans think the name a play on "You, too?" rather than on a high-altitude American spy plane that could read the license plates on cars entering the Kremlin (and that, like rock music, is still operational; words and parachute by Francis Gary Powers). Numerals are a vital part of many names of musical groups. Besides *U2* and *2 Live Crew*, we have *Sum 41, blink-182, 3 Doors Down* and *9 Inch Nails*.

A bluegrass winner is "O Death," by Ralph Stanley, which offers a chilling evocation by a man begging to be spared a little more time. Such serious bluegrass songs, some evoking and providing comfort for the 9/11 mood, contrast mightily with such derogatory ditties we used to strum: "I'd Rather Pass Another Kidney Stone Than Another Night With You" and a feminist favorite, "Shut Up and Talk to Me."

Dig it or deplore it, the music industry is a fecund source of lexical terms—if you can make out the words.

I was delighted to see attention given to the song "Frim Fram Sauce." However, I was disappointed that you neglected to mention the author of that song, Joseph Ricardel.

Vincent Ricardel
New York, New York

Shafafa is an Arabic word which means lace, what belly dancers wear, and refers to partial nudity.

Heskel M. Haddad, MD
New York, New York

Blessings on thee, verbal man, for spelling out that wonderfully incomprehensible word "ussin-fay." After years of poring through old Nat King Cole sheet music, we had given up ever seeing it in print. For a time, we thought it might be the name of some nightmarish recipe called "the Awesome Fate," but Diana Krall's recent rendition of the song proved that false.

We do feel, however, that you may be trying too hard to link each silly name to an actual food item. We like to think the song depicts a woman of moderate means (who has grown up on "fish cakes and rye bread") sitting in a fancy restaurant, trying to order exotic dishes and fumbling over the names. In that case, "frim fram" loosely translates into, "y'know, that wonderful sauce I had one time that went with the whatchamacallit fish." And the same could be said for "shafafa" (although that could possibly be a gross mispronunciation of "chiffon"). The use of the Pig Latin "ussin-fay" for "fussin" fits right in with this interpretation.

Diana Krall says it's all about sex, and that's certainly the way she sings it. But Carmen McRae, in her 1983 rendition, says it's all about attitude and a heaping plateful.

Floyd Gumble and Carol Adamson

Carmel, New York

I love that Frim Fram sauce! I think I have solved the mystery of "shafafa on the side." I think shafafa is from Arabic, i.e., a Semitic triconsonantal root (there's an Israeli place name "Beit Shafafa"), naturalized into some African language (the way Swahili does a lot of). The root "sh-f-f" yields meanings of either "lips"—your lips on the side—or "diaphanous garments, filmy clothes"—Give me that teasing deception, courting ["fussin roun" as in Thurber], and your lips [or sexy clothes] on the side.

Leslie S. B. MacCoull

Society for Coptic Archaeology

Tempe, Arizona

Pound Sand. When Tony Blair called George W. Bush on the day after September 11 to pledge his support, the British prime minister said he assumed the United States was considering an immediate response. According to a report in the *Sunday Age* of Melbourne, Australia, giving an anonymous Blair adviser as a source, Bush replied, "We're thinking about that," but he did not want to "*pound sand* with millions of dollars in weapons" to make himself feel good.

Historians a decade hence will probably be able to determine if President Bush actually used that expression in a call that was surely recorded by both men. But two insider accounts of the week following the attacks on the U.S. show that it was in active use in the White House. According to Bob Woodward and Dan Balz of the *Washington Post*, Andrew Card, the chief of staff, asked rhetorically in a Camp David meeting on September 15, "What is the definition of success?" The reporters then paraphrased Card's answer: "He said it would first be proving that this was not just an effort to *pound sand*—as the president had repeatedly made clear." In *Time* magazine's version of the same meeting, "A quick cruise-missile response was ruled out as ineffective. White House chief of staff Andy Card called this the '*pound sand*' alternative."

From this we can deduce that the president in all likelihood did use the phrase that tense week, perhaps repeatedly. What did he mean by it?

Following the clue of context, the Bush administration usage of *pound sand* means "waste time, act ineffectively," influenced by the expression used pejoratively by bomber pilots about meaningless missions, "making the rubble bounce."

That is a variant of the phrase's original meaning. "I find it interesting," e-mails Wayne Butler from Marblehead, Massachusetts, "that writers in family newspapers would use such phrases as 'turn in the barrel' and '*pound sand*' when the origin and/or complete phrase is so well known." (That was after I had written that it was somebody's "turn in the barrel," forgetting that the phrase originated in the punch line of a dirty joke. I apologize for blanking out on that; the phrase seems to have crossed into general usage from its sexual origin, similar to today's innocent use of *wuss* for "one who is unmanly" or *schmuck* for "jerk.")

In the same way, *pound sand* has escaped its earlier scatological association. Along with *go pound salt*, the imperative now has the dismissive sense of "buzz off; go jump in the lake"; it has lost its taboo connotation of "do something humiliating to oneself."

As used earlier by politicians, the phrase is not taboo. When Clark Clifford in the last days of the 1948 election campaign told his boss, President Harry Truman, that a *Newsweek* poll of fifty reporters gave him no chance of beating Tom Dewey, the man from Independence replied: "I know every one of these fifty fellows. There isn't one of them has enough sense to *pound sand* in a rat hole." This salty derogation of the media was recalled by the first President Bush toward the end of his calamitous campaign in 1992; when he saw a sign that read "Annoy the media, elect Bush!" he laughed and said, "I feel like Harry Truman when he talked about fifty reporters, and he said not one of them knows enough to *pound sand* in a rat hole." (The elder Bush's assessment of media wisdom was not as accurate as Truman's.)

Truman did not coin the phrase. In volume 4 of the great *Dictionary of American Regional English* (*DARE*), the origin is tracked to someone's refusal to give a recommendation. A *Dialect Notes* issue of 1912 records "He wouldn't know enough to *pound sand* in a rat hole; so don't get him." The same source provides a variant recorded in 1923: "Don't know enough to *pound akerns* in a woodpecker hole."

This takes us into the world of metaphoric ignorance. *DARE* asked Americans across the nation how they would end the sentence "He hasn't sense enough to . . ." Among the most colorful answers were "to pour water [or sand] out of a boot with directions on the heel and the toes cut"; "to lap salt and drool"; "to pack guts to a hog"; "to tie his own shoelaces"; and "to find his rear end with both hands and a road map." By far the most frequent was "to come in out of the rain," with "to *pound sand* down a rat hole" finishing a strong second.

That's been the primary sense for years. However, the sense that is now becoming predominant, replacing stupefying stupidity, is "wasting time by doing something pointless." A 1975 usage found by *DARE* is "The lumber didn't come, so the carpenters *pounded sand* all afternoon."

That was the meaning of the phrase used by the president to the prime minister, and by the White House chief of staff to the crisis group assembled at Camp David—if all the backgrounders are true and the reporters are not *pounding sand.*

☙

Predator's Adjective.   In finding that Microsoft violated antitrust laws, Judge Thomas Penfield Jackson cited the 1890 Sherman Act, which requires the plaintiff to prove "that the defendant has engaged in *predatory* or anticompetitive conduct."

He ruled, "Viewing Microsoft's conduct as a whole also reinforces the conviction that it was *predacious.*" The *New York Times* headline writer preferred the more familiar adjective in the act, and went with "*predatory* behavior."

Which is it? The Latin root is *praedari,* "to prey upon." Since 1589, *predatory* behavior has been characterized by pillaging, plundering and robbery. Edward Gibbon, in his 1781 *Decline and Fall of the Roman Empire,* wrote of a general who "recalled to their standard his *predatory* detachments."

Predacious, more often spelled *predaceous,* came along in 1713 to be applied to animals. Samuel Johnson's friend and acolyte Mrs. Piozzi wrote in 1789 of "one *predaceous* creature caught in the very act of gorging his prey."

Today, *predacious* is almost always applied to the savagery of animals; *predatory,* which appears in databases one hundred times more often, describes the plundering or rapacious action of humans, extended to the monopolistic action of corporations.

Ironically, Microsoft's *Encarta* dictionary loosely defines both adjectives first as pertaining to animals; not so in the *Oxford English Dictionary* or *Merriam-Webster's Collegiate,* and their sequence of definitions is clearly backed up by my usage count.

Therefore, I say the judge erred in choosing *predacious;* Bill Gates's practices may be monopolistic, but to judge them to be savagely animalistic goes overboard.

☙

Preshrunk Flower.   In introducing Don Rumsfeld as his choice for secretary of defense, President Bush the Younger emphasized the designee's policy strength and ability to hold his own in council: "You bet General Powell's a strong figure and Dick Cheney's *no shrinking violet*. But neither is Don Rumsfeld." The phrase runs in the family; shortly after his election, President Bush the Elder said of the then newly chosen House Republican whip, Newt Gingrich: "I don't think he needs any lectures from me. He's not going to suddenly become a *shrinking violet*, but we don't want that."

Asked about the man selected to be Bush's secretary of veterans affairs (the government mistakenly puts no apostrophe after veterans), the retired commandant of the Marine Corps, Charles Krulak, said of Anthony Principi: "Tony is no *shrinking violet*. He'll tell it like it is and do what's right."

Why has this metaphor, used only in negation, become so vital to the vocabulary of the new administration? More to the linguistic point, when did violets gain their reputation for congenital shrinkage, and why?

The earliest use that my researcher, Elizabeth Phillips, can find is the 1827 play *Sylvia*, by George Darley. In it, the fairy queen Morgana says to the spirit Floretta: "I've seen thee stand / Drowning amid the fields to save a daisy, / And with warm kisses keep its sweet life in. / The *shrinking violet* thou dost cheer; and raise / The cowslip's drooping head."

The novelist Nathaniel Hawthorne, in his 1860 *The Marble Faun*, used the flower in a simile stressing shyness: "An old Greek sculptor, no doubt, found his models in the open sunshine, and among pure and princely maidens, and thus the nude statues of antiquity are as modest as violets."

Yes, but why is a violet more modest than, say, one of Everett Dirksen's favorite marigolds? A clue can be found in the poet John Byrne Leicester Warren's 1893 poem about Circe, a beautiful witch: "Thou art the *shrinking violet*, half afraid"—and here comes the explanation—"That, in rathe April born, / Where icy winds complain, / Hardly unfolds her petals to the morn / Between the rainbow and the weep of rain." Look up *rathe;* it's not a misprint of *rather* but an archaic word meaning "exposed too early, as in a flower that blooms in still-frigid spring."

That's the source of the trope: the violet may appear to shrink from the cold because it often blossoms early. Is this just a conceit of poets and novelists? Let's turn to a botanist. Dr. Wayt Thomas of the New York Botanical Garden gets to the root of the plant's seeming shyness: "A possible answer is that violets often hold their blooms underneath, or partly underneath, the foliage, so that the otherwise showy flowers are hidden."

However, President Bush should not use the metaphor too frequently. For freshness of imagery, I recommend "He's no drooping cowslip!"

Props.   When at a loss for words (a good title for a collection of these columns), I walk around the Washington bureau of the *Times* as deadline time approaches, hands in my pockets, head down but with ears attuned, trolling for linguistic leads. Reporters, too busy at their terminals to converse at length with a passing language maven, toss the latest locutions in my direction, as one would throw scraps to a hungry hound.

"*Props!*" barked Kit Seelye, never looking up. I snatched at the possibilities of meanings for the plural noun: (1) A shortening of *propellers,* a means of propulsion in the pre-jet era; no, nothing new about that. (2) A shortening of *properties,* articles on a stage set, an item like Yorick's skull in Hamlet's hand; that has centuries of use in greenrooms. (3) Supports like tent poles, or aides that "prop up" a political candidate; that's a current sense, but hardly on the qui vive or worthy of note. That leaves (4), (5) and (6): a shortening of *propaganda, propination* or *propaedeutics.*

My next stop was the news desk, where young clerks and interns communicate with all the latest and most mysterious locutions. "If I were to use the word *props* in a sentence," I said as if testing them, "what would you take it to mean?"

"Applause," said one. "Kudos," agreed another, apparently versed in classical Greek (which would have told him that *propaedeutic* means "about elementary instruction"). An editor, eyes fixed on his screen but always alert to his surroundings, gave a little grunt and then said, "Two hits in the last two months in the *Times.*" Without missing a beat, the helpful backfielder had searched the newspaper's recent archives and in a flash found both citations. One of the clerks (never say "copy boy," especially if she's a young woman) reached into the mouth of a printer as it spat out two pages and handed me the research it would have taken Sir James Murray and his minions at the *Oxford English Dictionary* years to assemble a century ago.

"I'd like to give *props* to my dawg D.J. Jazzy Jeff," the president of CBS Television, Leslie Moonves, told advertisers as reported by Jim Rutenberg of the *Times* last month, "for waking us all up this morning." (When an interviewee pronounces the word *dog* as "dawg," it is permissible in the more informal sections of the paper to render it as pronounced.)

This month, before her performance at a Battery Park festival helping to revitalize downtown New York, the singer Sheryl Crow offered her respects to the heroic Fire Department: "I want to give *props* to Ladder 9, Engine 33—my buds."

From these examples it can be deduced that the verb currently most closely associated with the noun *props* is *give.* Now the etymologist rushes back to his library and plunges into other databases and slang booklets for early usages and semantic development.

In April 1992 (where have I been?) in a *Seattle Times* article on graffiti, latrinalia and hip-hop lingo, Marc Ramirez defined *to give props* as "to honor or owe respect to. Writers sometimes *give props* to other writers or crews in their pieces by including their tags or initials." Three months later, the music industry phrase appeared in *Ebony* magazine: "*Give* him *props.* "

I have nondatabase resources. Definitions of two senses were provided in the fifth edition (1997) of "A Dictionary of Cal Poly Slang," compiled by the students of intercultural communication at California State Polytechnic University, Pomona, under the direction of Dr. Judi Sanders. One sense is "friends: I got *props* who can back me up if I need them." The second, and ultimately dominant, sense is reported with the origin implicit: "Proper respect. The class gave me much *props* during the presentation."

That's it: *props,* coined on the West Coast in the music business, is a slang term for "proper respect" and is now sweeping the country, or at least my newsroom. (Consequently, *propination* means "a toast to someone's health.")

With a somewhat less hangdawg expression, I cruised the bureau again, giving *props* to the with-it clerks, until I heard shoes.

Jack Cushman, the weekend editor, mentioned that he heard someone say, "My wife has *shoes* with that." That didn't impress me (my wife has shoes with that outfit, too), but the editor repeated the word in a broader-context phrase: "Very worrisome *shoes*."

Short for *issues*! Another significant lexical find. We have seen how the scholarly-sounding word *issues* has for a decade swept aside the prosaic *problems* and obliterated the euphemism *challenges*. Even the feminist slogan "You got a problem with that?" has been emended to "You got an *issue* with that?"

To retain its freshness or insidership, a voguism frequently has to mutate, usually by clipping the first syllable. (Your children refer to you as *rents*, not *parents*.) Thus do we now have the second syllable of *issues* acting for the entire word. How to express it in print? This does not work: *'sues*. Nor does this: *'ssues*. The printed word must reflect the pronunciation, which could be *shooz* or *shoes*.

In my judgment, the clipped form of *issues* is best expressed in print with an apostrophe to indicate the lost syllable, followed by the group of letters that most familiarly evokes the sound. Thus, if you wish to pay proper respect to issues of great moment while appearing to be in that moment, you can say, "I give *props* to *'shoes*."

Props *(Cont'd).*   More than one hundred e-mailers responded to my column about *props*, a slang term with its origin in "proper respect."

"I thought you were going to mention Aretha Franklin's usage of the word on her 1967 hit single 'Respect,'" observes Dan Williamson of the Department of Philosophy at San Jose State University. "I think she sings, 'Give me my *propers* when I get home.' Despite the somewhat down-and-funky implications, I could swear that's really what yo' music-biz pals are really thinking."

Bernard Schneider of Falmouth Foreside, Maine, recalled that "during a recently aired Ed Bradley interview of the artist on *60 Minutes*, he inferred that her artistic plea for *propers* was for adoration and attention of a sexual nature."

That torrent of informed correction drove me to J. Redding Ware's 1909 *Passing English of the Victorian Era,* which touches lightly on the term as "erotic."

Reached during a tour that took her through Washington, Franklin is having none of that. Her use of *propers* (which many heard as *profits*) in the lyric was her own, not in the words originally written and performed by Otis Redding in 1965.

"I do say *propers,*" says the queen of soul. "I got it from the Detroit street. It was common street slang in the 1960s. The person's saying it has a sexual connotation couldn't be further from the truth. 'My *propers*' means 'mutual respect'—what you know is right."

Proteomics.   Remember the word urgently whispered into Dustin Hoffman's ear in the 1967 movie *The Graduate*—the secret that would lead him on to great fortune? Of course you do: "*plastics!*"

At the World Economic Forum in Davos, Switzerland, this year's word —the linguistic key to the future—was whispered into my ear by a great brain scientist: "*proteomics!*"

As in *genomics,* the study of the genetic material in the chromosomes unique to a specific organism, the accent is on the *om.* Pronounced "pro-tee-OM-iks," the hot new word in the cutting-edge community means "the study of the way proteins expressed by genes interact inside cells, especially to determine differences in protein action between diseased cells and healthy ones."

We need to know this, not so much to understand the sequencing of the human genome as to be able to drop the word into cocktail-party conversation.

(Nobody goes to *cocktail parties* anymore, because ever-fewer people are being served individually mixed cocktails, since it is easier for waiters to pass out glasses of wine; instead, we go to *receptions,* a word that conceals today's standardized boozing. However, *cocktail* remains an adjective describing a perfect little black dress and *cocktail-party* lives on as a compound adjective modifying *conversation,* the phrase meaning "idle chatter." I have digressed.)

The term *proteome* ("proteins that are encoded and expressed by a genome") was coined in 1994 by Marc Wilkins, then a graduate student at Macquarrie University in Sydney, Australia. On the analogy of *genome/genomics* came the formulation *proteome/proteomics.* Reached in Sydney, Wilkins—now with Proteome Systems there—defines *proteomics* as "the study of proteins, how they're modified, when and where they're expressed, how they're involved in metabolic pathways and how they interact with one another."

Frankly, if I were a biotech genius faced with the challenge of coining a word for "the study of proteins expressed by genes," I would have come up with the easier-to-say *proteinomics.* That has the smooth consonant *n* between the vowels *e* and *o,* as in *economics.* The *-omics* suffix is most comfortable following an *n:* you often heard *Nixonomics, Reaganomics* and *Clintonomics* but not *Fordomics, Carteromics* or *Bushomics.*

The *New York Times* reporter Nicholas Wade, soon after the widely hailed publication of evolution's set of instructions, wrote in June 2000, "Understanding the role of every human protein—*proteomics*—will be one of the goals of the post-genome era." (Are we post-genomic already? Genome, we hardly knew ye.) A *Times* business reporter, Sana Siwolop, followed up with an article about "an early leader in the field of *proteomics,* which many scientists generally regard as the next step after genomics research. *Proteomics* involves the large-scale study of the proteins that are made by genes."

As I whispered the magical word denoting the lucrative field into every available ear in Davos, one listener nodded and whispered back, "*optical semiconductor!*" His badge identified him as Michael Dell, the computer man. It seems that a regular *semiconductor,* like the chip in today's computers, is based on electricity, but an *optical semiconductor* is based on light, of which nothing is faster. This fellow Dell thinks the phrase *optical semiconductor* will be on everyone's lips in a few years, and I pass it along here in case people betting on *proteomics* lose their shirts.

However, eight syllables are a mouthful; how about *opticonductor,* or shorter still, crossing the *opticon*? You don't have to understand this stuff to name it.

Proteomics very soon will be over, and superseded by metabolomics, name-dropped by a colleague here. Proteins are, after all, only a subset of all the chemicals that bounce and diffuse around the inside of a cell. These metabolites, for example, sugars and lipids, are the products, substrates, stimulants and repressors of proteins and genes.

And when metabolomics is over, we'll go back to good ol' cell biology.

Doug Yu
School for Biological Sciences
University of East Anglia
Norwich, United Kingdom

I am a lowly college student with only a couple of semesters of Greek, but I may be able to offer a good reason why the "omics" suffix is most comfortable following an "n." My understanding is that the suffix is actually "nomics," coming from the Greek "nomos," meaning custom or law.

Ross O'Connell
Amherst, Massachusetts

You of all people! Nothing is faster than light, so an optical semiconductor is based on light, than *which nothing is faster, not* of *which.*

Gerald M. Levitis, MD
New York, New York

When you write that nothing is faster than light, haven't you impaled yourself on the horns of a Lurking Amphiboly? It is like saying that nothing is better than mom's cooking, a terrible indictment of the old lady's cuisine. Fill my tank with nothing! It is faster than light and a good deal cheaper.

J. J. Kilpatrick
Washington, D.C.

Proteomic Fix.   I wrote, "An optical semiconductor is based on light, of which nothing is faster." Fourteen members of the Gotcha! Gang, including James J. Kilpatrick, journalism's master philologist, noted that "nothing is faster *of* light" is meaningless, and that if I meant "nothing is faster *than* light," I should have written, "light, *than* which nothing is faster." They are correct. Some days never end.

Push-Back.   Douglas Feith, a high-level Pentagon official, took me aside at a reception and whispered a single noun in my ear: "*Push-back.*" I felt like Dustin Hoffman getting the one-word advice about plastics in *The Graduate.*

He's right; the noun *push-back* is everywhere. The vogue began with the verb form among secretaries of state: Henry Kissinger often spoke of seeking "to *push back* the shadow of nuclear catastrophe." In 1998, Madeleine Albright spoke of "one of the major reasons to *push back* on Saddam," and in May of this year, Colin Powell said, "I have to *push back* a little when you say America is not willing to give its lives."

The Pentagon has now nounified it. Asked if he realized the uproar that would be caused when the public learned that the army was buying its black berets from China, the army's chief of staff, General Eric Shinseki, gulped and said, "I think we expected there would be some *push-back*." It spread quickly. Asked if she spoke her mind about environmental affairs to the president, Christie Todd Whitman said: "He wants strong people. He wants *push-back*." Senator Tom Daschle explained the Democrats' failure to stop the Bush tax reduction with "We did our level best . . . in providing as much *push-back* as we could."

The old word *resistance* has put up no resistance. Not even *opposition* will oppose the hot new word shoving everybody around the capital. If ever France is again overwhelmed by an enemy, we can expect its courageous partisans to go underground and organize *le Push-back.*

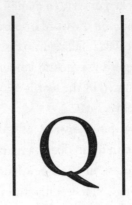

Quote Unquote.   Like it or not, you are going to learn something today. *Period*.

That written sentence fragment, *period,* is another way of signaling "And that's that" or "So there." Writing the word *period* at the end of a sentence uses the name of a punctuation mark to emphasize the work of a punctuation mark; in this case, writing *period* stresses finality or inescapability.

Now take that trick a step further: Say the punctuation mark aloud. By using the mark in speech, you not only call attention to your oral emphasis, but you also make it possible to transcribe the word for that symbol to paper or to your computer screen, and lo! You have the "quote-unquote" phenomenon. The word for the thing becomes the thing itself. (The semanticist Korzybski would flip.)

Here's how it works. The NBC host Matt Lauer asks a guest, "What do people in Great Britain think about this journalist, or *quote-unquote,* journalist?" Or Representative Bill Thomas of California tells a television interviewer, "There are other ways to get tax relief, not just within, *quote-unquote,* the president's plan." These usages of verbalized punctuation are sometimes accompanied by "air quotes," a visual signal of wiggling two fingers on each hand (recalling to some geezers the victory sign of a departed president).

The meaning of the spoken or written *quote-unquote* (wiggle, wiggle) is "so-called," casting aspersion on the word or phrase that follows. In American English, however, *so-called* is falling into disuse; it has the flavor of usage by speakers whose English is a second language. *Quote-unquote*—as a complete phrase, not separated by the words quoted—is now our primary derogator. A sneer is built in.

The joyously anticapital poet Edward Estlin Cummings (who styled himself e. e. cummings, "with up so floating many bells down") pioneered the use of the verbalized mark in 1935. Few students of the third-person singular of the state of being will forget his stunning "The Isful ubiquitous wasless&-shallbeless quote scrotumtightening unquote omnivorously eternal" etc. Were that being written today, e.e.'s poetic formulation, if he thought it scanned, would be "*quote-unquote* scrotumtightening."

The *Times*' recording room has rules for those of us who have to phone in our copy when modems fail. "Say 'period,' 'comma' and all other punctuation," Chris Campbell instructs. "Never say '*quote-unquote*' unless that's exactly what you want transcribed. Say 'open quote' before the quoted material and 'close quote' after it. At the end of a paragraph, say 'graf' or 'new graf.' " Thus, I would dictate the Bible's opening as "Cap I In the beginning no comma cap G God created the heaven and the earth period new graf cap A And the earth was without form comma and void semicolon and darkness begin itals was unitals upon the face of the deep period." (I don't know why the second *was* is in italics, but that's how the King James Version has it.)

In the heyday of network radio (comma? Yes, after two prepositional phrases) the two words were fused to be used before the quotation. "In the 1940s, the words *quote* and *unquote* were used frequently on the radio," the lexicographer David Guralnik told me long ago.* "There had to be some method of separating the words of the announcer and the person quoted. The problem came with short quotations: 'The president said, *quote*, Nuts,

*David Guralnik, one of the great lexicographers, died May 19, 2000.

unquote.' It worked much better to say, 'The president said, *quote-unquote,* Nuts.' "

Ronald Reagan popularized that device in his speeches in the '80s, deriding "*quote-unquote* tax reforms." But copy editors soon began adopting a variant: *quote-endquote,* hyphenated and with the *un* changed to *end* and sometimes placed after the quoted term. Georgia's Democratic senator, Zell Miller, was quoted in the *New York Times* a month ago saying, "I was hurt and mad at some longtime friends, *quote-endquote,* who had been so loud and harsh and vehement in their criticism about my doing the tax cut and Ashcroft."

Some users are going all the way to *quotes* before the quotation, leaving out the *un* or *end* and relying on speech inflection to indicate the quotation's end. This won't work in print. As my editor says, *quotes,* it's confusing and I'd better not do it and at this point you don't know whether I'm quoting him or me.

My solution: for plain quotation with no sneer intended, go back to "he said, *quote,* those were the days, *unquote.*" Specifically for casting aspersion—heaping ridicule on what follows—it's OK in informal use to write or say "what some pluralizing people like to call *quote-unquote* aspersions."

As a pastor, I think I can help you! As I understand it, any time that you see a word (like "was") in italics in the KJV, it indicates that there is no corresponding word in the original Hebrew or Greek text, but that an English word is required to complete the sense of the sentence. The literal Hebrew words would be more accurately rendered "The earth without form and void," but the word "was" is then added in order to make the sentence grammatically correct in the English.

Robert Stutes
Humble, Texas

I would like to offer a plausible reason for the second "was" in Genesis being italicized.

In the original Hebrew, the first was *is explicit; the actual past tense of the verb* to be *(haytah,* in Hebrew*) is used. This is not the case in the second use of the verb. The word "was" is only implicit there, and a strict interpretation of the Hebrew would render "and darkness upon the face of the deep." The translator of the King James Version apparently used the italics here to indicate his quote-unquote itals alteration unitals of the original.*

Sol Kanarek
Flushing, New York

R

Ramp Up.   Among verbs you might have thought had growth potential, *increase* is diminishing. *Accelerate* is slowing down. *Augment* has been subtracted from our vocabulary. *Grow* itself, especially in its use about the economy, has been stunted.

The vibrant new verb climbing over the backs of its ever-feebler synonyms is *ramp up*.

"With the advent of Bush II," wrote Hendrik Hertzberg in the *New Yorker*, ". . . the push was on for SDI [Strategic Defense Initiative]— renamed National Missile Defense, or NMD—to be, in Pentagon jargon, '*ramped up*.'"

Not just Pentagon jargon. The homeland security aide Tom Ridge, explaining why he issued another nationwide terrorism alert, explained, "This information is related to Al Qaeda or bin Laden, or else we wouldn't have *ramped* it *up*."

Journalism, too, has seized on the term. The *Wall Street Journal* noted that "the Justice Department is *ramping up* to investigate Enron as Congress is also mounting major investigations." Brian Duffy, when he took over as editor of *U.S. News*, said, "We're hoping to *ramp up* the investigative stuff and enterprise stuff."

Stuffily, the Internet has spread the word throughout the software sphere. "Getting *ramped up* to sell Keywords . . . is imperative," said the boss of RealNames, Keith Teare (presumably the moniker he was born

291

with). In Bangalore, India, Irfan Ali, the president of CommWorks (when I create a program to jam together words with a capital in the middle, I'll name it RunOn), announced proudly that his "staff will be *ramped up* to 100 in the next couple of years."

Usage in the opposite direction lies dormant. In 1981, the Reagan energy secretary John Edwards said his department "should be streamlined, *ramped down.*" In February 2002, a conservative Republican senator from Oklahoma, Don Nickles, took that different direction. He looked at income tax rates and asked aloud, "How fast can we *ramp* those *down*?"

Who is there to restrain this kudzulike growth of *ramp, up* and *down*? A myriad of readers (including those who prefer the adjective form, as in "myriad readers") have urged this department to take to the ramparts. In Old French, *ramper* was "to creep or crawl." Its first appearance in English was in a 1390 poem: "A litel Serpent on the ground / Which *rampeth* al aboute round." Three centuries later, John Milton contributed to its meaning of crawling upward: "Surely the Prelates would have Saint Pauls words *rampe one over* another, as they use to clime into their Livings and Bishopricks." Shakespeare's contemporary Ben Jonson used it to lead off the couplet that has become the epitome of realism: "*Ramp up* my genius, be not retrograde; / But boldly nominate a spade a spade."

In its upward crawl, *ramp* sent out a tendril that became *romp,* "to frolic." Another, fiercer offshoot was first cited in Spenser's "He *rampt* upon him with his ravenous pawes." This meaning led to the stylized figure of the lion on many emblems being called *rampant* and was the root of the noun and verb *rampage.* In English slang, to *ramp* was to swindle or rob.

Meanwhile, the noun form was climbing the semantic ladder in fortifications, as a slope connecting ascending levels and making attackers vulnerable to arrows. This led to a meaning of "passageway enabling passengers to board a ship," later applied to airplanes and the slip roads leading on or off highways. The noun meaning influenced the meaning of the verb (to *ramp* is no longer "to play the slut"); the eager adoption in the computer world may have been associated with *ramp* function in electronics, "an electrical waveform in which the voltage increases linearly with time," as they like to say at CommWorks in Bangalore.

Will today's laserly focus on a vogue verb *ramp down* its usage? Or will its frequency continue to rise in a creepy, crawly climb? I am *amped* about this, without the *r*, which brings us to *amped up*.

A *Times* colleague, Clyde Haberman, who has been an assiduous *ramp-up* watcher, also notes the use of a similar-sounding expression, *amp up*, its past tense (very tense) *amped*.

The gutsy American Olympic skier Picabo Street did not win her third medal at Salt Lake City. She told reporters after her final run, "I was really *amped* as I waited," but had turned lethargic; another reporter said she had been *amped up*.

The speed skater Kip Carpenter, who placed third in his race, told the *Boston Globe*, "I was *superamped* and superpumped." Writing in *Sports Illustrated* about Olympic snowboarding, Austin Murphy noted that one participant was "*amped* on adrenaline."

In basketball on the same day, far from the Olympics, Kaitlin Bergen of the Bogota (N.J.) Bucs was telling the *Bergen* (no kin) *Record:* "In the first half I came out real sloppy. I think I got myself too *amped* to play" before coming back to help her team win.

The expression is synonymous with *hyped, wired, charged, pumped*, all of which also can take an *up*. "The roots may lie in amplified music," speculates Haberman.

Maybe. *Amp* has an electric connotation, both from "amplitude modulation" (AM radio) and from *ampere*, the measurement (named in 1881 after the scientist André-Marie Ampère) of steady current produced by one volt applied across a resistance of one ohm. More likely, it is rooted in drug lingo: a 1972 warning to addicts defined *amped* as "high on stimulants, usually amphetamines." But the first syllable of that word is pronounced "*amf*," not "*amp*"; another possibility is a shortening of *ampul*, a sealed container of a drug to be injected.

As often happens, the sinister derivation is forgotten as the word gains general usage: *amped* now most often means "excited, frenetic," and has probably been influenced by what is to many youths the thrilling noise of the amplifier. This is good, as the expression appears to be ramping up.

You seem to have a congenital unwillingness to accept the possibility that electrical engineers and their lingo can be the source of the new words and usages. When I told you years ago, with documentation, where "in the loop" came from—feedback theory—you scoffed. You give tepid acknowledgment today of the remote possibility that ramp functions in electrical system analysis may have led to the broader use of "ramped up" and "ramped down." If you had been an electrical engineer or any other knowledgeable participant in the military and space technology explosion of the past half century, you would have no doubt of the validity of that explanation.

You quote Clyde Haberman's timid speculation that "amped" might have some connection to amplified music. Well, it did. Rock guitarists and garage bands of the '50s and '60s enamored à la Tim Taylor for "more power," kept buying bigger and bigger amplifiers—"amps" for short—and speakers for their instruments (and vocal microphones), leading to the inevitable appreciative professional judgments of "Man, he's really amped," when each new level of building shake and cochlea rape was attained.

We may be nerds, but we are not out of the loop. Or, more accurately in my case, have not always been out of the loop.

John Strother
Princeton, New Jersey

Recuse.   "Chairman Pitt should *recuse* himself from any role in the Enron debacle," said Scott Harshbarger, president of Common Cause, about Harvey Pitt, the Securities and Exchange Commission chairman, because he had once represented Enron's accounting firm, Arthur Andersen, as an attorney. This verb is in frequent use by officials and judges eager to disqualify themselves from taking action in areas that may present a conflict of interest.

The ancient verb, from the Latin *recusare*, "to reject," is listed in the *OED* as "rare," in an entry written a century ago. Oxford editors, revising it today, are citing a use in a Louisiana court in 1829 and will report that the reflexive form (*recuse* yourself) is now in active use in America and South Africa, though not in Britain. The reflexive use was resuscitated in 1949 by the *New Republic,* with this advice to Democratic representatives: "If you go to a caucus, and they try to hogtie you on something too strong to gulp down, *recuse* yourself. . . . To *recuse* is to refuse to follow, to reject. . . . It's there for your protection."

During the Carter presidency, when I noted with satisfaction that Attorney General Griffin Bell had *recused* himself on some matter affecting his boss, a typographical error caused the reflexive verb to be changed to "rescued," and Bell waved the clipping before a cabinet meeting: "It says here I *rescued* myself, and come to think of it, that's what I did."

Redefinitions I.   The *Houston Chronicle* in 1994 was first to publish a word that captivated playful theologians: *Frisbeetarian,* one who believes that when you die your soul goes up on the roof and gets stuck.

This was followed four years later by a contest in the *Washington Post* asking readers for "redefinitions" of words. Some of my favorites:

coffee (n.), a person who is coughed upon.
asterisk (v.), to inquire about danger.
esplanade (verb form of the noun), to attempt an explanation while drunk.
negligent (adj.), a condition in which a woman absentmindedly answers
    the door in her nightie.
abdicate (v.), to give up all hope of ever having a flat stomach.

Word games teach in tricky ways. Language mavens who peruse this space were long ago advised to let a simile be their umbrella. In tense times, lighten up.

Redefinitions II.   We've had a gratifying early turnout to the appeal for redefinitions. Here are some fresh meanings for stale words:

intuition (n.), "knowledge that your salary won't cover the cost of your children's education" (Gail Elsant).

commute (v.), "travel to and from work without speaking" (Mark Mappen), topped by a second try, *trampoline* (n.), "legal claim made on the property of a homeless person."

approbation (n.), "fear of early release from prison" (Fred Bothwell) and "punishment that fits the crime" (Alice McElhone).

coordinates (n.), "a couple of preachers" (Geraldine Nelson).

grammarian (n.), "well-spoken grandmother" (from someone whose e-mail name is Cdella3; I respect any Cinderella's desire for anonymity).

defibrillator (n.), "lie detector" (Miriam Forman).

ineffable (adj.), "a guaranteed Grade-A term paper" (Matthew Batters, who submits a noun, *vilification,* "the inexorable spread of Greenwich Village").

warship (n.), "adoration of the navy" (Sheila Blume, whose second entry, *suffragettes* [n.], "cheerleading squad for de Sade High," is rejected with all suitable horror).

liturgy (n.), "throwing the sermon on the sidewalk" (Emily Barsh).

judicious (adj.), "Passover recipes" (Frank Corwin).

bashful (adj.), "being harsh or abusive toward someone" (K. Gray).

alphabet (n.), "the most aggressive wager on the table" (Andy Goodman).

miniscule (adj.), "the odds of *minuscule* being spelled correctly" (John Foshee).

chestnut (n.), "a male too interested in the female figure" (Claire Ball).

Finally a couple of redefinitions from Michael Edelman somewhere in e-mailville: *rebuffs* (n.), "polished athletic shoes," and *kindred* (adj., changed to n.), "fear of family reunions."

Keep 'em coming; it lightens up coverage of war words.

Redefinitions III.   In honor of Super Bowl XXXVI, here are some sports redefinitions.

superficial (n.), "a really good referee" (Mel Siedband).

beleaguered (adj.), "stuck in the semipros" (Eric Mencher).

contrapuntal (adj.), "foolishly advocating passing instead of kicking on fourth down" (Alfred Greenberg).

hermit (n.), "girl's baseball glove" (Judith Werben).

saturnine (n.), "baseball team that plays on weekends" (Ed Grimm).

truncate (n.), "tailgate party given by compact-car owner" (anonymous).

wrinkle (n.), "a small hockey arena" (Robert Forbes).

haiku (n.), "signal to center from Japanese quarterback" (Tony Wight).

Enjoy the game. Hope a *nail-biter* is in the works. *Haiku!*

Redefinitions IV.   There's no stopping wordplay. Coiners of these redefinitions get nothing but eternal life in the data bank.

altruism (n.), "the tendency to believe everything you hear" (Gary Parnell).

condescending (n.), "a prisoner going down a flight of stairs," and *liability* (n.), "the capacity for prevarication" (Ed Grimm).

madras (n.), "an Indian sleeping mat" (Robert Forbes).

equinox (n.), "a cross between a mare and a bull," and *apology* (n.), "the study of primates" (Robert and Mary Rubalsky).

cantaloupe (n.), "parental nonconsent" (Joan Jaquish).

destabilize (v.), "let the horses out of the barn" (anonymous).

precursor (n.), "a profane tot" (Leon Freilich).

Regime Changes.   Secretary of State Colin Powell laid it on the rhetorical line: the Bush administration "is committed to *regime change*" in Iraq. He repeated to the Senate that "a *regime change* would be in the best interests of the region." That's a euphemism for "overthrow of government" or "toppling Saddam."

Why, then, did he not say "we intend to throw him and his motley crew of mass murderers out of Baghdad, replacing them with a government that will allow the Iraqi people free elections"? Because that sort of talk is undiplomatic or even impolitic. *Overthrow* and *topple* are hot, vigorous verbs; *regime change* is a cool, polite noun phrase suggesting transition without collateral damage.

A *regime* is a government you don't like. (It can also be a strict diet of grapefruit and pasta, which you don't like either, but that's a different sense.) The *old regime* is always pejorative, coming from the French revolutionaries' gleeful derogation of the government of the last Bourbon kings as *l'ancien régime*. The word's coloration is negative; no politician seeking a "fresh start" or a "clean sweep" goes on to call for a *new regime*.

"If the case for *regime change* is clear," writes Michael Eisenstadt in the *National Interest*, "the way forward is not. The debate in Washington about *regime change* in Iraq has become highly partisan." (The title of his article is "Curtains for the Baath," a play on the name of Saddam's Baath political party; this suggests further headlines like "Going to the Mat with Baath," "Baath Throws in Towel," etc.)

Where did this euphemism begin? The earliest citation I can find in the Nexis data bank is in a 1980 Associated Press story predicting "risk to business from *regime change*." After kicking around in foreign-policy journals for a decade, it was picked up by *Daily Variety* in Hollywood, as it followed "the *regime change* at MCA Music." Diplolingo is now wresting the phrase back from the general usage.

Another military euphemism, *collateral damage*, was used above. This was not a subliminal plug for Arnold Schwarzenegger's latest movie epic of vigilante revenge. It was an introduction to a phrase used in restrained apology for casualties among civilians or to destruction of other than military targets. It was also used by the mass murderer Timothy McVeigh— "there's always *collateral damage*"—in dismissing contrition for the children his truck bomb killed in Oklahoma City.

The adjective *collateral*, "parallel," came to mean "ancillary, subordinate"; as a noun, it is a pledge of security alongside a debt to ensure payment. The essential meaning is now "on the side of." Where the adjective is used to modify *damage,* the meaning becomes "unintended, inadvertent." It is in the same league of hesitant regret as *friendly fire.*

The phrasedick Fred Shapiro at Yale tracked it back in its current sense to a 1961 usage by Thomas Schelling in *Operations Research* magazine: "Measures to locate and design our strategic forces so as to minimize *collateral damage.*" Reached at the University of Maryland, where he is now a distinguished professor, Schelling says, "I used it because it seemed to be the common terminology." He disclaims coinage of that and of *counterforce* and *second strike,* also often attributed to him; such modesty is rare. (When I coin something, I make sure all the nattering nabobs of negativism know it.)

In running the traps with Shapiro's help at the American Dialect Society, I get word from John Baker that *collateral damage* was used in a British court in 1820. It had been cooking along quietly in legal usage until the 1990s, when it exploded into military parlance.

Retraction.   In Gore's historic Second Telephone Call, Bush (snippily or not) asked if he intended to *retract* his concession. This was often reported as "called to *rescind* his concession." Any difference?

Retract, from the Latin *trahere,* "to draw," means "to take back; to withdraw." It is most often used now in connection with correcting misstatements and avoiding libel suits.

Rescind's root is *scindere,* "to split, divide," and means "to revoke, annul, cancel, expunge, abrogate." It has more of a legal connotation than *retract.*

Because a political concession is a gracious accommodation rather than a legal surrender of rights, the use of *retract* in this case was correct.

Riff and Raffish.   "POTUS Speaks" is the title of one of the early freshets in what will become a torrent of inside-the-Clinton-White-House memoirs. The acronym *Potus* (in newspaper style, capitalized and lowercase because it is longer than four letters) stands for the office to be occupied by the man we elected a couple of weeks ago.

I was present, if not at the birth of the acronym, then at least when the spoken word was in its infancy. As a new White House speechwriter in 1969, I noticed the letters on one of the labels next to the five buttons on a telephone extension in the Cabinet Room and wondered aloud, "Who's this guy Potus?" A member of the White House Communications Agency (we pronounced WHCA "Whacka") explained that since the Johnson administration, the phone line from the Oval Office was marked with the initials for "President of the United States."

It stood to reason: A stark *Nixon* might have seemed presumptuous, and there wasn't enough space on the label for *President*. An abbreviation like *Pres.* or *Prsd't* would have looked funny; *Prez* was too jazzy and *Prexy* overly informal. Hence *Potus*, sported proudly on the telephone of all close-in White House aides. I left in 1973 and turned out a novel a few years later about a blinded chief executive; a problem was, what should the bachelor president's love interest call him? A first name would seem presumptuous and "Mr. President" unromantic. Solution: *Potus*, which was suitably irreverent without being awkwardly familiar.

Time and technology march on. In real life a generation later, Monica Lewinsky told a grand jury that when the president called her from the Oval Office, the word *Potus* would appear on her caller ID. Similar acronyms have sprung up: *Scotus* is journalese for "Supreme Court of the U.S.," and more recently, the first lady became known to staffers as *Flotus*.

Now to a word used in the memoir by Michael Waldman, *Potus* Clinton's chief speechwriter. He describes the moment in his chief's first speech to Congress in 1993 when Clinton departed from the somewhat disorganized text. "He began to *riff*," writes Waldman, "to ad-lib, to revise entire paragraphs. . . . [economic adviser Gene] Sperling and I were scanning our single-spaced copies of the speech. 'He's ad-libbing! He's ad-libbing the State of the Union!' we shouted, and gave each other a high-five."

Whence *riff*? *Rife* means "abundant," probably associated with *riff*'s sense of "the belly"; much fashion attention is now focused on exposing the belly button, or navel, in the *midriff*.

But for our immediate purposes, *riff* originated as a jazz term, one meaning of which is an ostinato phrase, a musical figure, often syncopated, used throughout a composition at the same pitch. First cited in 1935, *riff* is a solo improvisation that, when often repeated, becomes identified with the player who can "leave that bit in" until it becomes part of a routine.

The meaning of the musical term was then extended to any rhetorical improvisation or flight of oratory, as in a *New Yorker* use in 1970 of "some lovely comic *riffs*."

Now comes the confusion. "Putin Offers Help to Belgrade on Election *Riff* " was a headline in the *New York Times*. A simple typographical error, no? The intended word was surely *rift*, meaning "a split, division, fissure." But a quick database search reveals dozens of uses of *riff* (perhaps influenced by *tiff*, "minor argument") to mean *rift*.

This "is hardly an error that we could consider a hapax legomenon," says Bryan Garner, author of the *Dictionary of Modern American Usage*. (That Greek phrase is used by irritated biblical exegetes to mean "only time used in a text" and often means they have to guess at the meaning.) Because the confusion of *rift* with *riff* is happening so frequently, notes the lexicographer sternly, "the modern use of *riff* in that sense appears to be nothing more than rank word-swapping resulting from sound association."

Word-swapping, like spouse-swapping, is a no-no. Let us resist, holding fast to the distinction: when the president-elect swings into a familiar unity pitch, that's a *riff*; when he tells a wing of his party that thought it deserved cabinet posts to get lost, that starts a *rift*.

On the third hand, if any politician uses a vulgarity or deliberately dresses like a slob— but in a kind of attractive way—he is said to be *raffish*.

The French writer Frédéric Dard was "known for his *raffish* prose style," wrote Eric Pace in a *Times* obituary. This adjective first appeared in a letter from Jane Austen in 1801: "He is as *raffish* in his appearance as I would wish every disciple of Godwin to be." William Godwin was a brilliant, unkempt Dissenter, husband of the early feminist Mary Wollstonecraft, and he struck admirers as delightfully unconventional.

Raff may come from *raft*, in one sense "a large collection of rubbish," and I won't belabor the reader with a whole *raft* of citations.

But see how the language meanders through time. Is the *raff* of *raffish* connected to the *raff* of *riffraff* ? Yes. The *riffraff* are the "rabble," the elitist's scornful dismissal of the disreputable or seemingly worthless elements of society. "You would inforce upon us the old *riffe-raffe* of Sarum," wrote the poet Milton in 1641.

Riff and *raff* are half-rhyming quasi-nouns from the Old French *rifler,* "to rifle, ransack," and *raffler,* "to ravage, snatch away," applied to things of little value.

Today's piece is less of a snobbish improvisation for society's elite than a *raffish riff* for the *riffraff.*

When President James Monroe borrowed books from the Library of Congress, he placed the letters "PUS" after his name to indicate "President of the United States."

Kurt S. Maier
The Library of Congress
Washington, D.C.

If you ever have occasion to write about the origins of "Potus" again, you should know that it was created, I believe, during the Johnson administration—by an AT&T repairman. The phone company man was installing direct connections on the consoles of certain members of LBJ's staff with a red button and the repairman felt that was insufficient designation; thus came Potus, *because* President of the United States *would not fit on the console panel.*

It was soon adopted by staff when discussing White House affairs while lunching at San Souci or Paul Young, using the term "Potus" in case anybody was listening. LBJ's secretary, Marie Fehmer, later verbalized it, and once when I had to see the President and asked what he was doing, she said: "Go right in. He's just potusing *around."*

Joseph Laitin*
Bethesda, Maryland

*Joseph Laitin, adviser to six presidents and former ombudsman of the *Washington Post,* died Jan. 19, 2002.

I recall distinctly reading the news of the death of President Franklin Roo-
sevelt in 1945. News of the president's travels was always restricted by
wartime censorship, but when he died, the newspapers reported the slow
journey of the train carrying the late president from Warm Springs, Georgia,
to Hyde Park. The news stories reported that the train dispatchers were noti-
fied to give priority to the presidential train, which had the special designa-
tion POTUS. I think that the acronym was used whenever President
Roosevelt traveled by train, which was the way presidents traveled in those
days.

William Shank
Ardsley, New York

A comment on riff-raff. *In the Bible we find the phrase "a mixed multitude"*
in a derogatory sense (Exodus 12:28). The Hebrew original says EREFF
RAFF. *Not a hapax legomenon.*

Eric G. Freudenstein
Riverdale, New York

Roll Out.   "Early in its foreign *rollout*," reported *Daily Variety*, a movie
titled *X-Men* hauled in $3.4 million over an opening weekend.

A restored version of the Rolling Stones' concert film *Gimme Shelter*, issued on its thirtieth anniversary, "will begin a nationwide *rollout* in a few
markets," according to a Reuters dispatch from Los Angeles.

The *Asian Wall Street Journal* spread the word throughout the Far East: "*The
Broken Hearts Club* will have a slow U.S. *rollout* beginning in major cities."

What is this movie marketing term that has so captivated the merchants
of dreams in Hollywood? Where did it begin, and what did it come to
mean?

"*Roll out!*" as every Army veteran of World War II grimly remembers,
was the unwelcome barracks call that pierced the blessed stillness of the
morning. Accompanied by the admonition to "grab yer socks," the phrase
has a literal meaning of "roll out of bed." It was often followed by a sar-

donic "rise and shine," a metaphoric allusion to the sun, and a few minutes later by "fall out on the company street!"—an order to assemble outside, in front of the barracks.

The transitional metaphor to its use in Hollywood probably came from the aircraft or automotive industries, as vehicles *rolled out* of hangars or off assembly lines. Ira Konigsberg, author of the *Complete Film Dictionary*, suggests a more ancient origin: "The point of the term is to suggest the growing appearance of the film much like the expansion of a carpet when it is *rolled out*."

How is a *rollout* different from a release? "A typical Hollywood release is a wide release to a national public all at once," says Konigsberg, "because of the reliance on national television advertising. *Rollouts* are for independent, foreign or more specialized Hollywood films that need to build interest by word-of-mouth or simply must earn the right to proceed to larger audiences."

A *rollout*, then, like its synonym *platforming*, is a process of release, taking place in stages. This useful term for gradual release or step-by-step development was picked up by marketers in other fields. The magazine *Martha Stewart Living* led to *Martha Stewart Weddings*, which gave birth to *Martha Stewart Baby*, and Ms. Stewart told *Advertising Age* last month, "There probably will be a *rollout* from there."

Political usage in the recent campaign, however, vitiated the nice distinction between the simultaneous general release and the calibrated *rollout*. "One prominent Republican strategist said that the *rollout* of Mr. Cheney had been disappointing," wrote Eric Schmitt of the *Times* in August. "Gore's handlers are plotting yet another *rollout* of their candidate," wrote Howard Fineman in *Newsweek* a month later.

This sense suggests only "introduction," and frays the carpet's specific edge. But politics likes to seize on with-it words and fuzz up their meanings.

I would not be surprised if the term "roll out" made its way into entertainment marketing etc. through direct mail. I believe that direct marketers have

used the verb phrase and the noun *"roll out"* for ten years or more to refer to
the culmination of direct mail testing.

A careful direct marketer of any significant size will test several response
rates that they generate. When one proves—often by a margin of less than
1 percent—to pull a greater response than the others, the marketer will
order most of the productive package to be rolled out, that is, sent to the full
mailing list of potential customers.

Don Hill
Radio Free Europe
Prague, Czech Republic

&

Roll's Roles.   Todd Beamer was a passenger on the doomed Flight 93,
taken over on September 11 by terrorists who intended to use the aircraft
as a missile to destroy the White House or the Capitol. He had a telephone
line open to an operator in Chicago, who reported hearing him recite the
Lord's Prayer before he led a group of heroic passengers to rush the suicidal hijackers. Then Beamer said: "Are you guys ready? *Let's roll.*"

President Bush recalled that moment in the eloquent peroration of a
speech in Atlanta last month. "We will always remember the words of that
brave man expressing the spirit of a great country," he said. "We will no
doubt face new challenges, but we have our marching orders. My fellow
Americans, *let's roll.*"

A song with that title was promptly distributed to radio disc jockeys. In
a Philadelphia football stadium, a fan called "the sign man" unfurled a
banner with the words "*Let's roll . . .* out" to tumultuous applause. "The
words are everywhere," reported Britain's *Guardian*. "They have become
America's favorite bittersweet and articulate bumper sticker."

The phrase in its currently popular sense means "let's get going; let's
move." The original sense of *get rolling* had to do with the wheels of con-
veyances, horseless and otherwise, and dates back to the 16th century. The
crapshooter's *roll 'em* was introduced early in the 20th century, and the
moviemakers' command to cameramen, "*roll 'em*" (answered in an old

joke by "anytime you're ready, C.B.!"), was first recorded in 1939. Five years later, in his novel *The Man With the Lumpy Nose,* Lawrence Lariar wrote: "'Do me a favor and go home and write it!' McEmons stood over the reporter menacingly. *'Get rolling!'"* (I have an editor like that.) But the specific phrase *let's roll* in its current meaning was first cited in the 1952 novel *The Tightrope,* by Stanley Jules Kauffman: "'*Let's roll,* dreamer,' said Perry."

In 1950 and 1951, the blues artist Cecil Gant (aka Private Gant, the GI sing-sation) came out with two songs that brought *roll* on to the music scene. "We're Gonna Rock" was a remake of a lesser-known 1947 song by Wild Bill Moore, and repeated the words "We're gonna rock, we're gonna *roll*" for most of the song. The second was "Rock Little Baby" (the title bottoms on "rockabye your baby"), which included the line "Rock little daddy, send me with a rock and a *roll.*" By June 1951, the disc jockey Alan Freed promoted the revolution in popular music that became known as *rock 'n' roll.* The phrase "Let's *rock and roll*" was an excited call to dance to that music. Later—and this is the etymological conjecture of a confirmed foxtrotter—with the *rock* clipped out, the phrase became a more general exhortation to nonmusical movement or action.

In a related development, as transition-hungry writers like to put it, a new sense of to *roll up* wheeled into the lexicon. It was expressed this month by ABC's Sam Donaldson: "It looks like the Taliban is being *rolled up.*" The verb phrase *roll up,* which might have begun in the showroom of a carpet salesman, later became the action of arriving in a carriage or automobile, and now has the meaning of "to defeat" or "to conclude" (expressed by film directors in a noun form as "that's a wrap"), akin to the military meaning of "to mop up" (though no soldiers say "that's a mop").

The old verb *roll*—from the Latin *rota,* "wheel"—like Ol' Man River, is unstoppable, creating new meanings as it goes, recently elevating itself by association with a historic moment. With the poet Byron, we can wish it ever more power: "*Roll on,* thou deep and dark blue Ocean— *Roll!*"

ℭ

Run the Table.   "It may be tougher for Mark Green to *run the table* than a lot of people realize," wrote Bob Herbert of the *Times,* drafting an op-ed column about the Democratic nominee in 2001 for the New York mayoral election.

"I don't think any of us went in thinking we were going to *run the table,*" said Michael Strahan, the New York Giants defensive end, referring to a string of pro football victories last year that led some fans to believe the team could finish the season as Super Bowl champions.

On election night in last year's presidential race (was it only last year?), the phrase's attraction won over, in rapid succession, Dan Rather of CBS ("Gore . . . virtually has to *run the table* of states that are still undecided"), Jeff Greenfield of CNN ("George Bush now has to *run the table*") and Tim Russert of NBC ("If Gore wins Florida, Bush has to *run the table* and win Iowa, Nevada, Oregon, Wisconsin . . .").

Where is this metaphoric table, and who runs it? Does it have, as some readers suggest, a poker origin? Because I was accused in my youth of having a "pool-hall pallor," my hunch was that the origin was the table covered by green felt. I aimed an etymological cushion shot at Tom Shaw, managing editor of *Pool and Billiard Magazine* and co-author of *The Complete Idiot's Guide to Pool and Billiards.* (The book does not profess to be a comprehensive guide; the adjective *complete* modifies *idiot,* the reader, not the *guide.*)

"To *run the table,*" defines Shaw, "is to clear the table of all the balls and thereby to win the game. The phrase began to be used about forty years ago, but the usage picked up in the last decade or so."

To run the lexicon of this sport's table: *billiards* comes from the French *bille,* "stick," which is called a *cue,* from the French *queue,* "tail." The long stick, which reminded some early users of a tail, can be used to make a ball hit another ball in a form of the game known as *carom billiards,* played with only three balls by real hustlers on a table with no pockets. A more popular variation is known as *pool,* using fifteen object balls to be knocked into the table's pockets. *Pool* is from the French *poule,* "hen," in which the winner takes the bets of all the players, thereby scooping up "the pool." This sense is the same used in the winner-take-all-stakes betting called "the office *pool*," also used as a modifier in journalism's "*pool* reporters." The meaning is "combined resources," though the connection with chickens is obscure.

A famous variation of pocket billiards, or pool, is *snooker*, played with twenty-one smaller balls, mostly red. In the 19th century, a *snooker* was a newly joined and easily fooled British cadet; the name was applied to this form of pool in 1875 by subalterns in India. It is now a verb meaning "hoodwink, dupe," as if at a pool table by a table-running hustler.

In "Run the Table" you said, "The phrase began to be used about 40 years ago . . ."

I recall at the University of Virginia in 1950 seeing an exhibition of pocket billiards by Willie Mosconi. He did "run the table" consistently. He won the U.S. pocket billiard championship nineteen times between 1941 and 1956, "running the table all the while." His highest run (in an exhibition) was 526 balls.

We did use the phrase at that time. For instance, we had one fraternity brother about whom we joked that at any Sunday buffet, he would "run the table"—that is, of course, to eat everything in sight.

Although the U.S. men's pocket billiards championship began in 1878, the present competitive form of the sport known as "straight pool" did not become the official game until 1912. However, I'm sure that the winners from that date on won by "running the table."

Charles A. Carroll
New York, New York

Your lexicon of billiards is inadequate, to put it mildly. "Carom" in English is "cannon." British billiards is played with three balls on a table without pockets. One scores by potting a ball, going off, or by a cannon—hitting both the other two balls with your ball. In France, billiards is played on a table without pockets and one scores only by various types of cannon.

The verb "snooker" has a specific meaning. At times in the game one has to hit a particular colour. If one is prevented because other balls are in the way, one is "snookered." The equivalent in old-fashioned match-play golf was "stymied." Both words can be used figuratively. One can deliberately "lay a snooker" for an opponent. A player extracts himself from a snooker by coming off the cushions or swerving the ball (difficult).

Ken Mackenzie
Levallois-Perret, France

First, cloth that covers billiard tables does not contain any felt. The cloth uses a combination of wool and nylon or in some cases 100% wool.

The next, I wonder if your use of the word hustler *in describing carom billiards players is appropriate, indeed what you intended to imply. A hustler is a person who tries to induce another player to gamble over the outcome of a billiard game by not revealing his or her true skills. It is a derogatory term; and indeed, one billiard writer described it as being little more than petty thieves. Carom billiards is the most complex, fascinating and difficult of all the cue sports; and those few who still play this beautiful game are far removed from the world of the hustler.*

Finally, in regards to the term snookered, *in the billiard world this term is used to describe a situation when a shooter finds the cue ball in a position from which he cannot make a direct hit on the intended object ball; he is* snookered, *not deceived, just blocked from a direct route to make a legal shot.*

Richard L. Hehir, MD
Syracuse, New York

Ruok? I'm Gr8!   Between the superstar Britney Spears and the 13-year-old singer Brittney Cleary, nobody will ever spell France's northwestern region of Brittany correctly again. But Miss Cleary, of Nashville, in her song "I.M. Me," has engaged in text messaging, a combination of initialese and the euphonic use of the alphabet that deserves scholarly attention.

WAN2TLK? In e-mailese, BRB stands for "be right back," IMHO means "in my humble opinion" and LOL signifies "laughing out loud." That's merely initialese. But it gets livelier: "anyone" is shortened to NE1, XLNT flashes "excellent," "thanks" is snipped to TX and "be seeing you" to BCNU. G2G means "got to go." WERV U BIN? RUOK? (To my knowledge, texmess lacks a message for "I can't go on with this because I have to do my homework.")

The cartoonist William Steig pioneered this technique in books beginning in the '60s. His angry man shouts at a woman, "URODS!" She yells back, "URSN9!" My favorite is his little green men from Mars labeled NMELEN.

It also comes from license-plate tomfoolery. A man in white shorts asks 10S NE1? A polite driver's plate shows XQZ ME. An optimist: IM42N8. A Wonderland rabbit: ML8 ML8.

E-mailese may be old wine in new bottles, but it's not a fad because it won't go away. Give it a HAND, initialese for "have a nice day."

How R U? It's good 2 B back home after the dogs and I spent last year out West. Every day I look out the window and C the birds. The trees and flowers, 2. G but there R lots of trees and flowers. I called my new friend J in Las Vegas last week. Xcuse me, but I have 2 go 2 the bathroom and P. That's because I just drank a cup of T. Last night I got hungry so I 8 a sandwich. Y don't you write me a note if you get a chance?

If this is the direction e-mail is taking the language, then I want no part of e-mail.

Robin Holske
Boscawen, New Hampshire

You describe a variety of "so-called text messaging" and you state that the earliest example of that art dates from the 1960s.

I recall an example that antedates your example by a wide margin; that is, if priority is important.

This bit appeared in the Sunday comics of the Detroit Times *when I was ten or twelve years old:*

Barney Google, a long-ago comic strip character, is seated at a table in a restaurant and he asks the waiter, "FUNEX"? The waiter replies, "SVFX." Barney then asks, "FUNEM?" The reply is "SVFM." Barney then says "OKMNX."

For some time thereafter OKMNX became a reply among my school-mates.

Benjamin Pecherer
Lafayette, California

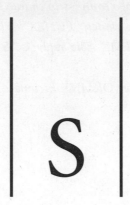

Save the Prunes.   Has *prune* become a dirty word? The California Dried Plum Board, formerly the California Prune Board, is in the midst of a campaign to change the age-old name of its product.

"Unfortunately, the stereotype among the women that we're targeting," says Richard Peterson, executive director of the former prune association, "is of a medicinal food for their parents, rather than a healthful, nutritious food for women who are leading an active lifestyle." (He means "an active life." And "medicinal food" avoids the word *laxative*.)

Urged on by Sunsweet, which has been stewing about the way the word's connotation has been harming its black-wrinkled-fruit market, the United States government is going along with the language manipulators. The Food and Drug Administration noted that the anti-prune-name lobby promised to "coordinate a unified transition of product names, beginning with dual labeling that would include both names (prunes and dried plums) on labels to educate consumers who do not know that prunes are a type of dried plum."

To protect those consumers ignorant of prune-plum nomenclature, Christine Lewis, the labeling official in the FDA's Center for Food Safety, wrote last year that she would hold the then Prune Board to its pledge to "track consumer awareness of the fact that dried plums are, in fact, prunes."

After the consumer has been force-fed the change for two years, the word *prunes*—even the poetic alliteration *pitted* prunes—will disappear forever.

But our fact-driven labeling czar is no pushover: "We do not concur," she wrote, "with the alternate name *'dried plums'* used on other foods such as prune juice, canned prunes and prune butters." Perhaps that is because the term *dried plum juice* is a contradiction in terms too grotesque for even the federal government.

In last year's supplemented application to the FDA, the then Prune Board noted precedents in the changing names of foods: the *kiwi fruit,* for example, never got off the ground when known as "the Chinese gooseberry"; *hazelnuts* used to be called "filberts." The *garbanzo bean,* with its romantic Spanish heritage, is shoving aside the familiar term "chickpea," while the *wiener* or *frankfurter* is better known and hawked in the United States as the "hot dog." But those were rooted in regional or dialectical differences, not deliberate attempts to impose linguistic change.

"Prunes by any other name would taste the same," wrote the AP farm reporter Philip Brasher, alluding to the Shakespearean Juliet's rose, "but they might sell better." The then Prune Board might make its case about the name's negative connotation by citing a line in *Henry IV, Part 2:* "He lives upon mouldy stewed prunes."

On the other hand, in direct rebuttal to the mouldy market research about the antipathies of young women to plums in their dried state, Pompey in *Measure for Measure* says: "Sir, she came in, great with child, and longing . . . for stewed prunes. Mistress Elbow . . . being great-bellied, and longing, as I said, for prunes. . . ." This proves that pregnant women—making up a market not to go untargeted—have been drawn to prunes for at least four centuries.

That is not to overlook the wrinkle problem. Prunes are undeniably associated with wrinkles, which we can call "character lines" all we like, but nobody wants to look like the old Dick Tracy character Pruneface. In a review of *Once Bitten,* a 1985 spoof of vampire films, the *Seattle Times* wrote of the character played by Lauren Hutton, "She'll turn into an old *prune* if she doesn't get a transfusion of virgin blood soon."

Accordingly, the industry can ask: if apricots, when dried, can be called *dried apricots,* why can't plums, when similarly freed of moisture, be called *dried plums?* The etymological response: the plum grows on a tree named the *Prunus domestica.* The root of that roundish fleshy drupe we call a *plum* is the Latin *prunum.* We've been calling a *prune* a *prune* since 1345, and the name is sure to outlast the California Dried Plum Board, if not the name *California* itself.

Not everyone in that power-deprived state is targeting the language. I asked the California Raisin Marketing Board if the raisin growers will soon petition the Food and Drug Administration for permission to label their product *dried grapes.*

"Never!" shot back Judy Hirigoyen, director of marketing for the raisin combine. "We think it's cool to have wrinkles."

On top of your splendid and sufficient blasting of dried plums, *there is a second overwhelming objection. As we learn in Dickens'* Little Dorrit, *Mr. Dorrit's daughter's governess discovered circa 1857 that the way to give a pretty shape to the lips of growing girls was to repeat certain words, namely:* Papa, potatoes, poultry, prunes *and* prism. *Should prunes be outlawed or become obsolete, the formula would fail. Its rhythm and completeness are the secret of its worldwide success.*

Jacques Barzun
San Antonio, Texas

The reference to prunes in Measure for Measure *does not really relate to a pregnant woman's being attracted to the fruit. Pompey's comment is an insult, indicating that Mistress Elbow has a venereal disease. Prunes were considered good medicine for such ailments.*

Kenneth Greif
Waterbury, Connecticut

In Cleveland, where I used to live, the plums of the type that are made into prunes are sold as "fresh prunes."

Sam Thorton
Huber Heights, Ohio

℃

Say What?   "Why don't you incorporate a running endnote feature on anachronisms in movie scripts?" suggests Hendrik Hertzberg, senior editor of the *New Yorker*. (I tell him how to edit his magazine; he tells me how to write my column. Our readers benefit mightily.) My anachronism file is limited to the classic example of Cassius's mention of a clock striking in Shakespeare's *Julius Caesar,* set in a time before clocks had been invented. Fortunately, Hertzberg includes a specific example to enliven his broad policy guidance.

"Movie art directors go to incredible lengths to make sure the details are right in period films," he notes. "Yet the dialogue is often studded with ear-stinging anachronisms. I noticed this most recently in the new Woody Allen movie about the 1930s jazz guitarist Emmet Ray."

He referred to a scene in *Sweet and Lowdown* in which the actor Sean Penn is in a car with a group of black musicians; one of them, after making an observation, adds, "*You know what I'm sayin'?*"

"The phrase *you know what I'm saying?*" Hertzberg writes, "a substitute for *y'know?,* is a hip-hop coinage never heard before the 1980s, I believe." Close, but no cigar. (That's probably a carnival phrase used after a failure to ring a bell in a test of strength, but I wish I had a citation, you know what I'm sayin'?) In the summer of 1978, it was noted in this space, "The summarized continuation, or indication of a continued series, has long been a staple of kids' talk: *et cetera et cetera* was followed by *blah-blah-blah* and more recently by *and all that stuff;* the current locution is *you know what I'm saying?*"

During the past generation, the meaning of the vogue phrase changed from "and similar examples" to "will you give me some assurance, verbal or by some nonverbal signal, that you comprehend at least part of what I have been trying to tell you?" This new meaning is also expressed as *y'un-nerstan'?* but *you know what I'm sayin'?* is far more prevalent, with 3,000 citations in the Dow Jones database since that first one in print in 1978.

In 1996, the Texas columnist Joe Bob Briggs surveyed the range of hot reassurance interrogations—from the ubiquitous *you know what I'm sayin' here?* to the older *you get my drift?*—and wondered, "Did we go through some kind of national anxiety attack where the entire population decided that nobody was listening?"

The phrase is also a form of white noise, or meaningless sound to fill up a moment between phrases. When the British heavyweight boxer Julius Francis was beaten decisively by Mike Tyson in January 2000, the human punching bag told an interviewer: "I tried in there, *you know what I'm sayin'?* I tried."

Although the question was posed for hundreds of years, its emergence in the popular culture in this meaningless sense was surely, as Hertzberg believes, a phenomenon that began only a generation ago. Its use in a film set in the 1930s is thus an anachronism, a word rooted in Greek for "error in chronology."

For those moviegoers who spot such ear-stingers, and whose recourse until now was only to mutter, with Hamlet, "The time is out of joint": "O cursed spite, / That ever I was born to set it right."

Say What? II.   In imperial Japan before World War II, members of the "thought police"—*Shiso Keisatsu*—fanned out to suppress dangerous thinking in the populace. The thought police were disbanded by General MacArthur when he imposed freedom of speech on occupied Japan. The name of the group was later chillingly immortalized by George Orwell in his 1949 novel *1984.*

Enter now the *time police.* This dread group of moviegoing vigilantes is dedicated to suppressing anachronism now so freely engaged in by screenwriters.

Anachronism is the placement of a word of the present in the mouth of a person of the past. The newly organized *time police* have asked me to help them put a stop to it because the practice is subverting our society's orderly sense of sequence.

"In *Schindler's List,*" writes Eric Myers of New York, "in the space of ten seconds, the character played by Ralph Fiennes refers to a *scam* twice, then says, 'Who's *scamming* who?' This, in Germany during World War II?"

I would have focused on "who's *scamming whom*" and missed the anachronism, but he's right: *scam* is carnival lingo for "trick, deception, swindle" and probably did not cross into general slang until the early '60s.

Timecop Myers, after thus dispensing of Steven Spielberg, turns his attention to Woody Allen: "In *Bullets Over Broadway,* he has a distraught John Cusack moaning, 'I'm very *conflicted!*' I don't think anybody used that kind of psychobabble in 1928."

True; according to *Merriam-Webster, conflicted* came into use by psychotherapists in 1967 to describe a condition of clashing emotional impulses. By 1980, it was applied to senses ranging from "indecisive" to "at sixes and sevens" to "paralyzed by an internal tug of war."

In the Oscar-winning 1981 film *Chariots of Fire,* recounting the triumph of British track stars of the 1924 Olympics, one of the heroes rails at the prejudice that prevails in the *corridors of power.*

"It's a ringing phrase that sets off a thrilling scene," notes Richard Beebe of Middlebury, Connecticut, "but *corridors of power* didn't come into common usage until forty years after the movie's setting, when it was coined by C. P. Snow as the title for his 1964 novel of British politics." (Actually, it was coined in the BBC's magazine, the *Listener,* in 1962, but popularized by Snow's title two years later.)

Writers of television miniseries are included in this glorious game of Gotcha! Charles Kluepfel, a Timecop patrolling the sets of Bloomfield, New Jersey, notes an anachronism in CBS's *Sally Hemings: An American Scandal,* a drama loosely based on Thomas Jefferson's relationship with one of his slaves: "Jefferson starts showing some children various specimens of bones, and the teleplay writer has him say, 'This is a skull fragment of the *humongous* mastodon.' But the word *humongous* was coined during my lifetime, and *Random House Unabridged* gives the times of first usage as 1965-70."

Back to the movies. In the 1993 version of *Tombstone,* about the legendary gunfight at the OK Corral, the dying Doc Holliday croaks to Wyatt Earp that he should grab the girl and not look back, and Earp replies sadly, "Thanks for always *being there,* Doc."

Barbara Arnstein of Whitestone, New York, suggests that the gunfight venue's name might be the "I'm OK, You're OK Corral." The locution to *be there for you,* meaning "capable, reliable, to be depended upon," reached the general lingo in the 1920s, and its most recent sense of "to be nurturing, comforting" began with a religious overtone in 1981. Both senses came along years after Holliday joined Sheriff Earp to gun down the Clanton Brothers gang, who were, in a more sinister sense, there for him.

Say What? III.   Beware the urge to be ultracorrect.

Most power-writers know that the phrase *corridors of power* is identified with C. P. Snow, author of the 1964 novel of that name. In a recent article, I noted this, but after looking into the *OED,* added, "Actually, it was coined in the BBC's magazine, the *Listener,* in 1962, but popularized by Snow's title two years later."

Comes now Mary DeForest of Denver to set me straight. In a 1956 novel, *Homecoming,* Snow wrote, "The official world, the *corridors of power,* the dilemmas of conscience and egotism—she disliked them all."

In his preface to *Corridors of Power,* Snow explained: "By some fluke, the title of this novel seems to have passed into circulation during the time the book itself was being written. I have watched the phenomenon with mild consternation.

"The phrase was first used, so far as I know, in 'Homecoming.' . . . Mr. Rayner Heppenstall noticed it, and adopted it as a title for an article about my work. If he had not done this, I doubt if I should have remembered the phrase myself; but when I saw it in Mr. Heppenstall's hands, so to speak, it seemed the appropriate name for this present novel."

Snow knew it had become a cliché, but all must share the burden. As he put it, "I console myself with the reflection that, if a man hasn't the right to his own cliché, who has?"

Scandalexicon.   Every scandal has its own vocabulary. Today's column is not about scandal; it reports and judges only the vocabulary. In the current anger and agony roiling the Catholic Church, here are some of the words that should be used and pronounced with care:

Pedophile is central and is usually mispronounced. If you were like me until this was written, you would have pronounced the vowel sound in the first syllable as *eh* as in "pedal" or "pedometer." Why are we mistaken? Because the Greek word *pæd*, pronounced to rhyme with the fourth syllable of "encyclopaedia," means *child*, the abuse of whom the word is about. The Latin word *ped*, rhyming with "head," means "foot." But what's at issue here is not a foot fetish. Thus, the first syllable of *pedophile* should—and for decades after its 1951 coinage, did—take a long *e*, as in "pediatrician," not a short *eh*, as in "pedicure."

So it is correctly pronounced "PEE-duh-file," right? Only if you're a purist. San Diego's Charles H. Elster, a leading pronunciator, informs me that "the rules haven't changed, but usage has"; doctors in the 1960s began switching to the schwa, and now general dictionaries are split: *Merriam-Webster* sticks with the *ee*, while *Webster's New World* and *American Heritage Dictionary* list both, with the more recent *eh* preferred. Elster is going with the flow to "PEH-duh-file"; I'll hang tough with "PEE-duh-file," because it's etymologically sound and I like to correct people.

The Greek word *pedophilia* literally means "child love." It is a sexual abnormality in which the preferred object of the potential predator is a child, though the *pedophile* or less frequently used *pedophiliac* is not required to act on that perversion. (Psychiatrists call it an abnormality, moralists a perversion.)

Is the *pedophile*'s object (or as moralists would say, victim) a male child or a female? Although the original meaning of *pæd* or *paid*, "child," covers both, notes a Princeton professor, Joshua Katz, "in English there's been an extension: the critical thing is the youth, not the sex of the youth. A *pederast* is the Greek-based word for an adult male who desires boys only." (This synonym for *sodomist* has long been pronounced "PEH-duh-rast"; there's an irritating inconsistency here, which is why it is hard for me to rail at "PEH-duh-file" as a mistake.)

If the lust of both *pedophile* and the outdated *pederast* is directed at children, what about an adult's desire for teenagers? Until 1988, this was a void in our vocabulary; it was filled by Tariq Rahman, professor of linguistics at

Quaid-i-Azam University in Islamabad, Pakistan, with *ephebophilia*. He noticed its 1980 citation in a paper in French about the ancient Greek treatment of postpubescent boys written by Félix Buffière: "les *ephèbophiles*, comme certains les nomment"—as certain people have named them. An *ephebos* was an Athenian youth of eighteen or so in training for citizenship; the new word is pronounced "ef-FEE-bo-file." No dictionary I've seen has it, but the 1999 *Merck Manual* defines *ephebophilia* as "attraction to youths" who are "postpubescent."

That's almost the way the Reverend Donald Cozzens pronounced its application to priestly predators last month on *Meet the Press*. Speaking of the abuse of minors not limited to prepuberty or to boys, he clipped the "ef." The moderator Tim Russert seized on the new locution, clipping it as well, and so *pheebofile* was born—because Tim is linguistically infallible. Another formation of this noun is *pheebophilia*, which I define as "the desire by an adult for an adolescent" with no sex of luster or lustee specified and spelled with two *e*'s (as did the NBC transcript) so that sloppy pronouncers cannot do to it what they have done to *pedophile*.

You refer to alternate pronunciations of the first vowel sound in the noun pedophile. *You label one lone* e, *and the other* eh. *You name the second pronunciation schwa. The sound is actually a mid front lax vowel,* [ə]. *Schwa is the reduced vowel sound in the second syllable, which you represent as "uh," and which phonologists represent as* e.

Ellen Measday
Livingston, New Jersey

Thank you for pointing out the difference between a pedophile and an ephebophile. Distinguishing between the two is important, morally, legally and psychologically.

Ronald Colvin
Philadelphia, Pennsylvania

This is my first foray as a member of the Gotcha! Gang. You referred to the vowel in the first syllable of the "PEH-duh-file" pronunciation as being a schwa, but the schwa is a sound that occurs only in unaccented syllables, like the first syllable of "about." The dictionary says the schwa symbol is sometimes used for the related stressed vowel that occurs in "cup," but it would never be used for the short "e" of "bed" or "pedophile."

Sandra Wilde
Portland, Oregon

🍂

Secret Plan.   In a rousing speech to an AFL-CIO convention in New Jersey, Vice President Gore used the attack word *secret* seven times. It is now his favorite adjective, having temporarily replaced *risky* (as in the phrase, pronounced as one word, *riskytaxscheme*).

He was blazing away at Governor Bush's proposal, not yet detailed, to allow individuals to divert a portion of their Social Security taxes into the stock market. Gore charged that Bush believed "it would be best not to let you, the voters of this country, in on the *secret plan* before the election. . . . He is suppressing the details of how his plan would work and refusing to divulge what his *secret plan* really is." At a subsequent news conference, he evidently felt that *secret* was not pejorative enough and added, redundantly, a "private *secret plan.*"

That sinister phrase—*secret plan*—has resonance to veteran rhetoricians and students of presidential campaigns. In the 1968 primaries, candidate Richard Nixon was searching for a way to promise he would extricate the United States from its increasingly unpopular involvement in Vietnam. The key verb to be used was *end*, though it would be nice to get the verb *win* in some proximity to it.

One speechwriter came up with the formulation that "new leadership will *end* the war and *win* the peace in the Pacific." Nixon made it part of his stump speech, and the juxtaposition of *end* and *win*—though it did not claim to intend to *win* the war, but only the peace—drove his major opponent for the GOP nomination, Governor George Romney of Michigan, up the wall.

When a UPI reporter pressed Nixon for specifics, the candidate demurred; the reporter wrote that it seemed Nixon was determined to keep his plan *secret,* though he did not quote Nixon as having said either *secret* or *plan.* But this gave Romney a chance to slam back at his opponent's promise. In what became the centerpiece of his stump speech in the snows of New Hampshire, Romney demanded to know, "Where is your *secret plan?*" That question skillfully presupposed an assertion of not just a general promise but also a detailed plan, and soon it became widely accepted that Nixon had said, "I have a *secret plan* to end the war."

Years later, when a *New York Times* columnist attributed that direct quote to Nixon, a White House speechwriter challenged him to find the quote in anything taken down by pencil or recorder at the time. The pundit searched high and low and had to admit the supposed remark was unsourceable. (Look, the Nixon speechwriter was me and the columnist was later my colleague, Tony Lewis; I didn't have to research this.)

During Ronald Reagan's run for re-election in 1984, Democrats took a leaf from the Romney playbook and charged him with having a *secret plan* to raise taxes after the election. This forced Reagan to say defensively he would raise taxes only "as a last resort" and reminded politicians that the old *secret-plan* charge had legs.

Even Gore, a few weeks before he leveled the tried-and-true phrase at Bush, showed he was aware of its old-chestnuttiness. In a hilarious, deadpan, self-mocking speech to the Gridiron Club in Washington, he was widely reported to have said he had a *secret plan* to win the White House: he would claim credit for all the good stuff that had happened in the past eight years and dissociate himself from the bad stuff.

Meanwhile, George W. Bush has been using an attack word of his own to characterize the Gore approach to Social Security: "For eight years," he wrote in a fund-raising letter, "Clinton/Gore has had history's greatest opportunity to reform Social Security. They chose to *demagogue* the problem, not repair it."

I kept this letter, sent to me by its recipient, Leila Hadley Luce of New York, to note the use of the beslashed singular subject *Clinton/Gore,* followed properly by the singular verb *has,* but then followed incorrectly by *they. Clinton/Gore* is a team and takes an *it.*

But Mrs. Luce's covering note questioned the use of the "new verb," *to demagogue*. Originally a noun, this was formed from the Greek *demos,* "people," and *agogos,* "leading"; it meant "leader of the mob" and now has the derogatory meaning of "a politician who appeals to people's emotions." The noun can be used attributively to do the work of an adjective: Robert Southey in 1812 denounced "the venom and the virulence of the *demagogue* journalists."

Governor Bush cannot be faulted for using *demagogue* as a verb. It was coined in that form by James Harrington in his 1656 utopian theory, *Commonwealth of Oceana.* He picked up the noun coined five years earlier by Thomas Hobbes and wrote of a time "when that same ranting fellow Alcibiades fell a *demagoging* for the Sicilian war." In 1890, the *Cincinnati Commercial Gazette* wrote of President Benjamin Harrison, "The president never thought of *demagoging* the matter."

Note the lack of a *u* in those usages of what most of us would until recently spell as *demagoguing.* But we live in a non-U world; just as *catalogue* and *dialogue* have been dropping their *ue* endings, so too will *demagogue* soon enough be spelled d*emagog,* with its gerund *demagoging.*

It's a hard word for the mob to handle; *demagogic* is pronounced with the final *g* soft, rhyming with *logic,* but *demagoguery* has the final *g* hard, rhyming with *toggery.* (Get away from that e-mail key; there is such a word. It means "clothing.")

Will Gore now assail Bush for harboring a *secret plan* to attack him for *demagoguery?* Will Bush lash back in a debate by demanding he spell it? Both sides are now armed.

See-Through Vogue Words.   Back when he was merely the Clinton administration's treasury secretary, Harvard's new president, Larry Summers, was asked by a vituperative columnist (me) how he planned to protect the privacy of bank depositors. "We're more concerned with *transparency,*" he countered.

"You can't turn around these days," writes the *Washington Post* columnist Marjorie Williams, "without encountering the Bush administration's favorite buzzword: *transparency*."

She's right; my dossier on this term is fattening. "Part of the problem in dealing with North Korea," President Bush told South Korea's president, Kim Dae-jung, is that "there's not very much *transparency*." Not to be out-vogue-worded, Kim later hoped that "the North Korean missile issue will be resolved with *transparency*."

In Senate confirmation hearings for deputy secretary of state, Richard Armitage fervently expressed his support for the five unassailable towers of political virtue: "democratization, *transparency*, open governance, women's issues, empowerment."

But perhaps pellucity's pollution has peaked. "We have noticed a definite increase in the term *visibility*," notes Sheri Prasso, editor of the section of *BusinessWeek* titled UpFront (one word, capital modishly in the middle, playing on the meanings of *up-front* as "honest, forthright" as well as "found in the opening pages of the magazine"). "The lack of *visibility* is cited by CEOs and other corporate types when they talk about earnings projections for the last half of the year."

"*Visibility* is really poor for the back-end of the year," said Timothy Koogle, the departing CEO of Yahoo, last month. (The year's *back-end* is still referred to by the geriatric set as "fall" and "winter." The noun *back-end* is a back-formation from *back-ended*, created by the need for an opposite to *front-ended*, a variant of *front-loaded*.)

In the struggle against the tenacity of opacity, will *visibility* overtake *transparency*? I don't see it.

Sensual.   Maneuvering my shopping cart through the brassiere section of a Wal-Mart in Charles Town, West Virginia (on the way, I swear, to men's ultrarelaxed jeans), I was struck by the brand name of a Hanes underwear product: *Sensuale*.

By adding an *e* to the word *sensual*, the manufacturer not only gives a frenchified twist to the term but also enables the "lightly lined underwire" to be trademarked. Nothing incorrect about that. But a close examination of the package reveals this selling pitch: "Sensuous styling that's sure to allure."

Which is it, then—*sensual* or *sensuous*? Is there a difference? Yes; just as in *underwire* and *underwear,* the distinction is worth preserving.

Sensual has to do with the pleasurable gratification of the senses; for five centuries, it dealt with sexual appetites and carnal desires. "He loves," sneered a disapproving prude in 1618, "as far as *sensual* love can go." To this day, a *sensual* person is one more inclined to revel in physical pleasures than to get a charge out of moral rectitude.

The poet Milton was not blind to this connotation of lewdness. However, writing in 1641 about the difference between soul and body, he needed a neutral adjective to apply to the body that meant "pertaining to the senses" of touch, taste, sight, smell and hearing. So he dropped the *-al* from *sensual* and substituted *-ous,* writing, "The Soule ... finding the ease she had from her visible, and *sensuous* colleague the body."

The poet Coleridge announced in 1814 that he would reintroduce Milton's word "to express in one word what belongs to the senses"; ever since, usagists have differentiated *sensual,* "indulgent in physical pleasure," from *sensuous,* "descriptive of aesthetic appreciation." You get a *sensual* kick out of watching an R-rated movie and a *sensuous* kick out of listening to music or sniffing the cookies in Grandma's oven.

Shouldst Milton be living at this hour, he would surely take umbrage at the misuse of his uplifting adjective by the bra makers at Hanes. They are alluding to the luxurious feeling of their lightly lined Sensuale product, implying, as in the *OED*'s sense 3, "a luxurious yielding up of oneself to passive enjoyment."

I noodled this around with Steven Pinker, the director of the Center for Cognitive Neuroscience at MIT. He does not see the semantic difference to be holding up. "The distinction was blown to smithereens in the early 1970s," he says, "when 'J' published *The Sensuous Woman,* which as I recall suggested some interesting new uses for Jell-O and Saran Wrap. Apparently there have been attempts to reserve *sensuous* as a synonym for 'sensory'—pertaining to the senses in a clinical way, as in 'sensory physiol-ogy'— but they have failed."

Not with me, they haven't. I like the distinction. It reminds me of the difference between *continual* and *continuous*.

Even Pinker, a descriptivist, goes along with me part way on that: "The most consistently respected meaning difference between *continual* and *continuous*," he notes, "is that *continuous* can be used for spatial as well as temporal *continuity* ('a *continuous* line of trees'), whereas *continual* can be used only for temporal *continuity*. We see this in the spatial adjective *discontinuous* ('a *discontinuous* line')."

Prescriptivists like me go all the way. We say *continual* means "repeat-edly," like the plumber upstairs going bang, bang, bang when you're trying to sleep. Pinker agrees that although *continuous* is nine times more com-mon in writing, *continual* "is said to be used for iterated events." (*Iterate* means "repeat, say again"; I think he treats *reiterate* as semiredundant.)

Continuous, on the other hand, is like the steady whine of a buzz saw in operation. *Continuous* "is said to be used for a truly gapless state or condi-tion, such as heat, war or illness. One can sense this in the contrast between 'John is working *continuously*' (without interruption) and 'John is *contin-ually* working late' (every day)." Pinker has counterexamples, but I refuse to become confused.

Remember the difference between *-al* and *-ous*. Suffixes count. It's fine being *imperial* (having an empire) but not being *imperious* (overbearing). Those who observe these distinctions are virtually virtuous.

Shall We Trance?   "Scott Henry packed the *trance* tent," reported Kelefa Sanneh of the *Times,* "with a set built on simple melodies, pounding beats and dramatic contrasts." The article was about an annual dance party held in New York as a kind of mall of music. "*Techno* and *trance* both eschew syncopation," the writer explained. "The listener is tempted to imagine that the thumping will continue forever. By contrast, styles based on syn-copation tend to produce shorter, more volatile tracks, often built around vocal performances—songs, in other words." I like that sudden simplification of the pretentious "vocal performances" with "songs," but the writer's wry phrase "in other words" doesn't work with the single word "songs." You wouldn't switch to the singular "in another word" because that would lose the easy, colloquial sense of "to put it in plain English." I'd try "that is, 'songs.' " (In this compulsive copyediting, am I being too picky? You should see my e-mail.)

Forget about *techno,* already being pushed aside by *electro.* Keep your ear on *trance* (in another word, *noise,* as the incognoscenti would mutter). Its meaning is not the same as the noun first used by Chaucer in the 14th century to mean "swoon, a suspension of consciousness." But the author of *The Canterbury Tales* also used it as a verb to mean "to skip or prance; to tramp rapidly."

This lays a shaky etymological basis for *trance* music, which was first cited in the *Guardian* in 1970 about shamanist tribal music played in Ethiopia. It surfaced again in the mid '80s as a name for what Joe Brown described in the *Washington Post* as a combination of "electronic instruments with traditional acoustic sounds, creating a sense of well-being, even euphoria." This New Age music was followed by a more distinct beat as an aid to meditation, and in recent usages of *trance dance* the beat has apparently taken over.

But do not take this as the latest in the musical vocabulary. A decade ago, the *Boston Globe* coined *mash-ups* to describe a mixture of styles in a kind of creatively corrupt collage. In the *New York Times* a few weeks ago, Neil Strauss referred to "the first significant new musical genre to be lifted out of the underground," called "*mash-ups* or bootlegs," mixing two or three quite different recordings by established stars, often in contravention of copyright law. Some bootleggers become furious at others who *mash up* their "white labels" with other bootlegs.

One practitioner of the *mash-up,* this time using rock and the voice of a famed television news anchor, is Mark Gunderson of Columbus, Ohio. He cheerfully told the *Houston Press* that he coined the name for the light-fingered stunt: *plagiarhythm.*

℃

Shoveling Coalition.   Afghanistan's "Northern *Alliance*" was a collection of ethnic groups with the joint purpose of opposing and defeating the Taliban. Its victory was made possible by the coalition of outside forces led by, and mainly made up of, U.S. troops and aircraft.

Is there a semantic difference between an *alliance* and a *coalition*?

Yes, and we'd better get it straight before the United States and its allies (or coalition partners) hit the next state harboring terrorists.

An *alliance* is a formal joining of long-term interests, usually expressed in a treaty (even when derogated in 1914 by Germany's Theobald von Bethmann-Hollweg as "a scrap of paper"). The North Atlantic Treaty Organization, and especially its English-speaking component, is informally but accurately called "the Atlantic *Alliance*."

A *coalition* is a temporary alliance, an ad hoc arrangement between or among nations or groups to effect some immediate end. That describes the force assembled by the U.S. in the Persian Gulf war in 1991. But when our NATO allies sought assurances from Defense Secretary Donald Rumsfeld last month that the war on terrorism would not extend to countries other than Afghanistan, he replied: "The mission determines the *coalition*. The *coalition* doesn't determine the mission."

Neither word properly denotes the collection of forces in the recent war in Afghanistan. It was a U.S.-initiated air-sea mission, with U.S. and British commandos on the ground as spotters and organizers for the ground troops of the Northern *Alliance,* which was really a local coalition; other nations offered grudging moral support or intelligence tips or a willingness not to shoot down our aircraft using their airspace. It was said that calling it a *coalition* was diplomatically useful, but the word to describe such unilateral cooperative intervention has yet to be coined.

To provide a service to world synonymy, I turned to Henry A. Kissinger for a differentiation of the two terms that do exist to describe unions of forces or nations in league.

"An *alliance*," he responded, "is a group of states assembled for an agreed purpose with specific obligations to deal with that contingency.

"A *coalition* is a group of states avowing a common purpose, but which may leave the specific obligations it entails open and indeed subject for negotiation when the contingency to which the common purpose applies arises."

Shtick.   Senator Joseph Lieberman was the newsmaker guest at the thirty-fifth anniversary of the Godfrey Sperling Breakfast, sponsored by the *Christian Science Monitor*. Before getting down to political business, the first Jewish candidate to be nominated for national office by a major party said, "Let me do *shtick* for a while." He then engaged in some mild ethnic humor, just as he did at the Gridiron Dinner, where he told of watching a Jewish pornographic film titled *Debbie Does Neiman Marcus,* about which he said, "There was no sex, but I felt guilty anyway."

Lieberman used the Yiddishism *shtick* to mean "comic routine; line of patter." It is rooted in the German *Stück,* with an umlaut over the *u.*

(About umlauts: In this case, that mark of two dots above the vowel indicates that it is to be pronounced from the front of the mouth. *Uh,* as in the English *stuck,* comes from back in the throat; *oo,* as in *stooge,* is farther up front. An umlaut—pronounced "OOM-lout," meaning "changed sound"—also separates the sound of a vowel from the different-sounding vowel that follows, as in reënter, though in English we tend to replace the umlaut with a hyphen. We will now re-enter the subject of this *Stück.* Like you, I have stumbled through life without knowing what an umlaut signifies and looked it up today only because language is my *shtick.*)

In the aforesaid "language is my *shtick,*" the sense of *shtick* is not the original "piece," nor the extended "comic routine"; rather, it is the sense absorbed into the English language of "characteristic bit of business" or, more generally, "specialty."

"Welcome to the season of *shtick,*" writes Holman W. Jenkins Jr., columnist for the *Wall Street Journal,* in an article deriding other pundits for knee-jerk narratives about the bursting of the stock market "bubble" coming as a complete surprise.

"For the purposes of the *shtick* . . . the small investor is an eternal rube who can't be expected to have taken a skeptical view of the bubble," Jenkins writes. "The devil theory of the bubble turns on the notion that investors got bad advice from Wall Street.... In fact, the *Wall Street Journal's* first use of the term 'Internet bubble' occurred in 1995, four years before the Nasdaq peak.... The underlying message of the *shtick* is that the small investor is nothing but a victim and a twit."

Asked for his definition of the Yiddishism, Jenkins replied, "A hackneyed act or comedian's routine that's getting a little tired." Because he was adept at etymology, I asked for the origin of the economic sense of *bubble*. "The South Sea bubble," he said instantly. "My best guess is that *bubble* in that financial context just naturally arose from the connection to the sea."

For background on the South Sea bubble, Robert Menschel, the Goldman Sachs partner whose research for a book titled *Markets, Mobs, and Mayhem* has made him an authority on investor psychology, referred me to Charles Mackay's 1841 work, *Extraordinary Popular Delusions and the Madness of Crowds*. In it, the British historian detailed Holland's "tulip-mania," France's "Mississippi madness" and the predations of England's "South Sea Company."

This last was formed in 1711 to exploit a monopoly on British trade with South America and the islands of the South Seas. Though unprofitable, the company traded its stock for government bonds and took responsibility for the national debt, triggering a wave of speculation, a spate of imitators and a belief that unlimited credit expansion could sustain prosperity. When mass mania subsided and stocks plunged in 1720, the ensuing failure of the banking system was characterized as "the bursting of the South Sea bubble." The poet Alexander Pope wrote that "avarice creeping on, / Spread, like a low-born mist, and hid the sun."

Now the word *bubble* is widely used to describe the run-up in the late '90s of Internet and related technology stocks. It was given a boost in 1984, when Britain's prime minister, Margaret Thatcher, warned, "If you go into what I call a *bubble* boom, every *bubble* bursts."

The financial usage of bubble *was full-blown long before the 1720 South Sea Bubble, and it has no connection to sea foam. In fact, it conclusively predates the South Sea Bubble by at least half a century! The great Restoration come-dies by Congreve, Etherege and Wycherly are rife with the word, as both noun and verb "to bubble" (to cheat or to trick) was common usage in En-gland by 1675, when Wycherly wrote his salacious comedy,* The Country Wife. *Scams and financial hype were called "bubbles" at least as early.*

In the sense of an ephemeral or deceptive illusion, "bubble" already ap-pears prominently in Macbeth *(1607). In Act I, Scene iii, Banquo says, "The earth hath bubbles as the water has, and these are of them. Whither are they vanished?" Macbeth answers, "Into the air, and what seemed corporal melted as breath into the wind. Would that they had stayed!" It's quite pos-sible that these lines drew pained chuckles from the wealthier members of his audience for Shakespeare may well have been punning on the financial sense of "bubble." He might have had in mind the Muscovy Company (founded in 1555, which had never yielded the fabulous Russian fortune its 201 mer-chant shareholders had hoped for), and Sir Walter Raleigh's expeditions (which cost Raleigh alone at least 40,000 pounds), of the Virginia Company, which had financed the Jamestown expedition just the year before* Macbeth *was produced.*

In any case, Shakespeare seems to have foreseen the lament of NASDAQ investors down to a T.

Chances are, "bubble" wafted over to England from Holland, where the first modern stock market began around 1602. Joseph de la Vega, who de-scribed the Amsterdam exchange in 1688 in his Confusion de Confusiones, *speaks often of "windhandle," or "dealing in wind" (trading shares not in the speculator's possession, as was done even then by short-sellers). What's more, de la Vega writes of "inflating" stocks by offering to buy them above market price, just as "God with one breath breathed life into Adam." This image— puffing up prices by blowing them full of air—seems the most likely origin of the financial term "bubble."*

Incidentally, Mackay's Extraordinary Popular Delusions and the Mad-ness of Crowds *is a splendid read, but as history is notoriously unreliable. It has been superseded by much more trustworthy works like Charles Kindel-berger's* Mania, Panics and Crashes *(1978), Peter Graber's* Famous First Bubbles *(2000) and the definitive* The South Sea Bubble *(1960), by John*

Carswell, a British polymath of Safiresque reach (my favorite book by him is
his monograph on Coptic tattoos, I kid you not).

Jason Zweig
Investing Columnist
Money Magazine
New York, New York

𝒞

Sidekicking.   When Vice President-elect Dick Cheney (only intimates
call him Richard) took a strong public position on national missile defense, he was quick to add that he did not want to infringe on the turf of
"my old *sidekick* Colin Powell," the secretary of state-designate.

The *Washington Post* columnist Jim Hoagland, suspecting that the incoming vice president was asserting foreign-policy dominance, promptly
popped him one: "Even the terminology betrayed Cheney's ambitions
and intentions. Gabby Hayes was Roy Rogers's '*sidekick*.' Rogers was
not Hayes's sidekick, just as Don Quixote was never Sancho Panza's *sidekick.*"

Hoagland might also have cited George W. Bush's comment during the
campaign referring to Karen Hughes, then his communications director,
as "my *sidekick*"; that suggests a relationship of principal to aide. Was Cheney dissing Powell or respecting him as a colleague?

The first citation of the old slang with a seeming western flavor was in a
1904 story by O. Henry: "Billy was my *side-kicker* in New York"; in 1906,
Helen Green wrote, "The Red Swede . . . sat over a pint of champagne with
Dopey Polly . . . and his *side kick,* the Runt." (Such colorful nicknames are
now frowned upon.) Some speculate that *side kicks,* two words, was a
phrase derived from the outside pockets of an overcoat; in underworld
slang, it referred to an accomplice.

Close study of the history of the word indicates the primary meaning to
be "partner" or "close friend," with only a second sense carrying a connotation of "junior partner" or "subordinate," from "one who walks or rides
alongside." A vice president would not call a president a *sidekick,* because

they are not political equals, but could use the word about a colleague in the administration's cabinet without seeming to pull rank.

Skutnik.   When a person's name turns into a word, that's called an eponym, from the Greek *epi,* "upon," and *onyma,* "name."

The University of California at Santa Barbara had a panel about the media (from the Greek for "really high-class buncha guys"). When CNN's Jeff Greenfield assured the crowd, "I haven't planted a *skutnik* here," I stopped him: I had heard of a *sputnik,* the Russian word for the first Soviet satellite, but what was a *skutnik*?

Greenfield directed me to his book *Oh, Waiter! One Order of Crow!* about the media failure on election night: "A *skutnik* is a human prop, used by a speaker to make a political point. The name comes from Lenny *Skutnik,* a young man who heroically saved lives after the Air Florida plane crash in Washington in 1982 and who was introduced by President Reagan during his State of the Union speech."

The introduction of heroes became a staple in presidential addresses to joint sessions of Congress. In 1995, the columnist William F. Buckley was one of the first to use the name as an eponym: "President Clinton was awash with *Skutniks.*"

The play on *sputnik* aside, the word should be spelled *Skutnik* in deference to the original honoree. Watch for one the next time around.

Sleeper.   In the stock market, a *sleeper* is an undervalued security. Among publishers, a *sleeper* is a book that sells for years without being advertised. Movie moguls think of it as a film that surprises by grabbing audiences, and in politics a *sleeper* is a seemingly unimportant amendment that would cost billions if not spotted by alert opponents. In horse racing, when a horse has been held back in previous races to build up the odds— and then is allowed to go full speed to win its owner's big bet—that horse is a *sleeper.*

That word of so many senses (and don't forget the garment with no opening for toes that sleepwear manufacturers produce for toddlers) has awakened new interest with its most sinister meaning: "a spy long in place but not yet activated."

"Hollister . . . was a *sleeper*," wrote the mystery novelist Holly Roth in a 1955 book that used that word as its title, "a member of the Communist Party whose whole life was dedicated to the one big moment." In 1976, the *Times of London* observed, "There almost certainly exists within our political establishment, what is known as a *'sleeper'*—a high-level political figure who is in fact a Soviet agent, infiltrated into the system many years ago."

As the cold war ended, the word surfaced again with a slightly different meaning: in 1990, Professor Paul Wilkinson, a British terrorism expert, told the Press Association that Iraq was unrivaled in the technique, with *sleeper* squads, known as "submarines," already in position.

Benjamin Weiser reported in the *New York Times* on Dec. 22, 2000, that a former U.S. Army sergeant, Ali A. Mohamed, testified to a federal grand jury investigating the bombing of two U.S. embassies in East Africa that the Saudi terrorist Osama bin Laden used the technique: "In 1997, [Mohamed] told the FBI about networks of terrorists," wrote Weiser, "known as *'sleepers,'* who lie low for years but do not need to be told what to do." The reporter quoted an FBI document released in court holding that Mohamed knew "that there are hundreds of *'sleepers'* or 'submarines' in place who don't fit neatly into the terrorist profile."

Four years after that FBI report was written, the word *sleeper* moved from spookspeak jargon into the general language. "The pattern of bin Laden's terrorism," wrote Evan Thomas and Mark Hosenball in *Newsweek* two weeks after September 11, "is to insert operatives into a country where they are *'sleepers,'* burrowed deep into the local culture, leading normal lives while awaiting orders."

Slippery Slope.   "In bioethics," writes Robin Henig, a science writer from Takoma Park, Maryland, "a *slippery slope* implies a certain inevitability to scientific progress, an inability to put a stop to progressively more loathsome applications of knowledge once we receive knowledge in the first place. When did the term come into use, and what has it meant other than the way we use it today in bioethics?"

In politics: Archbishop Desmond Tutu, in decrying the undemocratic methods of Zimbabwe's president, Robert Mugabe, said that the African nation was "on the *slippery slope* of perdition." (By using "of," he used *perdition* to mean "eternal damnation"; had he said "to," it would have meant "hell.") The Nobel laureate Tutu liked that phrase: "When you use violence to silence your critics . . . you are on the *slippery slope* toward dictatorship."

Civil libertarians in the United States use it, too: Otis Moss III, pastor of the Tabernacle Baptist Church in Augusta, Georgia, warned that President Bush and his attorney general "stand upon a *slippery moral slope* as they attempt to respond to this horrific act [September 11] with legal procedures that shred the foundation of our Constitution."

Sometimes a cigar is just a cigar. Before the ever-popular phrase was extended into metaphor, it was used by poets who liked the alliteration to mean, simply enough, a muddy hill on which one could break one's neck. Herman Melville in his 1876 *Clarel*: "The steeds withstand the *slippery slope* / While yet their outflung fore-feet grope." And Robert Frost in 1916: "As standing in the river road / He looked back up the *slippery slope* / (Two miles it was) to his abode."

But the key task of the phrasedick is to find earliest uses of the current sense of "a course that leads inexorably to disaster." The *OED* tracks it to a 1951 novel, but new retrieval technology lets us do better than that. The economist Herbert Heaton wrote in 1928 that Canadian "cards and bills alike found themselves on the steep *slippery slope* of war finance." And thanks to the Cornell Making of America database, we have this 1857 use from *Chamber's Journal*: "When the educated person of middle class is reduced to pennilessness . . . what but this gives him the desire to struggle again up the *slippery slope* of fortune?"

In both those citations, the meaning is closer to "the greasy pole," a figure of political speech popularized by Benjamin Disraeli to describe the difficult climb and easy fall from power. The current sense of "first step in what will be a long slide" probably surfaced in the early 20th century, possibly in an article by a writer in a 1909 *Quarterly Review,* published in London: "the first step down that *slippery slope* at the bottom of which lies a parliamentary government for India." If you want to join the phrasedick fellowship, send along an earlier usage and get an effusive accolade.

Nowadays, as Ms. Henig notes, the phrase is often used in controversies about ethics. "It does not make sense to ban stem-cell research where abortion is completely legal and fertility clinics destroy untold embryos," wrote Marcel D'Eon in the *StarPhoenix* of Saskatoon, Saskatchewan, last month. "And it demonstrates what opponents of abortion have been saying for more than 30 years: we are on a *slippery slope.* Who knows where it will lead?"

Logicians are very cautious about *slippery slope* arguments because it is impossible to know beforehand, with absolute deductive certainty, that an "if-then" statement is true. President Dwight Eisenhower in 1954 came up with the "falling domino" principle: "You knocked over the first one, and what would happen to the last one was the certainty that it would go over very quickly." This "domino theory" was later much derided by opponents to our defense of South Vietnam.

I notice that the word "phrasedick" is a favorite of yours. I assume you intend it to mean a person who investigates origins and associations of phrases, as in "phrase detective." The second syllable was used in that meaning more popularly in my youth ('40s and '50s) than it is today, when, as you surely know, it more commonly suggests a vulgar definition. I'd hate to think of you in that way.

Madeline Hamermesh
Minneapolis, Minnesota

Slug It Tout.   Headline writers—at their best, the language's poets of the succinct—sometimes give in to the urge to accentuate a minor sense of a temptingly short word. In response to the television news producers' "If it bleeds, it leads," some writers of our headlines are in danger of adopting its counterpart: If it fits, it hits.

"Bush *Touts* Welfare-to-Work Proposal During Ohio Trip" was an AP headline this month. It was soon followed in the *Washington Post* by a headline over an article from Michigan, "Bush Steps Into the Classroom to *Tout* New Education Law."

We're talking about the English verb *tout*, pronounced "towt," not the French word for the adjective "all," pronounced "too," as in "le tout New York," meaning "anybody who is anybody among the glitterati." The English *tout* is hot, not just in headlinese but also in the body of articles. A *Washington Times* reporter, object of no pleas to squeeze, picked up on the vogue verb with "The president was scheduled to travel to Pennsylvania today to *tout* another component of his budget: $11 billion to fight bioterrorism." A reporter for the *New York Times* noted that Senator Robert Torricelli of New Jersey supported a deduction of college tuition payments from federal income taxes with "He and his advisers *tout* this whenever possible."

An AP deskman, asked about the meaning of *touts* atop the wire service article about welfare-to-work, quickly replied, "It means 'speaks in favor of.'" Others would defend their use of *touts* as meaning "recommends, urges passage of, advocates, supports, presses for" or even "praises, hails." Those are not the primary meanings of this colorful colloquialism. Words carry connotations; because of its larcenous, racy origin, this verb lugs along an aura of slyly phony enthusiasm.

Touter began as a noun in the English village of Tunbridge Wells in 1754. "Here are a parcel of fellows," wrote Samuel Richardson, "mean traders, whom they call *touters* and their business *touting* . . . riding out miles to meet coaches . . . to beg their custom while here." The racetrack association came early, as *Sporting* magazine in 1812 defined a *touter* as "a person who hides up between the furzes on the heath to see the trials of horses." The novelist Charles Dickens, in his 1844 *Martin Chuzzlewit*, used it to mean "a thieves' scout" when he wrote of "thimble-riggers, duffers, *touters*, or any of those sharpers . . . known to the Police."

Clipped to the single-syllable *touts*, these sneaky souls can still be spotted coming back from the furzes on the heath at some of our huge race-ways to *tout*—the verb—a horse to an unsuspecting bettor, thereby to ma-nipulate the odds or get a piece of the winnings. (A generation ago, I bought a double-breasted pinstripe suit; A. M. Rosenthal, then the execu-tive editor of the *Times,* said, "You're supposed to look like a newspaper-man, not a racetrack *tout,*" and I have not worn it since.)

From this sleazy background we get the current extended meaning of the verb to *tout:* "to publicize blatantly, to praise extravagantly; to impor-tune often for a selfish or sinister purpose." Politicians have been known to do that, of course, and opinionmongers have the right to use it freely. Though it is terse and punchy, its judgmental appearance in a headline is to be (to use the favorite verbs in headlinese) assailed and decried. What's a good substitute for *tout*? *Discuss* has no sell in it, and *advocate* is too bookish; if you're reaching for dignified pushiness, try *promote.*

Slurvian.   What students of the New York accent now categorize as "first-stage Slurvian" was reported in the 1938 Federal Writers Project "Al-manac for New Yorkers." An example given was *onnafyah.*

The definition of *onnafyah,* as consumers of hurried meals in Manhat-tan know, is "a short order is being prepared." The metaphor of a burger sizzling on the grill has since been extended to a more general "it'll be ready in a minute," whether or not applied to food. This brings to mind another first-stage Slurvian expression, *jeet?,* a quick way of asking some-one if he has eaten.

Slurvian is not limited to New York City. The most famous example of slurred speech embodied in dialect is the southern *y'all,* which has its equiv-alent in New York Slurvian *alluhyuz.* (That's if the emphasis is on the *all;* if the speaker wishes to stress the plural *you,* the phrase becomes *alluhyooz.*) And in California, *g'yonit* signifies "get on it," meaning "get moving."

These amalgams and other familiar interrogatory compressions—*tsamatta?, hootoadjadat?, whaddyanutz?*—have no meaning other than the phrases when separated: "What's the matter? Who told you that? What are you, nuts?" Of greater semantic interest are the phrases that gain a separate sense when deliberately slurred. We will now consider "second-stage Slurvian."

Linguists will not soon forget *fuggedaboudit*. Although the transliteration of the New Yorkese phrase has appeared on T-shirts around the country, the expression is not being dropped by Noo Yawkiz, which so often happens when a dialect phrase becomes adopted by outsiders. That is because the slurred words do not mean only the literal "forget about it"; rather, the phrase is second-stage Slurvian for "don't bother me with that" or a more figurative "it'll be a cold day in hell before I buy that cockamamie notion."

The closest Slurvian synonym to *fuggedaboudit* is *gedaddaheeuh,* which long ago lost its initial meaning of "leave the premises" and now conveys disbelief shot through with an abiding disdain. Standing alone, *gedaddaheeuh* means "I don't believe you" or the more vivid "don't give me that baloney." But when used in the start of a sentence like "*Gedaddaheeuh* wid yer fancy talk," the disbelief turns to vehement rejection, in the sense of "I vigorously reject your highfalutin language."

The sense of the compressed phrase is no longer the sum of its individual words; the compressed phrase conveys a meaning all its own. Another example of the semantic change called "figurative extension" that grew out of New York speedspeech is *noprollem,* which originally meant "I can do it easily" but now can be a modest response to gratitude with the primary sense of "you're welcome."

Derision at such elision is misplaced. The University of Pennsylvania's William Labov, whose classic 1966 study, *The Social Stratification of English in New York City,* demonstrated that the city is a melting pot of various dialects, should be delighted. (I have been unable to pinpoint the locale of *gerareheeuh,* a variant of *gedaddaheeuh;* fresh street research is needed.)

The lexicographer Sol Steinmetz notes that the Brooklyn accent differs from Noo Yawkese: "*Oily boid* is Brooklynese," he says, "as any Manhattanite or Bronxite will inform you in no *unsoyten toyms.* There is no standard New York pronunciation of words like *car, bad* and *off.* What we think of as 'New Yorkese' is the least prestigious of the various social dialects, or the one that differs or deviates most from standard American English. That is why New York speech has a low prestige even among its own speakers."

Off. I just pronounced that as I wrote it, and it sounded like "awf," as in *awful,* not like "off" as in *offal.* For help on this, I turned to the pronunciation maven Charles Harrington Elster, author of *Is There a Cow in Moscow?* (Yes, but there is no *zoo* in zo-ology.)

"New York tawk features a diphthongal *aw* sound," Elster observes, "that in heavy New Yorkese sounds almost disyllabic." (Before a Parisian reader of this column in the *International Herald Tribune* expostulates, "*Gedad-daheeuh avec ton baratin,*" let me translate. A diphthong is the gliding sound of combining vowels, as in the *oy* in the head-smacking Yiddish *oy veh. Disyllabic* means "having two syllables.") "It's impossible for me to transliterate this elongated *aw* here, but ask a dyed-in-the-wool New Yorker to pronounce *dog* and *coffee* and you'll come close.

"New Yorkers are also renowned *r*-droppers," Elster says. "Day eat wid a *fawk,* day walk onna *flaw,* an day drink adda *bah.* The superintendent of their apartment building is *da soopuh,* and the *New York Times* is *da pay-puh.*" He agrees that "their propensity for slurvy pronunciation can sometimes be nothing short of miraculous. When I lived in New York, I remember how conductors on the Long Island Rail Road managed to slur the name of a certain station, Woodside, into the unintelligible *wuss-eye* (the eye of a wuss?)."

On hamburger that will "be ready in a minute," I fear you are paying your researchers too much, thus forcing them into restaurants that employ wait-persons who do not use the expression heard virtually universally in the Big Apple, namely, "It's coming right out," or "it'll be right out."

Ask someone who eats in a luncheonette, a Chinese restaurant, a greasy spoon, or other places where the bourgeoisie take their nourishment.

As for "r" droppers, the real epidemic hereabout comes in the form of the "t" droppers, people who intone Atlanna, Toronno, innerception, cenner in their manner of slurring speech.

What next?

Melvin Poretz
Merrick, New York

I haven't heard "gerareheeuh" in close to seventy years, and I've probably never seen it in print before. Unfortunately, I don't live there anymore, and so I can't do any street research for you, but I suspect there is a Yiddish connection. Mr. Weisberg, the landlaw nexdaw, used it alluhtime when he wahnid us to gedawf his propuhdy. Actually, it was more like "gerahfumheeuh," but we got the idea. Perhaps the Slurvian phrase developed from the German/Yiddish "heraus," meaning "out" or "outside," which sounds a bit like "get out."

Donald Berger
Hollywood, Florida

You mention that you have been unable to pinpoint the locale of ger-areheeuh, a variant of gedaddaheeuh. *I think it may come from the annals of immigration from Eastern Europe. I seem to recall an article entitled "Hungarians," by I remember not whom, in* The New Yorker *about 35 years ago. The author describes his first days in public school in the United States, at which point he knew no English. So he transliterated the schoolyard expressions he heard into Hungarian, attempting to observe how they were used:* sarap *seemed to mean, "be quiet," and* gerarahir *seemed to mean, "Go away." Flip (or roll) the "r" and it sounds right.*

Lisa H. Newton
Fairfield University
Fairfield, Connecticut

When you talk about New Yorkers dropping "r's" you know perfectly well that New Englanders do the same, and perhaps they corrupted the New Yawkuhs, or perhaps they all got it at once. I spent forty years of life in Boston, where they also ADD "r's" where they do NOT belong (as in Kennedy's "Cuber"). Not having lived in New York for any length of time, I'm not sure what New Yorkers do about adding "r's" inappropriately. All I know is that I still say "fowdy" for forty, after twenty-five yeahs on the West Coast, although by now I do not say "Californier," and sort of miss being called "Sheiler."

Sheila Madden
Berkeley, California

You previously did a column, as I recall, on words that mean something different in other parts of the country, but are pronounced the same way. I have noticed a few. For example, in New York, a wok *is a cooking instrument. In Chicago, you* wok *the dog (or* dagh?) *(In New York you* wuak *the* duag). *A friend in Iowa told me proudly, "My brother is a* liar!" *That is a strong Midwestern pronunciation for those who pass the bar!*

I would suggest a real-life addition to your column about such New Yorkisms as fuggedaboutit. *I used to work for a college president. He was from the Bronx and the college is in the Bronx. I was the chief financial officer. He used to ask,* yagotdanumbizz? *When the situation was more urgent, he would ask,* yagotdafreakinnumbizz? *Remembering that he was a college president with a PhD, he also referred to a large building on campus as the* lieberry. *When that was a subject of urgency, it became* dafreakinlieberry.

Michael J. McTague

Bronx, New York

"Gerareheeuh" I know as "gerradeheeuh," I think that comes from Brooklyn. The evidence is in the name of one of the founders of Murder, Inc., usually printed as Gurrah Shapiro. In earlier days, when he proposed selling a shopkeeper "protection," the response was "gurradeheeuh." After a while, I think, people just paid off, but the name stuck.

Robert W. Bertcher

East Rockaway, New York

As I remember hearing or reading, the original expression was "gurrareheeuh," supposedly coined by Louis (Lepke) Buchalter (a Brooklyn-based Jewish gangster of the '20s with a heavy accent). He allegedly used it so often that they started to call him Lepke "Gurrah" Buchalter, but probably not to his face.

Annette Picard

Les Monts-de-Corsier, Switzerland

The Lower East Side mobster Louis Lepke Buchalter had a henchman, Jacob "Gurrah" Shapiro, a mean-spirited thug with a gruff, heavy accent who or-

dered people to "get out of here." It came out as "Gurrah." My father was a laundryman. He has the unenviable distinction of having paid protection money to Shapiro in the '20s.

Leonard Kian
Grand Rapids, Michigan

May I add a footnote to your word list of Slurvian? You speak of the well-known Brooklyn accent signalized by "the oily boid." Modern Brooklynites only exaggerate what all of New York and New Jersey inherited from the Dutch, whose eu sounds halfway between our er in early and oi. It's now gone, but one could still hear that gentle sound in the speech of Nicholas Murray Butler and Robert Livingston Schuyler, both at Columbia in my time.

Jacques Barzun
San Antonio, Texas

Smashmouth. "The word *smashmouth* is everywhere," notes the *Times* education reporter Edward Wyatt: "the XFL, the title of a book about the presidential campaign, even in a certain columnist's column. Everywhere, that is, except for the online *OED*. Worth a look?"

The XFL is a professional football league, co-owned by the World Wrestling Federation and NBC, that makes a fetish out of ferocity, with teams sporting macho and self-mocking names like "the New Jersey Hit-men" and "the Memphis Maniax." The book is a campaign-trail memoir by Dana Milbank titled *Smashmouth: Two Years in the Gutter With Al Gore and George W. Bush.* The columnist is a right-wing vituperator who usually eschews vogue words, but in this case wrote of "the sort of *smashmouth* campaign that the Democrats perfected."

The word's meaning goes beyond "aggressive." It is a new and especially vivid synonym of "brutal, savage, violent," stopping just short of "heinous" and "barbaric." However, in the XFL it has a self-mocking quality, and in politics it does not always carry such an offensive connotation. "Such nasty, *smashmouth* politics are said by the goody-goodies to be destroying our democracy," goes Milbank's thesis, "alienating the electorate and suppressing voter participation. I believe the opposite is true: that nasty is nice on the campaign trail, that it's cool to be cruel."

Football metaphors are as mother's milk to politicians: no etymologist has yet come up with the origin of *level playing field*, but football's *game plan* was adopted by campaign strategists, and both politicians and quarterbacks relish the military metaphor of *throwing the bomb*.

Although coinage of *smashmouth* is often attributed to Mike Ditka, the former Chicago Bears tight end and coach, that CBS sportscaster vigorously, almost aggressively, denies being the originator. The word is a compound adjective, which calls for hyphenation; in current use, however, it is most often treated as one word, as if it were an attributive noun like *blood* in "blood sport." It cannot properly be written as two words if used as a modifier.

The earliest citation on the databases (can a hacking baseball player slide into a database?) is a September 1984 usage by Jim Wacker, the Texas Christian University football coach, who told David Casstevens of the *Dallas Morning News* that the "physical game" played by his TCU Horned Frogs was "*smash-mouth* football."

Two months later, the columnist George Will praised Wacker for having "the finest sense of nuance in language since Flaubert, or at least since Woody Hayes," and applied the coinage to politics: "As the clock—the merciful clock—runs out in this final quarter of what feels like a 27-quarter presidential game, Messrs. Mondale and Reagan are playing *smash-mouth* politics. Vigorous, they are."

In 1994, the term was adopted as the name of a rock group, whose members told the *Wall Street Journal* reporter Stefan Fatsis that they liked the way the sportscaster John Madden used it. Above the topically etymological story (everybody wantsa get inna de act), a headline writer reviewed the progress of the locution in one of the *Journal's* characteristically chatty subheads: "*Smash-Mouth:* Sick of the Term? Sorry, There's No Stopping It—Blame the XFL If You'd Like, But It's Old and Seems to Fit the Popular Culture Well."

NBC's Web site claims its XFL is "the type of '*smash mouth*' [sic] football that fans crave . . . returning football to its tougher roots." A league spokesman, Jeff Shapes, says: "It's the type of football played in the National Football League in the '60s and '70s. Football fans breathe and drink *smashmouth* football." He adds hastily, "Obviously, it doesn't mean literally that anyone's mouth is being smashed."

Snippy.   "You mean to tell me, Mr. Vice President," George W. Bush said incredulously to Al Gore on election night, "you're *retracting* your concession?"

"You don't have to be *snippy* about it," Gore responded.

This interchange on the most tumultuous night in the history of American politics was reported by aides who heard one side of the conversation, or might have been listening on telephone extensions; we do not yet know if the call was also surreptitiously recorded. Neither candidate disputed the accuracy of the above account by Kevin Sack and Frank Bruni in the *New York Times*. The Associated Press report, almost but not exactly the same, had Bush saying, "Let me make sure I understand—you're calling me back to *retract* your concession?" and Gore replying, "You don't have to get *snippy* about this."

In the interest of global public understanding and linguistic history, however, this department is obliged to unearth the origin and meaning of the Gore charge of *snippy*.

The earliest definition, in Nathaniel Bailey's 1727 dictionary, is "parcimonious" (now spelled *parsimonious* and considered a bookish term for a cheapskate) and "niggardly" (now used less frequently because some confuse it with a racial slur). In John Bartlett's 1848 *Dictionary of Americanisms*, it is defined as a "woman's word" for "finical," probably rooted in the sense of *fine* as "small," which has now become *finicky* and is a derogation meaning "excessively meticulous."

That cannot be what Al Gore meant. Let's go back to basics: to *snip*, from the German *snippen*, originally meant "to snatch quickly" and came to mean "to clip or cut off, often with a scissors." (This produced a *snippet*, a tiny piece of a thing, later extended to a short bit of prose or, in Dryden's use, "some small *snip* of gain.") The action of clipping or cutting off small pieces led to *snippety,* "fragmentary, scrappy," with a temporary detour to *sniptious,* and finally to *snippy,* metaphorically cutting off pieces, thereby seeming "curt, supercilious, fault-finding, airish," its meaning influenced by the "irritable, tart, short-tempered" sense of *snappish.*

Snippy, like *snappish,* begins with the sneaky "sn" sound, characteristic of *sniveling, snide* and *snarling.*

Earlier generations might have taken *snippy* to mean "brassy, cheeky, saucy"; now the wide-ranging senses are expressed as "touchy, flip, smart-alecky, disrespectful, on your high horse, having an attitude."

The American election results were "the fault of the American people," a French broadcaster suggested. "They seem to have ignored their responsibilities to be clear on what and whom they want." The *Washington Post* columnist Jim Hoagland's riposte: "Now that is *snippy.*"

To snip, *you wrote, comes from the German word, "snippen," but there is no such word; what you meant is "schnippen." That, however, does not mean "schneiden" in the sense of "cut," but obviously stems from the noun "Schnupfen," which is the German word for "cold," but is more related to "snuff" and leads us straight to the meaning of your* snippy *and the German "schnippisch." In the 16th century, exactly 1550, Hans Sachs—he of the* Meistersinger—*used it in the sense of "to breathe in air" by way of throwing your head back in a show of hauteur. There is your "disrespectful," "smart-alecky" or even better "on your high horse."*

As a verb, "schnippen" is only used in the context of snapping your fingers. Whereas the snip *in the sense of "cut" has a little "s" inserted after the "p"— and then it is down to one "p" only—as in "schnipseln" or "Schnipsel" (n.) (snippet).*

Christine Brinck Joffee
Munich, Germany

Sorry. I *regret* not having previously explored the etymology of *apology.* You'll have to *excuse me,* but I refuse to say I'm *very sorry.*

We have just run the gamut of English words that the Bush administration used or refused to use in extricating from China twenty-four service-members in *detention* (suggesting a brief hold in custody, usually on political grounds), *internment* (longer denial of freedom without imputation of criminality) or *captivity* (longest, connoting punishment, synonymous with *imprisonment*).

Note the relatively new term *servicemember,* which alternated with the two words "crew members." That was used because "members of the armed services" is a mouthful. Reporters could not use *servicemen* because that now-sexist term would not include three of the navy aircraft's crew who are women; hence the Pentagon locution, not yet in most dictionaries, *servicemembers*. President Bush persisted in using "our servicemen and women."

After the collision of the Chinese fighter plane and the American EP-3E Aries (Latin for "ram") reconnaissance plane, Secretary of State Colin Powell, soon followed by President Bush, expressed *regret* at the apparent loss of life of the Chinese pilot. The root of *regret* is the Old English *grætan,* "to weep." As a verb, it means "mourn, lament"; as a noun, it means "sorrow" but is not a form of contrition, admitting sin or guilt; rather, *regret* is condolence without culpability.

The Chinese demanded not merely *bao qian* (bow chen), as in "sorry I was late," but the much graver *dao qian,* a phrase that begins a formal *apology.* The Greek *apologos,* "a full account," led to the Latin *apologia,* "justification." *Apology* began in English in 1533, meaning "a speech in defense" with the "*Apologie* of Syr Thomas More, Knyght." That sense of vindication was soon replaced. In current use, to *apologize* means "to express regret at a mistake or wrongdoing; to accept responsibility for a misdeed."

No deal, said the United States; an *apology* is not in order. Although Premier Jiang Zemin suggested, in English, that a mild *excuse me* might be acceptable, other authorities in China demanded the confession implicit in *apology*. On National Public Radio, Daniel Schorr jocularly suggested a solution: *apologrets*. Nice try; didn't fly.

Resolution came in the form of linguistic ambiguity that allowed both sides to claim victory. In using the syllable *qian* in his translation of our letter referring to our unauthorized landing at a Chinese airfield, the American ambassador, Admiral Joseph Prueher, some scholars said, allowed the Chinese to infer an admission of wrongdoing. After our crew was released, Secretary Powell retorted, "We should not be fooled by Chinese propaganda that says they got an *apology*."

The key word was *sorry,* later adverbially emphasized as *very sorry.* (Fortunately, it never came to *really, really sorry, no foolin'.*) It's the informal alternative to *sorrowful,* based on *sorg,* which first appeared in *Beowulf* around 725, meaning "grief, sorrow, care." *Sorry,* with its *-y* suffix—meaning "full of" but also used to form pet names—seems more colloquial than *regret.* It was seized upon by the Chinese as "a form of apology," enabling them to claim satisfaction.

Then came the *-ident* controversy among American spokesmen. "It's an *accident,* it's a very regrettable *accident,*" said Richard Boucher, State Department spokesman, four days after the collision, "and we're trying to resolve it . . . without blowing it into an international *incident.*"

The next day, Sun Yuxi, China's Foreign Ministry spokesman, twice used *incident* to describe the episode, matter, subject or occurrence. Nor did hard-liners here like the State Department's insistence on *accident;* in their judgment, the aggressive, reckless endangerment of American surveillance aircraft ordered by the Chinese high command for months was intended to create an *incident.* President Bush straddled, claiming we "did nothing to cause the *accident*" and in the same statement referring to "the kind of *incident* we have just been through."

In diplolingo, an *incident* is no trivial happening; it is like the striking of a match, no conflagration in itself but an event that could inflame passions. Curiously, the word works as both dysphemism and euphemism: Americans were repelled in 1940 at the fictional account of lynching called *The Ox-Bow Incident,* but when Chinese Communist officials want to minimize what Westerners call "the massacre at Tiananmen Square," they call that crushing of student-led protest "the *incident* of June 4, 1989" (in Chinese, *liu si,* "six four"). The lexicographer Eric Partridge wrote in 1960 that "if a businessman speaks of *incidents* when he means quarrels, he has been influenced by journalism."

Sou.   If you were president of the United States, and someone asked you to describe—in one word—what kind of state the Union was in, what adjective would you select?

White House speechwriters struggle with that almost every year. Judson Welliver, who did the writing for Calvin Coolidge under the title of "literary clerk" (and who should get the credit for Silent Cal's reputation for eloquence), elected to use nouns. "It is exceedingly gratifying," said the cool-keeping chief executive in 1925, "to report that the general condition is one of *progress* and *prosperity*." No powerful, state-defining adjective.

When it came to Harry Truman, the operative word was the modest but solid *good*. "I am happy to report to this 81st Congress"—the one after "that Republican, 80th do-nothing Congress"—"that the state of the Union is *good*." The following year, the plain-spoken Truman said that it "continues to be *good*."

Dwight Eisenhower avoided the characterizing adjective, preferring to say that the state "continues to vindicate the wisdom of the principles on which this Republic is founded." I thought that evaded the responsibility of the top man to give the country a grade. John Kennedy came back to the Truman tradition, but with a nice buildup: "I can report to you that the state of this old but youthful Union, in the 175th year of its life, is *good*." Lyndon Johnson copped a plea at one point—"the state of the Union depends, in large measure, upon the state of the world." As Vietnam wracked his administration, he used a thoughtful adjective in 1968: "I report to you that our country is *challenged*, at home and abroad." Richard Nixon, in his next-to-last "SOU," as we speechwriters called the annual messages (written, as Thomas Jefferson preferred) or addresses (spoken, as Woodrow Wilson preferred), used a defensive adjective, a conservative adjective and an uplifting adjectival phrase. "The *basic* state of our Union," his writers wrote in February 1973, just before the Watergate scandal took hold, "is *sound,* and *full of promise*." The use of the defensive modifier *basic* may have reflected a concern that the apparent, or surface, state was not so sound or *full of promise*.

Gerald Ford, two years after what he had called "our long national nightmare," recalled Harry Truman's word and admitted dolefully but honestly, "I must say to you that the state of the Union is *not good*." The following year, he called the state "in many ways a *lot better*—but still *not good enough*." In his last such address, in 1977, Ford assessed the nation's state as *good,* adding with pride, "We have a more perfect Union than when my stewardship began."

Jimmy Carter thrice preferred the Nixonian *sound,* an adjective often used to reassure the public about the economy, as in "sound money," and also in the firmness of "sound judgment." A digression about *sound:* the noun, from the Latin *sonum,* means "the sensation of what we hear." Don't listen to that. The sense here of the adjective *sound* comes from the second syllable of the Old English *gesund,* "health"—similar to the German *Gesundheit!* wished upon sneezers. In 1601, Robert Johnson wrote about the French king that "Francis the 1 left his credite *sound*." More recently, as an Arthur Andersen executive testified before Congress, "This policy toward document disposal reflects *sound* audit practice." In that sense, *sound* means "financially healthy"; curiously, in these health-conscious times, no president has yet said the state of the Union is *healthy*.

In each of Jimmy Carter's uses, he chose to change one word in the language of the Constitution, which requires the president to "give to the Congress information of the state of the Union," and said "the state of *our* Union."

Ronald Reagan, during 1982's recession, looked ahead: "In the near future the state of the Union and the economy will be *better—much better*." The following year, he admitted that "our economy is *troubled*," but said that "the state of our Union is *strong*." This picked up the Carter *our,* which ever since has been most often preferred by presidents, but chiseled in granite the adjectives *strong* and *stronger*.

Although Ford showed that it was possible to say *not good,* no president has said or is ever likely to call our state *weak*. The first President Bush used "*sound* and *strong*" in 1990, combining Nixon-Carter with Reagan, but the following year departed from tradition to use the word *union* in a sense that illuminated his "thousand points of light": "The state of our Union is the *union* of each of us, one to the other—the sum of our friendships, marriages, families and communities."

Bill Clinton put the constitutional phrase into a question and then answered it in 1994: "What's the state of our Union? It is growing *stronger*, but it must be *stronger* still." In 1996, he said "the state of the Union is *strong*" and in the next two years repeated that phrase, reverting to his initial *our Union*, but sticking to *strong*. In 2000, with the economy still booming and surpluses projected as far as the eye could see, Clinton concluded his string of SOU addresses with "the state of our Union is the *strongest* it has ever been."

George W. Bush last month also used *stronger*, but his speechwriter Michael Gerson used it in a creative way, pointing to a seeming paradox: "Our nation is at war, our economy is in recession and the civilized world faces unprecedented dangers. Yet the state of our Union has never been *stronger*." This anomaly was apparent in the victory in Afghanistan and was largely brought about by "the might of the United States military." In Bush's first SOU, he was able to point out how a justified pride in our power and national will overwhelmed both the economic strains and the dangers of terrorism. The favorite adjective of recent presidents to characterize the nation's state—*strong*—was thus unarguably applicable. Do presidents and their writers think about the one-word summation of the state of the Union (always capitalized) when the time for the report required by the Constitution rolls around? Do they read the way their predecessors handled it and chew over whether to stick with previous usage (*Good? Sound? Strong?*), or play off one of those usages, or come up with something fresh? As this history should show, you bet they do.

Squeezewords.   Rush Limbaugh, the radio philosopher, was appalled. Thousands of his listeners were sending in messages protesting the increased number of commercials on his program. Because he was talking the same amount of time every day, and the show ran the same three hours, how could this be?

Then a surreptitious form of editing was revealed to him. "A new kind of digital technology," wrote Alex Kuczynski in the *New York Times,* "was literally snipping out the silent pockets between words, shortening the pauses and generally speeding up the pace of Mr. Limbaugh's speech." The irate radio commentator stormed, "I think it is potential doom for the radio industry." Since then, he tells me: "I have amended that. They will reduce the pauses judiciously, no more than a minute and a half per hour. I want to see if the nuances are affected—after all, a pause can be pregnant."

Decades ago I did something similar to Humphrey Bogart. He had a habit, as do many of us, of punctuating his ad-lib phrases with *uh.* (This has since been replaced with "I mean" and "y'know," which serve the same function of demonstrating a presence while not saying anything.) When Bogie had a couple of drinks, the *uh*'s came thick and fast. In the '50s, after taping an interview with him for the Armed Forces Network, I did him a favor and laboriously snipped all those stammering self-interruptions out of the tape. When our talk was broadcast, he was surprised at how articulate he sounded.

In most cases, I would do the same today as a courtesy to interviewee and listener. I'll even clean up a grammatical error when taking notes for a written interview, thereby preserving a source and avoiding [sic-sic-sic] wiseguyism. But secret snipping for commercial gain is another kettle of fishiness. Not only is it sneaky, but the silent squeeze also weakens discourse by removing dramatic pauses.

A related danger is not a result of nefarious squeezing by money-grubbing time-savers, but of the hurried laziness of speakers. Let's not be stiffs about this: in pronunciation, the English language has always tended toward contraction. Old-timers cannot recall ever having heard *business, colonel* or *Wednesday* pronounced with three syllables. *Chocolate,* which geezers recall as "CHOCK-a-lit," has become "CHAW-klit"; its central syllable melted away in our mouths. In a 1949 article in the *New Yorker* (now the Nyawka), John Davenport commented on "Slurvian," the language of what linguists call syncope ("SING-kuh-pee"). In this laid-back lingo, *syrup* becomes *surp, Americans* are *Merkins,* and "no, Ma'am" *gnome.* His *forn,* for *foreign,* was picked up by the Central Intelligence Agency, and now "no foreign distribution" is stamped NOFORN.

In our time, such speeding up must not go unremarked. In today's compulsive compression, other majestic and sonorous words are losing their central syllables. In *The Big Book of Beastly Mispronunciations*, Charles Harrington Elster argues that "syncopated pronunciations tend to improve the fluidity of speech" and cites "VEJ-tuh-bul" for *vegetable*, "FAM-lee" for *family* and "DY-pur" for *diaper*. (Only babies say "change my 'DI-a-per.'")

This has not taken place in a *vacuum*. (That word was once pronounced "VAK-u-um," but our natures abhorred it, and it's now "VAK-yoom.") However, Elster still cites as objectionable to cultivated speakers such squeezings as "AK-rit" for *accurate*, "YOO-zhul" for *usual*, "claps" for *collapse* and "VUR-bij" for *verbiage*. (I would add an "ASS-ter-ik.") He takes a pop at me for countenancing an *r*-less "TEM-puh-chur," and he's right: from now on, I'll take my "TEM-pra-chur."

In this political season, two locutions have come under the sustained pressure of the squeezers. One is *President*, the three-syllabled office much coveted by campaigning candidates. I never minded Lyndon Johnson's southern pronunciation of the last syllable in his warm "I am yo' *President*"; that is a legitimate dialect variation. However, the near-universal adoption of *Prezdent* seems to me to diminish the office.

A special target for the squirrels of squeeze has been *Social Security*. This generation, promised six full syllables with no cutbacks, was willing to accept "Soshasecurity." But what of the candidates who promise the salvation of "Sosh-security" or preserving untouched the indexed benefits of "Sosa-CURE-ity"? Dwayna M. Wisdom of Union City, New Jersey, notes other variations from "SoSecurity" to "Soshacurity."

How can anyone pledge expanded benefits to a contracted program? Cock a wary ear to the way the candidates squeeze this revered phrase in coming debates. Then cast your vote for *Prezdent*.

Stovepiping.   The new bête noire of the military, and of the most modern managers, is *stovepiping*.

"Flat organizations work better than vertical organizations," decrees the

Pentagon's manpower analysis handbook. "It should be noted that *stovepiping* is not inherently evil, but the burden of proof should be on the *stovepiping* function to demonstrate that it is not."

Lt. Gen. Ed Rowny (Ret.) urged in the *Wall Street Journal* that Tom Ridge, director of the Office of Homeland Security, be given authority to order widely dispersed bureaucracies into coordinated action. Ridge's present problem? "Rampant *stovepiping*—different agencies under different command."

Rowny was present at the time of the creation of the word. When he was working for James Forrestal in forming the Defense Department in 1947, he notes, "we all went up and down our particular chain of command, but when it came time for the Army to cooperate with the Navy, we'd *stovepipe*—go up to the top of the pipe and then back down, instead of cross feeding."

The noun *stovepipe* is a vertical cylinder carrying a stove's smoke up through the roof. As an adjective modifying *hat,* it describes the tall top hat that Lincoln wore. Now that business schools use the participle form, *stovepiping,* in derogation of managers who fail to look around, the question arises: what do rising managers call horizontal cooperation that avoids direction from the top? *Floorboarding* comes to mind.

Strip Search. "Republican leaders are sure to fight hard to either defeat the bill or *strip out* parts," wrote the *Orlando Sentinel.* The CNN correspondent Chris Huntington said, "If you *strip out* certain charges, they're reporting a profit of 12 cents." *Fortune* magazine quoted Andy Fastow, an Enron executive, as having said, "We *strip out* price risk; we *strip out* interest risk; we *strip out* all the risks."

Gypsy Rose Lee, where are you? *Strips* is an acronym apparently coined by a bump-and-grind ecdysiast enthusiast at Treasury for "Separate Trading of Registered Interest and Principal of Securities." To *strip* a bond is to remove its interest-paying coupons and sell the principal of the bond separately. What you have left is a zero-coupon bond and a separate bunch of coupons. "To *strip out*," says Professor Robert Jarrow of Cornell, "is to infer the value of the zero-coupon bonds underlying the value of a coupon bond. It relates to Treasury Strips that the Federal Reserve Board trades."

That specific financial meaning has been removed—*stripped out,* if you will—in the vogue use of the phrase by scandalmongers on the periphery of the Enron story. It now means "snatched away from, in the dead of night."

Stuff.   *Stuff* is hot. It began a few years ago, with *stuff-stuff-stuff* temporarily replacing "et cetera, all that jazz and on and on." The word received a boost when Richard Carlson titled a series of books *Don't Sweat the Small Stuff,* an expression first popularized as a book title in 1988 by Michael Mantell. The word was applied to character by Tom Wolfe a decade before in his book about astronauts, *The Right Stuff.*

But those uses carried the meaning of "things" or "material." In its latest vogue sense, *stuff* is racing through the lingo of the software industry as the word to denote all the extra goodies provided with the purchase of a computer, usually in the phrase "plus lotsa great *stuff.*" There may be a mocking quality to the use of the simple old word by the nerds of the newest technology, as if to say, "This is too complicated for me to explain to the likes of you in my space-time continuum."

Vogue-Word Watchers will note that I did not observe that *stuff* was "in." *In* is out—way out. (*Way,* in its adverbial sense of "exceedingly," is *way* voguish.) As categories for cutting-edge terminology, *in* and *out* are as archaic as *U* and *Non-U,* as behind the times as *avant-garde.* Remember *edgy,* last year's word for what you had to be? It's in the graveyard of nonce words, behind the tomb of *state of the art.*

Those on the qui vive who need to flaunt their with-it-ness in the face of the stodgily au courant have turned to *hot,* with the extreme of "forwardly fashionable, at the center of attention" expressed as *way hot* or *hot-hot.* (In the nomenclature of the new, forget *cool,* which is no longer *hot.* Lists that used to classify people and places as In and Out are now labeled "What's Hot and What's Not.")

In "Hot New York"—an assessment of the latest socialites, chefs, designers, "Web guys" and media bosses—the *New York Observer*'s editors observed that "heat is *hot*" and defined it as "the ethereal stuff that makes a man or woman in this town shine." It is not power but notoriety—an especially transient or raffish aspect of celebrity—that determines the degree of heat: "As one of the largest shareholders of AOL–Time Warner, Ted Turner certainly is as powerful as most world leaders," observed the temperature-takers, "but in terms of heat, he's Mr. Freeze."

This department is blessed with the Vogue-Word Watchers, shock troops of the Lexicographic Irregulars with eyes sharpened and ears cocked to catch the *hot-hot* in midflight. "What's the sudden attraction to *traction*," asks my *Times* colleague, the business reporter Tim Race, "in business and political contexts?" Example from a West Palm Beach Democrat during the recent Long Count: "If Gore gets any *traction*, you'll see a special session." *Traction* is a word originally meaning "the action of pulling" that came to mean "the adhesive friction of a vehicle on the ground" and has been extended further in politics to "the grip of a campaign on the public attention." I have used it too often and stand corrected.

"We need something more than this *feckless*, photo-op foreign policy," declared Senator John McCain on the stump in October. Vogue-Word Watcher Darren Gersh of Chevy Chase, Maryland, asks: "Often users of *feckless* seem to be looking for an SAT synonym for 'clueless.' Only a few seem to be aiming at the dictionary definition of 'ineffective, or lacking purpose.' By the way, if you are *feckless*, can you be feckful? And is having feck a good thing?"

You bet; the Scotticism comes from *effect*, rooted in the Latin *facere*, "to do." If you're *feckless*, you don't do nuthin'. Good word; needs rest; try *feeble*. As for the archaic *feckful*, go with the modern *effective* or *efficient*.

"Can something be done about this word *robust*?" demands James MacGregor Burns, the great historian at Williams College in Massachusetts. The adjective has been married to *economy*; Matthew Winkler, editor in chief of Bloomberg News, recently denounced it because "it means whatever you want it to mean. Do we mean growing demand, increasing demand? Then why don't we say that?" Professor Burns's theory is that "the word has risen with prosperity and will promptly decline if there is a recession." (In the lexicon of the Old Economy, a roboom is followed by a robust.)

The vogue word rooted in the Latin *robur,* "strength," is now hot in diplomacy, where even a demarche can be *robust,* and especially in the wide world of Webese (forget the passé *cyberlingo*). The *Dictionary of Computing and Digital Media* (I was a pioneer in digital media, but it was then called "fingerpainting") defines *robust* as describing "a system with the ability to recover gracefully from exceptional inputs and adverse situations. A robust system is almost bulletproof." The word is rapidly becoming *feckless.*

"Don't sweat the small stuff" was very big in Northern California, specifically in Walnut Creek (just outside of Berkeley), at Del Valle High School, in 1963—well before 1988.

There may have been some bigger connection to Big Events in the phrase: several of the members of Del Valle's 1964 graduating class went on to participate in the Free Speech Movement at Berkeley in the fall. And the rest, of course, is history.

Kate Buford
Irvington-on-Hudson, New York

Summitese.   "A parley at the summit" was what Winston Churchill called for a half-century ago. He envisioned an intimate get-together of a few world leaders and not a paperbound conference "zealously contested by hordes of experts and officials drawn up in a vast cumbrous array."

The summit in Moscow between Vladimir Putin and Bill Clinton would not be to Churchill's taste; hordes drawn up in a vast cumbrous array (what a mouth-filling derogation of staff) will be whispering in summiteers' ears.

Whoops! In referring to the summit, I have transgressed. "As a noun," reads the ordinarily sensible *New York Times Manual of Style and Usage,* "*summit* may designate the level or format of a meeting (the issue will go to the *summit*) but is jargon when used as a synonym for meeting (they held a *summit*)."

As they say in the Pentagon, I nonconcur. (*That's* jargon.) The stylist's resistance to linguistic change is laudable—new terms should have to fight their way into general acceptance over time—but players in the poker game that is language have to know when to hold 'em and when to fold 'em. *Summit* is no longer merely an attributive noun modifying *meeting* or *conference;* usage over fifty years has turned the modifier into that top-level conclave itself. Cancel the *meeting.*

With that settled (at least in my mind), we can turn to the summit in Moscow and diplomacy's fierce struggle of verbs about a controversial arms control treaty: *abrogate* versus *withdraw.*

In 1972, the general secretary of the Soviet Union's Communist Party, Leonid Brezhnev, and President Richard Nixon signed a treaty to limit antiballistic missile systems. The ABM treaty, in its Article XV, says, "Each Party shall, in exercising its national sovereignty, have the right to *withdraw* from this Treaty if it decides that extraordinary events . . . have jeopardized its supreme interests." Six months' notice is to be given "prior to *withdrawal.*"

Hard-liners in the United States point to a new missile threat from rogue nations, learnedly mutter *rebus sic santibus*—"circumstances have changed"—and add that the Soviet signatory of 1972 no longer exists. Unless the Russians agree to let us build a limited missile defense against a terrorist attack (a defense not powerful enough to affect Russia's deterring missile forces), then we should *withdraw* from the treaty.

Softer-liners counter that such unilateral action would undermine all arms control; instead, they hope Clinton in Moscow will seek minor amendments to the treaty to allow a limited U.S. defense that would not cause the Russians to worry that their missile force could be stopped. (I am being excruciatingly evenhanded here.) They warn of a worldwide reaction against us if the United States abrogates the treaty.

The choice of verbs—*withdraw* or *abrogate*—tips the reader to the point of view. *Abrogate* means "to cancel, annul, quash, void, to abolish authoritatively." The word is harsh; in William Tyndale's 1526 translation of the Epistle of Paul the Apostle to the Hebrews, we see the controversial "In that he sayth a new testament he hath *abrogat* the olde."

Withdraw, in contrast, means "to retract, to take back or away" or "to remove"; in another sense, it means "leave the room." Robert Henryson, in his 1480 *Testament of Cresseid,* came up with a gentle line still remembered fondly by copy editors afflicted with prolix writers: "*Withdraw* thy sentence, and be gracious."

A *New York Times* editorial opined, "Mr. Bush would *withdraw* loans and credits to Russia over its crackdown in Chechnya and *abrogate* the Antiballistic Missile Treaty." Though in the newspaper's view both steps would be "dangerously confrontational," its use of *withdraw* regarding loans and *abrogate* about the treaty suggests that it would find the latter step more troubling.

"*Abrogate* has a pejorative connotation," says Anne-Marie Slaughter, a revered professor of international law at Harvard, "in the sense that it means 'to end the treaty not in accordance with the treaty's terms.' It suggests a much more active decision to end the treaty and is much closer to the term *breach* than the term *withdraw.*"

That's what Senator Barry Goldwater had in mind when he took a case against President Jimmy Carter to the Supreme Court, claiming the president had unlawfully *abrogated* a treaty with Taiwan. In turning down his appeal, the Court avoided the hot verb and refused to intervene in what it called Carter's *termination* of the treaty.

At the current Moscow summit, the word *abrogate* is used by the Clinton briefers only to say what they would not do and what the Republicans might do. The GOP candidate, Governor Bush, last year used the harsh word to indicate what he might be prepared to do, but this year he has sidestepped the semantic trap, preferring *withdraw.*

Which verb will triumph? Keep your eye on a dark horse coming up on the outside: *amend.* If Clinton gets Putin to agree to change the ABM treaty, he will declare success and send the amendments to the Senate. In response, GOP leaders have already chosen a hospital term to describe their reaction to any modest amending: *dead on arrival.*

I have been thinking about abrogate *and* withdraw. *It seems to me that you withdraw from a multilateral treaty because there are others left to observe it and you abrogate a bilateral treaty because it takes two to tango.*

You will immediately say ah yes but the ABM treaty specifically speaks of "withdraw" and "withdrawal." I think the framers of the treaty were looking for a euphemism less harsh sounding than abrogate.

That's how it strikes me. I can't prove any of it.

Daniel Schorr
National Public Radio
Washington, D.C.

Supreme Court Stumble.   In oral argument before the Supreme Court, the Gore attorney David Boies focused on the intent of the voters. Questioning him, Justice Anthony Kennedy noted that a general "intent" ran throughout the law and drove that point home with an adage: "Even a dog knows the difference in being stumbled over and being kicked."

Just one of those homely old sayings, untraceable to its source, like JFK's "Victory has a thousand fathers, but defeat is an orphan"? At my urgent request, Fred Shapiro, editor of the *Yale Dictionary of Quotations*, tracked it down. Here it is, from the 1881 book *The Common Law*, by Oliver Wendell Holmes Jr., in a passage about intentional violence: "Vengeance imports a feeling of blame, and an opinion, however distorted by passion, that a wrong has been done. It can hardly go very far beyond the case of a harm intentionally inflicted: even a dog distinguishes between being stumbled over and being kicked."

Holmes, the "Yankee from Olympus," was appointed to the Supreme Court by President Theodore Roosevelt and retired in 1932 at age ninety. His use of a homely figure of speech is evidently familiar to members of the current court.

Switcheroo.   During the war of commercial spots between George W. Bush and John McCain, Bush quoted the *Wall Street Journal,* saying Mc-

Cain's campaign was "crawling with lobbyists," and McCain slammed back with a charge that the Bush spot "twists the truth like Clinton." When the McCain manager offered to call a truce, Bush reportedly replied, "It's the old game of *switch-and-bait:* say one thing and do another."

The name of the old game, as Bush quickly realized, is the reverse: *bait-and-switch*. In this dodge, an advertiser entices a customer into the store with a low price on an attractive item, but then says, "We're out of it," and tries to sell a higher-priced item.

"If a product or service is advertised at a price that seems too good to be true," advises the Better Business Bureau of Los Angeles, "this may be a 'bait' ad. Then, if the merchant refuses to show you the advertised item, to take orders for it or to deliver it within a reasonable time . . . take this as a sign you are being 'switched.'" The point to remember in applying it metaphorically in politics is that the *bait* always comes first. Then comes the *switch*.

Bush has been criticized for his overuse of alliteration. As William Kristol noted on MSNBC's *Hardball* program, "compassionate conservatism" was followed by "prosperity with a purpose" and then by "a reformer with results." But to me, alliteration always attracts. My favorite was the unforgettable 1920 passage by Warren G. Harding, promising "not heroics but healing, not nostrums but normalcy, not revolution but restoration, not agitation but adjustment, not surgery but serenity, not the dramatic but the dispassionate, not experiment but equipoise."

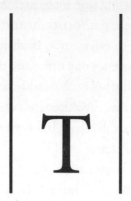

That Said. "The South Carolina primary between Mr. Bush and Mr. McCain in 2000," wrote Eleanor Randolph, the *New York Times* editorialist, discussing Representative Lindsey Graham's current campaign for the Senate, "left Republicans in his state bitter and divided. *That said,* both President Bush and Senator McCain have already campaigned for his election to the Senate."

In olden times, those two sentences would have been written as one, with the first clause subordinated: "*Although* the South Carolina primary ... left Republicans ... divided, both Bush and McCain ... campaigned for his election. . . ." Or they could have remained as two sentences, with the second beginning *however* instead of with the voguism *that said.*

Coming out of a meeting in the White House with President Bush about the war in Afghanistan, Tom Daschle, the Senate majority leader, told reporters: "I don't believe there was adequate notification. *Having said that,* we will move on." He could have begun his second sentence, which undermines the first, with the wishy-washy *on the other hand,* the stark *in spite of that,* the smooth *all the same* or the bookish *nevertheless,* but the word-conscious Democratic leader chose—with his characteristic consummate care—the other form of the self-referential voguism sweeping the country: *having said that.*

This absolutive participial construction now spreading like wildfire

362

through our discourse was brought to my attention by the Floridians Sylvia and Morton Holstein. They noted an article I wrote wearing my other hat, in my op-ed capacity as vituperative right-wing scandalmonger, and considered my harangue inconclusive, lacking the zinger at the end that satisfies both advocate and audience. "As the journalists like to say," they wrote, "'*having said that*'—and then go on to the real meat of the subject. Well, Mr. Safire, having said that—now what? Can we expect a follow-up?"

This is it. I was also alerted to the voguism by Samuel P. King somewhere in e-maildom: "The latest abomination is the substitute for *however* in its many forms—*having said that, that having been said,* et cetera. That said, I guess I'll just have to get with it."

We turn now to Professor John Lawler in the linguistics department of the University of Michigan: "*That said* is an abbreviated form of the absolutive participial phrase '(With) that (having been) said.' " (You were wondering where I got that "absolutive participial" from? You think I make up this stuff? If I had taken Latin, I'd be able to explain the closely related ablative absolute.) Lawler goes on to the essential meaning of *that said:* "It announces a change of subject, often despite whatever was just said."

But let us plunge deeper into the vocabulary of vacillation. Writers of opinion articles know how to use what we call a *to-be-sure graf.* After making an argument, some of us feel the urge to show that we are not simpletons—that we know the counterarguments, have taken them into due consideration, but still maintain our positions. In goes the *to-be-sure graf,* a paragraph disarming our opponents with its "Yes, we know all that folderol on the other side" and thereby reducing the volume of irate e-mail.

To be sure is a rhetorical device to set up and counter the opposition after your initial point has been made. You often present the other side's position as a straw man easy to knock down and then repeat your opening argument with great force at the end. This *to-be-sure* trick is described by grammarians as "concessive"—that is, I'll give you this; it costs me nothing and makes me appear reasonable.

However (to use an old construction), *that said* is a device that works in the other direction. The point to be negated is made first: "My opponent is a great guy, a real patriot and a quick study." (End of concessive construction.) "*That said,* he doesn't know what he is talking about." In the Daschle usage quoted above, a refinement was added to make the message "He was mistaken; *that said,* I forgive him and will take credit for my compassion." (President Bush does this, too; listen for it at news conferences.)

Are we ready for the definition of the two faces of today's phrase?

One sense of *that said* is "however" and balances what goes first with what goes afterward, as in the objective Randolph usage that opened today's voguism watch. In its much more frequent sense of "nevertheless, in spite of that, even so" and the lusty "contrariwise," *that said* clears the air and clears the throat for casting aspersions on all that has preceded it. The subliminal message is "I have done my duty by touching all the bases to show my profound understanding of both sides, and the buttering-up I have just completed gives me the right to now lay upon you what I really think."

To be sure, *that said* has its good side.

Titular.   As he took the oath of office, George W. Bush not only assumed the powers of the presidency but also became the *titular* head of the nation. That presumes the meaning of "the *titular* head" to be "the one who holds the title."

Ah, but the word has a connotation that makes politicians shudder: it resonates as merely "nominal; in name only." A *titular* leader is understood to be the one who may have the formal title but is not the real or actual wielder of power. For that reason, the expression "*titular* head of the party" is reserved for the person who won the party's nomination but not the election.

"The *titular* leader has no clear and defined authority within his party," said the Democrat Adlai Stevenson in 1956. "He has no party office, no staff, no funds. . . . Yet he is generally deemed the leading spokesman of his party." When Alf Landon, the 1936 GOP nominee, told the House minority leader, Joseph Martin, in 1940 that FDR had just offered him the post of secretary of war, Martin later wrote: "I advised him not to accept. He was, after all, the *titular* head of the Republican Party."

Now it is Al Gore's turn to bear the burden, or dubious honor. But even that title may be under challenge from the former president with whom he served. "Clinton is still the *titular* leader of the Democratic Party, having rudely shoved aside Al Gore," opined the cable-TV pundit Mort Kondracke at year's end. National Public Radio's senior correspondent, Daniel Schorr, used the title in a more nuanced fashion when saying that Gore "should be the *titular* leader of the party, and is—and yet I somehow feel you're going to see a lot more of Bill Clinton."

Dick Morris, the political analyst who once advised Clinton, said that Senator Hillary Clinton will be "the *titular* leader of the Democrats in the Senate." (This was the first time, and perhaps the last, that the title was given to a woman.) I think it was a misusage: if the former first lady becomes the most powerful force in the Senate, then the elected leader of the Senate Democrats, Tom Daschle, would be derogated as merely the *titular* leader, which would imply that Senator Clinton held the real power.

To No Avails.   Because George W. Bush was frequently answering questions on a variety of subjects from reporters on his campaign plane, his aides noticed that their chosen message of the day at major events was not getting through. "Because Gore wasn't doing *avails* like that," said Karen P. Hughes, "the networks were using shots from his events."

Peter Marks, a *New York Times* reporter, noted, "Unlike the campaign of Vice President Al Gore, which has strictly limited the candidate's access, Mr. Bush and his advisers have provided a steady diet of the kind of '*availabilities*' that reporters crave."

When were *press availabilities* born? How do these differ from *news conferences*? When did they get clipped to *avails*?

In June 1980, Representative John B. Anderson was running for president as an independent. "The congressman continues to receive substantial local attention," wrote Warren Weaver in the *New York Times,* "from the daily sessions at each campaign stop that his staff labels as 'press availabilities.' " Three months later, as Ronald Reagan's lead over Jimmy Carter narrowed in polls, easy access to the GOP candidate was curtailed; the *Toronto Globe and Mail* noted that "all *'press availability'* sessions with the former California governor have been dropped."

Reagan understood the shade of difference in the lexicon of access. "I have had now over 120 interviews since I've been in office," he said in 1983, "and numerous *press availabilities.*" An *interview* is a talk with one reporter or a small group. A *news conference* (changed from *press conference* by President Richard Nixon, who believed the event should not belong to the press but to the newsmaker) is usually called to make an announcement and to take questions on that and other subjects. A *press availability* is actively passive; that is, political figures open themselves to general questioning, putting the burden of creating news on the press. It is less focused on the candidate's preferred message and is therefore, from a campaign's point of view, riskier.

In 1992, Mary Schmich of the *Chicago Tribune* noted that Senator Bob Kerrey "faced the media in a routine campaign free-for-all known as a *'press avail.'* " Two years later, Howard Wilkinson of the *Cincinnati Enquirer* wrote: "The flacks who surround political candidates like to call it a *'press avail.'* . . . No one in the glamorous and fast-paced world of high-power politics has time to say six syllables when one or two will do."

Without the word *press,* the word *availability* has a different meaning in today's politics: "commercial time available for purchase by advertisers." But in American political history, that word has profound resonance as a derogation of opportunism. In 1840, Senator Thomas Hart Benton of Missouri said scornfully of the Whig candidates William Henry Harrison and John Tyler, "*Availability* is the only ability sought by the Whigs." And lexicographic objectivity forces me to report that Ralph Waldo Emerson wrote in an essay the next year, "Conservatism . . . goes for *availableness* in its candidate, not for worth. . . ."

You reported on the usage of the word avail *as shorthand (or shortspeak) for* availability. *My dictionary defines* avail *as, to be of use or advantage. So, now we have two words, both nouns, both spelled the same, both pronounced the same. Should this be sanctioned, or sanctioned?*

Frank O'Donnell
Rockville Centre, New York

Unilateralist. "I hope the notion of a *unilateral* approach died in some people's minds here today," President George W. Bush told a NATO news conference in Brussels, bridling at having been saddled with the dirty diplomatic word. "*Unilateralists* don't come around the table to listen to others. . . . *Unilateralists* don't ask opinions of world leaders." In case anybody didn't get his point, he gave a definition: "A *unilateralist* is one that doesn't understand the role of NATO." Were it not for the ghost of the Nixonian "I am not a crook," he would surely have added, "I am not a *unilateralist*."

Why the revulsion at this word? Because the adjective means "undertaken by one," which is diplomatically quite incorrect, or "one-sided," which carries an overtone of arrogance. Born in botany to describe a cluster of flowers growing on one side of a stalk, it bloomed in diplolingo a half-century ago: "*Unilateralism*, to coin one more gobbledygook term," wrote Arthur Schlesinger Jr. in 1951 in its disparagement, "has become the new isolationism. Go it alone; meet force with maximum force; there is no substitute for victory . . . these are the tenets of the new faith."

A year ago, Senator Joseph Biden, now the Democratic chairman of foreign relations, tagged the GOP ticket as "*unilateralists* if not isolationists." That was the theme that France's prime minister, Lionel Jospin, picked up this spring: "This is not an isolationist administration as has been the case before in the Republican tradition," he noted. "This is more like a *unilateralist* administration."

Uni- means "one"; *multi-* means "many." A few years ago, Republicans were criticizing the Clinton administration for being too *multilateral,* following the lead of the U.N. and other groups of nations. Just as the *uni-* prefix implies arrogance, *multi-* implies meekness, requiring Clinton's secretary of state, Madeleine Albright, to come up with a toughening modifier: "assertive *multilateralism*."

Rather than reaching for a softening qualifier ("acquiescent *unilateralism*" leaps to mind) and despite an opening offered by the European trade commissioner, Pascal Lamy ("One man's *unilateralism* is another's determined leadership"), the Bush team decided to deny it flatly. Its preferred self-description is neither isolationist nor interventionist, but *internationalist.*

As the smoothing-over was decided on, one word muscled its way into vogue: *emollient.* In the *New York Times* in December, R. W. Apple Jr. and Steven Erlanger separately wrote of "*emollient* words" used by Bush to soften hard lines. Last month, British analysts became entranced with the word: "At his first major meeting with skeptical European leaders," wrote Anton La Guardia in the *Daily Telegraph,* "Mr. Bush struck an *emollient* note." My colleague in columny, Anthony Lewis, who I suspect reads the British press, noted that "the *emollient* Bush words about loving the environment did not match the reality of the administration's destructive actions."

Get to know this soothing locution, both noun and adjective, which is not nearly as stinging as "astringent" and is the opposite of "abrasive." The Latin *molli* is "soft"; Alexander Pope wrote in 1727 of poetry's "*emollients* and opiates." Pour it over your *unilateralism,* rub it in and cozy the world along.

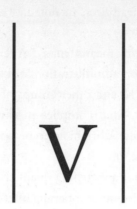

Vapors. When Hubert Védrine, France's foreign minister, dismissed President Bush's "axis of evil" metaphor as "simplistic," Secretary of State Colin Powell retorted that his French counterpart was "getting the *vapors* and whatnot."

Bush liked that response. At a news conference in Tokyo, asked to explain the foreign furor over the "axis of evil"—the most memorable phrase so far in his presidency—the president lobbed the ball to Powell: "You might want to ask him what he meant by 'the *vapors*.' " The secretary was lexicographically prepared: "It's a 19th-century Victorian term, if you wish to look it up. . . . It was meant to say, 'Let's not swoon.' "

An invitation to look anything up is my meat; I did, and one common meaning is substantially as Powell defined it: a sighing, wrist-to-forehead fainting away, historically done by a delicate flower of a woman. (To *swoon* is "to be overcome by rapture," rooted in the Old English *geswogen,* "unconscious," and popularized in descriptions of teenage girls at the early performances of Frank Sinatra at New York's Paramount Theater.)

Ah, but the *vapors* has a variety of meanings and a long history. The *Century Dictionary* defined it a century ago as "a disease of nervous disability in which strange images seem to float hazily before the eyes, or appear as if real . . . the 'blues': a term much affected in the 18th century, but now rarely used." Synonymy was provided by Henry Fielding in his novel *Amelia,* written in 1751: "Some call it the fever on the spirits, some a nervous fever, some the *vapours,* and some the hysterics." In *Robinson Crusoe,* Daniel Defoe's hero evoked the hallucinatory connotation: "These things fill'd my Head with new Imaginations, and gave me the *Vapours* again." It is a manifestation of what was first called "melancholia"; in President Lincoln's time, "the hypo," and later "depression."

Why *vapors,* which has to do with gaseous, misty or steamy exhalations? Because the mental state of low spirits was thought to originate in the stomach or spleen (in men), or the uterus (in women), for which the Greek word is *hystera,* bubbling up to the brain and causing morbidity. In a "discourse concerning chocolata," Henry Stubbe wrote in 1662 that "by the eating of those Nuts, she feels the Hypochondriacal *vapours* . . . to be instantly allayed." Though this belief that internal emanations were the basis for nervous disorders was rejected during the rise of psychiatry, the old idea that mental states are affected by chemical products of the body has made a comeback (as did the lay term "blues").

In current use, *vapors* is a word used jocularly, not in allusion to depression but often to suggest mild hysteria or unmanly weepiness. When applied to men, it carries a feminine overtone: the writer Peggy Noonan told Maureen Dowd of the *New York Times* in 1991 of White House aides "who are utterly at the mercy of the lunar tides and utterly affected by the *vapors* and by an almost feline desire to look man to man at one's enemy and scratch his little eyes out." Two years later, Dowd returned to the expression in its evocation of the past no longer relevant: "In the old days, if a woman wished to escape a difficult encounter, she could plead a case of the *vapours* and retire to her Victorian fainting couch."

That trivializing sense can also be applied to governments: writing about an abortive attempt by Iraqis in 1995 to overthrow Saddam Hussein, Claire Berlinski noted this month in the conservative *Weekly Standard,* "Moments before the plan was to be effected, the Clinton administration, seized by an attack of the *vapors,* changed its mind."

Afterthought: In the medical lexicon, the names of ailments and diseases are often changed to get more formal or avoid the sort of kidding-around that became attached to the *vapors.* Thus, *grippe* is now "influenza," *dropsy* is "edema" and *lumbago* is "lumbar pain."

Apoplexy, whose adjective form, *apoplectic,* came to mean "red-faced with rage," is now called "stroke" (like *apoplexy,* from the Greek *plessien,* "to strike") because this third largest killer in the United States was nothing to treat lightly.

The best example of the laugh associated with this abandoned term was Ethel Merman's famous ad-lib when playing in Irving Berlin's *Annie Get Your Gun:* Annie Oakley was to show her marksmanship by shooting a duck; the stage gun did not go off, but the duck fell on cue. Merman, never the sort to get the vapors over a show-biz mishap, walked over to the prop, held it up and said, "Whaddya know—*apoplexy!*"

Visit With.   "Vice President Cheney has a completely open door" to members of Congress, said the Bush counselor Karen Hughes last month on ABC's *Nightline.* "He's always available to visit with any member who'd like to *visit with* him."

Press Secretary Ari Fleischer recalled the days when George W. Bush, as governor of Texas, would "drop by and *visit with* various legislators of both parties."

John McCain's recent get-together with the Democratic leader, Tom Daschle, was described in the *New York Times* as "Mr. Daschle's highly publicized weekend *visit with* Senator John McCain." Elizabeth Becker, a *Times* colleague, notes that "the political use of *visit with* is rampant. Not *visit to,* or just *visit,* and rarely *meet*—always *visit with.* Where is it from?"

The South. Lyndon Johnson used that venerable southern Americanism when he introduced the Voting Rights Act of 1965, telling a joint session of Congress he was grateful for the chance "to reason with my friends, to give them my views and to *visit with* my former colleagues."

What does the preposition *with* do to the verb *visit?* It milks out most of the action, making the verb intransitive and changing its tone from purposeful to neighborly. "To say that John McCain *visited with* Tom Daschle," says Leonard Zwilling, general editor at the *Dictionary of American Regional English (DARE),* "implies a friendly exchange of views, as opposed to *met with,* which could just as well suggest that they had a flaming set-to."

Visit does not mean *visit with.* You can *visit* a place or a person, but you can *visit with* people only. In his 1927 *We,* the aviator Charles A. Lindbergh, who had just visited France, wrote of "Perryville, Mo., where we *visited with* some of Klink's friends."

In his *Merriam-Webster's Dictionary of English Usage,* E. Ward Gilman adds a nice distinction: "To say that you *'visited with'* someone usually implies not only that you conversed, but that you went a bit out of your way for the sake of some friendly talk." Senator Wayne Allard of Colorado sensed that distinction earlier this month, thanking Defense Department nominees "for taking time to drop by my office and *visit with* me personally."

Let moguls continue to *take meetings;* let confrontationalists visit imprecations on one another; let trustees descend on colleges with stern *visitations,* and let Lady Macbeth fear "no compunctious *visitings* of nature," but remember—today's successful politicians sailed smoothly into the era of sweet, nonpartisan *visits with.*

Voguism I.   What's with *voguism*? The reader will ask: "Is it a word? Why isn't it in my dictionary?"

It is not synonymous with *nonce word,* which is "a term used once for some special occasion." Rather, *voguism* is a not-so-new neologism that was created in this space in 1982. Though picked up and used once by *Newsweek,* the word has since languished, out of print and out of sorts. It is today getting another chance at linguistic life because it meets a need—not a "felt" need, but a real one—in an age when words and phrases come and go like overnight celebrities. (When was the last time you used the '80s *state of the art* or the '90s *at the end of the day*? There was a time you couldn't get through a New York talk-show minute without them.)

We need a term that goes beyond *vogue word* to encompass whole phrases like *having said that.* In my personal lexicon, *voguism* means "a word or phrase in fashion, used by writers who are with-it and then repeated endlessly by politicians and public intellectuals unable to assert their relevance without it; a breeze-by bromide, a cliché without staying power."

Dictionaries, limited to reporting words in use, need citations to trigger inclusion in future editions. At the end of the day, only adoption by other language mavens will determine how *voguism* fares.

Although it won't affect your semantic analysis of that (having been) said, *it might be useful to note that it appeared in British English a few decades before it surfaced in the U.S.*

As for voguism, *it would seem to be a voguism for* cliché. *You'll find* vogue word *in the* OED, *and I suspect that* voguism *is to* vogue word *(or* expression*) as* Briticism *is to* British word *(or* expression*).*

Laurence Urdang
Old Lyme, Connecticut

Voguism II: This Day Is Over.　"A few months ago," writes Joan Swirsky from someplace (look, if you're going to send me e-mail, it would help regional dialectologists if you said where you're from), "it seemed that every talking head I saw on TV started using the expression *at the end of the day*. I thought of writing you about the derivation, but time went by. Then I saw Terry McAuliffe interviewed by Tim Russert. Without exaggeration, McAuliffe used that expression at least twenty times, like it was his tic!"

You are indeed exaggerating, Swirsky, wherever you are. The chairman of the Democratic National Committee, Terry McAuliffe, used the phrase only seventeen times in the twelve minutes he spoke on the air: "*At the end of the day* we won on the issues"; "*At the end of the day* if all the votes were counted"; "There was no swap *at the end of the day*." This off-putting tic, as Swirsky accurately described it, continued until the end of his appearance, distracting viewers from his earnest message.

Fifteen years ago, I cited George Washington's early use of this phrase in a 1797 letter and suggested that its vogue use in the '80s was getting out of

hand. After heaping ridicule on it as an affectation and a cliché, I concluded: "*At the end of the day* is hot. But you'll see, when all is said and
done . . ."

Evidently, this did not do the trick. Although the phrase is now banned
at the DNC, it has become a staple of speakers determined to take a lofty,
daylong view of what they consider to be other people's feeding frenzies.
Like *famously,* another vogue term savaged here six years ago, it marches
on. A language maven finds this humbling.

Voguism III: Three Little Words.   Soon after Governor George W.
Bush became the likely Republican nominee, Vice President Al Gore
blasted his opponent's proposed tax cut as a "*risky tax scheme* that would
threaten our prosperity." A few days later, he assailed the Bush plan "to
blow the entire surplus on a *risky tax scheme* that would benefit the
wealthy." A database search shows Gore using that phrase 164 times in the
past two years, 44 in the last month alone.

Its provenance can be found in the Democratic campaign of 1996. In his
debate with GOP vice-presidential nominee Jack Kemp, Gore zapped the
tax-reduction plan put forward by Bob Dole as a "*risky tax scheme* that
would blow a hole in the deficit." Because Gore evidently believes this attack phrase to be effective, it is worth analyzing.

Risky, an adjective coined in 1827 by the novelist James Fenimore
Cooper, suggests danger without going so far as "dangerous, unsafe" or
"perilous." It suggests a knowledge of the hazard ahead that can be
avoided by prudent action. Although the noun *risk* in a financial sense is
acceptable, the adjective *risky* is intended to engender wariness or suspicion.

In American English, *scheme,* especially as a verb but also as a noun,
suggests a crafty or secret plan to attain a sinister end. This is not the case
in Britain, which treats the noun *scheme* as synonymous with "project, enterprise, plan." However, the verb on both sides of the Atlantic has a larcenous tinge, as "to effect by contrivance or devise by underhanded means."
A long-ago cartoon showed an ambitious IBM employee setting aside the

company's slogan, "Think," with another sign: *"Scheme."* That sly sense of the verb has slopped over the noun in America.

Candidate Gore plans, or *schemes,* to keep *risky tax scheme* in his verbal arsenal. As Mr. Bush comes up with words equally effective, they will receive equal etymological treatment here.

Voguism IV: Bold Initiative.   Readers who enjoyed the exhaustive exegesis in this space of Al Gore's use of *risky tax scheme* were promised a similar study of favored words of his opponent, George W. Bush.

We have an entry culled from a column by Gail Collins in the *New York Times,* wherein my colleague wondered "whether Mr. Gore is right in charging that the Bush tax plan is 'risky,' or Mr. Bush is more correct in dubbing it *'bold.'* "

As far back as 1997, the governor described his tax plan to the Texas legislature as "this complex, *bold,* aggressive plan." The *Dallas Morning News* promptly hailed his "*bold* tax plan." In a presidential primary debate in New Hampshire in late 1999, Bush described his tax proposal as "a good, *bold,* practical plan." One of his early competitors, Senator Orrin Hatch, later saluted the Bush proposal to reduce taxes by $483 billion over five years as "*bold* but responsible."

Hatch's qualifier—"but responsible"—was intended to strip any possible riskiness out of the Bush plan (or, as Gore keeps deriding it, "scheme"). It indicates the senator's subtle awareness of the adjective's ability to trouble the easily daunted.

The word, of Teutonic origin and first spelled *bealde,* appeared in Old English about the end of the first millennium. Shakespeare, in 1593, felt it necessary to place it near a synonym: "when their brave hope, *bold* Hector, marched to field." But even as the meaning of "brave" took firm hold, Shakespeare recognized that the word had acquired a different sense, of "overly audacious, too forward": in his 1605 *King Lear,* he wrote of "men so disordered, so deboshed and *bold.*"

Bold, applied to a person, today connotes "pushy," sometimes "fearless," but on the edge of "reckless"; applied to an idea, however, the connotation is slightly stronger than audacious and just short of courageous. It's better to have *bold* ideas than timid ones.

But watch out for cliché fusion: the Dow Jones database spits out 1,802 hits in the past decade on *bold initiative*. William Godwin coined *initiative* in 1793 to mean "the first step in some enterprise" and (prefiguring debate in the art world centuries later) wrote, "Sensation . . . possesses the *initiative*." The overuse of *bold* to modify Godwin's word vitiates its potency. An alternative to *initiative* is *undertaking*, but that may have fallen by the wayside as the managers of funerals became known as *undertakers*. (They now prefer *morticians*.)

Bold suffered a decline in use for some years (*brave, undaunted*, and *intrepid* were preferred) but made a comeback in the great example of the split infinitive of our time: the *Star Trek* plan "to *boldly* go where no man has gone before." In *Star Trek: The Next Generation*, the *man* was changed to *one;* that was a *bold* initiative.

Wave of the Wand.   Under "Enhanced Security Measures," the White House Web site lists, among other items, "random *hand-wanding* of passengers at the gate."

The *Toronto Star* wrote in 1989 about a "physical search which includes *hand-wanding* and X-raying." When a guard at an inspection post at Kennedy Airport in New York failed to give a passenger a once-over with a handheld electronic search instrument, the terminal was evacuated. "The employee was conducting pat searches," an airline spokesman told the *Daily News*, "but was not *wanding* passengers."

Wand is a noun meaning "stick," its root in the verb *wend* or *wind*, connoting a slender, twisting rod. Since the 15th century, *wand* has evoked images of a magician or a fairy casting a spell.

No more. In 1979, the *Bookseller* reported on "the light pen, or '*wand*' that could read machine-readable codes on books." But it was a series of short jumps from handheld devices to bar-code scanners to electronic instruments that detect metal objects in a person's clothing. Now you can't board a plane without being *wanded*. (Those with beards or Middle Eastern looks are among the ten most wanded.)

The word *hand* is being dropped from *hand-wanded* because the essence of the search by the *wand* is personal: security people do not put whole human beings through the baggage-scanning machine. The *wand*, properly wielded, does not touch the person. The other verb, in which the body is searched by hand, is *frisk*. That sense goes back to Cockney rhyming slang, "to *frisk* a cly," the allusion to which escapes me.

You referred to the expression frisking a cly *as Cockney rhyming slang. Slang it is; rhyming it ain't.*

Cly is slang for seize or steal; a clyfaker *is a pickpocket. So* frisking a cly *is searching a pickpocket.*

Graeme McLean
New York, New York

The Victorian pickpockets and cutpurses referred to their victims as their "clients." Inevitably, the term "client" was shortened to cly. *Sometimes pickpockets worked* on the fly *against a moving target, but they also worked* on the frisk. *When a crowd assembled to watch some public spectacle, a pickpocket would stand next to his victim and then he would (here comes the interesting verb)* fimble *him, using only his fingertips to probe surreptitiously until he located the victim's note-case (as wallets were often called in those days). The subtle pat-down before the actual snatch was called* frisking the cly.

F. Gwynplaine MacIntyre
New York, New York

Weapons-Grade.   Are you in favor of *same-sex* marriage? Have you recently gone through *wrong-site* surgery leading to a *near-death* experience? Do you search a *drop-down* menu to find a *with-it* shop so that you can look (to use a compound adverb) *drop-dead* gorgeous in your *bare-midriff* dress?

When the vogue for compound adjectives was just getting under way, the hyphenated terms were usually literal: a *white-collar* worker wore a white shirt to the office, and a *blue-collar* worker's collar at the factory was often blue. The literal meaning is expressed today in *disco-inspired* tees (formerly T-shirts) and Gucci's *under-the-breast* corset. But the hyphenations could also be metaphoric: *lace-curtain* Irish required some knowledge of social history, much as *baby-boom* generation does today. Early on, the precedent was established permitting the stringing-together of several words: the *going-out-of-business* sale of the Depression is matched in word number by *out-of-the-box* thinking today.

Now the hyphenation of modifiers rules the linguistic roost. This *rule-roosting* device—See? Nothing to it—satisfies the need for the new: "Hyphenation gives the impression," says Frank Abate, former editor in chief of the U.S. Dictionaries program at Oxford University Press, "that the compound is novel, imaginative or requires some background knowledge." He notes that some of these double-word modifiers grow out of adverbial phrases: in "technology at the cutting edge," the adverbial phrase is swung around in front of the noun to become *cutting-edge* technology; in the same way, "you can track changes in real time" becomes *real-time* data.

The compression of modification suits headline writers and e-mail correspondents, whose shortness of space or haste in composition makes them the language's leading squeezers. A statement like "a host is on duty at our Web site continuously" is whittled down to *24/7/365*-hosting. Some compound adjectives are dying: *push-button* convenience is passé, and *solid-state* electronics, which substitutes transistors for vacuum tubes, is not needed in an age that assumes *vacuum* to be a noun for a device that sucks up dirt. *State-of-the-art* anything died from overuse, and *world-class* is out of the competition, falling back into the nonce-word category. And parody has weakened *industrial-strength*.

I am not the only language maven to notice this. At Astrakhan State Pedagogical University, located in the Volga River delta, Maya Ryashchina has found three patterns: noun plus postpositive, as in *hands-on* manager and *heads-up* tennis; verb plus postpositive, as in *drive-by* killing; and a modal verb plus infinitive, as in *can-do* mentality, *must-have* wine and *must-see* film. (Go, Astrakhan S.P.U.!)

Euphemizers have reached out for compound adjectives. Adults of generous girth or a tendency toward obesity (whom the insensitive used to call "fat people") wear *big-and-tall* clothes for men, *plus-size* for women.

The soul-satisfying impetus for our compound-modifying discourse . . . it's getting to me . . . begin again. The biggest boost to the use of hyphenated adjectives in the way we write has come from the military. In that *target-rich* environment, we find the World War II use of *company-grade* and *field-grade* officers. In the 1960s, *zero-defect* quality control and *zero-tolerance* policies made their mark, promptly picked up by politicians. "An unfortunate inclusion in the U.S. legislation," biologists observed at the Royal Society of London in 1967, "was the use of the term 'zero tolerance,' which implied a nil residue level." (In the scandal affecting the Catholic Church today, a *zero-tolerance* policy toward pedophile priests is in the headlines.)

What single term epitomizes the triumph of the compound adjective? The hands-down winner (in the old days, I would have written, "The winner, hands down," and come to think of it, that's more emphatic) is *weapons-grade.*

This was coined in a 1952 policy statement by the Atomic Energy Commission calling for "nuclear plants which are economically independent of government commitments to purchase *weapons grade* plutonium." It was not then hyphenated; that was done a year later by the scientist George L. Weil, the colleague of Enrico Fermi at the University of Chicago who physically initiated the first nuclear chain reaction. Weil started a linguistic chain reaction as well: the meaning became "fissionable material of a quality for use in nuclear weapons," and its serious meaning now applies to biological agents as well.

As with all horrific words, it was quickly absorbed into popular culture. Voted the "catch-all superlative" of last year by the American Dialect Society, *weapons-grade* has been used to modify everything from a Toyota's torque output to Elvis Presley's charisma. Allan Metcalf, the Dialect Society's executive secretary, explains, "*Weapons-grade* salsa would mean really hot."

The week preceding your article my ninth-grade classes and I had been reading Julius Caesar *and noted Cicero's observation that the night before*

Caesar's assassination was a "strange-disposed time," as well as Cassius' comment that "certain of the noblest-minded Romans" had chosen to embark with him on "an enterprise / Of honorable-dangerous consequence."

In the past week, we have completed Act II where troubled Brutus enviously looks at his sleeping servant Lucius and comments "enjoy the honey-heavy dew of slumber" and Caius Ligarius is willing to follow Brutus with a "heart new-fired."

Apparently, not only did the Bard invent so much of our vocabulary, he also was the inventor of the compound-adjective!

Elyse Aronauer
Flushing, New York

Welcome Back, Rogue.   On June 19, 2000, a date that will live in euphemism, the diplomatic language was deliberately and suddenly attacked by Secretary of State Madeleine Albright. Speaking on public radio's *Diane Rehm Show,* she abandoned the tried-and-true Kissingerism *rogue states,* preferring instead to refer to nations like Libya, Iraq and North Korea as *states of concern.*

Peppered with questions about this calculated change in nomenclature, a hard-pressed State Department spokesman, Richard Boucher, replied, "We have different policies toward different places because the key issue here is not to categorize." He was clearly uncomfortable with the linguistic shuffling.

Rogue is a 16th-century English canting word, used by beggars and vagabonds, that is obscure in its origin, though it may be a variant of the name Roger (as in the limerick about the girl from Cape Cod that concludes, "'Twas Roger the Lodger, by God!"). As a noun, *rogue* is synonymous with, and carries the delicious old flavor of, "knave, scoundrel, villain." As an adjective, it means "mean" or "uncontrollable."

We have a rollback. In his budget address to a joint session of Congress, President George W. Bush denounced "*rogue* nations intent upon developing weapons of mass destruction." Speaking at the dedication of the USS *Reagan* the following week, he made clear that the ringing locution or cliché is back in language's good graces: "Our present dangers . . . come from *rogue* nations."

Mary Ellen Countryman, the National Security Council spokeswoman with the most salutatory name in the new administration, told Al Kamen of the *Washington Post* that *rogue nation* was "a term that means something to people."

Right. No longer will criminals fear being portrayed in a *states-of-concern's gallery,* nor will vicious beasts driven out of the herd be called *states-of-concern elephants.* Nor, thanks to the Bush rollback, will tomorrow's actors playing Hamlet begin a soliloquy, "O what a state of concern and peasant slave am I."

Whatever It Takes.   I have long been of two minds about the word *ambivalent.* But the time has come to take an unequivocal stand on *ambiguity.*

As far back as 1982, an investment banker named Leo Dworsky wrote in the *Christian Science Monitor* that the Middle East could withstand "more downright *strategic ambiguity.*" In 1995, Joseph Nye, then a top Pentagon official, used the phrase in a speech to the Asia Society about the extent of America's defense commitment to Taiwan. As long as Taiwan did not press for independence, any attack by China on the island would have "grave consequences"—which may or may not include use of United States forces. Two years later, James Baker, the former secretary of state, unambiguously defined the phrase at a Rice University conference as "We don't tell anybody what we might do."

House Republicans led by Representative Christopher Cox, however, said that *strategic ambiguity* "virtually invites conflict." They recalled that when Dean Acheson left South Korea out of a list of countries the United States would defend, the Communists "miscalculated" and invaded. A Clinton assistant secretary of state, Winston Lord, was uncomfortable with the phrase, but said it was "like the Energizer Bunny—it keeps going and going."

Then along came President Bush's affirmative response to a question about defending Taiwan if attacked. "With the full force of American military?" Charles Gibson of ABC asked. Bush replied, "Whatever it takes to help Taiwan defend itself."

When a State Department spokesman said that this was no change in policy and Bush reiterated his expectation that Taiwan would not be provocative, the *New York Times* reported that this was "making it *ambiguous* whether the United States still holds to '*strategic ambiguity.*' " Hardliners countered that the best deterrent to war was clarity, not vagueness.

The Latin *ambigere* means "to be undecided"; synonyms of *ambiguity* include "uncertainty, doubtfulness, inexplicability." The addition of *strategic* makes the uncertainty appear cunning, a deliberate policy of "keep 'em guessing." But *strategic,* long a global intensifier in national security circles, lost puissance when "*strategic* partner," as applied to China, fell into disfavor and was disavowed by Democrats.

Cool compromisers in Washington's think tanks are suggesting on deep-six background that Bush geopolitical thinkers adopt a policy of "*tactical ambivalence*" in the framework of "*strategic* clarity." Those adjectives and nouns can be switched around to fit changed circumstances caused by nuke-ular threats.

Willkie Lives.   After Al Gore denounced the *old guard* and other powerful interests, the relatively moderate Joe Lieberman was asked if the Democratic proposals would cause him to take a populist line. "Political rallies tend not to be places for extremely thoughtful argument," he told the *Wall Street Journal.* Rather, he said that the Gore policy proposals were "quite moderate" and added, "You have some rhetorical flourishes."

That reminded political-history buffs of Wendell Willkie, GOP nominee in 1940 against FDR, who warned in the campaign that "if the present administration is restored to power for a third term, our democratic system will not last another four years." After his defeat, Willkie undertook a diplomatic mission for President Roosevelt and was asked how he could square his cooperation with his earlier charges. In testifying before Congress in a way that infuriated Republicans, Willkie grinned and let the cat out of the political bag: "It was just a bit of campaign oratory."

Today, that's called "rhetorical flourishes."

Wired.   After Bill Clinton expressed contrition at a preconvention interview at a church gathering in Illinois, the Reverend Bill Hybels, one of his pastoral advisers, put his hand on the president's shoulder and prayed with him, saying, "Thank you, God, that you *wired him up* the way you did."

Wired bids fair to be the most multisensed "hot" word on the American linguistic scene. No other old word has more new meanings. Up to 1980, according to a search engine that puff-puffs its way through all the libraries in the world, 61 books had *wired* in the title, but in the past twenty years, almost 400 more have been added. The noun began in the Latin *viere*, "to plait," and the Greek *iris*, "rainbow." The Old High German *wiara* meant "fine gold work." As a verb, its early definitions—"fasten or strengthen with a metal tie" and "connect in an electrical circuit"—remain, but in our technological time the wound-together word has burst into a rainbow of senses.

Wired for sound, applied in the '50s to people wearing hearing aids, was the name of a 1986 song by Michael W. Smith and Wayne Kirkpatrick. This was in the Christian contemporary rock section of music stores, deploring the difficulty of studying the Word of God amid the cacophony of "a world that's *wired for sound*."

An entirely different meaning of *wired for sound* was emerging at the same time: "The joint is *wired*. . . ." wrote J. D. MacDonald in a 1957 novel, *A Man of Affairs*. "The next step is cameras and infrared and tape recorders, I guess." The single word *wire* stood for "electronic eavesdropping." A person fitted with a surreptitious recording device to help others spy on conversations is said to wear a *wire*. This was what Monica Lewinsky refused to do for investigators for the independent counsel looking into her relationship with the president.

Meanwhile, beginning in 1969, another meaning was taking root: "high on amphetamine drugs; manic." A mild precursor of this, reported by John Farmer in his 1890 slang dictionary, was "irritated; provoked." The sense of its modern offshoot, not necessarily drug-related, ranges from "edgy, jumpy, uptight" to "pumped up, visibly nervous" to "feverishly excited." It was the title of Bob Woodward's 1984 book, *Wired: The Short Life and Fast Times of John Belushi*.

A sense also first cited in 1969 is from the computer world: "having circuits connected permanently and designed for an unchangeable function." *Scientific American* noted in 1981 that "it is a rule of thumb in computer science that an operation can be executed fastest when it is *hard-wired* into the computer rather than specified as part of a program." Why "hard"? Because that differentiates it strongly from the software, which is not part of the machine's wiring.

This computer meaning was quickly transferred to neuroscience and applied to the workings of the brain. "These cells are *hard-wired* and ready for action," wrote the *New Scientist* in 1971, "as soon as the kitten opens its eyes." In a few years the professor of astronomy Carl Sagan was writing, "The brain is completely *hard-wired:* specific cognitive functions are localized in particular places in the brain," an assertion since largely confirmed by imaging technology, though experience or accident can cause "rewiring" to take place. This year, the *New York Times* architectural critic Herbert Muschamp, writing about the Neurosciences Institute in La Jolla, California, noted that the Nobel laureate Gerald Edelman's institute was "partly inspired by Dr. Edelman's theory that the brain's architecture is shaped by our experiences. Tell me what you like, and I will tell you how you're *wired.*"

That sense was later applied to more general opinions or abilities. When Joseph Lieberman was chosen by Al Gore to be his running mate, Rabbi Avi Shafran told the *New York Times* that concern about Jewish visibility in politics was "sort of *hard-wired* into our system, for better or worse." Similarly, a coach for the University of California Bears recently told the *San Francisco Chronicle* that he had high hopes for a young player because "he's *wired* the right way for a quarterback"—that is, he had the stable temperament and quick reactions suited to that position.

As the Internet came into being, another new sense was applied: "adept at the use of the computer, tuned into the culture of the Internet." In Paris, a group that had tried to launch a magazine called *Electric Word* was reaching for a new name for a magazine addressed to the cyberworld. Jane Metcalf said to John Rosetto, John Plunkett and Barbara Kuhr, "*Wired.*" George Shirk, editor of that successful publication's independent offshoot, *Wired News,* sees their role as heralds of "the Virtual Class, people in technology, finance, marketing, media, law, politics and education who are driving the Digital Revolution."

A related sense, beyond the specific Internet culture, is "part of a network of people with related interests; integrated into a social set or part of an informatrix." A more pejorative side to this is "set up to take advantage of high-level contacts": a deal that is rigged, its outcome arranged beforehand not on the basis of merit or fair competition, is subject to the charge of being *wired*.

Thus, the question "Is he *wired*?" can mean "Is he sure to get the job?" Or "Is he tense, excited, on 'speed'?" Or "Is he au courant, with-it, where it's at?" Or "Is his brain's activity predetermined?" Or "Is he fitted with a secret microphone?" Or "Is he temperamentally disposed for this?" Or "Is he on the Net?"

How will this past participle of a short verb, in future permutations, further transform its meaning and vivify our tongue? Nobody, no matter how well connected, can tell which senses will prevail and which will pass into archaisms. Stay *wired*.

Wordplayers.   What do you call somebody who continually applies his nose to the grindstone, eschews the distractions of fun and games and otherwise occupies himself with those moneymaking endeavors that make Jack a dull boy?

A *workaholic*, of course. But what did we call that addiction to work—that obsessive attachment to long hours and briefcases voluntarily stuffed with homework—before Wayne E. Oates, in a burst of linguistic innovation in 1968, titled an article in a pastoral magazine, "On Being a 'Workaholic' "?

We had no word for it. The language suffered from a gaping hole. Not until this Southern Baptist pastor from Louisville, Kentucky, came up with his coinage could English speakers succinctly express themselves. "I have dubbed this addiction of myself and my fellow ministers as *workaholism*," Oates wrote, and later defined his term as "the compulsion or the uncontrollable need to work incessantly."

He based it, obviously, on *alcoholic*. In so doing, the coiner made a new suffix out of *-oholic*. But the question of spelling arises: if the suffix is adopted from *alcoholic*, why did Oates not spell his word *workoholic*? That was the spelling of a parallel formulation adopted the same year to describe those bittersweet-toothed souls who cannot do without a chocolate fix: *chocoholic*. But *choco* lent itself to the *-oholic*; why did Oates prefer the *a*?

I cannot ask him because Wayne Oates was one of those who died in the past year, remembered in history not so much for his fifty-seven books and hundreds of published articles, but for his undisputed coinage of a necessary word. That's the way it goes in the word dodge; if you coin a good one, it becomes the lead of your obituary no matter what else you did.

Same for Herbert Freudenberger, the eminent psychologist who died last month in New York. Was he noted for his work with people who lost self-esteem, became bored, discouraged and sloppy? Or for his free clinics for drug addicts, or for his court-ordered analysis of the murderous Charles Manson? No. The headline in the *New York Times* read "Herbert Freudenberger, 73, Coiner of 'Burnout,' Is Dead."

He first used the word as the title of a 1974 book, subtitled *The High Cost of High Achievement*, which he wrote with Geraldine Richelson, defining *burnout* as "the extinction of motivation or incentive, especially where one's devotion to a cause or relationship fails to produce the desired results." In his native Germany, from which he fled in 1938, the term is *aus gebrant*, literally "burned out."

Burnout had been a 1940s term for "the sudden loss of power in a jet or rocket engine." By the '50s, it had been largely replaced by *flameout,* giving Dr. Freudenberger a chance to give it a new life with his psychological sense. Though he did not coin the word itself, as Mr. Oates did with *workaholic,* he gave *burnout* the sense by which it is known today.

Another man known to the word trade died in 1999. (We don't use euphemisms like "passed away" or "departed this vale of tears"; when you die in this business, you die.) He never tried to pass himself off as a serious linguist or lexicographer, but his wordplay delighted his readers, stimulated interest in the world of words and sometimes instructed us with a light-verse touch.

The advertising and promotion man Willard Espy is best known for his almanacs of *Words at Play,* compiled and reissued by Merriam-Webster six months ago. Having fun with words can involve creative rhymes ("I do not roister with an oyster") and nonce coinages ("my family was a scribacious lot"). As players of Scrabble and workers of crossword puzzles know, games are a good way to discover the glories of lexicography.

My favorite Espy production is "To My Greek Mistress," an odd ode. "All you need to read off this verse as if it were English," he noted, "is a vague recollection of the Greek alphabet." (Begin by remembering that Ψ is pronounced "psi," and P is pronounced "rho.")

> With many a Ψ ate a Π
> That you had baked, my dear;
> This torpor N I you—
> I'm feeling very queer.
> Ο Φ Ο Φ upon your Π!—
> You Δ cruel blow!
> Your dreadful Π has made me X;
> My tears fall in a P;
> I would have Λnother lass
> Who baked that Π, I vow;
> But still I M and M for you,
> As sick as any cow.

Translation for those stimulated to brush up their Greek:

> With many a (sigh) I ate a (pie)
> That you had baked, my dear;
> This torpor (new) (I owe to) you—
> I'm feeling very queer.
> O (fie) O (fie) upon your (pie)!—
> You (dealt a) cruel blow!
> Your dreadful (pie) has made me (cry);
> My tears fall in a (row).
> I would have (lammed a)nother lass
> Who baked that (pie), I vow;
> But still I (moo) and (moo) for you,
> As sick as any cow.

Oops! The term aus gebrant *is literally non-existent. The correct spelling of the verb* ausbrennen *in the perfect tense is* ausgebrannt. *Interestingly, in my native Danish, the term for burnout is the very close* udbraendt. *It is only speculation on my part whether Danes can thank Herbert Freudenberger for a common verb's expanded figurative meaning.*

Lotte Martin
Vero Beach, Florida

Words at War.   "You are about to embark upon a great *crusade*," General Eisenhower told his troops on the eve of D-Day; he later titled his memoirs *Crusade in Europe*. American presidents liked that word: Thomas Jefferson launched "a *crusade* against ignorance," Theodore Roosevelt exhorted compatriots to "spend and be spent in an endless *crusade*" and FDR, calling for a "new deal" in his acceptance speech at the 1932 Democratic convention, issued "a call to arms," a "*crusade* to restore America to its own people."

But when George W. Bush ad-libbed that "this *crusade*, this war on terrorism, is going to take a while," his figure of speech was widely criticized.

That's because the word has a religious root, meaning "taking the cross," and was coined in the 11th century to describe the first military expedition of the Crusaders, European Christians sent to recover the Holy Land from the followers of Muhammad. The rallying-cry noun is offensive to many Muslims: three years ago, Osama bin Laden maligned U.S. forces in the Middle East as "*crusader* armies spreading like locusts."

In this case, a word that has traditionally been used to rally Americans was mistakenly used in the context of opposing a radical Muslim faction, and the White House spokesman promptly apologized. In the same way, Vice President Dick Cheney was chided for referring admiringly to Pakistanis as "Paks." Steven Weisman of the *New York Times* asked, "Is it conceivable that he would have used a similar slur with the Japanese?" The shortening *Paki* is taken to be a slur, even when criticized as "*Paki-*bashing," and *Paks* only slightly less so. In past military cooperation with Pakistan, U.S. servicemembers used *Paks* as they would use *Brits* or *Aussies,* nationality nicknames no more offensive than *Yanks.* Cheney probably picked up *Paks* in his Pentagon days, but innocent intent is an excuse only once; now he is sensitized, as are we all.

In the same way, when the proposed Pentagon label for the antiterror campaign was floated out as "Operation Infinite Justice," a spokesman for the Council on American-Islamic Relations noted that such eternal retribution was "the prerogative of God." Informed of this, Defense Secretary Donald Rumsfeld quickly pulled the plug on the pretentious moniker.

Who coins these terms? Nobody will step forward; instead, software called "Code Word, Nickname and Exercise Term System" is employed to avoid responsibility; it spits out a list of random names from which commanders can choose. This avoidance of coinage responsibility leads to national embarrassment (which is finite justice). "Operations," said Winston Churchill, "ought not to be described by code words which imply a boastful and overconfident sentiment."

Apropos of Churchill: in Bush's well-received address to the joint session of Congress calling for a "war on terror," the president said with impressive intensity, "We will not tire, we will not falter and we will not fail." This evocation of an earlier rhetoric of resolution (which his aides, who turned out the speech in nine hours, insist was not researched) could not have been lost on Prime Minister Tony Blair, an honored guest in the audience. In a speech broadcast to America on Feb. 9, 1941, Churchill said: "We shall not fail or falter; we shall not weaken or tire. . . . Give us the tools, and we will finish the job." (Note where the Brit placed the *shalls* to heighten the expression of resolve, and the *will* expressing futurity before the stressed finish. Bush held to the more American *will not,* in front of the emphasized *tire, falter* and *fail.*)

The Bush speech showed a heightened concern for connotation. In an exegesis of his prepared speech, this former speechwriter looked for the words not chosen. For example, Bush castigated the power-seeking terrorists as those who "follow in the path of Fascism, Nazism and totalitarianism." The word left out of the series beginning with Fascism and Nazism is, of course, *Communism;* however, the administration is seeking help from Russia and other former Soviet republics, in which many former and present Communists live—hence, the less specific, all-encompassing *totalitarianism.* The tactful substitution preceded the most original phrase in the speech, pointing to the end of the path of all those isms: "history's unmarked grave of discarded lies."

The other noun that was not there in the Bush address to Congress was *defense,* as in the hottest phrase in Washington today, *homeland defense.*

The earliest citation I can find is by China's Xinhua News Agency, reporting on April 11, 1977, about "the mobilization of the puppet army and the '*homeland defense* reserve forces'" by South Korea. Twenty years later, a panel of experts recommended to Defense Secretary William Cohen that a new armed-forces mission considering biological threats be called Defense of the Homeland.

In February 2001, a commission headed by former Senators Gary Hart and Warren Rudman delivered a prescient report that the nation was vulnerable to terrorist attack. It called for a cabinet-level agency amalgamating customs, law enforcement, Coast Guard and other nonmilitary federal agencies coordinating *homeland defense.* The Hart-Rudman report received little attention in the media or at the White House.

On the eve of the president's speech, White House sources told the Associated Press he would create a "*Homeland Defense* Security Office"—a coordination group, not a whole new department. At the last minute, the word *defense* was dropped. Why? I'm told because it "sounded defensive," and, more probably, "protecting the internal security of the homeland would be confused with the war-making mission of the Department of Defense."

Thus, in the new lexicon of the war on terror, *security* means "defense"; *defense* means "attack."

You stated crusade *and* crusader *were coined in the 11th century. They were not. Those who took the cross in the First Crusade (as well as the second) were called "pilgrims"; their bloody journey to Jerusalem being a "pilgrimage."*

It was not until about the time of the preaching of the Third (1188) that the venture became a "crusade" (croseria) and the adventurers "crusaders" (crucesignati). Just as our doughboys who fought in 1918 could not know what they were involved in, neither could Europe's knighthood know in 1095.

Ronald Colvin
Philadelphia, Pennsylvania

I think you messed up your "shall" and "will" definitions. Surely Churchill was just expressing simple futurity with, "We shall not fail . . . shall not weaken. . . ." It was a given. His resolve and determination were expressed with " . . . we [bloody well] will finish the job." With the tools, nothing can (shall) stop us.

I was taught that first-person "will" and second- and third-person "shall" signified determination. Simple futurity was first-person "shall" and second- and third-person "will." And if you don't believe me, see p. 58 of Strunk and White [The Elements of Style].

Graeme McLean
New York, New York

My English teacher at Grafton Street Junior High School, Worcester, Massachusetts, was a superb grammarian and affectionately called "Bulldog" Brogan, because of his large, fierce teeth and facial expressions. One of the grammatical distinctions that he taught his classes has been invaluable to me as an attorney in being able to construe the meaning of statutes and in drafting documents. According to him, for the ordinary future tense, "shall" is used for the first persons singular and plural and "will" is used for the second and third persons singular and plural. However, to express obligation or determination these auxiliary verbs are reversed.

It is true that in contemporary oral and even written American usage, "shall" is not used to express future tense, even for the first-person singular. However, I have noticed in recently reading Edith Wharton's House of Mirth *that Ms. Wharton is very careful to follow Mr. Brogan's prescriptions.*

You are wrong in your analysis of the quotations of Bush and Churchill. As I will show, both speeches observe the distinction that I have specified in ¶1 above. First of all, when Churchill states, "We shall not fail or falter; we shall not weaken or tire," he is expressing an optimistic prediction about how the English will behave. He is using the straightforward future tense. But notice how in the final sentence you quote, "Give us the tools and we will finish the job," Churchill uses "will" with the first-person plural to express the determination and resolve of the English people. Now Churchill is dedicating the English nation "to finishing the job."

On the contrary, Bush's speechwriters wisely have short-circuited the Churchillian language, in consideration of the speaker and his American audience and the sixty years that have elapsed since the time Churchill delivered his speech. Still, there is in President Bush's speech the powerful, though simplified, echo of Churchill in "We will not tire, we will not falter, we will not fail." Here, Bush speaks with confidence of the resolve of the nation. He proclaims the "will" of the people to do what is necessary. These three four-word sentences serve as a litany for the American people, instead of the more leisurely alternatives used by Churchill ("fail or falter" and "weaken or tire"). Bush utters a battle cry. There is a crescendo in the use of the short,

Anglo-Saxon verbs that resonates with the alliteration and assonance of the final "falter" and "fail," which is a brilliant reversal of the sequence of the use of these two words by Churchill.

Donald V. Morano
Chicago, Illinois

Yee-Haw.   When Paul Beier, a mountain lion expert at Northern Arizona University, was told that 11,000 biodiverse acres of Irvine Ranch in Southern California were set aside by conservationists, he exclaimed to the *Los Angeles Times:* "*Yee-haw!* That is fantastic news."

When the actor-director Jodie Foster recently won a celebrity's game on *Jeopardy,* she, too, let out a *yee-haw,* as did Oprah Winfrey when interviewing lucky survivors of near-death experiences.

And when the Dow Jones industrial average poked its head above 10,000 late last year, the *Cincinnati Post* quoted a happy Wall Street watcher saying, "You can quote me this way, '*Yee-haw,*' with a hyphen in the middle."

A hyphen does indeed belong between the *yee* and the *haw* of this joyous expression. What does the exclamation mean? The *New Oxford American Dictionary* is the first to include it: "An expression of enthusiasm or exuberance, typically associated with cowboys or rural inhabitants of the southern U.S."

The *haw* is often pronounced *ha.* The *Leicester Mercury* of Britain headlines an article about "the 10 worst country-and-western song titles ever recorded" as "*Yee-ha* Howlers." (The odious "Did I Shave My Legs for This?" was runner-up to the poignant farewell ditty "Get Your Tongue Out of My Mouth 'Cause I'm Kissing You Goodbye.")

What happened to the old western favorites *Yippee!* and *Yahoo!*? They're buried at the O.K. Corral.

The earliest citation of *Yippie!* is supplied by *Merriam-Webster*, from an *Everybody's* magazine of 1914: "*Yip-pee*, Andreas! I've done it!" Popularized by the novelist Sinclair Lewis in his 1920 *Main Street*, it is generally believed to have a much earlier origin in cowboy usage, though I cannot find any examples. In the 1960s, the *yippies*, based on an acronym of the Youth International Party influenced by the laid-back *hippies*, drained much of the cowboy flavor out of the word.

Yahoo has a literary origin. The satirist Jonathan Swift, in his 1726 *Gulliver's Travels*, gave that name to a race of brutal men subservient to highly intelligent horses, the onomatopoeic *Houyhnhnm*. It was taken up by political writers in the last century and applied to anti-intellectuals, usually right-wingers.

Meanwhile, out west, riders of the purple sage used the word in the farrago of interjections and exclamations beginning with *y*: *yippy-aye-ay, yowee, yea, yo*. There may be an association with *yell*.

In the 1990s, *yahoo!* was taken over by the Internet service provider of that name. Its Web site explains that the company's founders, David Filo and Jerry Yang, drolly designated their server "Yet Another Hierarchical Officious Oracle"—its initials spelled *yahoo*—but they liked the acronym's Swiftian meaning of "rude, unsophisticated, uncouth." Though the company preserved the exclamation mark in its title, evoking not the brutes in Swift's allegory but the yell of a man astride a bucking horse, *yahoo's* identification with the popular site has overtaken its sense as a cry of a man in the saddle.

With the synonymic underbrush thus cleared, we can now address the origin of *yee-haw!*

A clue can be found in a 1911 short story by Jack London, describing a rider on the ice drawn by sled dogs: "As they were driving in single file, without reins, he had to guide them by his voice, and it was evident the head-dog had never learned the meaning of *gee* and *haw*."

As equestrians know, *gee* (with a soft *g*) is usually a direction to a horse to go to the right, and *haw* to the left. To *gee up* and *gaddy-up* is to urge onward. "The regiment is somehow got back," wrote Thomas Lackland in *Homespun; or, Five-and-Twenty Years Ago*, an 1867 novel, "by *geeing* and *hawing* . . . while he '*gees*' and '*haws*' the yoke of cattle."

My speculation that the current *yee-haw* is bottomed on the horseman's *gee-haw* is supported by a 1967 citation from a Texan in the files of the *Dictionary of American Regional English*. "That suggests to me," says Leonard Zwilling of *DARE*, "that *yee-haw* might have something to do with the commands for a horse—to *gee*, go right, and *haw*, go left. On the other hand, it might have something to do with *gee-haw whimmey-diddle*, a toy found in the Appalachians."

For those who wish to do further philological research in the field, the World Gee Haw Whimmey Diddle competition is held annually at the Folk Art Center on the Blue Ridge Parkway near Asheville, North Carolina. The spinning toy, which can go left or right, is also known as the *ziggerboo* and the *flipperdinger*. As the first prize is announced, listen to what the winner yells.

Zemblanity.   Arms controllers know that the Russians have been setting off non-nuclear explosions at their nuclear test facility on the barren, frigid Arctic island of Nova Zembla, and thereby hangs a new word.

An old word is *serendipity,* "a happy discovery by accident." It was coined by Horace Walpole in 1754, based on the fairy tale of the three princes of Serendip, who "were always making discoveries . . . of things they were not in quest of." The Indian Ocean island of Serendip, later known as Ceylon, is now the nation of Sri Lanka.

A *Times Book Review* note about the novel *Armadillo,* by William Boyd, reads, "The novel's hero . . . is undone by an outbreak of *zemblanity,* the opposite of *serendipity,* in the multicultural hubbub of Cool Britannia." Newton Scherl of Englewood, New Jersey, writes, "I have tried without success to find *zemblanity* in any of my dictionaries." That's because it is not yet there.

"What is the opposite of Serendip, a southern land of spice and warmth?" asks Boyd in his novel. "Think of another world in the far north, barren, icebound . . . Zembla. Ergo: *zemblanity,* the opposite of serendipity, the faculty of making unhappy, unlucky and expected discoveries by design."

Writers from Jonathan Swift and Alexander Pope to Jules Verne and Salman Rushdie have used Zembla's wastes north of Siberia as symbolic of what Charlotte Brontë called "forlorn regions of dreary space." Now this site of testing of non-nuclear explosives at a nuclear facility has given birth to *zemblanity,* the inexorable discovery of what we don't want to know.

☙

Zhlub.   A recent *New Yorker* cartoon by David Sipress has an ordinary-looking woman addressing a wimpish man on the other end of a couch with "I want to start dating other *zhlubs.*"

About six months ago, Dennis Murray, a Fox News producer, told the *Washington Post* media reporter Howard Kurtz of his dismay at having to run even a brief shot of a truck caravan carrying ballots from Palm Beach County, Florida, to the state capital to be counted. "It was just funny, looking at it on the screen, like some poor *schlub* just moving something," he said. "What's the point? . . . Who cares?"

Which spelling is correct—the magazine's *zhlub* or the newspaper's *schlub?*

In his Yiddish dictionaries, Leo Rosten spelled it *zhlub,* from the Slavic *zhlob,* "coarse fellow." The sound is better transliterated as *zh* than as *sch.* That's this maven's call; in either case, the word rhymes with *rub.*

The senses today range from describing a person who is "ill-mannered" ("he acts like a *zhlub,* that *zhlub*") to "clumsy" ("Vassar-Shmassar, the girl's still a *zhlub*") to "oafish" ("what can you expect from such a *zhlub?*").

Jerk and *drip* are long gone; *nerd* and *dork* are passé. Is this the time of the *zhlub?*

☙

Zero Misteaks: The Gotcha! Gang Strikes Again

1/28/2001

"In your pick-apart work on the 2000 census," writes David Galef of the University of Mississippi's English Department, "you ruefully noted, 'Language has its limitations.' Make that *limits.*"

Yeah, right. (Make that "Yeah; right.") Although both *limit* and *limitation* mean "boundary" and by extension "point beyond which nothing is allowed or possible," *limitation* has a special sense of "lack of capacity; restrictive condition; handicap." A *limit* is like a line that marks an end, as in *city limits;* a *limitation* is a restriction that disables or nullifies, as in *statute of limitations.*

In an article about an investigation by Independent Counsel David Barrett into political influence in the Internal Revenue Service, I wrote that an immunized IRS employee was "singing like a birdie" and added parenthetically, "(hardly an original metaphor)."

"A *simile* is a figure of speech in which two essentially unlike things are compared," observes Henry A. Jackson III of Pittsburgh, "often in a phrase introduced by *like* or *as,* as in 'How like a winter hath my absence been' or 'So are you to my thoughts as food to life.' *Singing like a birdie* is not a metaphor, but is a simile." Right; and in Shakespeare's sonnet 75, "So are you to my thoughts as food to life" is more of an analogy than a simile.

He has me on the tropes. Both *metaphor* and *simile* compare one thing to another, but *simile* is specific, as in Shakespeare sonnet 97's "How like a winter," while *metaphor* is poetic, as in U. S. Grant's "I am a verb." Grant could have said, "I am a man of action, like a verb," which would have been a *simile;* instead, he let the reader take the metaphoric leap. A metaphor is like a fragrance that calls up a beautiful memory (which is a simile), while a simile lets a metaphor be its umbrella. (So I strain for effect. A grammarian's reach must exceed his grasp, or what's a metaphor?)

The world's only best-selling nonagenarian intellectual is Jacques Barzun; he is the kindest member of the Gotcha! Gang, a veritable cavalier of cavil. The author of *From Dawn to Decadence: 500 Years of Western Cultural Life, 1500 to the Present* noticed that I wrote, "If the Florida Supremes had named a Gore slate of electors, the Florida Legislature *would* have named its own; some electors in other states *may* then have been seduced into faithlessness." From San Antonio, the former Columbia University professor writes: "The needed word is not *may,* but *might,* to match the *would.* Write '*will name its own,*' then you *may* have your *may.*"

Yes; correct. *Might* is iffy, hypothetical, perhaps contrary to fact; *may* introduces a real possibility. Because my opening *if . . . would* was conditional, it should have been followed by the iffy *might*. Only if I had used the certain *will* should I have followed it with the possibly factual *may*. (It could be that I might get more mail on this, and may well be moved to answer it.)

"While I am at it," adds Barzun, "I may (or might) as well cavil at an aside in your language column. A *bee in the bonnet* is not quite the same as 'slightly crack-brained,' though it may imply it. The primary idea is 'obsessively intent on one idea.' It buzzes on one note. You're the man for fine distinctions: backtrack!"

*Gotcha*ed again. My irked gratitude to the Nitpickers' League knows no limits, because its members force me to learn my *limitations*.

Discussing U. S. Grant's poetic metaphor "I am a verb" you wrote: "Grant could have said, 'I am a man of action, like a verb.' . . . " But this would not have captured Grant's meaning. He was dying of throat cancer, in excruciating pain, unable to speak, struggling to complete his memoirs and thereby leave his wife financially secure after his death. He wrote to his doctors: "I think I am a verb instead of a personal pronoun. A verb is anything that signifies to be; to do; or to suffer. I think I signify all three." No longer a man of action in the conventional sense, Grant was eloquent to the last.

Marc Lange
Associate Professor of Philosophy
University of Washington
Seattle, Washington

6/24/2001

Now about those two dots above a vowel. In an aside that was a sly attempt to boost mail from speakers of German, I wrote that "an *umlaut*— pronounced 'OOM-lout,' meaning 'changed sound'—also separates the sound of a vowel from the different-sounding vowel that follows, as in *reënter*, though in English we tend to replace the umlaut with a hyphen."

I naïvely confused an *umlaut* with a *dieresis*. An *umlaut* in the German language is a diacritical, or distinguishing, mark placed above a letter to specify the sound. When the umlaut is on a *u*, the vowel is pronounced by pursing the lips to say "OO" and then trying to pronounce "EE." An umlaut on an *o* gives it the same vowel sound as the *u* in the English *turn*.

Thus, the German name *Müller* is pronounced "Mue-ller," and in English, we insert an *e* after the *u* to show that it is not pronounced like an ordinary *u*.

A *dieresis* denotes the separated pronunciation in English of two uncomfortably adjacent vowels. As the co-author of the world's greatest stylebook gently informs me, "It's 'reënter,' not 'rëenter,' and accordingly, three words earlier in the sentence, you mean 'precedes,' not 'follows.' "

An *umlaut* changes the sound of a German vowel; a *dieresis* splits two vowels that are pronounced separately in English. When two vowels snuggle together confusingly, a clarifying separation is indicated by the dieresis over the second vowel; in *naïve*, the two dots tell you to pronounce the word "nah-YEEV," not "knave" or "knive."

The same separation is needed when the two vowels are the same but are pronounced differently. Examples: with *reënter*, the *e* in *re* is pronounced "EE," while the first *e* in *enter* is pronounced "EH." The two dots over the second *e* tell you not to pronounce that as a single syllable, "REEN." And *zoölogy* is "zoe-ology" not "zoo-logy." As army recruiters say, please *coöperate* and *reënlist*.

I don't know about you, but when the vowels are the same, I'm ducking diereses and following *Times* style by switching to hyphens.

Your essay leaves the citizens of Hawaii in a state that can theoretically neither be spelled nor pronounced.

George Gerson
Westfield, New Jersey

1/13/2002

"Uofallpeople" is the name of the file I must grimly address today. It contains the pointing of fingers by the Gotcha! Gang at the language maven for errors in my columns last year.

On biblical quotation: Let me first get right with the Good Book. In a diatribe attacking senators who were giving John Ashcroft a hard time at his confirmation hearings (who knew?), I directed readers to Proverbs 1:15. My intention was to make the point that "a soft answer turneth away wrath." Unfortunately, as several pious readers noted, my numbers were switched around and that observation is in 15:1. (However, 1:15 advises us not to associate with thieves: "do not set foot on their paths." My quoted guidance, while not germane, wouldn't land you in jail.)

On death and taxes: In examining dysphemisms, I wrote: "When did the *inheritance tax* (a pro-taxing term) become the *estate tax* (a neutral term)? And who changed it to the *death tax,* which has a built-in antitax message?"

The Gotcha! Gangsters Robert Johnson and Harry Allan set me straight: an *estate tax* (federal or state) is imposed on the net value of the deceased person's property; an *inheritance tax* (nonfederal, some states) is levied on the heir who receives that property. Both are *death taxes.*

On Stalin's friend: In warning President Bush about trusting Vladimir Putin, I recalled a previous president's misplaced trust and quoted FDR as saying about Joseph Stalin, "I like old Joe." Wrong president. It was Harry Truman, recalling the Potsdam Conference, who said on June 11, 1948: "I got very well acquainted with Joe Stalin, and I like old Joe! He is a decent fellow. But Joe is a prisoner of the Politburo."

On comprise/compose/constitute: I wrote of Yasir Arafat's Force 17, his personal Tanzim militia, Hamas, Hezbollah and Islamic Jihad: "They *comprise* a terror coalition, supplying one another with arms, money and suicidal killers."

Greg Walker of the International Association of Chiefs of Police blew the whistle on this one, suggesting that I should have written *constitute,* meaning "make up." He's right.

The rule is that the parts *compose* the whole, and the whole *comprises* the parts. That's because *comprise*—from the Latin *comprehendere,* "to grasp all, to take in mentally"—means "include, contain, embrace" (as if from the outside in). Contrariwise, *compose* and *constitute* mean "to make up" (as if from the inside out).

Therefore, I should have written, "They *compose* ('form, produce') a terror coalition" or—equally correctly—"The terrorist coalition *comprises* ('includes, contains, embraces, brings together') not only Hamas, Islamic Jihad and Hezbollah but also Arafat's Force 17 and his personal Tanzim militia."

Loosey-goosey usagists say that the distinction is all but erased, and some great writers have even used the misleading construction *is comprised of,* but I belong on the ramparts on this one.

On the stickiness of wickets: I wrote about Prime Minister Tony Blair of Britain, "maneuvering his way through the *sticky wicket* of the Middle East."

One neither navigates nor maneuvers *through* such a soggy metaphor. The wicket, as I am informed gleefully by Lee Child, Jack Kenny and Ben Werschkul, is the ground on which the baseball-like game of cricket is played. When it is sticky, not in the sense of "tacky" but in the sense of "wet, slippery," the ball bounces on the ground in front of the batsman in unpredictable ways. This metaphor has been extended to a general meaning of "awkward, embarrassing, difficult," but as Mr. Child notes, "the key point is that the batsman is on a sticky wicket; he is perforce immobile in front of it; the bowler, himself knowing that the wicket is sticky, will be bearing down on the batsman with a wolfish grin." Therefore, it's *on,* not *through,* the sticky wicket.

Those of us in language's artful dodge who make a living correcting others must learn to strike a noble pose and take the gaff when we goof. Nobody stands taller than those willing to stand corrected. As FDR said, "If you can't stand the heat, get out of the kitchen."

Wait—no. That was Harry Truman.

6/09/2002

I have been semantically *unchaste.* In describing the difference between *celibate* ("single, unmarried") and *chaste,* I held that the latter meant "to deny all sexual intercourse."

Not so. As a horde of irate and probably married readers thundered, a person who engages in sex within marriage is *chaste*. Only when the inter-course is premarital, extramarital or postmarital can one be charged with being *unchaste*.

This *chastening* ("purifying") experience of being *chastised* ("pun-ished")—all rooted in the Latin *castus*, "pure, cut off from"—drags me into my annual exercise in self-flagellation. It provides a glorious if some-what sadistic moment for the Gotcha! Gang.

In an article about intervention in the Middle East, I wrote, "That is why a *dovecote flutters*." John Scanlon e-mails, "I can understand a dove flutter-ing, but wouldn't a *dovecote* sway?" True; a *cote* is akin to a cottage, a place of abode; birds flutter, but their cages and nests do not.

And while dealing with the Middle East, I misidentified Aipac as "the American Israeli Political Action Committee." Though this mistake can be found almost five hundred times on the Web, including on a United States Navy site, common misusage does not make it so. The name of the pro-Israel group is "American-Israel Public Affairs Committee." (Because po-litical action committees are so often denounced, and so many people make this mistake, maybe Aipac should change its name; send your e-mail to update@aipac.org, not to me.)

In my op-ed incarnation, I've been in a running battle with our intelli-gence agencies about their all-out campaign to discredit evidence of a visit to Saddam Hussein's spymaster in Prague by the suicide hijacker Mo-hamed Atta. I called the torrent of self-protective leaks by CIA and FBI sotto voce spokesmen "a misdirection play," and defined this as a move by an adept offensive lineman: "He blocks his man toward the center; as the defender pushes back hard, the misdirecting lineman gives way, seemingly overcome by the countercharge—as his running back scoots through the hole near the center left by the defender."

Watch out for those sports metaphors. "What you described as a *misdi-rection play*," e-mails an anonymous Sunday couch potato, "is really an *in-fluence block*. A *misdirection play* is when running backs and sometimes linemen flow in one direction and the ball carrier, usually after a delay, runs in the opposite direction."

I checked back with John Beake, VP of football operations at the NFL, who said, "It's not exactly a *misdirection play;* it's an *influence draw*." A call to Bill Brink at the *Times* sports desk suggested that that could be an *influence block* or *draw* taking place within a *misdirection play,* and my usage required no correction.

When a spook friend then called to say my column was "about a boo-boo," I said yeah, I know, some say it was an "influence block," but that's in dispute. No, my source said, the reason for all the CIA leaks to discredit the Atta-in-Prague story was "that the Company made a *boo-boo* in not passing on data about Atta to the FBI from Czech intelligence."

I immediately wondered: What is the origin of *boo-boo,* "blunder, egregious error"? Why are our spies and counterspies, engaged in the most serious business, using a reduplication that sounds like baby talk?

The etymology of *boo-boo* is a subject of fierce debate among leading lexicographers. The *Oxford English Dictionary,* its earliest citation from a 1954 article by Bill Henry, who wrote in the *Los Angeles Times* that Defense Secretary "Engine Charley" Wilson's "recent *boo-boo* . . . threatens to become historic," speculates that it's a reduplication of *boob,* meaning "fool" (and not in its sense of "breast," a vulgarism to be hooted at). The *OED* holds that *boob* is a shortening of *booby,* "a lubber, a nincompoop," from the Spanish *bobo,* "fool," in turn from the Latin *balbus,* "stammering." (I suppose that is the basis of *booby prize,* won for being especially stupid. It is a short linguistic leap from the ignorant *booby* to the erroneous *boo-boo.*)

Both *Merriam-Webster* and *American Heritage* take a different tack. They argue that *boo-boo* is an alteration of *boo-hoo,* "imitative of the sound of weeping." *Webster's New World* ducks any etymology and dismisses the second-order reduplication (changing the second letter to produce a rhyme) as an echoic colloquialism based in "baby talk."

To an undisputed error: In a recent dissection of compound adjectives, I wrote that "the hyphenation of modifiers rules the linguistic roost. This *rule-roosting* device. . . ." Neil Greenspan, a professor of pathology, e-mails, "You seem to have your new hyphenated entity backwards."

Betsey Walters of Lakeville, Massachusetts, in-chimes: "A *rule-rooster* would be a chicken balanced on a yardstick. A *roost-ruler* is a chicken in charge."

Just as bad, I defined *24/7/365* hosting as "a host is on duty at our Web site continuously." Gerald Dorman of Lindenhurst, New York, notes that "the Web server, or host, is not a person; it is a computer, serving out bits and bytes of data, not paté. What *24/7/365* means is that the server is up and running continuously." Other members of the Gotcha! Gang argued that logic directs the new continuum to be fashioned *24/7/52,* meaning "24 hours a day, 7 days a week, 52 weeks a year," but in language, logic is not roost-ruling (got it).

Many members of the Nitpickers' League who set me straight by writing to onlanguage@nytimes.com (the server is on duty *24/7/nowandthen*) precede their corrections with a kindly "Homer nodded." This is a loose translation of *dormitat Homerus,* "Homer nods," a phrase by the Latin poet Horace, suggesting that even great poets have senior moments. (The phrase was popularized by the English poet Alexander Pope in 1709 as "Those oft are stratagems which errors seem, / Nor is it Homer nods, but that we dream." I sometimes make a mistake on purpose, too, to demonstrate the power of my mail pull.)

As language changed, *Homer nods* became a mistake. Yesterday, to *nod* meant "to fall asleep momentarily, as the head falls forward," based on "to move the head up and down as a signal of affirmation." Today, to *nod* means only "yeah, OK, uh-huh." The original meaning of "to drift into dreamland" requires an additional word: to *nod off.* And so to bed.

I had always thought that the word boo-boo *originated as "bubo"—the infected, swollen lymph nodes that characterized bubonic plague. Childhood hurts and injuries are often referred to as boo-boos by parents who kiss and make them better. It is an easy jump from having a boo-boo to making a boo-boo—an error or mistake in judgment.*

Arlene Marin
Orangeburg, New York

You were indeed mistaken about chaste, *but you were quite right about the fluttering* dovecote. *Like "the house was in an uproar," it is a simple synecdoche, the container for the thing contained. No problem.*

Stephen Orgel
Department of English
Stanford University
Stanford, California

"Anybody can make a mistake." This plain English observation lacks the classical elegance of "Homer nods." It's also less colorful than the Japanese equivalent, Saru mo ki kara ochiru, *literally, "Even monkeys fall from trees [sometimes]."*

Dr. Glenn Murray
Pittsburgh, Pennsylvania

ACKNOWLEDGMENTS

The thankees are: Joan Houston Hall and Leonard Zwilling of the *Dictionary of American Regional English;* Fred Mish, Joanne Despres and Jim Lowe of Merriam-Webster; Jesse Sheidlower and Erin McKean of Oxford North America; John Paterson of the *OED;* Mike Agnes of Webster's New World; Joe Pickett and David Pritchard of American Heritage; Antonette di Paolo Healey of the *Dictionary of Old English;* and thankfully back from the dusty shelves of slangdom, Jonathan Lighter, editor of the *Historical Dictionary of American Slang.*

Others I call on for lexicographic support or advice include Sol Steinmetz, one of the world's great lexicographers and my favorite Yiddish expert; Fred Shapiro of the Yale Law Library; Gerald Cohen of the University of Missouri-Rolla; Ron Butters of the University of Georgia; Anne Soukhanov, editor-at-large of *Encarta Dictionary;* Wendalyn Nichols, formerly of Random House; Allan Metcalf of the American Dialect Society; Victoria Neufeldt of the Dictionary Society of North America; Connie Eble of the University of North Carolina; Bryan Garner, editor of *Black's Law Dictionary* and the *Dictionary of Modern American Usage;* Anatoly Liberman of the University of Minnesota; Paul Dickson; Christine Ammer; John Algeo; David Crystal of the University of North Wales; William Kretzschmar of the *Linguistic Atlas* project; Wayne Glowka of *American Speech;* Robert Burchfield, former editor of the *OED;* Samer Shehata of Georgetown; William Leap of American University; Mohammed Sawaie of the University of Virginia; Ed Callary of the American Name Society; Arnold Zwicky and Geoffrey Nunberg of Stanford; and Constance Hale, Laurence Urdang, Frank Abate, Michael Quinion and Charles Harrington Elster, the pronunciation maven.

411

My editors at the *New York Times Magazine* have been Rob Hoerburger, Abbott "Kit" Combs, Jeff Klein, Jaimie Epstein, Bill Ferguson, Jack Rosenthal, Adam Moss, Harvey Shapiro and Michael Molyneaux.

My group at Simon & Schuster includes Gypsy da Silva, Tom Pitoniak, Bill Molesky, Jim Stoller, Anthony Newfield, Barbara Raynor and of course, Michael Korda.

In addition to Kathleen Miller's research and Jeffrey McQuain's and Elizabeth Phillips's language aid, those helping me at the *Times*' Washington bureau include my assistant Anne Elise Wort, who keeps her eye out for current words, and Todd Webb, who tries to keep up with both snail mail and e-mail. The bureau's chief librarian, Barclay Walsh, and the librarians Marjorie Goldsborough and Monica Borkowski are always there to lend a helping hand or foot.

The copy-editing saviors of my political column who have kept the Gotcha! Gang at bay are Steve Pickering, Linda Cohn, Sue Kirby and Karen Freeman.

My gratitude to Jacques Barzun, architect of America's House of Intellect and a frequent correspondent herein, is expressed in the dedication of this book to him.

Sadly, another friend in usage, Alistair Cooke, died in 2004 at the age of 95. He founded what he called "Sanpickle"—the Safire Nit-pickers League—and I'll miss his good-humored savaging of my solecisms.

The final thankees are the Lexicographic Irregulars, the Squad Squad and—yes—the Gotcha! Gang.

Index of Names

Abate, Frank, 186, 380
Acheson, Dean, 383
Ackerman, Bruce, 174
Adair, Marshall P., 192
Adams, John, 101, 173
Adams, Sherman, 259
Adams, Thomas, 18
Adamson, Carol, 275
Ade, George, 134
Ælfred the Great, King, 262
Agnes, Mike, 88, 184
Ailey, Alvin, 210
Akchurin, Marat, 270
Albert, Marilyn, 51
Albright, Madeleine, 94, 156, 183, 286, 369, 382
Alexander, Sir James E., 262
Ali, Irfan, 292
Allan, Harry, 404
Allard, Wayne, 373
Allen, Robert S., 173
Allen, Steve, 199
Allen, Woody, 263, 315, 317
Allina, Franz, 236
Ames, Aldrich, 200–201, 203, 204
Amit-Kohn, Uzi, 50
Ampère, André-Marie, 293
Anderson, C. R., 250
Anderson, Joe, 68
Anderson, John B., 365–66
Angleton, James J., 204
Apple, R. W. Jr., 167–68, 369
Arafat, Yasir, 210–11, 404, 405
Archer, Bill, 188

Aristotle, 58, 59
Armstrong, Dave, 232
Arnold, Matthew, 143
Arnstein, Barbara, 317–18
Aronauer, Elyse, 382
Ashcroft, John, 174, 404
Assad, Hafez al-, 77
Atta, Mohamed, 406, 407
Atwater, Lee, 105
Auden, W. H., 187
Auermann, Nadja, 97
Austen, Jane, 301
Austin, Tex, 264
Avery, Tex, 99
Ayto, John, 189

Bacon, Francis, 169
Bailey, Nathaniel, 345
Baker, James A. 3rd, 383
Baker, John, 299
Baldwin, Hanson W., 139
Baldwin, Tom, 163
Balfour, Arthur James, 147
Ball, Claire, 296
Ball, Terence, 126
Balogh, Harry, 45
Balz, Dan, 276
Barnes, Fred, 174
Barnhart, David, 81, 199
Barrett, David, 401
Barsh, Emily, 296
Bartlett, John, 345
Barzun, Jacques, 21, 37, 47, 77, 90, 99, 115, 209, 266, 314, 343, 401, 402

413

Bates, Katharine Lee, 245–46
Batters, Matthew, 296
Baudouin, king of Belgium, 167
Beake, John, 407
Beamer, Todd, 305
Beck, Curt W., 122
Becker, Elizabeth, 372
Bede, Venerable, 42
Beier, Paul, 316
Bell, Griffin, 295
Bellow, Saul, 109, 213
Bender, Marylin, 87
Ben-Gurion, David, 147
Bennet, James, 211
Bennett, William J., 205, 206, 242–43
Benton, Thomas Hart, 366
Bergen, Kaitlin, 293
Berger, Donald, 341
Berger, Samuel R., 229–31
Berlin, Irving, 217, 372
Berlinski, Claire, 371
Berra, Yogi, 81
Bertcher, Robert W., 342
Bethmann-Hollweg, Theobald von, 328
Bezos, Jeff, 225
Biden, Joseph, 368
bin Laden, Osama, 65, 107, 135, 164, 218,
    291, 334, 391
Binsted, John, 176
Birnbaum, Jeffrey, 105
Bismarck, Prince Otto von, 172
Black, Conrad, 166
Blackstone, William, 21
Blaine, James, 237
Blair, Tony, 9, 63, 76, 210, 211, 250,
    275–76, 392, 405
Blake, William, 13
Bleier, Edward, 248
Blitstein, Ryan, 240
Bloch, Felix, 202
Blokov, Ivan, 65
Blome, Richard, 147
Bloomer, Amelia, 225
Blume, Sheila, 296
Bobrowsky, Matthew, 129

Bodian, Nat, 175
Bodoni, Giambattista, 17
Bogart, Humphrey, 35, 142, 352
Boies, David, 360
Bonaparte, Joseph, 14
Bonaparte, Napoleon, 14, 167, 229, 251,
    252
Bork, Robert H., 173, 174
Botha, R. F., 148
Bothwell, Fred, 296
Boucher, Richard, 94, 348, 382
Bowen, Arabella, 65
Boycott, Charles Cunningham, 225
Boyd, William, 399
Boyd, Zachary, 28
Bradley, Bill, 34, 263–64, 265
Bradley, Ed, 282
Brasher, Philip, 313
Brauchli, Marcus, 108
Breaux, John, 14
Breslin, Jimmy, 52
Brezhnev, Leonid, 358
Briggs, Joe Bob, 315
Brink, Bill, 407
Brogan, "Bulldog," 394
Brokaw, Tom, 135, 254
Brontë, Charlotte, 399
Brooks, David, 213
Brooks, Mel, 22
Brown, Barry, 117
Brown, David, 110
Brown, Helen Gurley, 145–46
Brown, Joe, 327
Brown, Tina, 90
Brown, Willis, 18
Bruni, Frank, 26, 345
Buchalter, Louis (Lepke), 342
Buckley, Roger, 261
Buckley, William F., 169, 207, 208,
    252–54, 333
Buffett, Warren, 9
Buford, Kate, 357
Burchfield, Robert, 2
Burke, Edmund, 165
Burkins, Glenn, 182

Burnham, James, 253
Burns, James MacGregor, 356–57
Burns, Scott, 79
Bush, Barbara, 94
Bush, George H. W., 94, 263, 269, 277, 279, 350
Bush, George W., 5, 13, 24, 26, 33, 35, 43–44, 62, 67, 81–82, 84, 105, 109, 110, 125, 126, 137, 138, 139, 145, 146, 164–65, 167–68, 169–70, 171, 174, 184, 188, 189, 190, 205, 206, 208, 213, 214, 218, 220, 231–32, 236, 241, 243, 270, 275–76, 279, 280, 286, 291, 299, 305, 307, 321, 322, 323, 324, 332, 335, 337, 343, 345, 347, 348, 351, 359, 360–61, 362, 364, 365, 368, 369, 370, 372, 375, 376, 382, 383–84, 390, 391–92, 394, 404
Bush, Jeb, 183
Bush, Vannevar, 157
Butler, Nicholas Murray, 343
Butler, Wayne, 276
Byron, Lord, 33, 306

Cain, James M., 144
Calhoun, Arthur Wallace, 73
Calhoun, John C., 172
Callender, James Thomson, 216
Cambronne, Count Pierre-Jacques-Etienne, 229, 231, 251–52
Campbell, Chris, 288
Capone, Al, 214
Card, Andrew, 106, 184, 276
Carleton, Jonathan, 155
Carlson, Richard, 355
Carlyle, Thomas, 168
Carpenter, Kip, 293
Carroll, Charles A., 308
Carroll, Lewis, 130
Carswell, John, 331–32
Carter, Bianca, 11
Carter, Jimmy, 22, 84, 243, 246, 249, 295, 350, 359, 366
Carter, Rosalynn, 172
Carville, James, 35, 49

Cassidy, Frederic G., 199
Casstevens, David, 344
Cellucci, Paul, 254
Celsius, Anders, 161
Chandler, Raymond, 144
Chapman, Stephen, 182
Charles, Hugh, 205
Chartier, Jean Pierre, 144
Chaucer, Geoffrey, 247, 327
Chavez, Linda, 138
Cheang, Alice, 130
Cheney, Dick, 26, 111, 134, 135, 139, 190, 279, 332, 372, 391
Cher, 182
Chetwynd, Lionel, 82
Child, Lee, 405
Chirac, Jacques, 156
Churchill, Charles, 14, 15
Churchill, Frank, 153
Churchill, Winston, 93, 148, 162, 172, 176, 266, 357, 391–92, 393, 394–95
Clanton Brothers, 318
Clausewitz, Carl von, 107
Clawson, Patrick, 212
Cleary, Brittney, 309
Cleveland, Grover, 160, 237
Clifford, Clark, 277
Clinton, Bill, 34, 47–50, 76, 77, 82–83, 86, 106, 133–34, 172, 181, 182–83, 185, 186, 188, 190, 206, 208, 215, 216, 217, 221, 224, 229–31, 239, 243, 263, 266–67, 269, 299, 322, 333, 351, 357, 358, 359, 361, 365, 369, 385
Clinton, Hillary Rodham, 49, 91–92, 106, 365
Clymer, Adam, 31, 132
Cochrell, Sam, 46
Cohen, Beverly S., 96
Cohen, Gerald, 23
Cohen, Noam, 53
Cohen, Richard, 35
Cohen, William S., 14, 392
Cole, Nat King, 271, 275
Coleman, Donald J., 59
Coleridge, Samuel Taylor, 325

Collins, Gail, 92, 254, 376
Colvin, Ronald, 37, 320, 393
Conan Doyle, Arthur, 12, 186
Conant, Jennet, 6
Conger, Eric, 56
Congreve, William, 331
Connally, John, 169
Connelly, Joel, 181
Connor, John, 8
Conrad, Joseph, 143
Cook, Elisha Jr., 35
Cooke, Alistair, 7
Coolidge, Calvin, 237, 349
Cooper, James Fenimore, 142, 186, 375
Corwin, Frank, 296
Cosby, Bill, 108
Countryman, Mary Ellen, 383
Couric, Katie, 239
Cowell, John, 222
Cox, Christopher, 383
Coyne, Andrew, 92
Cozzens, Rev. Donald, 320
Crabb, George, 65
Crow, Sheryl, 281
Crowe, William, 107
Crowley, Timothy, 108
Cummings, Edward Estlin (e. e. cum-
    mings), 272, 288
Cunningham, Paul, 120
Cuomo, Mario, 214
Curry, Ann, 239
Cusack, John, 317
Cushing, Richard Cardinal, 33
Cushman, Jack, 282
Custer, George Armstrong, 238, 240
Cylke, Chris, 5

Dae-jung, Kim, 324
Dalzell, Tom, 81
d'Angerville, Mouffle, 228
d'Angio, Carl, 57
Danzig, Richard, 222
Dao, James, 264
Dard, Frédéric, 301
Darley, George, 279

Daschle, Tom, 63, 64, 90, 125, 286, 362,
    365, 372
Davenport, John, 352
Davis, Gray, 84, 85
DeBeck, Billy, 136
Decatur, Stephen, 77
Defoe, Daniel, 371
DeForest, Mary, 318
Dell, Michael, 284
de Mille, Agnes, 160
D'Eon, Marcel, 336
Descartes, René, 67
Despres, Joanne, 258
Deutelbaum, Marshall, 144
DeVito, Danny, 143
Dewey, Thomas E., 181, 277
Dickens, Charles, 135, 176, 314, 337
Dickinson, Emily, 72
Di Clemente, John, 79
Dionne, E. J. Jr., 173
Dirksen, Everett, 279
Disraeli, Benjamin, 159, 335
Ditka, Mike, 344
Dole, Bob, 375
Donaldson, Sam, 306
Donato, Marla, 239
Doolittle, J. William, 103
Dorman, Gerald, 122, 408
Dowd, Maureen, 107–8, 182–83, 206, 371
Draco, 174
Dreier, David, 233
Duffy, Brian, 291
Dukakis, Kitty, 94
Dukakis, Michael, 94, 105
Dunne, Finley Peter, 63
Durbin, Richard, 62
Dworsky, Leo, 383

Eagleburger, Larry, 32
Earp, Wyatt, 317
Edelman, Gerald, 386
Edelman, Marian Wright, 232
Edelman, Michael, 296
Edelson, Noel M., 121
Edwards, John, 292

Egan, Cardinal Edward M., 33
Ehrlichman, John, 84
Eisenhower, Dwight D., 171, 243, 336, 349, 390
Eisenstadt, Michael, 298
Eldblom, Nancy, 126
Elias-Narvaez, Edwin, 116
Eliot, T. S., 8
Ellis, Joseph, 60–61
Elman, Mischa, 88
Elsant, Gail, 296
Elster, Charles Harrington, 319, 340, 353
Emerson, Ralph Waldo, 366
Epstein, Ed, 227
Erlanger, Steven, 369
Espy, Willard, 389
Etcoff, Nancy, 189
Etherege, Sir George, 331
Evans, Bergen, 234
Evans, Cornelia, 234

Farley, Christopher John, 273
Farmer, John, 386
Farrell, James T., 62
Fauci, Anthony, 83
Fax, David, 121
Feeney, Sheila Anne, 62
Fehmer, Marie, 302
Feinaigle, Gregor von, 104
Feinsilver, Lillian, 87
Feith, Douglas, 286
Fermi, Enrico, 381
Ferris, Gerrie, 68
Fielding, Henry, 370
Fiennes, Ralph, 316
Filo, David, 397
Fineman, Howard, 304
Finn, Holly, 14
Fireman, Richard, 114
Fitzgerald, F. Scott, 47, 50, 138, 182
Fitzgerald, John J., 23
Flaubert, Gustave, 344
Fleischer, Ari, 110, 241, 372
Flisser, Eric, 119
Foggin, Mark, 118

Forbes, Robert, 297
Forbes, Steve, 189
Ford, Gerald M., 135, 169, 350
Ford, Tom, 98
Forman, Miriam, 296
Forrestal, James, 354
Forster, E. M., 61
Foshee, John, 296
Foster, Jodie, 316
Fournier, Edouard, 229
Fournier, Ron, 241
Fowler, H. W., 1–2
Fox, Maurice, 115
Fox, Robert, 13
Francesco, Steven, 9
Francis, Julius, 316
Francis I, king of France, 350
Frank, Nino, 144
Franklin, Aretha, 282–83
Frankum, Robert, 268
Fraser, Lady Antonia, 132–33
Freed, Alan, 306
Freeman, Mary E. W., 188
Freilich, Leon, 297
Freudenberger, Herbert, 388–89, 390
Freudenstein, Eric G., 303
Fried, Harvey, 113
Friedman, Richard D., 60
Frost, Robert, 335
Fry, Christopher, 20
Frye, Northrop, 34

Gabriel, Joyce, 145
Galef, David, 400
Gans, Herbert J., 112
Gardner, Erle Stanley, 35–36
Garment, Len, 30
Garner, Bryan, 301
Garrett, Jack E., 43, 119
Gaston, Tim, 154
Gates, Bill, 8, 9, 123, 278
Gehrig, Lou, 172
Gelshenen, Estelle, 267
Gersh, Darren, 356
Gershwin, Ira, 272

Gerson, George, 203, 403
Gerson, Michael, 351
Gibbon, Edward, 278
Gibson, Charles, 384
Gibson, Mel, 213
Gilbert, Matthew, 64
Gilman, E. Ward, 373
Gingrich, Newt, 188, 269, 279
Ginsburg, Ruth Bader, 199
Godwin, William, 301, 377
Goebel, George, 199
Goggins, William O., 66, 157
Gold, Ben, 118
Golden, Harry, 87
Goldfine, Bernard, 259
Goldstein, Norm, 141
Goldwater, Barry, 169, 181, 359
Gonzales, Elian, 247
Goodman, Andy, 296
Gorbachev, Mikhail, 207
Gore, Al, 18, 19, 25, 34, 43, 82, 137–38,
    184, 188, 189, 242, 250–52, 255–57,
    263–64, 265, 299, 304, 307, 321, 322,
    323, 343, 345, 356, 360, 365, 375, 376,
    384, 386, 401
Gorman, James, 24
Gottlieb, Annie, 188
Graber, Peter, 331
Graham, Lindsey O., 107, 362
Graham, Peter, 42
Grant, Ulysses S., 237, 252, 401, 402
Gray, K., 296
Grbac, Elvis, 44, 45
Green, Helen, 332
Green, Mark, 307
Green, Robin, 52
Greenberg, Aldred, 297
Greene, Graham, 194
Greenfield, Jeff, 307, 333
Greenhouse, Linda, 101
Greenspan, Alan, 78
Greenspan, Neil, 407
Greenstreet, Sydney, 35
Greenway, David, 249
Greer, Germaine, 187

Greif, Kenneth, 314
Grieg, Edvard, 124
Grimm, Ed, 297
Grimond, Johnny, 93
Groninger, Tim, 116, 119
Gumble, Floyd, 275
Gunderson, Mark, 327
Guralnik, David, 288

Haag, Marcia, 58
Haberman, Clyde, 293, 294
Haddad, Heskel M., 96, 126, 274
Hafner, Katie, 196, 197
Hagel, Chuck, 213
Hague, William, 63
Haig, Alexander M. Jr., 241
Haldeman, Bob, 84
Hall, Joan, 136
Halliwell, James O., 28, 153
Hamermesh, Madeline, 194, 336
Hamilton, Alexander, 101, 215, 216
Hammerstein, Oscar, 272
Hammett, Dashiell, 24, 35–36, 144, 248
Hand, Learned, 208
Hanssen, Robert, 200, 201
Harding, Warren G., 101, 235, 361
Hari, Mata, 201, 203
Harrell, Evans, 67
Harriman, Averell, 168–69
Harrington, James, 323
Harris, Joel Chandler, 24
Harris-Adler, Rosa, 65
Harrison, Benjamin, 323
Harrison, William Henry, 366
Harshbarger, Scott, 294
Hart, Fred H., 256
Hart, Gary, 392
Harvey, T. J., 210
Haselberger, Gil, 235
Haskel, Ben and Doris, 208
Hatch, Orrin, 170, 376
Hauser, Eric, 265
Hawkins, David, 127, 240
Hawthorne, Nathaniel, 279
Hayes, Gabby, 332

Hayes, Woody, 344
Heaton, Herbert, 335
Heflin, W. A., 28
Hehir, Richard L., 309
Heimert, Andrew J., 41
Hely, Dan, 127
Hemings, Sally, 317
Hemingway, Ernest, 34, 194, 229
Hemmer, Bill, 139
Henig, Robin, 334, 336
Henneberger, Melinda, 80
Henry, Bill, 407
Henry, O., 46, 332
Henry, Patrick, 101, 102
Henryson, Robert, 183, 359
Heppenstall, Rayner, 318
Herbert, Alan, 162
Herbert, Bob, 231, 307
Herr, Michael, 64
Herrick, Robert, 33
Hertzberg, Hendrik, 191, 291, 315
Heywood, John, 271
Hiatt, Fred, 247
Hill, Don, 305
Hines, Cragg, 264
Hirigoyen, Judy, 314
Hiss, Alger, 72
Hoagland, Jim, 140, 332, 346
Hobbes, Thomas, 243, 323
Hoffman, Dustin, 283, 286
Holland, Philemon, 166
Holliday, Doc, 317
Holmes, Oliver Wendell, 21, 126
Holmes, Oliver Wendell Jr., 360
Holske, Robin, 310
Holstein, Sylvia and Morton, 363
Holt, Thaddeus, 142, 203
Homer, 20, 408, 409
Hone, Horace, 153
Hoover, Herbert, 236
Horace, 33, 34, 35, 408
Horn, Laurence, 113
Horton, Peter, 263
Horyn, Cathy, 98
Hosenball, Mark, 334

Howard, Juwan, 68
Hughes, Charles Evans, 59–60
Hughes, Karen P., 164, 332, 365, 372
Hull, Jane Dee, 63
Humphrey, Hubert H., 270
Hunt, Al, 163–64
Huntington, Chris, 354
Hussein, Saddam, 212, 227, 242, 286,
    297, 298, 371, 406
Hutton, Lauren, 313
Hutton, R. H., 9
Huxley, Aldous, 44, 270
Huxley, Thomas, 9
Hybels, Bill, 385
Hyde, Henry, 32
Hyde, Nina, 182
Hymers, John, 119

India.Arie, 272–73
Ingraham, Laura, 82
Ireland, Patricia, 146

Jackson, Andrew, 172
Jackson, Henry A. III, 401
Jackson, Thomas Penfield, 278
Jacobs, Joseph, 153
James, Mrs. A.G.F. Eliot, 260
James, Brad, 240
James, William, 207, 208
Jansen, G. H., 12
Janus, 100–102
Jaquish, Joan, 297
Jarrow, Robert, 354
Jefferson, Thomas, 101, 173, 215, 216,
    317, 349, 390
Jeffery, Peter, 70
Jenkins, Holman W. Jr., 329–30
Jennings, Peter, 108, 139, 261
Jespersen, Otto, 1
Jiang Zemin, 230, 231, 347
Joffe, Gerardo, 74
Joffee, Christine Brinck, 346
Johnson, Lyndon B., 302, 349, 353, 372
Johnson, Robert, 350, 404
Johnson, Samuel, 161, 184, 278

Jones, Chuck, 99
Jones, Liz, 151
Jonson, Ben, 292
Jordan, Vernon, 170
Jospin, Lionel, 368
Juliana, queen of the Netherlands, 167
Jurkowitz, Mark, 261

Kagan, Robert, 165, 205, 208
Kahn, David, 56
Kamen, Al, 92, 383
Kanarek, Sol, 290
Kaplan, Jacques, 87
Karpinski, Richard, 198
Karr, Mary, 256
Katz, Joshua, 319
Keller, Julia, 189
Kemp, Jack, 169
Kennedy, Anthony, 360
Kennedy, Ethel, 252
Kennedy, Jane, 68
Kennedy, John F., 27, 159, 215, 219, 265,
    341, 349, 360
Kennedy, Patrick, 193
Kenny, Jack, 405
Kermode, Frank, 59
Kerrey, Bob, 366
Kerry, John, 191
Keys, Alicia, 272, 273
Khaldun, Ibn, 43
Khomeini, Ayatollah, 212, 218
Khrushchev, Nikita, 265
Kian, Leonard, 343
Kilpatrick, James J., 285, 286
Kindelberger, Charles, 331
King, Larry, 133, 137
King, Samuel P., 363
Kipling, Rudyard, 93
Kirkpatrick, Wayne, 385
Kirshner, Ralph, 268
Kisselgoff, Anna, 130
Kissinger, Henry A., 9, 25, 123, 127, 128,
    252, 286, 328, 382
Klein, Michael, 218
Kluepfel, Charles, 317

Knight, John P., 155
Knyghton, Henry de, 186
Kondracke, Morton, 111, 365
Konigsberg, Ira, 304
Koogle, Timothy, 324
Korzybski (semanticist), 287
Krall, Diana, 271–72, 275
Krauthammer, Charles, 164, 205, 206,
    208
Kreienkamp, Gerry, 161
Krepon, Michael, 13
Krinn, Malvin, 126
Kristensen, Kai, 123
Kristof, Nicholas D., 86
Kristol, William, 165, 361
Krugman, Paul, 92
Krulak, Charles, 279
Kuczynski, Alex, 352
Kuhr, Barbara, 387
Kurtz, Howard, 134, 400
Kyl, John, 213

Labov, William, 339
Lackland, Thomas, 397
La Guardia, Anton, 369
Laitin, Joseph, 302
Lake, Ricki, 81
Lamy, Pascal, 369
Landau, James A., 199
Landon, Alf, 365
Lang, Fritz, 144
Lange, Marc, 402
Lariar, Lawrence, 306
Laribee, Sheri, 234
Lauer, Matt, 49, 287
Law, Cardinal Bernard F., 33
Lawler, John, 363
Lawrence, Martin, 81
Lawson, Dennis, 50
Leahy, Pat, 174
Leary, Timothy, 270
le Carré, John, 200
Lederberg, Joshua, 64–65
Lee, Robert E., 199
Lee, Gypsy Rose, 354

Lee Kwan Yew, 196
Leffall, LaSalle Jr., 255
Legatt, Alan D., 75
Letterman, David, 133
Levin, Gerald M., 27, 28
Levitis, Gerald M., 285
Levy, Chandra, 51
Lewinsky, Monica S., 49, 92, 213, 300
Lewis, Anthony, 369
Lewis, Christine, 312
Lewis, Neil A., 185
Lewis, Paul, 112
Lewis, Sinclair, 397
Lewis, Tony, 322
Lieberman, Hadassah, 132, 133
Lieberman, Joseph, 14, 131, 132, 191,
    206, 208, 213, 242–43, 251, 258–59,
    329, 384, 386
Lieberman, Stan, 268
Lighter, Jonathan E., 62
Lim, Robyn, 230
Limbaugh, Rush, 351–52
Lincoln, Abraham, 91, 127, 173, 209, 210,
    215, 217, 354, 371
Lincoln, Crawford, 258
Lindberg, Christine, 62
Lindbergh, Charles A., 373
Lipton, Lauren, 260
Litvinov, Maxim, 22
Lloyd, Christopher, 162
Lockhart, Joe, 183
London, Jack, 397
Long, Rob, 213
Longfellow, Henry Wadsworth, 11
Loquendi, Norma, 102–3
Lord, Winston, 383
Lott, Trent, 63, 64, 174
Louis, Joe, 45
Luce, Leila Hadley, 322–23

MacArthur, Douglas, 316
MacCoull, Leslie S. B., 275
MacDonald, J. D., 385
MacFarquhar, Neil, 104
MacIntyre, F. Gwynplaine, 48, 379

Mackay, Charles, 330, 331
Mackenzie, Ken, 309
MacMurray, Fred, 79
Madden, John, 344
Madden, Sheila, 341
Madison, Dolley, 126
Madison, James, 101, 126
Madonna, 64
Mahler, Gustav, 123
Maier, Kurt S., 302
Mailer, Norman, 227–28, 238
Mandelson, Peter, 9–10
Manson, Charles, 388
Mantell, Michael, 355
Mao Zedong, 34, 35, 172
Mappen, Mark, 296
Marie Antoinette, 228–29, 231
Marin, Arlene, 408
Marke, Percy, 187
Marks, Peter, 365
Marmon, William, 8
Martin, Edward, 23
Martin, Henry, 35
Martin, Joseph, 365
Martin, Lotte, 390
Martin, Steve, 154
Martineau, Harriet, 172
Mary Magdalene, 214
Mathews, Mitford, 106
Mathewson, Christy, 62
Matthews, Chris, 27, 205
Matthews, Victoria, 155, 162
Mauldin, Tim, 125
McAuliffe, Anthony, 251
McAuliffe, Terry, 374
McCain, John, 34, 63, 105, 164, 170, 171,
    172, 205, 208–9, 356, 360–61, 362, 372
McCawley, James, 237
McCloskey, Rev. John, 36
McCormack, Brian, 26
McElhone, Alice, 296
McGee, George, 255
McGrory, Mary, 27
McIntyre, Tom, 68
McKhann, Guy, 51

McLaglen, Victor, 239
McLean, Bethany, 90
McLean, Graeme, 379, 393
McMyne, Frank, 234
McNulty, Kevin, 250
McQuain, Jeffrey, 38, 88
McQuillen, Dick, 120
McRae, Carmen, 275
McSally, Martha, 220
McTague, Michael J., 80, 342
McVeigh, Timothy, 298
Meade, George, 199
Measday, Ellen, 320
Mednick, Mark, 46
Melia, Daniel F., 79
Melville, Herman, 252, 335
Mencher, Eric, 297
Mencken, H. L., 119–20, 176
Menschel, Robert, 330
Mercer, Johnny, 239, 272
Merman, Ethel, 372
Merrill, Daniel, 125
Metcalf, Allan, 381
Metcalf, Jane, 387
Meyers, Aloysius, 167
Meyers, Ron, 88
Milbank, Dana, 241, 343–44
Miller, Henry, 213
Miller, Jonathan, 133
Miller, Judith, 170
Miller, Kathleen, 44
Miller, Zell, 18, 289
Milton, John, 30, 202, 292, 302, 325
Mish, Fred, 236, 238, 267
Mitchell, John, 84
Mohamed, Ali A., 334
Mondale, Walter, 214, 344
Monroe, James, 302
Moonves, Leslie, 281
Moore, Thomas R., 257
Moore, Wild Bill, 306
Moran, Bugs, 214
Morano, Donald V., 395
More, Syr Thomas, 347
Morris, Edmund, 61

Morris, Mark, 130
Morris, Richard, 49, 365
Morrison, Philip, 139
Morrow, Lance, 47
Morse, S. A., 254
Mosconi, Willie, 308
Moses, Isaac, 142
Moss, Otis III, 335
Moynihan, Daniel Patrick, 257
Mubarak, Hosni, 77
Mufson, Steven, 193
Mugabe, Robert, 335
Muir, Gerry, 56
Muldoon, Gary, 214
Murphy, Austin, 293
Murray, Dennis, 400
Murray, Glenn, 409
Murray, Sir James, 281
Muschamp, Herbert, 386
Mussorgsky, Modest, 123
Mwanawasa, Levy, 19, 20
Myers, Eric, 316–17
Myers, Richard, 107

Nader, Ralph, 19, 126
Neisuler, Susan, 78
Nelson, Geraldine, 296
Nelson, Ted, 157–58
Netanyahu, Benjamin, 95
Newbold, Gregory, 95
Newman, Paul, 108
Newton, Harry, 31
Newton, Lisa H., 341
Nicholas II, Czar, 270
Nicholson, Jim, 236
Nicholson, Jock, 121
Nickles, Don, 292
Nisenholtz, Martin, 197
Nixon, Richard M., 25, 34, 169, 211, 229,
    231, 256, 300, 321–22, 349, 350, 358,
    366, 368
Noonan, Peggy, 110, 371
Norris, Floyd, 235
Norton, Thomas, 186
Novak, Robert, 145

Nunberg, Geoffrey, 93

Oakley, Annie, 372
Oates, Wayne E., 387–88
Obeidi, Sue, 67
Obrecht, Robert, 57
O'Connell, Ross, 285
O'Donnell, Frank, 180, 191, 367
O'Hara, John, 98
Olasky, Marvin, 169–70
Olson, Barbara, 163
Olson, Ted, 163
Organ, Claude H. Jr., 255
Orgel, Stephen, 409
Orwell, George, 316

Pace, Eric, 301
Page, Clarence, 68
Pahlavi, Shah Mohammad Reza, 211
Palmer, Mark, 91
Parham, Betty, 68
Park, Malcolm, 117
Parker, Ross, 205
Parnell, Gary, 297
Partridge, Eric, 348
Pataki, George, 139
Paul of Venice, 222
Paulshock, Bernadine S., 110
Pearson, Drew, 173
Pecherer, Benjamin, 311
Pelikan, Maria, 222
Peterson, Richard, 312
Peugeot, Frederic, 185
Pfaff, William, 94
Philippsohn, Steven, 226
Phillips, Elizabeth, 279
Phillips, John, 154
Picard, Annette, 342
Pickett, Joe, 160, 267, 268
Pinker, Steven, 325–26
Pinter, Harold, 132–33
Piozzi, Mrs., 278
Pitt, Harvey, 294
Plato, 59
Plunkett, John, 387

Podesta, John, 182, 183
Poe, Edgar Allan, 235
Pollack, Milton, 41
Pollock, David, 12
Pope, Alexander, 330, 399, 408
Popik, Barry, 23, 81
Poretz, Melvin, 340
Porter, Cole, 272
Potter, Stephen, 264
Poulos, Nick, 140
Powell, Colin, 11, 12, 82, 165–66, 169,
    192, 193, 194, 279, 286, 297, 332, 347,
    348, 370
Powers, David, 27
Powers, Francis Gary, 274
Powers, Thomas, 226
Prasso, Sheri, 324
Presley, Elvis, 381
Principi, Anthony, 279
Prueher, Joseph, 348
Pusey, Merlo, 60
Putin, Vladimir, 62, 241, 270–71, 301,
    357, 359, 404

Quayle, Dan, 80, 190

Rabin, Yitzhak, 50
Race, Tim, 356
Rafshoon, Gerald, 131
Rahman, Tariq, 319–20
Raleigh, Sir Walter, 331
Ramirez, Marc, 281
Randolph, Eleanor, 362, 364
Raspberry, William, 18
Rasputin (Grigory Novykh), 270
Rather, Dan, 307
Ravel, Maurice, 123
Raver, Anne, 92
Ray, Emmet, 315
Raybould, Andrew, 128
Raymond, Eric, 198
Read, Fran, 115–16
Reagan, Ronald, 22, 61, 84, 106, 169, 171,
    174, 206, 207, 232, 268, 289, 322, 344,
    350, 366

Redding, James, 125
Redding, Otis, 283
Reddy, Rhonda, 10
Redmond, Paul, 29
Rehm, Diane, 94
Rehnquist, William H., 102, 108, 199
Reich, Brian, 147
Reichenbach, Bodo, 74
Renzulli, Frank, 52
Reuther, Walter, 83
Ricardel, Joseph, 274
Ricardel, Vincent, 274
Rice, Adam, 89
Rice, Condoleezza, 62
Richards, Bill, 198
Richardson, Samuel, 337
Richelson, Geraldine, 388
Richey, Warren, 102
Ridge, Tom, 111, 291, 354
Rios, Essa, 10
Ripken, Cal, 172
Roberts, Cokie, 183
Robinson, Edward G., 79–80
Robson, Barbara, 165
Rockefeller, Nelson, 169, 181, 237
Rodman, M. H., 38
Rogers, Roy, 332
Roker, Al, 132
Romney, George, 321, 322
Ronell, Ann, 153
Roosevelt, Franklin D., 162, 164, 173,
    215, 219, 237, 256, 303, 365, 384, 390,
    404
Roosevelt, Theodore, 55, 360
Rose, Eric, 255
Rosen, Joe, 127
Rosen, Saul, 47
Rosen, Steven J., 12
Rosen, Stephen, 81
Rosenberg, Ethel and Julius, 72
Rosenthal, A. M., 338
Rosenthal, Fred, 120
Rosenthal, Jack, 7, 132
Rosetto, John, 387
Rosten, Leo, 104, 204, 400

Roth, Holly, 334
Rothschild, Lord, 147
Rousseau, Jean-Jacques, 228–29
Rove, Karl, 43, 105, 168, 169
Rowe, Nicholas, 150
Rowny, Ed, 354
Rubalsky, Robert and Mary, 297
Rubin, Robert, 77–79
Rudman, Warren, 392
Rukeyser, Louis, 24
Rumsfeld, Donald, 13, 65, 107, 135, 137,
    166, 176, 236, 279, 328, 391
Rushdie, Salman, 399
Russert, Tim, 13, 132, 307, 320, 374
Rutenberg, Jim, 281
Ryashchina, Maya, 380

Sabin, Albert, 22
Sabol, Barbara, 232
Sack, Kevin, 345
Saffir, Herbert S., 255
Sagan, Carl, 386
Samuelson, Robert J., 235
Sanders, Judi, 81, 281
Sanneh, Kelefa, 326
Scalia, Antonin, 1–3, 53–60
Scanlon, John, 406
Schaible, Damian, 271
Scharfenberg, Kirk, 249
Schelling, Thomas, 299
Scherl, Newton, 399
Schickel, Richard, 144
Schiffer, Rabbi Ira J., 177
Schlesinger, Arthur Jr., 270, 368
Schlesinger, Richard, 81
Schlessinger, Laura, 125
Schmich, Mary, 366
Schmitt, Eric, 26, 304
Schneider, Bernard, 282
Schneider, William, 251
Schnur, Dan, 105
Schorr, Daniel, 167, 347, 360, 365
Schroeder, Robert, 60
Schulz, Charles M., 136
Schuyler, Robert Livingston, 343

Schwartz, Roger M., 99
Schwarzenegger, Arnold, 298
Sciolino, Elaine, 159
Scott, Dickson, 190
Scott, Vernon, 92
Scott, Sir Walter, 132, 186
Scowcroft, Brent, 46
Seelye, Katharine Q. "Kit," 42, 280
Seicol, Noel H., 191
Seymour, Horatio, 215
Shafran, Rabbi Avi, 386
Shakespeare, William, 17, 20, 34, 37, 94,
    136, 170, 202, 223, 224, 234, 235, 247,
    280, 292, 313, 315, 331, 376, 382
Shank, William, 303
Shapes, Jeff, 345
Shapiro, Fred R., 23, 85, 103, 181, 186,
    299, 360
Shapiro, Jacob "Gurrah," 342–43
Sharon, Ariel, 210–11, 241
Shaw, George Bernard, 37, 44
Shaw, Joseph, 35–36
Shaw, Tom, 307
Sheehy, John J., 221
Shehata, Samer, 12
Shelley, Mary, 112, 113
Shelley, Percy Bysshe, 113
Sheraton, Mimi, 22
Sheridan, Richard Brinsley, 194
Sherr, Lynn, 245
Sherwood, Patricia M., 152
Shinseki, Eric, 286
Shirk, George, 387
Shore, Karen, 234
Short, Clare, 10
Siber, Richard, 197
Sides, Joseph D., 114
Sidorkin, Alexander "Sasha," 66
Siedband, Mel, 297
Siegal, Allan M., 31
Siegmeister, Bobby, 154
Silber, William, 123
Simon, Neil, 247–48
Sinatra, Frank, 272, 370
Sinclair, Upton, 270

Sipress, David, 400
Siwolop, Sana, 284
Skutnick, Lenny, 333
Slatin, Stephen, 114, 116–17
Slaughter, Anne-Marie, 359
Slung, Michele, 190
Smith, Bob, 256
Smith, Charlotte, 126
Smith, Jack, 182
Smith, Martin, 105
Smith, M. Gregg, 141
Smith, Michael W., 385
Smith, Perry, 13
Smitherman, Geneva, 68
Snow, C. P., 317, 318
Sontag, Susan, 205
Southey, Robert, 323
Spano, Susan, 130
Spears, Britney, 309
Spellman, Francis Cardinal, 33
Spenser, Edmund, 292
Sperling, Gene, 300
Spiegel, Sam, 132–33
Spielberg, Steven, 64, 317
Spitalny, Phil, 100
Stalin, Joseph, 404
Stanley, Henry, 82
Stanley, Ralph, 274
Stanwyck, Barbara, 80
Steig, William, 310
Stein, Herbert, 8
Steinblatt, Jim, 273
Steinmetz, Sol, 137, 197, 205, 221, 339
Stentor, 174
Sterne, Laurence, 17
Stevens, Wallace, 50
Stevenson, Adlai E., 19, 168, 251, 364
Stewart, Alison, 61
Stewart, Jim, 51
Stewart, Martha, 304
Stone, Julian, 114
Strahan, Michael, 307
Strauss, Neil, 327
Street, Picabo, 293
Streeten, Paul, 133

Streisand, Barbra, 64
Strother, John, 15, 47, 152, 250, 294
Strunk, William Jr., 393
Stubbe, Henry, 371
Stutes, Robert, 289
Sullivan, Andrew, 28
Sullivan, Jim, 90
Summers, Larry, 323
Sun Yuxi, 348
Su Shih, 130
Swift, Jane, 254
Swift, Jonathan, 109, 166, 397, 399
Swirsky, Joan, 374
Swope, Herbert Bayard, 59

Tagliabue, John, 29
Tarlowe, Stuart, 26, 180
Taylor, Tim, 294
Taylor, Zachary, 19
Teare, Keith, 291
Tenet, George, 110
Tennyson, Alfred, Lord, 182
Thackeray, William Makepeace, 94
Thatcher, Margaret, 19, 330
Thomas, Bill, 287
Thomas, Evan, 334
Thomas, Wayt, 280
Thomson, Hillary, 46
Thorton, Sam, 314
Thurber, James, 275
Tinker, Joe, 62
Titus Livius, 166
Tobin, Roger, 115, 122
Tolchin, Charles P., 178–79
Tolchin, Martin, 233
Torricelli, Robert, 337
Trajkovski, Boris, 141
Trausch, Susan, 26
Trillin, Calvin, 138
Trollope, Anthony, 94, 145, 264–65
Troupin, Peggy, 122
Truman, Harry S, 148, 187, 256, 257, 277,
    349, 350, 404, 405
Tsongas, Paul, 269
Tucker, Jack, 131

Tufts, James Hayden, 206
Turan, Kenneth, 144
Turner, Ted, 356
Tutu, Archbishop Desmond, 335
Twain, Mark, 24, 212, 256
Tyler, John, 366
Tynan, Kenneth, 132
Tyndale, William, 359
Tyson, Mike, 316

U2, 274
Unterricht, Sam, 85
Urdang, Laurence, 20, 25, 27, 41, 89, 162,
    250, 374

Van Buren, Martin, 19, 45
Van Wouw-Koeleman, Hans, 153
Védrine, Hubert, 156, 370
Vega, Joseph de la, 331
Veit, Richard, 73
Verhovek, Sam, 225
Verne, Jules, 399
Vickery, Mike, 13–14
Virgil, 154
Voegelin, Eric, 253

Wacker, Jim, 344
Wade, Nicholas, 284
Wagner, Richard, 104
Waldman, Michael, 300
Walker, Greg, 404
Walker, Ivan, 220
Wallace, Mike, 139
Wallingford, Dick, 187
Walpole, Horace, 241, 399
Walsh, Edward, 208
Walters, Betsey, 408
Walters, Logan, 26
Ward, Samuel Augustus, 245
Ware, J. Redding, 283
Warren, John Byrne Leicester, 279
Washington, George, 101, 215–17, 374
Wasserman, Robert and Claudia, 16
Wasserstein, Wendy, 146
Waxman, Seth, 95

Weaver, Warren, 366
Weeks, Albert, 270
Weil, George L., 381
Weintraub, Steven H., 106
Weis, Judith, 127
Weiser, Benjamin, 334
Weisman, Steven, 391
Wellington, Duke of (Arthur Wellesley),
    14, 167, 251
Welliver, Judson, 349
Wells, H. G., 207
Welsh, Charles, 257
Wenner, Jann, 82
Werben, Judith, 297
Werschkul, Ben, 405
Wharton, Edith, 145, 394
White, E. B., 393
White, John D., 123
Whitman, Christie Todd, 286
Whitman, Walt, 270
Whitney, Craig, 156
Wiener, Norbert, 155, 226
Wight, Richard M., 249
Wight, Tony, 297
Wilde, Sandra, 321
Wilder, Billy, 79, 144
Wilenitz, Israel, 243
Wilkins, John S., 195
Wilkins, Marc, 284
Wilkinson, Howard, 366
Wilkinson, Paul, 334
Will, George, 269, 344
Will, Mari Maseng, 232
Willebrands, Johannes, 33
Williams, Brian, 18, 184

Williams, John, 123
Williams, Marjorie, 146, 324
Williams, Robin, 143
Williamson, Dan, 282
Willkie, Wendell, 384–85
Wilson, "Engine Charlie," 109, 407
Wilson, Woodrow, 349
Winchell, Walter, 23
Winfrey, Oprah, 316
Wisdom, Dwayna M., 353
Wise, David, 227
Wise, Jeff, 61
Witherspoon, John, 215
Wittmann, Marshall, 134
Wolfe, Tom, 72, 150, 355
Wolff, Michael, 90
Wollstonecraft, Mary, 301
Wonder, Stevie, 182
Woodward, Bob, 276, 386
WuDunn, Sheryl, 86
Wurman, Richard Saul, 116
Wurtele, Morton G., 191
Wyatt, Edward, 343
Wycherly, William, 331

Yang, Jerry, 397
Yew, Lee Kwan, 196
Young, Edward M., 128
Yu, Doug, 285

Zeldin, Boris, 271
Zuckerman, Stuart, 46
Zweig, Jason, 332
Zwicky, Arnold, 181
Zwilling, Leonard, 372, 398

Index of Terms

abdicate, 295
abrogate, 358–60
accelerate, 291
acronyms, 5–7
acute, 119
adages, 159–60
Afghan/afghanis, 218
African-American, 131
age, 257
agent in place, 200, 204
agita, 52
agnostic, 8–9
aha!, 247–48
ahem, 91–94
alliance, 328
alliteration, 14–15, 361
alluhyuz, 338
alphabet, 296
Al Qaeda, 164, 211, 218, 291
altruism, 297
amazon.com, 225
ambiguity, 383–84
amend, 359
"America the Beautiful," 245–46
amped, 293–94
ankle-biter, 44
ante-man, 257
ante up, 257
antiterrorism, 10–11
apology, 346–48
apoplexy, 372
approbation, 296
Arab street, 11–12
archaic, 162

architect, 115–16
arch pause, 91–94
artifice, 265
assassination, 219
assonance, 15
asterisk, 295
asymmetric warfare, 13–14
asymmetry, 13–14
attendant, 30–31
at the end of the day, 374–75
augment, 291
aus gebrant, 390
avails, 365–67

baby-boom generation, 380
bait-and-switch, 361
baldfaced lies, 16–17
ballistic, 117
barefaced lies, 16–17
barnburners, 18–19, 45
bashful, 296
bated breath, 19–21
bathetic, 214
begging the question, 125
being there for you, 315–16
beleaguered, 297
belt-and-suspenders approach, 79–80
benevolent compassion, 53–60
bialy, 22–23
biblical quotation, 404
Big Apple, 23
big enchilada, 84–85
billiards, 307–9
biting the bullet, 140–41

blanched, 186
blatant, 16
bleeps, 24, 25
blendwords, 226–28
blips, 24–25
blond/blonde, 131–32, 191
blood and iron, 172
blue-collar worker, 379
body man, 26–27
boggles, 89–90
bold, 376–77
boldfaced lies, 16–18
boo-boo, 407, 408
borking, 173, 174
box cutters, 163
brazen hussy, 162
breach, 359
British garage, 273
broadband, 27–29
bubble, 330–32
buck stops here, the, 256, 257
bull, 186–87
bundling, 29, 31
burnout, 388–89
Bushisms (G. H. W.), 269
buzz cut, 190

cache, 30, 31
can, 220–21
can-do mentality, 380
cantaloupe, 297
captivate, 210
captivity, 347
cardinals, title migration of, 33
carom billiards, 308, 309
carpe diem, 33–35
carpenters, 190
cashmere, 259–60
cast-iron man, 172
celibacy/chastity, 36–38, 405–6
census forms, 38–41
certiorari accepted, 102–3
chador, 67
chads, 41–43, 160–61
chastity/celibacy, 36–38, 405–6

chat chute, 43
chestnut, 296
chocoholic, 388
chorine/chorus girl, 160
chuddies, 190
clam up, 228
class warfare, 43–44
clean your clock, 44–47
client/cly, 379
cliffhanger, 44
Clintonisms, 47–50, 133–34, 215,
    216–17, 229–31, 266–67, 269, 299, 351
coalition, 328–29
cocktail parties, 283–84
coffee, 295
Cold Case squad, 51–52, 161
collateral damage, 298–99
come heavy, 52
commute, 296
compassion, 53–60
compassionate conservative, 168,
    169–70
compose/comprise/constitute, 404–5
condescending, 297
conflicted, 317
congenital, 124
connection, 61–62
contrapuntal, 297
contemptible, 82
continual/continuous, 326
control freak, 63–64
cookie pushers, 30, 192
cookies, 30
cool, 239, 355
coordinates, 65–67, 296
corridors of power, 317, 318
cote, 406
counterterrorism, 10–11
courtesy titles, 99–100
court packing, 173–74
creamed, 45
crescendo, 124
crusade, 390–91, 393
cutting-edge technology, 380
cyber, 226

damage control, 106
damned lies, 16
dancer, 160
dancing, 1
dangle, 201, 202
dark, 143–45
dashes, 71–74
dastardly, 164
date wars, 74–77, 408
dead drop, 200–201, 227
Dead Letter Office, 161–62
dead on arrival, 359
deathcare industry, 94–95
death tax, 232, 404
deer park, 227–28
defeathered, 45
defense, 393
defibrillator, 296
demagogue, 322–23
destabilize, 297
detention, 347
deuterochiliast, 199
dieresis, 402–3
differentiate, 60
dirigiste, 77–79
dirty lies, 16
disaffected, 208–9
disenchanted, 208–9
disenfranchised, 184
disenthrall, 209, 210
diva, 274
dodge, 265, 266
Domain Name System, 223–25
dominatrix, 63
don't go there, 80–81
doofus, 82–83
double agent, 203–4
dovecote, 406, 409
downhome, 149
drive-by killing, 380
drubbing, 45
dumb-ass, 82–83

e-books, 178
ecology, 126–27

e-fraud, 226
electronica, 273
Elmer Fudd trapper hats, 98–99
e-mail terms, 310
em dash, 73
emollient, 369
employee, 193
enchanted, 208–9
engineer, 119–20
enjoy!, 86–89
enroned, 90–91
epicenter, 114, 140
equinox, 297
er, 91–94
eschatology, 253
esplanade, 295
estate tax, 232, 404
euphemisms, 94–95
eviscerate, 95–96
expletives, 25
exponential growth, 114–15, 122,
     123

farewell addresses, 214–17
fast track, 233
feckless, 356
federalism, 101–3
fibs, 16
fightback, 10
film noir, 144–45
finagle, 104–5
firewall, 105–6
flagrant, 16
flat-out, 16
fog of war, 106–8
fog the glass, 155
foot-and-mouth disease, 108–9
for crying out loud, 137
foreign service, 192–93
for Pete's sake, 137
forthcoming, 111
for the love of Pete, 137
forward-leaning, 110–12, 241–42
Franken-, 112–13
freak, 63–64

freedom, 56–57
"Frim Fram Sauce," 271–72, 274, 275
Frisbeetarian, 295
frisking, 379
fuggedaboudit, 339
fulminations, 113–29
fussin', 271–72, 275

galumphing, 130
gambit, 265
gedaddaheeuh, 339, 341
gee, 136
gee-haw whimmey-diddle, 398
geeing and hawing, 397
geek, 241
genomics, 283, 284
gerunds, 1–3
get rolling, 305
gigged, 133–34
gimmick, 265
glitterati, 181
global warming, 233
gofer, 26
good grief, 136
goodness gracious!, 135–37
gooey, 214
"goo-goo" character, 59
goomah/goombah, 52
gosh, 136
gotcha, 137–39
gotcha journalism, 138
go-to guy, 134–35
grammarian, 296
great balls of fire!, 136
great Caesar's ghost!, 136
great day in the mornin', 136
great Scott!, 136
ground zero, 139–40
grow, 291
grunge, 273
Gucci Gulch, 99
gunmen, 141–42
gunsel, 35–36, 142
gushy, 214
gypsy, 160

haiku, 297
hands-on manager, 380
hand-wanding, 378
harbor, 164–65
hard-core rap, 273
hard-wired, 386
having it all, 145–47
having said that, 362–63, 373
heads-up tennis, 380
heavenly days, 137
hella, 240
hell's bells, 137
hermit, 297
hijab, 67
hijackers, 163
history, 10
holy, 137
homeboy, 149
homeland, 147–49
homeland defense, 392–93
homely, 149
hooey, 186, 187–88
hoof-and-mouth disease, 108–9
hooking up, 149–52
horrific, 219
hot, 355–56
house music, 273
huff, 154
humongous, 317
hurr, 152–53, 155
hustler, 309
hyper, 155–58
hypermarket, 156
hyperpower, 156, 158
hypertext, 156–58
hyphenated compound words, 379–82
hypothesis, 127
hysterical, 210

identify, 89
immanentize the eschaton, 253
incident, 348
inclusion, politics of, 169
increase, 291
indifference, 9

industrial-strength, 380
ineffable, 296
infamy, 162–63, 219
influence block, 406–7
inheritance tax, 232, 404
intent, 360
interactive, 27
internment, 347
interregnum, 21–22
intuition, 296
invest, 165–67
investigate, 166
investiture, 166, 167
inveterate, 202
iron chancellor, 172
iron curtain, 172
iron fist, 167–69
iron horse, 172
iron man, 172
iron rice bowl, 172
iron triangle, 170–72
-ism, 189
-itis, 191

Janus words, 100–102
Jew, 131–32
jihad, 211–12
judicious, 296
justice, 164

kamikaze, 163
kibosh, 176–77
kindred, 296
kit and caboodle, 85

lace-curtain Irish, 379–80
La-La Land, 181–82
laser, 6
laydown dates, 179–80
leave no child behind, 231–32
Left Coast, 180–82
legacy, 182–83
legitimacy, 183–84
le mot de Cambronne, 229, 231, 251–52
lesion, 120

let's roll, 305–6
"Let them eat cake," 228–29
lies, 16–17
ligging, 184–85
limit/limitation, 400–401
"lingua interruptus," 74
liquor store, 258–59
liturgy, 296
livid, 185–86
lockbox, 188–89
lookism, 189–91
losers, 155, 159
lot lizards, 195
lounge, 193–95
lounge lizards, 194
lumbering, 32

mad cow disease, 109–10
madras, 297
main man, 26, 27
mainstream, 169
man, the, 26
maneuver, 265
man with the briefcase, 26
maser, 6
mash-ups, 327
maudlin, 214
mawkish, 214
may/might, 401–2
m-commerce, 196–98
mental-health consumers, 233–34
mercy me, 137
merde!, 229, 251
metaphor, 401
methodology, 120
micromanager, 63
might/may, 401–2
military-industrial complex, 171
millenarians, 198–99
mine run, 199–200
miniscule, 296
minority, 85–86
misdirection play, 406–7
mishmash, 104
Miss/Ms./Mrs., 99–100

moderate/moderation, 168–69
module, 115
mole, 200–202
mole hunt, 227
moral certainty, 207
moral clarity, 205–8
moral equivalence, 206–7
moral relativism, 207
most favored nation, 232, 233
muddied/muddled, 206
mujahedeen, 211–12
mushball, 213
"Mush from the Wimp," 246, 249
mushy, 212–14
must, 221
must-see film, 380
my countrymen, 214–15
myopia/myopic, 126, 128–29
My stars!, 137

nail-biter, 44
need to, 220–21
negative pregnant, 222–23
negligent, 295
neo-soul, 273
Netspionage, 226–28
neutral, 9
new guard, 250–52
noncommittal, 9
noodge, 242–43
noprollem, 339
normalcy, 235
normal trade relations, 232
nuance, 241–42
nuclear, 243–44
nudge, 242–43
nudnik, 243
nut, 64

obsolete, 162
obviate, 41
off the wall, 185
ohhoh, 247–48
oh-oh, 248
old guard, 250–52, 384

omigod, 136
one fell swoop, 234–35
one-upmanship, 264
onnafyah, 338
on pins and needles, 20, 21
on the blower/hook/horn, 250
operation, 255
Operation Enduring Freedom, 235–36
operator, 31
orchestration, 122–23, 124–25
organic, 114, 116–17, 119, 121, 273–74
-osis, 191
out-of-the-box thinking, 380
outright, 16
over, 10

package store, 258–59
Pakistani, 218–19, 391
paraleipsis, 216, 252
parallel parking, 151
parameter, 121, 124
parlous, 261
participles, 1–3
party time, 256
pashmina, 259–60
patients, 233–34
pedophile, 319–20
pejorative, 208
penultimate, 119
people of color, 68
percentages, 263
perception management, 227
perilous, 261
periodically, 118
petrology, 253–54
phrasedick, 336
ping, 262–63
plagiarhythm, 327
platforming, 304
ploy, 263–66
plus which, 266–68
polenta, 214
politics of personal destruction, 269–70
pool/pool table, 307–8
possessive forms, 1–3, 180

post-grunge, 273

Potus, 299–300, 302–3

pounding sand, 276–78

precursor, 297

predatory conduct, 278

pregnant pause, 222

press availabilities, 365–66

presumptive/presumptuous, 81–82

prevarication, 16

print-on-demand books, 178

procedure, 254–55

pro-choice, 233

pro-life, 232–33

props, 280–83

proteomics, 283–86

prunes, 312–14

puppy lick, 152

push-back, 286

pushing the envelope, 150

put up or shut up, 255–57

put your money where your mouth is,
     256–57

quantum jump, 115, 122, 124

quote unquote, 287–89

radar, 6–7

raffish, 301–2

ramp up, 291–94

rankles, 89

rathe, 279

rats in the barn, 18–19

rebuffs, 296

receptions, 283

recuse, 294–95

redefinitions, 295–97

regime change, 242, 297–98

regime lethal, 227

regret, 347

rescind, 299

resistance, 286

retraction, 299

riff, 300–302

riffraff, 302, 303

rigamarole, 187

risky tax scheme, 375–76

robust, 356–57

rogue states, 94, 382–83

roll 'em, 305–6

rollout, 303–5

roll up, 306

romped, 45

rout, 45

ruching, 98

rule-roosting device, 407–8

run of the mill, 199–200

run the table, 307–8

ruse, 265

saturnine, 297

scamming, 316–17

scheme, 375–76

schizophrenia, 124

schwa, 320–21

screaming meemies, 20, 21, 198

screenager, 190

seaboard, 181

seasonable/seasonal, 7–8

secret plan, 321–22

security, 393

seize the day, 33–35

seize the moment, 33–35

semiconductor, 284, 285, 286

sensual/sensuous, 324–26

sentence fragments, 236–38

September 11 attacks, 14, 139–40,
     148–49, 163–65, 219, 335

serendipity, 399

servicemember, 347

shafafa, 272, 274, 275

shall/will, 392, 393–95

shnook, 202, 204–5

shoes, 282

short words, 175–76

shovelware, 198

shpilkes, 20

shrinking violet, 279–80

shrug, 190

shtick, 329–30
sickthink, 202, 227
sidekick, 332–33
signal site, 201
simile, 401
SIS, 203
ska-punk, 273
skeevy, 52
skiff, 226
skip trace, 201–2
Skutnik, 333
sleeper, 333–34
slippery slope, 334–36
slogans, 236–38
Slurvian, 338–43
smashmouth, 343–45
snaffle bit, 98
snippy, 345–46
snooker, 308, 309
sodomy, 1–3
soppy, 214
SOU (state of the Union), 349–51
soul music, 273
spam, 29–30
squeezewords, 351–53
squishy-soft, 214
-stan, 218
stand pat, 256
state-of-the-art, 380
state of the Union, 349-51
states of concern, 382
steeling, 170
steel magnolia, 172
sticky wicket, 405
stovepiping, 353–54
stratagem, 265
strategic ambiguity, 383–84
strategic partnership, 229–31
streaming media, 198
street, the, 11–12
stripping out, 354–55
stuff, 355–57
subterfuge, 265
suck face, 151

sufragettes, 296
suicide bombers, 163–65
summit, 357–58
super, 240
superficial, 297
surgery, 255
surreptitious, 228
swash, 97
symmetry, 13–14
syncopate, 261
synecdoche, 409
synergy, 115

tactic/tactics, 265, 266
take meetings, 373
Taliban, 164, 165, 211
tautology, 161
termination with prejudice, 201
terp, 160
terrorism, 10–11, 139–40, 141–42,
    163–65, 210–11, 219
text messaging, 310
that said, 362–64, 374
theory, 127, 128
'til the last dog is hung, 50
time police, 316–18
Tinseltown, 181, 182
titular, 364–65
to be sure, 363
to-be-sure graf, 363
toggery, 323
tongue sushi, 151
tonsil hockey, 150, 151
toque blanche, 97–98
toques, 98–99
totalitarian, 63
tout, 337–38
traces, 201
track record, 127
traction, 356
trampoline, 296
trance, 326–27
transparency, 323–24
triangle, 171–72

triangulation, 49
truncate, 297

uber, 240
uh-huh, 248
uh-oh, 248–49
uh-uh, 248
um, 91–94
umlaut, 402–3
uncaring, 9
unconcerned, 9
unilateralism/unilateralists, 368–69
upcoming, 111
up-front, 324
up the wall, 185
USA PATRIOT bill, 5

vapors, 370–71
vested, 167
vested interest, 167
vestment, 166
visceral reaction, 95
visibility, 324
visit/visit with, 372–73
voguisms, 282, 363, 373–77

wanding, 378
warship, 296
way cool, 238–40, 355
way hot, 355–56
way out, 238

weaponized, 83
weapons-grade, 381
Well, I swan, 137
West Bank, 233
wet work, 201, 204
What gives?, 98
white-collar worker, 379
whole enchilada, 84, 85
wile, 265
will/shall, 392, 393–95
wimp, 246–47
winners, 154–55, 159
wired, 385–87
withdraw, 358–60
women of cover, 67–68
woof tickets, 68–70
workaholic, 387–88, 389
world-class, 380
wrinkle, 297

yahoo, 397
yee-haw!, 396–98
ye gods and little fishes, 137
yoga, 121–22
You know what I'm sayin'?, 315–16

zemblanity, 399–400
zero tolerance, 381
zhlubs, 400
zounds!, 137